OFF THE BEATEN PATH® SERIES

Texas

FOURTH EDITION

by June Naylor

The Globe Pequot Press

Guilford, Connecticut

The prices and rates listed in this guidebook were confirmed at press time. We recommend, however, that you call establishments before traveling to obtain current information.

Maps provided are for reference only and should be used in conjunction with a road map. Distances suggested are approximate.

Copyright © 1994, 1997, 2000, 2002 by June Naylor

Off the Beaten Path is a registered trademark of The Globe Pequot Press.

Cover and text design by Laura Augustine
Cover photo by David Davis
Maps created by Equator Graphics © The Globe Pequot Press
Illustrations by Carole Drong

ISBN 0-7627-1244-9
ISSN:1537-0526

Manufactured in the United States of America
Fourth Edition/Fourth Printing

For my parents—
I am grateful for your love and your
abundant Texan legacies.
And for Carolyn, Janie,
and Anna Claire—
here's to all
the Texas adventures
ahead of us.

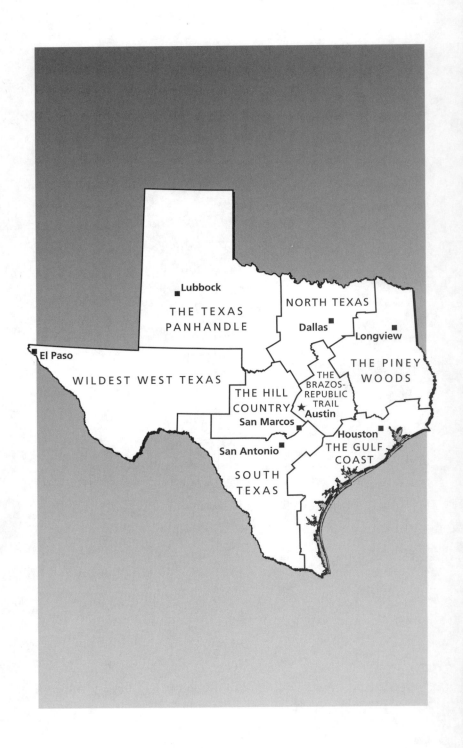

Contents

Acknowledgments

Working on the fourth edition of this book was a pleasure, mostly because it allowed me to rediscover the backroads and oft-overlooked corners that make Texas live up to its vast legend. I owe a great debt to the kindly folks who work in tiny museums, cafes, shops, and inns in such towns as Leakey in the Hill Country, Uncertain in the Piney Woods, Fort Davis in the Big Bend, and Snyder in the Panhandle; it's people like this, in places like those, who make writing about Texas a joyful privilege. As for the support at home, I have endless gratitude for my parents, who cheer my every piece of work, and the friends (Mike, Mike, Trish, Renee, and Barbara) who make me keep my sense of humor—and still love me even during those moments when I seem to have misplaced it.

Introduction

John Steinbeck wrote in *Travels with Charley*, "Texas is a state of mind. Texas is an obsession. Above all, Texas is a nation in every sense of the word."

Sam Houston—first president of the Republic of Texas and hero in the defeat of Santa Anna—would have loved Steinbeck.

But for all its staunch independence, Texas is one big welcome mat. Folks coming to call from elsewhere are often taken aback when greeted on the street by total strangers with a "Hidy," "Howdy," or "Hey." There's no catch—Texans are just greeters by nature.

Let's go ahead and dispel some myths: Texas is flat if you don't count those ninety-one mountains that reach over a mile into the sky; Texas is dry if you ignore 3.07 million acres of inland water made up of streams, rivers, lakes, springs, creeks, and 624 miles of Gulf of Mexico shoreline; and Texas has no trees if you overlook those 23 million acres of woodlands.

Texas is proud of its state flower, an odd, stalky gypsy called the bluebonnet. It arrives overnight in spring, thickly coating fields and highway shoulders in a spectacle of deep blue that would have given Renoir a lump in his throat. The bluebonnet first pops up in the Rio Grande Valley and the Big Bend in February, launching a six-month pilgrimage that eventually tints the high Panhandle plains. The bluebonnet's colorful pals every spring are the bright orange Indian paintbrush and the pink primrose.

Mesquite, the Texas tree that looks to be fragile in its slenderness, is actually a hearty survivor that thrives on the harshest land. It multiplies easily, makes a great flavoring for barbecue fires, produces a delightful blossom honey, and provides shade and food for cows and deer. On top of all that, its gnarled, thorny countenance completes the perfect ranch portrait.

Texas's farm-to-market roads serve not only today's farmers, but also those wanderers who just want to absorb the gentle, uncluttered environs. The first such road opened in 1941, and now there are more than 3,000, making up 41,000 highway miles of the state's total of 73,000. The shortest, FM 2413 in Robertson, is 528 feet. Two of the prettiest farm-to-market vistas are in the Piney Woods of east Texas and the Trans-Pecos wilds of west Texas.

When eating in Texas, be aware that Mexican meets Southern, Cajun greets soul, and, somehow, dissimilarities welcome one another. From such mingling, Southwestern cuisine rides a crest of fame, and country cooking soars higher than ever on all palates.

Trust places with signs that say IF YOU LEAVE HERE HUNGRY IT'S YOUR OWN FAULT, and put your faith in waitresses who are concerned you haven't been eating right and insist you need that piece of pie to keep up your strength. Also, if it sounds absurd, it's probably good; if it sounds French, it probably isn't Texan.

For fried alligator tail, a tender delicacy, look around east Texas lake joints, which also serve up lightly fried catfish with green tomato relish and jalapeño hush puppies. Barbecue, a critical Texas staple, is best from the old places in central Texas's Taylor, Lockhart, and Luling. If you can find barbecued pork or beef ribs, brisket, goat, shrimp, or sausage, eat it up.

How about buffalo? It's a tasty treat, lower in fat and cholesterol than beef, and a wonderful way to eat Wellington, burgers, and steaks. No bull. The best wurst turns up in thickly German towns such as New Braunfels and Fredericksburg, while kolache heaven is spread out over the Czech communities of West and Caldwell.

A word about chicken-fried steak: Sounds weird, but this could be the national food of Texas; go for it only if it's fork-cutting tender and its breading is homemade and light. And whence came chili? San Antonio or Fort Worth? Both claim it. Beef or venison, spicy or mild, beans or no, there's plenty of it for the sampling at cook-offs all year long. Just don't confuse it with chile, which can be a fire-hot stew if eaten on one of Texas's two Native American reservations, or a velvety green or creamy red pepper sauce if found in one of south Texas's Hispanic-infused towns. Now, you'll get plenty of argument from fajita lovers, but the best Mexican eats are breakfast goods—migas, empanadas—found in cafes and bakeries.

For fruits of the Texas earth, look to Weatherford and Stonewall for peaches, Pecos for cantaloupes, and the Rio Grande Valley for citrus. For the nectar of Texas gods, we have nineteen vineyards and wineries, among them international award winners Llano Estacado Winery in Lubbock and Fall Creek Vineyards in Tow.

As Bubbas will tell you, this is one recreation-crazed state. In water action alone, there's rafting, canoeing, and kayaking on Hill Country rivers and the Rio Grande, while sailing and sailboarding are Corpus Christi favorites, surfers flock to Galveston, catamaran rentals are booming business on South Padre Island, and fishing charters and tournaments subsidize the Port Aransas economy.

Texans are always looking for an excuse to have fun. There are festivals celebrating black-eyed peas, mosquitoes, flowers, berries, hush puppies, rattlesnakes, bluegrass music, fall foliage, and fire ants. Cowboys have a Christmas ball, Native Americans have a championship pow-wow, and Scottish clans gather in kilts.

When exploring the sprawling state, it's usually helpful to do so by region. Eight easily defined areas—each with its own personality and shape—will keep you busy, to say nothing of intrigued.

In north Texas, all Dallas and Fort Worth have in common are a shared river, 27 miles of freeway, and the world's busiest airport. Which is just the beauty of the area—in about a half hour you can be some place drastically different. Dallas is larger, more dashing, and aggressive. It glitters and bustles and has a lifestyle ridden with haute cuisine and couture. Fort Worth defines Texas succinctly: business-people wear boots and make deals over barbecue, and cowboy-hatted police officers ride horses on their downtown beats. Dallas's revolving Reunion Tower, the Cowboys and Mavericks, internationally flavored dining, and incomparable shopping bring Fort Worth folks over for visits. Conversely, Fort Worth's restored Stockyards and world-renowned art museums, the Caravan of Dreams and its acclaimed jazz stage, and the family-style Mexican food at Joe T. Garcia's bring Dallasites over in hordes.

East Texas's Piney Woods is something of an extension of the Old South, with several of the Republic of Texas's birthmarks. San Augustine and Nacogdoches are vintage towns packed with earliest history, while Jefferson appeals with its old riverboat town and antiques shop charm. Marshall, a stop on stagecoach and Victorian train lines, has restored mansions and bed-and-breakfasts in lovingly refurbished homes. Train buffs delight in traveling between Rusk and Palestine on the Texas State Railroad's steam locomotives. Tyler grows a third of America's commercial roses, and Canton brings up to 50,000 people each month to its century-old First Monday Trade Days. Four national forests jam the region, and the Big Thicket National Preserve is home to a precious virgin forest where twenty kinds of wild orchids and carnivorous plants and 300 varieties of birds coexist in an impenetrable natural fortress.

Some of Texas's deepest heritage is found in the humid, lush environs of the Texas Gulf Coast. Sam Houston's ravaged army rid the Republic of Santa Anna's Mexican troops on a field named San Jacinto, where now stands a breathtaking, 570-foot commemorative monument against the backdrop of Texas's largest city. Houston is an oil city, home to the NASA-Johnson

INTRODUCTION

Space Center, the Astrodome, and a sizable selection of theaters, museums, and shops.

A short drive east, Galveston is the uppermost of Texas's significant beach communities. Once known as the Wall Street of the Southwest, the island-city boasts one of the nation's largest collections of restored Victorian buildings. The Strand, the 1894 Grand Opera House, Ashton Villa, and the *Elissa,* a square-rigged tall ship, highlight a long list of attractions. Padre Island is a long, thin finger of sand protecting the Texas coast from Corpus Christi to the Rio Grande. Most of the island's 113-mile stretch is national seashore, populated by 350 species of birds, sand dunes, and sea oats. The King Ranch—the largest privately owned ranch in the world—sits inland from the sailboarding, sailing city of Corpus Christi. South Padre Island is a resort town glistening with new high-rise hotels and sleek condos, boutiques, and sun-bleached houses. Teens jam the beaches in spring, families ride the waves in summer, and anglers work the bay and beach year-round.

Brownsville is the state's southernmost point and one entrance to Mexico. Slightly west, the communities of McAllen, Weslaco, and Mission are the heart of Texas's huge citrus industry and the home of Winter Texans, snowbirds from the Midwest. San Antonio, the most common gateway to south Texas, fairly reverberates with the passion of Texas's European origins and the tenacious Hispanic culture still enjoying growth. Some explorers make their way down to Langtry, home to the revered Judge Roy Bean, whose justice was once the only law west of the Pecos. In this southwestern corner find the world's Spinach Capital, the state's oldest winery, the dramatic set of the epic film *The Alamo,* and an opalesque lake shared by two friendly countries.

If the spiritual heart of Texas is to be embraced, it will happen in the Hill Country. Spring-fed rivers course beneath limestone cliffs, through rolling hills dotted with live oak and wildflowers. It is a region for escape, for reflection, for rejuvenation. Small towns in the Hill Country embrace a serenity not quite duplicated elsewhere. Fredericksburg and New Braunfels gleam with their German heritage, displayed in the shops, historic lodgings, and plentiful wurst and beer. Kerrville is home to the Y.O. Ranch, and Burnet claims the Vanishing Texas River Cruise.

At the heart of Texas, figuratively and literally, is Austin, the state capital and an integral part of the Brazos-Republic Trail. This is an easy city to enjoy, one favored for its music and nightlife, where pleasures unfold from lakes and wooded hills, cultural centers at the University of Texas, and the National Wildflower Research Center. To the east are more small towns forming the core of the old republic.

John Wayne should have been required by law to make all his westerns in the Texas Panhandle. The genuine, traditional Texan style is so thick here you could cut it with a knife. In the High Plains a great treasure is the shockingly beautiful and huge Palo Duro Canyon. An exciting musical drama plays under the stars there in summer, and real working cowboys take folks out to the canyon's edge for a Cowboy Morning Breakfast.

Texas's western heritage is defined and illustrated with great care at the Panhandle Plains Museum in Canyon and at the Ranching Heritage Center in Lubbock. Another Lubbock asset—wines produced from its sandy but rich land—is offered for sampling at three award-winning vineyards.

West Texas is a vast area distinguished by attractions as diverse as ancient Native Americans and pioneer forts, mountains, and unexplained moving lights—this is a region that could take years to truly explore. El Paso is a reservoir of Native American, Hispanic, and Anglo influences characterizing the city's architecture, art, food, shopping, and pastimes.

Due east from El Paso, Guadalupe Mountains National Park contains a wealth of scenery, from McKittrick Canyon and its blazing fall foliage to Guadalupe Peak, Texas's highest point at 8,749 feet above sea level. Fort Davis lies between the Guadalupe Mountains and the Big Bend's Chihuahuan Desert. Home to Fort Davis National Historic Site with its restored cavalry fort, Fort Davis sits beside the Davis Mountains State Park and its romantic Indian Lodge, and it claims Prude Ranch, a place with restorative qualities; McDonald Observatory, with fascinating "Star Parties"; and miles of cool, clean mountain air and vistas gained by a 74-mile mountain loop road.

The Big Bend is the site of a rugged, 800,000-acre national park, encompassing a wild stretch of the Rio Grande beloved by geologists, naturalists, and outdoorsy types who want to spend a day, week, or month camping and rafting in jagged canyons.

After driving around a spell, you'll notice bumper stickers with the image of the Texas flag emblazoned by the word "Native" or "Naturalized." Texans, whether born or transplanted here, like to advertise their Lone Star State status.

Such boasts shouldn't detract from the amiable intent—it's simply a friendly state, as the official motto proclaims. It won't take you long to find that out for yourself.

Texas Fast Facts

- Texas is the largest of the contiguous states, with 266,807 square miles
- Only Alaska has more fresh water than Texas
- There are four national forests in Texas
- The King Ranch in Kingsville is the largest ranch in Texas and is slightly larger than the state of Rhode Island
- Texas has 23.4 million acres of woodland
- Houston, Dallas, and San Antonio are among the nation's ten largest cities
- Texas has more than 200,000 alligators
- More than eighteen million people call Texas home, making this the second most populous state
- State capital: Austin
- State motto: Friendship
- State nickname: Lone Star State
- State mammal: armadillo (small); longhorn (large)
- State bird: mockingbird
- State tree: pecan
- State flower: bluebonnet
- State dish: chili
- State gem: blue topaz
- State fruit: red grapefruit
- State dance: square dance
- State song: "Texas, Our Texas"
- State plant: prickly pear
- State pepper: jalapeño
- State reptile: horned lizard
- State fish: Guadalupe bass
- State flying mammal: Mexican free-tailed bat
- State grass: sideoats grama

- State insect: monarch butterfly
- State seashell: lightning whelk
- State ship: battleship *Texas*
- State sport: rodeo

Important Dates in Texas's History

1519 Spain is the first of six nations to claim Texas.

1685 France claims the Rio Grande as the western boundary of its Louisiana Territory, based on the exploration of La Salle.

1821 Upon winning independence from Spain, Mexico acquires Texas.

1836 After holding off a Mexican army of thousands for thirteen days in the Battle of the Alamo, 188 "Texans" die. A month later General Sam Houston leads the Texas army in the successful Battle of San Jacinto to win independence from Mexico.

1845 Texas joins the U.S. as the twenty-eighth state.

1861 Texas secedes from the U.S., joining the Confederates in the Civil War.

1865 Texas rejoins the U.S.

1901 Oil is discovered at Spindletop.

1953 Dwight D. Eisenhower becomes first Texas-born president of the United States.

1963 John F. Kennedy is assassinated in Dallas; Lyndon B. Johnson, born in Stonewall, becomes the thirty-sixth president.

1965 National Aeronautics and Space Administration (NASA) opens the Lyndon B. Johnson Space Center in Houston.

1966 Barbara Jordan is the first African-American elected to the Texas Senate.

2001 George W. Bush becomes the forty-third U.S. president.

Web Sites Worth Visiting

Amarillo: www.amarillo-cvb.org

Austin: www.austintexas.org

Big Bend: www.visitbigbend.com and www.bigbend.com

Corpus Christi: www.cctexas.org

INTRODUCTION

Dallas: www.cityview.com/dallas

Fort Worth: www.fortworth.com

Lubbock: www.lubbocklegends.com

South Padre Island: www.sopadre.com

State parks: www.tpwd.state.tx.us

Speed Limits: The maximum speed limit is 70 miles per hour during the day and 65 at night on all numbered highways in rural areas. Lower limits are posted on many highways; limits on urban freeways are between 55 and 70 miles per hour.

Texas State Parks: The Texas Parks and Wildlife Department offers 122 parks. Texas State Parklands Passport affords visitors discounted entry fees. A Gold Texas Conservation Passport grants unlimited park entry to members for a $50 annual membership fee.

The parks department has a centralized reservations office for camping. Call the office at (512) 389–8900 from 9:00 A.M. until 8:00 P.M. Monday through Friday and from 9:00 A.M. until noon on Saturday.

Texas Travel Information Centers: The Texas Department of Transportation operates travel information centers in twelve locations across Texas. Each center is staffed by professional travel counselors and offers thousands of pieces of free literature, including the excellent *Texas State Travel Guide,* road maps, and lodging guides. All services are free, and the centers are open daily from 8:00 A.M. until 5:00 P.M., except New Year's Day, Thanksgiving Day, Christmas Eve, Christmas Day, and Easter Sunday.

Find the travel centers located in Amarillo on I–40; Anthony on I–10 (near the New Mexico state line); Austin at the Capitol Complex; Denison on U.S. 75/69 (near the Oklahoma state line); Gainesville on U.S. 77/I–35 (near the Oklahoma state line); Langtry on U.S. 90 at Loop 25; Laredo on I–35 (near the Mexican border); Orange on I–10 (near the Louisiana state line); Texarkana on I–30 (near the Arkansas state line); Harlingen on U.S. 77 at U.S. 83; Waskom on I–20 (near the Louisiana state line); and Wichita Falls on I–44 (near the Oklahoma state line).

For information on travel destinations and road conditions, call the travel consultants at (800) 452–9292.

Admission Fees: Note that in many cases, attractions are noted with a phrase such as, "A small admission fee is charged." Generally this means that admission fees are between $1.00 and $10.00 per person. The notation, "Admission is charged" usually means that the fee is above $10.00.

The Brazos-Republic Trail

*A*train whistle blows steadily, and soon loudly, through the fragile darkness. Just before dawn, a rooster begins its intonation, and moos soon follow. Days begin early in the country, breaking clean and fresh—the sky, grass, and picket fences seem unusually pure along central Texas's Brazos and Colorado rivers, through a region spreading just to the east of the Balcones Escarpment and the state's fabled Hill Country. German, Scottish, and Czech immigrants made their way to new homes through this rolling corridor, toughing out a life that could become hazardous when conflicts with Mexicans and Native Americans arose. Here, dairy and cotton farmers and horse ranchers carved lives with their families and friends, thanks in part to their own determined spirit and that of the Texas Rangers.

It was through this part of the frontier, once called Tejas by the Mexicans and Indians, that pioneers crafted a Republic, a sovereign nation that gave rise eventually to the Lone Star State. Today's explorers find great and lasting remnants of that period in peaceful towns that make wonderful discoveries on the way to someplace else, and in a fine capital city whose enduring beauty and character make it a popular place for people who love art, history, rhythm and blues, comfort food, lakeside scenery, and even bats—yes, the nation's largest urban bat colony lives under the Congress Avenue bridge spanning the Colorado River in Austin.

Heart of Texas

*H*illsboro, resting at the center of Hill County, is a town of 8,500, established as a trade center and county seat in 1853. People who've passed through remember most the **Hill County Courthouse,** built in 1890 to replace the original log cabin structure. The flamboyant, cream-colored design on the town square mixes styles to include classical revival, Italianate, and French Second Empire. A vintage *Saturday Evening Post* story called the courthouse "a monstrosity," while *Harper's* countered with a description declaring the ornate structure "like an outstanding cathedral." Tragically, the courthouse was destroyed by fire on

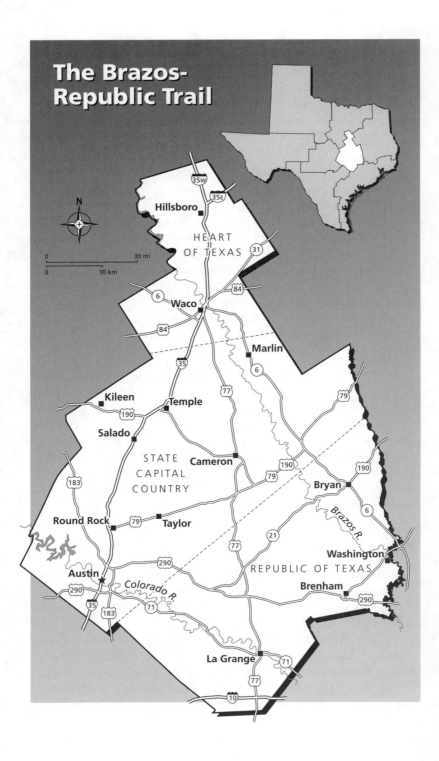

THE BRAZOS-REPUBLIC TRAIL

JUNE'S FAVORITE ATTRACTIONS ON THE BRAZOS-REPUBLIC TRAIL

Ant Street Inn, Brenham

Hill County Courthouse, Hillsboro

Inn at Salado, Salado

Kreuz Market, Lockhart

Lady Bird Johnson Wildflower Center, Austin

Round Top

Spoetzl Brewery, Shiner

Star of Texas Museum, Washington

State Capitol Building, Austin

Village Bakery, West

New Year's Day, 1993; however, the town and some of its powerful children—such as country singer Willie Nelson—rallied quickly to raise funds to restore the masterpiece to its original glory. Work was under way at once, and now the gorgeous creation of Texas limestone reigns over Hillsboro again.

The courthouse square in Hillsboro features a handful of shops, as well as the **Texas Theatre** (107 South Waco Street, Hillsboro 76645, 254–582–FILM), a twin-screen movie house showing first-run films. On the north side of the square, Franklin Street Antique Mall is ornate and inviting. Around the corner the Hillsboro Chamber of Commerce (115 North Covington Street, Hillsboro 76645, 254–582–2481) occupies a delightfully renovated period train depot.

Roughly a block north of the square, at the corner of North Waco Street and West Paschal Street, the old jail (1893–1983) is now the **Hill County Cell Block Museum**, (254) 582–2481. Inside find varied Native American artifacts. Open 10:00 A.M. until 2:00 P.M. Saturday from April through November. Admission is free. And 5 blocks north of the square on North Waco Street, the Old Hillsboro Cemetery is covered with ancient cedar trees and filled with wonderful old headstones and monuments, marking those buried here between 1856 and 1940.

June's Texas Anecdotes

*B*razos Republic: All through my childhood I was told that one of my ancestors was among the signers of the Texas Declaration of Independence. I knew that the portrait of the stern-looking man hanging in my maternal grandparents' home was that man, and I have visited his beautiful, aged headstone in the cemetery in Nacogdoches. As are my relatives, I have always been proud of this connection to Texas's roots. But until I visited the museum at Washington-on-the-Brazos, I never really felt a surge of emotion. When I saw the replica of that famous document, with William Clark Jr., delegate from Sabine County, named at the bottom with Sam Houston and the other forty-nine delegates, I actually felt my heart pounding. And there on the wall, too, was my great-great-great-great-grandfather's face, along with other sketchy pictures of the men who shaped our state's history on March 2, 1836.

3

Just a few blocks east of the square is *Tarlton House of 1895* (211 North Pleasant Street, Hillsboro 76645, 254–582–7216). Inside the 7,000-square-foot Queen Anne Victorian are seven king rooms and one double, all with private baths. There are 12-foot ceilings, east Texas pine floors, four gorgeous stained-glass windows, and seven ornate fireplaces with hand-carved mantels and Italian tile. Lavish breakfasts include casseroles, soufflés or stuffed French toast, fruit, scones, and marmalades. Special offerings consist of murder-mystery weekends; stress-relief weekends for women, including manicures, massages, and the like; and couples weekends, which include golf outings or museum trips.

People also come to Hillsboro for a much more modern pursuit—finding deals at *Prime Outlets of Hillsboro,* at 104 I–35 Northeast, Hillsboro 76645, (254) 582–9205. The fifty-plus stores here include Nike, Liz Claiborne, and Guess?, among other big names, all offering discounts from 20 to 75 percent off retail prices. The outlet center is open Monday through Saturday 10:00 A.M. until 8:00 P.M. and Sunday 11:00 A.M. until 6:00 P.M.

On Saturday and Sunday, visitors can hop aboard Hillsboro's double-decker bus, exactly like those for which London is famous. The sightseeing tour bus makes free shuttle runs between the outlet mall and downtown Hillsboro, from 11:00 A.M. until 4:00 P.M. on Saturday and from 1:00 until 4:00 P.M. on Sunday. The driver will accept tips, of course.

Another weekend bonus in Hillsboro is that of dining at the *Hillsboro Country Club Restaurant* (Country Club Road, north of Craig Street, 254–582–2112). The public is invited to dine from a menu of appetizers, sandwiches, baked potatoes, charbroiled black angus steaks, and specialty pies at lunch on Friday, Saturday, and Sunday and at dinner on Friday and Saturday. Reservations are a good idea.

Festival fans will want to note that Hillsboro hosts *Bond's Alley Arts and Crafts Festival* each year on the second weekend in June at Bond's Alley, a historic site adjacent to the courthouse square.

Take a side trip to *Corsicana,* 41 miles east of Hillsboro on Texas Highway 22. Although established in 1849, the Navarro County seat didn't see much action until oil was accidentally struck here in 1894 when the city was drilling for water. This set off quite a boom, and one of Texas's first refineries was built here in 1897. Today the city of about 23,000 is known far and wide as home to Collin Street Bakery (401 West Seventh Avenue, Hillsboro 75110, 903–872–8111), the fruitcake company founded in 1896. Each year 1.6 million fruitcakes are shipped to every state in the country and to nearly 200 foreign countries. You can also find a 10-cent cup of coffee here. Open 7:30 A.M. until 5:30 P.M. Monday

THE BRAZOS-REPUBLIC TRAIL

through Thursday, 7:00 A.M. until 6:00 P.M. Friday and Saturday, and noon until 6:00 P.M. Sunday.

Get a little history lesson at Corsicana's *Pioneer Village* (912 West Park Avenue, Hillsboro 75110, 903–654–4846), where Navarro County's surviving historic structures, filled with heirlooms, artifacts, and family treasures, make up this living-history village. Grounds include a Peace Officer Museum, a Civil War Museum, the Lefty Frizell Museum, various archives, an 1870 pioneer home, blacksmith shops, a general store, slave quarters, a barn, a carriage house, and an 1838 Indian trading post (the oldest structure in the park). Open from 9:00 A.M. until 5:00 P.M. Monday through Saturday and 1:00 until 5:00 P.M. Sunday. Admission is $2.00 for adults and 50 cents for children and free under six years.

About 10 miles south of Hillsboro, take time out to visit the tiny burgh of Abbott. Hometown of Willie Nelson, Abbott is a favorite stop for old-fashioned, mammoth turkey sandwiches at the *Turkey Shop* (on the east side of Interstate 35, 254–582–2015). Begun informally when the Tufts family began selling those sensational sandwiches to workers building the interstate in 1957, the restaurant opened in 1966. Son Robert is keeping the tradition strong today, selling sandwiches and offering a cafeteria line for diners needing plates of turkey, dressing, mashed potatoes, and green beans. Open from 8:30 A.M. Wednesday through Monday, it closes at 7:00 P.M. on Monday, Wednesday, and Thursday and at 8:00 P.M. on Friday, Saturday, and Sunday.

Texas Trivia

The Burleson County town of Caldwell, west of Bryan-College Station, hosts the annual Kolache Festival in September to celebrate Czech pastries and heritage.

Fifteen miles south on I–35 West—at the apex of the lines forming McLennan County—the tiny town of *West* on I–35 at Farm Road 2114 is a town of 2,500 residents rich in Czechoslovakian heritage. Folks in north and central Texas know where West, Texas, is, but most people think we mean west Texas.

First and foremost, West is famous for Czech food, especially kolaches—thick fruit-filled pastries—and homemade sausage. Travelers en route from Dallas or Fort Worth south to Austin and San Antonio invariably stop off in West to fill orders from friends back home who want plenty of kolaches. Consequently, the half dozen or so **kolache bakeries** on Main and Oak Streets always have pan upon pan ready to box, as well as frozen packages to go.

The Village Bakery at 108 East Oak Street, West 76691, (254) 826–5151, is one of the town's original Czech bakeries, opened in 1952. Kolache fruit varieties include peach, apricot, blueberry, prune, apple, and several others, as well as sausage, or klobasniki, kolaches, by far the most filling. The bakery sells coffee, juices, and soft drinks, and a few tables inside serve those patrons who can't wait any longer to get that kolache fix.

Around the corner, past a few good antiques shops, **Sulak's,** at 208 North Main Street, West 76691, (254) 826–7791, is a longtime favorite of central Texans and travelers alike. Opened in 1923, the Czech diner serves from 11:00 A.M. to 9:00 P.M. Thursday through Saturday. Best efforts are steaks, sausages, stews, bakery items, and Tex-Mex plates.

If you happen upon West on Labor Day weekend, join in the celebration at **Westfest,** one of Texas's favorite parties. Held at the West Fair and Rodeo Grounds at Main Street and Farm Road 1858, West 76691, (254) 826–5058, the Saturday-Sunday affair features authentic Czech costume contests, folk dancing—including polkas and waltzes—and the music of a nuclear-polka group, Brave Combo. Count on plenty of kolaches, sausages, and other comfort food.

Shortly after heading south again on I–35 from West, start watching for Farm Road 308, 10 miles south of West. You'll exit Farm Road 308 and head southwest to reach the **Homestead Heritage Visitors Center** at Brazos de Dios. Stay on Farm Road 308 for 3 miles, then turn north on Farm Road 933 for $1^1/2$ miles, then turn west on Halbert Lane. This is the center of information for a small farming community where traditional crafts and arts are preserved and practiced. From time to time there are workshops for pottery-throwing, basketweaving, soap making, woodworking, quilting, and spinning. At the visitors center, a two-story, dogtrot-style cedar building, you'll find a deli, bookstore, and shop selling early Texas longleaf pine furniture, quilts, wrought-iron fireplace tools, pottery, and food items. Reach the visitors center at (254) 829–0417; it's open from 10:00 A.M. until 6:00 P.M. Monday through Saturday. Gifted woodworkers produce furniture true to that of the pioneer period at the Homestead Heritage Furniture Shop; they'll take orders for their custom work or build furniture according to your specifications. For information call (254) 829–2060.

Back on I–35, **Waco** is another 7 miles south. A city of 106,600 straddling the historic Brazos River, Waco is a place destined to be noted in history books as one with a diverse heritage. Although Waco remains reminiscent of its cotton-cattle-corn heyday, few people will ever forget that the city was once prominent in international headlines for being the site of the tragic Branch Davidian episode in 1993.

Long populated by the Hueco Indians, from which the establishment took its name, Waco saw its first white explorers when a group of Hernando de Soto's men came through in 1542. Real civilization came when the Texas Rangers established a fort here in 1837, however. The town won the nickname "Six-Shooter Junction" later, when the Chisholm Trail was brought through the frontier post, but things have calmed down considerably, as the city is best known now for Baylor University and the Heart O' Texas Fair and Rodeo, held in early October.

Travelers enamored with Wild West history will love the *Texas Ranger Hall of Fame and Museum* (Fort Fisher Park, exit 335B off I–35, 254–750–8631). Inside there's a replica of that 1837 Texas Ranger fort, as well as dioramas and displays detailing the history of the Rangers since Stephen F. Austin founded them in 1823. A firearms collection, Native American artifacts, and western art are exhibited here, headquarters for today's Company F of the Texas Rangers. Camping and picnic sites are available in the thirty-seven-acre park. Open 9:00 A.M. until 5:00 P.M. daily. A small admission fee is charged for ages six and up.

Texas Ranger Hall of Fame and Museum

Waco's campiest attraction is the **Dr Pepper Museum** (300 South Fifth Street, Waco 76706, 254–757–1024), housed in the original bottling plant for Dr Pepper, a favorite Texas soda pop. The fountain drink was originally mixed at the Old Corner Drug Store here in the 1880s, when R. S. Lazenby, a Waco beverage chemist and drugstore customer, took interest in the new soda. After working with the formula for two years, he sold it commercially, and the formula is virtually unchanged. The original 1906 bottling plant-museum is on the National Register of Historic Places and features a restored period soda fountain and much Dr Pepper memorabilia, as well as audiovisual enhancement. It's open Monday through Saturday 10:00 A.M. until 5:00 P.M. and Sunday noon until 5:00 P.M. A small admission fee is charged for ages six and up.

On the campus of Baylor University—chartered under the Republic of Texas in 1845, and now the world's largest Baptist university—is the marvelous **Armstrong Browning Library** (700 Speight Street, Waco 76706, 254–710–3566). Inside find the largest collection of materials relating to Robert and Elizabeth Barrett Browning in existence, as well as fifty-six stained-glass windows depicting the famous pair's poetry. Open 9:00 A.M. until noon and 2:00 until 4:00 P.M. Monday through Friday and 9:00 A.M. until noon Saturday. Admission is free.

Travelers who are sports-minded will find the **Texas Sports Hall of Fame** (1108 South University Parks Drive, Waco 76706, 254–756–1633) of interest. Sports greats who competed on fields, courts, and tracks of Texas are honored, including Shaquille O'Neal, Jackie Robinson, Jack Pardee, and "The Tyler Rose," Earl Campbell, whose high school letter jacket is featured here. There are auto racing uniforms worn by A. J. Foyt and Johnny Rutherford; racing silks; a crop and saddle blanket belonging to Willie Shoemaker; game jerseys worn by Nolan Ryan, Bob Lilly, Mean Joe Greene, and Roger Staubach; and Rogers Hornsby's 1926 St. Louis Cardinals uniform. Highlights from films of college and professional sports are

The Oldest Profession

*T*he first legally regulated red-light district in Texas was, of all places, in Waco. It was also the second in the U.S., passing ordinances in 1889 that provided for the licensing of prostitutes and bawdy houses in a specified district

called the Reservation or Two Street. The one hundred or so women working on Two Street were regularly examined by physicians, but their businesses were shut down after a campaign in 1917, and the last house burned in 1964.

Dr Pepper Museum in Waco

shown in the museum's Tom Landry Theater. Open from 10:00 A.M. until 5:00 P.M. Monday through Saturday and noon to 5:00 P.M. Sunday. A small admission fee is charged for ages six and up.

There are several more points of interest in Waco, including the Bosque Brewing Co., Cameron Park Zoo, the splendid Earle-Harrison House and Pape Gardens, and the Taylor Museum of Waco History. For more information contact the Waco Convention & Visitors Bureau at (800) WACO–FUN or (254) 750–8696, or stop at the Tourist Information Center (take exit 335B off I–35, 254–750–8696); it's open from 8:00 A.M. until 5:00 P.M. Monday through Saturday and 9:00 A.M. until 5:00 P.M. Sunday.

Outdoorsy types can find Texas's oldest state park within close reach of Waco. ***Mother Neff State Park,*** a 259-acre spread in the scenic Leon River Bottom, was founded in 1916. It's reached by driving south from Waco on I–35 about 20 miles, then turning west on Farm Road and driving another 13 miles. You'll see the park upon reaching Texas Highway 236. There's good hiking in the park's Upland Hills and in ravines with shady, rock cliffs. There's good fishing and picnicking here, and photographers frequently find dawn and dusk subjects in raccoons, white-tailed deer, roadrunners, and armadillos. Call the park at (254) 853–2389.

Travelers who enjoy visiting historic cemeteries should make another little side trip from Waco to the town of ***Moody,*** 15 miles southwest via Farm Road 2113. The ***Naler Cemetery*** sign bears the dates 1870–1924; the fence is interesting, too, with wiring attached at gate posts with cogs for tightening.

Another 55 miles south of Waco on I–35, ***Salado*** (suh-LAY-doe) is a bucolic, creek-side stop in Bell County. Although only 1,500 residents call Salado home, it's a well-known jumping-off point for travelers en route to Austin. It was founded on a tract of land along the Chisholm Trail, originally in a grant by the state of Coahuila, Mexico, in 1830.

Scottish colonizer Sterling C. Robertson brought settlers to the area in the 1850s, and it fast became a thriving settlement with the opening of one gristmill inside the town limits and seven others in a 9-mile area. After the railroad bypassed Salado near the end of the century, however, forty-year-old Salado College closed, and the town nearly disappeared. Today there are nineteen state and eighteen national historic markers in town.

The town was named for central Texas's Salado Creek, one of five creeks so named in Texas, and this creek was the state's first designated natural landmark. The lovely waterway is fed by springs that are the northernmost of the huge Edwards Aquifer, surfacing here on the Balcones Fault. Within a few minutes' walk along the creek, it's easy to see why the town has become a retreat for artists, writers, historians, and craftspeople.

Some important folks have passed this way—Gen. Robert E. Lee, Gen. George Custer, and Gen. Sam Houston all stayed at an inn now called the *Stagecoach Inn,* in a shady grove just east of the interstate on Main Street near Royal Street. In fact, it was on the inn's front gallery that Sam Houston made one of his impassioned speeches, urging Texans not to secede from the Union.

The Stagecoach was the town's reason for surviving when times were toughest, and it's still a destination for travelers. The motel is a modern structure, but the restaurant is legendary, serving bounteous if plain lunches for $8.75–$10.75 and enormous dinners for $13.95–$20.25; specialties include baked ham, fried chicken, roast lamb, orange roughy, and filet mignon. Lunch is served from 11:00 A.M. to 4:00 P.M. and dinner is from 5:00 to 9:00 P.M. Call (254) 947–5111.

The Central Texas Area Museum on Main Street, facing the Stagecoach Inn, is busiest during the *Gathering of the Scottish Clans,* held annually in early November; it's open from 10:00 A.M. to 5:00 P.M. daily. The building holding the museum is well over a century old, and exhibits inside detail the history of central Texas. There's also the Wee Scot Shop inside, selling items of Scotland such as kilts and tartans. For information call (254) 947–5232.

After lunch or a look through the museum, wander a few yards north to the creek and follow the bank just a bit to the right. There you'll find *Sirena,* a bronze mermaid, sitting in a tiny inlet. She is lonely and sad, eternally trying to remove a hook from her fin. The creek's grassy bank continues east and is traced by a road winding through *Pace Park,* a willow-shaded place to take a picnic and relax with a book.

Tops of the bed-and-breakfast stops in town is the *Rose Mansion,* Main Street at Pace Park Road, (254) 947–8200. There are seven guest rooms, including three suites, all with private baths. Prices are $90–$130 for one or two. The lovely old home was built in 1873 and is wonderfully aged. Rooms are named for people important to Salado's past, such as General Custer. Antique furnishings are prominent, and books and games are abundant. Breakfast typically showcases something home baked and sensational.

Salado shops selling pottery, artwork, and cappuccino are found in clusters along Main Street, as are tea rooms, lunch cafes, and bed-and-breakfast retreats. For a complete listing call the Salado Chamber of Commerce at (254) 947–5040, or visit the Web site at www.salado.com.

Georgetown, a charming town of 22,000, sits about 20 miles south of Salado on I–35 at Texas Highway 29. The Williamson County seat is home to Southwestern University, Texas's oldest private institution of higher learning, founded in 1840. The university's gorgeous stone buildings, immediately east of the courthouse square on University Avenue, are positively European in architecture. The copper-domed county courthouse is its own masterpiece, and the square is lined with more than fifty Victorian-era buildings filled with gift shops, antiques stores, art galleries, and cafes. Some of the courthouse square shops to note are Handcrafts Unlimited, where quilters are observed on Thursday afternoons; The Windberg Gallery, offering American landscapes; and The Escape, where contemporary arts and crafts made by Texas and U.S. artisans are sold. Nearby, the Georgetown Firefighters Museum, at Ninth and Main Streets, features a 1922 vintage fire engine in mint condition. And right at the Georgetown exit off of I–35, the Mar-Jon Candle Factory offers tours and a gift shop.

It's not unusual to find Austin-bound travelers staying overnight in Georgetown. When big Austin events, such as the springtime South by Southwest Music Festival and the summertime Aquafest, claim most of Austin's lodging, people find Georgetown a good option. Choices include Claiborne House Bed & Breakfast Inn (912 Forest Street, Georgetown 78628, 512–930–3934); Page House Bed & Breakfast Inn (1000 Leander Road, Georgetown 78628, 512–863–8979); and Inn on the Square (104$^{1}/_2$ West Eighth Street, Georgetown 78628, 512–868–2203 or 888–718–2221). For more information contact the Georgetown Convention & Visitors Bureau at (800) 436–8696 or (512) 930–3545.

For a memorable barbecue experience, head east from Georgetown on Texas 29 about 17 miles until you reach Texas Highway 95. Turn south on Highway 95 and continue 7 miles to Taylor. Your destination is **Louie Mueller Barbecue** (206 West Second Street, Taylor 76574, 512–352–6206), which was, in the 1940s, a tiny tin shack in an alley behind the Mueller family's grocery. They opened the barbecue joint in order to sell meats that didn't move in the store, but before too long another barbecue stand was needed as the farming community grew. In 1959 the third and present location opened, and Bobby Mueller took over the business in 1974 when dad Louie retired. Bobby's son, John, joined the family operation in 1991, and the rest is history, as evidenced by the scads of newspaper and magazine articles from across the nation heralding the exceptional food, smoked daily on site in what can only be called a rustic setting. Meals start at about $7.00. Open from 9:00 A.M. until 8:00 P.M. Monday through Saturday.

From Taylor, head west on U.S. Highway 79, which takes you back to I–35. From there it's 18 miles south to Austin.

State Capital Country

Just 28 miles south of Georgetown lies Austin, the capital city, seat of Travis County, and haven for 488,000 people who love to kick back. But the sun worshippers seen today around Barton Springs, the eternally cool spring-fed pool in Zilker Park, were not the first to find this a great place to hang around. Spaniards decided it was the best place to build a mission in 1730, and that was after Native Americans had been established here for centuries.

The 1800s saw the creation of the fledgling settlement named Waterloo, and new Republic of Texas president Mirabeau B. Lamar liked the place so much he moved the seat of government here. A few ego struggles moved the capital back and forth from the Houston area until 1844, and the town was eventually named for the father of Texas, Stephen F. Austin.

Since 1882, students of higher learning have found the **University of Texas**—with an enrollment today of around 50,000—and the Austin environs a place to stay beyond the traditional four years, thanks to numerous graduate programs and jobs in state government. Indeed, with hilly scenery, an easygoing lifestyle, a wealth of homegrown music, and abundant Tex-Mex eats, Austin is easy to love and hard to leave.

The **LBJ Library and Museum** at 2313 Red River Street, Austin 78703, which is part of the university, is fascinating even for those who were not fans of the late President Lyndon B. Johnson. Great detail is used in chronicling his career, and personal items are quite interesting: There are early home photos, a fourth-grade report card showing excellent grades but a C in deportment, and a letter sent to his grandmother during his time at Southwest Texas State Teachers College, in which he expresses his deep desire to not be regarded as a black sheep. There are engagement photos of LBJ and Claudia "Lady Bird" Taylor, and there's an intriguing letter on Lady Bird Taylor's letterhead indicating her fear that Lyndon was thinking of a life in politics. The museum is open daily, 9:00 A.M. until 5:00 P.M. Call (512) 916–5136 for details.

Just east of the interstate, the *French Legation Museum,* 802 San Marcos Street, Austin 78702, was regarded as ostentatious when built in 1841 for the French ambassador to the Republic of Texas. Today the French provincial cottage of Bastrop pine and French fitments seems modest, but it suited the arrogant Comte Alphonse Dubois de Saligny, if just for a short time. It was learned that the irritable chargé d'affaires held a fraudulent title, and that was after he'd shown great disdain for his Native American visitors and Austin neighbors. He spent most of his time in New Orleans, which he found much more enjoyable, and historians estimate he actually spent eight weeks at most in the Austin home.

Today, the Daughters of the Republic of Texas operate the house-museum, situated behind grand iron gates atop a little hill and furnished with nineteenth-century antiques, a few of Saligny's belongings, and authentic items from a French Creole kitchen, such as copper pots and pewter tools. It's open Tuesday through Saturday 1:00 until 5:00 P.M. A small admission fee is charged. For details call (512) 472–8180.

A few blocks to the southeast, *Cisco's* at 1151 East Sixth Street, Austin 78702, is a true Austin institution, especially at breakfast. The Mexican bakery and cafe has small-town friendliness for regulars and newcomers alike, and the eye-opening dishes to know are huevos rancheros and

How Sweet It Is

*N*ext time you're in the grocery store buying ingredients for your favorite baked goodies, pick up flavoring from Adams Extract Co., founded in 1909. The Austin-based purveyor of good tastes produces twenty-seven extracts, including the widely famous vanilla, as well as Jamaican rum, butter, almond, peppermint, and lemon—and ninety-five seasonings. Look for recipes at www.adamsextract.com.

huevos migas, two sassy egg dishes. If you like something a bit heavier, order a basket of picadillos, which are homemade rolls stuffed with spicy beef. Lunches include traditional Mexican plates and chicken-fried steak; for a sweet, check out the bakery case in front. Note that Cisco's is a happy madhouse when the UT Longhorns have a home football game. It's open daily from 7:00 A.M. until 2:30 P.M.; call (512) 478–2420.

Northwest of downtown, *The Elisabet Ney Museum* at 304 East Forty-fourth Street at Avenue H, Austin 78703, awaits in one of the country's four existing studios of nineteenth-century sculptors. German immigrant Ney, a staunchly independent artist, came to the United States in 1873 and built this studio in 1892, naming it Formosa (meaning beautiful) after her studio in Europe. Some of her work is displayed here, while other pieces grace the Smithsonian National Museum of Art, various European palaces, and the Texas statehouse. Formosa was transformed into a museum by her friends and fans soon after her death in 1907. It's been restored but retains the rustic nature Ney loved. Art classes and audiovisual presentations are held here throughout the year. Visit the museum between 10:00 A.M. and 5:00 P.M. Wednesday through Saturday and between noon and 5:00 P.M. Sunday. Call (512) 458–2255 for information.

Also north of downtown is the new *Daughters of the Republic of Texas Museum* (501 East Anderson Lane/I–35 at U.S. Highway 183, Austin 78734, 512–339–1997). Exhibits pertain to the period in which Texas worked for independence as a republic, with historical collections of everyday life as well as guns from the fight for independence from Mexico. Open from 10:00 A.M. to 4:00 P.M., Monday through Friday and from 11:00 A.M. until 4:00 P.M. Saturday. Admission is $2.00.

If you need to be refreshed, head west of downtown to 400-acre *Zilker Park,* at 2220 Barton Springs Road, Austin 78703, home to the renowned *Barton Springs Pool.* The thousand-foot-long, rock-walled swimming hole—fed by Barton Springs, the fourth-largest natural springs in the state—is an oasis, always a chilly 68 degrees. In warm weather, the grassy, shady lawns sloping down to the pool are covered by lounging or Frisbee-tossing sun lovers. Beyond the pool you'll find the city's Botanical Garden Center, the Austin Nature Center, a miniature train, and 8 miles of hiking and biking trails. The park grounds are open daily from 7:00 A.M. until 10:00 P.M. The pool is open daily from 8:00 A.M. until 10:00 P.M. March 15 through October 15; a small admissin fee is charged. Call (512) 477–8672 for pool information and park information.

THE BRAZOS-REPUBLIC TRAIL

Right in the center of town on the UT campus, the *Harry Ransom Humanities Research Center* at Twenty-first and Guadalupe Streets has a remarkable collection of treasures. Visitors may view one of the nation's five complete copies of the Gutenberg Bible, as well as the world's first photograph—shot in 1826 by Joseph Niepce—in the fascinating Photography Collection, which contains more than five million prints and negatives. The literary collection includes autographed editions by Dylan Thomas and E. M. Forster, among several; and the Hoblitzelle Theatre Arts Collection exhibits items from Harry Houdini's personal correspondence to some Burl Ives folk recordings. The center is open Monday through Friday from 9:00 A.M. until 5:00 P.M. Call (512) 471–8944.

The state capitol building in Austin, dedicated on May 16, 1888, is the tallest capitol in the nation, measuring 309 feet and 8 inches from basement floor to the top of the Goddess of Liberty statue. That's about 7 feet higher than the National Capitol.

Also within Harry Ransom Center, the *Jack S. Blanton Museum of Art* (Twenty-third and San Jacinto Streets, 512–471–7324) is the university's fine arts museum and is counted among the top ten university art museums in the nation. The permanent collection includes more than 13,000 works spanning the history of Western civilization, from ancient to contemporary periods. The country's largest and most significant collection of Latin American art and the twentieth-century American art collection, which includes the Mari and James Michener Collection of American Paintings, are featured. The gallery is open from 9:00 A.M. until 5:00 P.M. Monday through Saturday and 1:00 until 5 P.M. Sunday. Admission is free.

In easy walking distance of the university, *Capitol Complex Visitors Center* (East Eleventh and Brazos, 512–305–8400) is well worth a visit. Built in 1857, the former General Land Office is the oldest government office building in Texas. Meticulously restored, it's now the Capitol Complex Visitors Center and Texas History Museum. Open 9:00 A.M. until 5:00 P.M. Tuesday through Friday and 10:00 A.M. until 5:00 P.M. on Saturday. Admission is free.

A few steps away, the *State Capitol Building* (Eleventh and Congress Streets, 512–463–0063) is a glorious work of Texas pink granite. When the legislature is in session, onlookers can watch policy history in the making. Free tours are given 8:30 A.M. until 4:30 P.M. Monday through Friday, 9:30 A.M. until 4:30 P.M. Saturday, and 12:30 until 4:30 P.M. Sunday.

Walk another block to the *Governor's Mansion* (1010 Colorado Street, Austin 78703, 512–463–5518), home to every Texas governor since 1856. Free tours of the antebellum house are given every twenty minutes from 10:00 until 11:40 A.M. Monday through Friday.

State Capitol Building

History buffs will be enthralled with the $80 million *Bob Bullock Texas State History Museum,* opened in April 2001. Surrounded by an exterior of six 11 x 16-foot concrete panels with sculpted bas-relief images that tell the story of Texas, the extraordinary museum is named for the beloved, late lieutenant governor. It houses three floors of exhibits that chart Texas's path. Find artifacts, photographs, art, an IMAX theater, and much, much more. Take extra film to document those sculpted panels, which portray a Native American leading a conquistador through the Palo Duro Canyon, a salute to the Alamo battle's purpose, and Texas-size achievements in the worlds of cowboys, trains, cotton, oil, and space exploration. Look for the smallest details, such as the horned toad near the conquistador's horse and the armadillo skittering out from a moon crater. Open 9:00 A.M. to 6:00 P.M. Monday through Saturday and 1:00 to 6:00 P.M. Sunday; 1800 North Congress Avenue, Austin, 78701, (512) 936–8746. Admission is charged.

Also downtown is the *Mexic-Arte Museum* (419 Congress Avenue, Austin 78701, 512–480–9373), which supports and promotes the Mexican/Latino art community. Exhibitions have shown the work of more than 5,000 artists, including that of Diego Rivera, Frida Kahlo, Juan Soriano, Jean Charlot, and others. Permanent exhibits showcase prints, photographs, textiles, masks, and artifacts. Open 10:00 A.M. to 6:00 P.M. Monday through Saturday.

A short drive north of the campus, find hundreds of gift items at *Clarksville Pottery & Gallery* (4001 North Lamar Street, Austin, 78734, 512–454– 9079). Begun in 1976 by a former university professor, the pottery offers handcrafted artwork in the form of jewelry, copper candlesticks, wooden boxes, clay jars, and much more by local, national, and international creators.

Among the growing number of fine stores just south of downtown is *Uncommon Objects* (1512 South Congress Avenue, Austin 78704, 512–442–4000), a place to pick up a great birthday or wedding present or to furnish your home. The store stocks hundreds of pieces of handcrafted items, such as tables and chairs, candlesticks, and mirrors, as well as antiques from Mexico and the Southwest.

The coolest new digs in town can be found at the *Hotel San Jose* (1316 South Congress Avenue, Austin 78704; 512–444–7322), a stylish inn carved from a 1930s tourist court that had gone to seed. The forty-room motel was turned into a model of retro refinement, with stained cement floors, Jetsons'-style modern furniture in the minimalist rooms, Indian cotton print spreads on thick platform beds, and butterfly chairs by the small, soothing pool. Potted cacti are everywhere, taking in the sun that peeks through handcrafted *latillas* and arbors along patios and walkways. Rooms come with high-speed Internet access, TV/VCRs, phones, and clock radios with CD players. Guests can get same-day dry cleaning, on-site massage therapy, and beer and wine in the poolside bar after 5:00 P.M. Dog bowls and dog beds are provided at the front desk for your canine companions. Rates are about $70–$175 and include a healthful continental breakfast.

Austin's selection of fine B&B lodgings is on the grow. For sensational views of Lake Austin, check into **River Oaks Farm** (2105 Scenic Drive, Austin 78703, 512–474–2288). A romantic old stone lodge sitting on the edge of Lake Austin, River Oaks Farm was built in the 1920s as a gentleman's hunting club. The Normandy-like farmhouse with three fieldstone buildings sits on an acre of beautifully landscaped, oak-covered grounds.

Right in the heart of town, **Lazy Oak Inn** (211 West Live Oak Street, Austin 78703, 512–447–8873) is an old plantation-style farmhouse built in 1911. Close to the capitol, Sixth Street, and the Convention Center, this B&B is decorated with antiques and eclectic furnishings. Nearby, The **Governors' Inn** (611 West Thirty-third Street, Austin 78705, 800–871–8908), built in 1897, is located 2 blocks from the UT campus and was once a fraternity house. There are ten rooms with private baths; a full breakfast is included.

To appreciate one of the state's finest sources of pride is to visit the **Lady Bird Johnson Wildflower Center** (4801 La Crosse Avenue, Austin 78744, 512– 292–4200), founded in 1982 by Lady Bird Johnson and called by *Texas Monthly* magazine her "visionary gift to Texas." Way back when her husband was still in the White House, Mrs. Johnson began her plan of beautifying America with roadside flowers. Her generous passion gave way to this extraordinary place, which remains the nation's only nonprofit organization committed to the preservation and reestablishment of native North American wildflowers, grasses, trees, shrubs, and vines in planned landscapes. Not only does the Wildflower Center maintain one of the largest collections of information about native North American plants for interested visitors, but it makes information available to more than 20,000 members across North America as well as landscape professionals and gardeners around the world. The Visitors Gallery, Research Library, and 232-seat auditorium all add to the educational experience of this unique facility.

Texas Trivia

There are 5,000 species of wildflowers in Texas. The bluebonnet is the state flower.

Relocated in 1995 to more sprawling land, the grounds are open from 9:00 A.M. until 5:30 P.M. Tuesday through Sunday. The Visitors Gallery is open from 9:00 A.M. until 4:00 P.M. Tuesday through Saturday and 1:00 until 4:00 P.M. Sunday. The store, Wild Ideas, is open from 9:00 A.M. until 5:30 P.M. Tuesday through Saturday and 1:00 until 4:00 P.M. Sunday. The Wildflower Cafe is open from 9:00 A.M. until 4:00 P.M. Tuesday through Saturday and 11:00 A.M. until 4:00 P.M. Sunday. A small admission fee is charged. Children under eighteen months are admitted free. Find the center's Internet site at www.wildflower.org.

Right downtown, the **O. Henry Museum** at 409 East Fifth Street, Austin 78701, occupies the quaint Victorian home briefly lived in by the master of short stories and surprise endings. His real name was William Sydney Porter, and he published an extremely short-lived publication called the *Rolling Stone* from his Austin residence in the 1890s. The museum contains some of Porter's personal effects, including a yellowing original of his *Rolling Stone,* and various period pieces. Writing classes for adults and children are held here from time to time, and each spring brings the O. Henry Pun-Off, a good time for all. The home is open Wednesday through Sunday from noon until 5:00 P.M. Call (512) 472–1903 for more information.

Just a few blocks from downtown proper, **Treaty Oak** (503 Baylor Street, between West Fifth and Sixth Streets) is the last of a cluster called Council Oaks, where treaties with Native Americans were

Bizarre Texas Stuff

*I*f Austin loves its wildflowers and live music, it's gone completely wild over its thousands of nocturnal winged residents. A stupendous bat colony—now the largest in urban North America—roosting on crevices beneath the Congress Avenue Bridge over the Colorado River has not only attracted a following of devoted observers, it's come under the watchful protection of Bat Conservation International (BCI). From BCI, Austinites and visitors have learned that these gentle and incredibly sophisticated animals pose no threat to bat watchers—as long as no one tries to handle the bats. In fact, on their evening flights from under the bridge, the Austin bats eat from 10,000 to 30,000 pounds of insects, including mosquitoes and numerous agricultural pests. Watching the nightly show of 1.5 million bats drag a flowing black curtain against the sunset is nothing less than spectacular; best viewing is from mid-March until early November, when the bats return to Mexico. As the nights become hotter and drier, the bats emerge earlier in the evening for food. For more information call the bat hot line at (512) 416–5700.

allegedly signed. It's thought that the historic Treaty Oak has grown from this Texas soil for more than 500 years, but the tree drew national attention and even sympathy when it was poisoned in 1989. Half the tree has been removed to save the remaining portion. Visitors come in a daily trickle to see notes, poems, and small gifts left by well-wishers.

Is it time yet to cool off again? If so, drive west from town on Texas Highway 71 about 16 miles to Farm Road 3238 and go south for 13 miles till you see **Hamilton Pool,** a Travis County park on Hamilton Pool Road. A swimming hole has been deemed the use of this stunning collapsed grotto since even old-timers can remember. There are 60-foot waterfalls cascading into the limestone-walled, jade green pool. County conservation authorities limit use to the first one hundred carloads into the park, so it's wise to go early or call ahead to see if there's room. You can picnic and hike there and book a guided nature tour. Open daily from 9:00 A.M. until 6:00 P.M.; admission is $5.00 per vehicle and visitors over sixty-two enter free. For details call (512) 264–2740.

Austin has a healthy relationship with beer, and you can see how one of the state's premier microbreweries does its magic at *Celis Brewery* (2431 Forbes Drive, Austin 78734, 512–835–0884). Tours are offered at 2:00 P.M. and 4:00 P.M. Tuesday through Saturday. It's free, first-come, first-served. Tours last thirty minutes and are followed by a tasting.

The brewpub known for good food, as well as suds, is *The Bitter End Bistro & Brewery* (311 Colorado Street, Austin 78701, 512–478–2337). Tucked into a renovated former warehouse, this appealing—and noisy—spot offers elaborate eats such as duck liver pâté, sausage, shredded barbecued pork, trout on bruschetta with capers and tomatoes, and the perfect beers to complement the flavors. Lunch can be $7.00 to $15.00, dinner from about $10.00. It's open for lunch from 11:00 A.M. until 2:00 P.M. Monday through Friday and for dinner from 5:00 until 10:30 P.M. Sunday through Thursday and 5:00 until 11:30 P.M. Friday and Saturday.

Fans of the PBS series called *Austin City Limits* know this town has music in its veins. Calling itself the Live Music Capital of the World, Austin offers dozens upon dozens of live music venues where you're likely to see groups you'll soon hear on the radio. To find out who's on stage when you visit, pick up a copy of the *Austin Chronicle,* an excellent alternative weekly, or check the weekend entertainment guide in the *Austin American-Statesman,* the city's daily newspaper. Almost any day of the week, the best acts are found at Antone's (2915 Guadalupe Street, Austin 78703, 512–474–5314), also known as Austin's Home of the Blues; and at Cedar Street

(208A West Fourth Street, Austin 78701, 512–708–8811), where martinis, imported cigars, and live jazz and swing are always served on the shady patio. The Continental Club (1315 South Congress Avenue, Austin 78704, 512–441–2444) has become an exceedingly hip hangout and a place where the musical mix is decidedly eclectic. There might be a polka band on stage, or there might be a crooner singing the sort of lounge music that makes you crave a martini, shaken and not stirred.

Town Lake, one of seven sapphire jewels formed by dams along this lower portion of the beautiful Colorado River, is toured aboard a paddlewheel replica called the *Lone Star Riverboat.* Excursions last ninety minutes and no reservations are required. Find the dock between the Congress Avenue and South First Street Bridges on the south shore of Town Lake. Tours depart at 5:30 P.M. Tuesday through Sunday and at 10:30 P.M. Friday, June through August; and at 3:00 P.M. Saturday and Sunday, September through November. Call (512) 327–1388 for more details; fees vary per tour.

A delightful view of the storied landscape spreading west from Austin's hills is bought with a ticket on the *Hill Country Flyer,* a train excursion operated solely by volunteers, which meets all state and federal rail inspection requirements. Steam railroading came back to central Texas when the Austin Steam Train Association put a restored vintage Southern Pacific steam locomotive plus a train of period passenger cars in operation as the Austin & Central Railroad. The Hill Country Flyer offers Saturday and Sunday excursions over a scenic 33-mile route from Cedar Park (on the northwest outskirts of Austin) to the hamlet of Burnet.

From March through Thanksgiving the train leaves at 10:00 A.M. from Cedar Park, making a two-hour trip to Burnet, where a three-hour layover is filled with lunch, antiques shopping, and a show by the Burnet Gunfighters Association. At 3:00 P.M. the train backs out of town, using a wye to turn the train for the return trip to Cedar Park, and arrives there about 5:30 P.M. After Thanksgiving the departure from Cedar Park is at 2:30 P.M., putting passengers in Burnet in time for dinner, followed by a stroll around the square to view thousands of Christmas lights. A 7:00 P.M. departure returns you to Cedar Park about 9:30 P.M. Make reservations by calling (512) 477–8468. Ticket prices vary.

To truly lighten up, unwind, and get centered, the destination of choice is the *Lake Austin Spa Resort* (1705 Quinlan Park Road, Austin 78732, 800–847–5637). A deluxe spa facility in a beautiful setting, the resort offers packages for three, four, or seven nights. Depending on your wants, your visit can include skin and body treatments; personal strength training sessions; nutrition consultation and healthy cooking classes; any assortment of fitness classes; body composition analysis; exercise options including kayaking, sculling, canoeing, and yoga; as well as meditation classes.

A $3 million expansion and renovation in 2000 yielded gorgeous suites, cottages, and rooms, many of which have private courtyards and/or porches with lovely views of the lake and hills. Landscaped gardens, a wonderful garden library, and the exquisite Healing Waters Spa ensure comfort and restoration in one of the most unforgettable surroundings in Texas. Inquire about special seasonal offerings, which may include authors' forums, healthful gourmet cooking, and friends and mother-daughter programs. Three-night deals start at about $1,100 and include all meals and most fitness programs. Spa offerings are usually extra. Learn more at www.lakeaustinsparesort.com.

Believe it or not, some people plan their entire visit in Austin around food. And it's no wonder, given the amazing selection of good restaurants. A must for dinner is *Fonda San Miguel* (2330 West North Loop, Austin 78756, 512–459–4121), a perfect slice of Old Mexico cuisine in a gorgeous villa setting. Exquisite chicken, steak, and fish choices are offered for dinner, from 5:00 until 9:30 P.M. Sunday through Thursday and until 10:30 P.M. Friday and Saturday. Sunday brunch is from 11:00 A.M. until 2:00 P.M. Meals typically are $15 to $30.

Hudson's on the Bend (3509 Ranch Road 620, Austin 78734, 512–266–1369) offers an unequaled Hill Country setting where haute Texas cuisine includes water buffalo enchiladas, kangaroo loin marinated in orange and cilantro, and crepes filled with smoked lobster, shrimp, and scallops. Do call ahead for reservations and plan to spend at least $20 per person. Open for dinner from 6:00 until 10:00 P.M. Sunday through Friday and from 5:30 until 10:00 P.M. Saturday.

Down-home food is found at *Stubb's Barbecue* (801 Red River Street, Austin 78701, 512–480–8341), an outpost of a beloved Lubbock landmark housed within a historic brick building, offering a great deck under the stars. Beef ribs, brisket, chicken, cole slaw, pinto beans, new-potato salad, and cold beer spell success. Open from 11:00 A.M. until 11:00 P.M. daily. Meals are about $7.00 and up. And at *Texas Chili Parlor* (1409 Lavaca Street, Austin 78701, 512–472–2828), you'll find the stuff legends are made of. This small, dumpy place is home to some pretty serious chili, rated X to XXX. You can get a bowl of chili or have it spread atop burgers or nachos. Clientele includes everyone from state politicos to university students and musicians. Meals start at about $5.00.

For more information on Austin, contact the visitors bureau at (800) 926–2282. Or visit Austin's Internet sites at www.austintexas.org and austin.yahoo.com.

For some of the finest barbecue ever, head back east to town and follow U.S. Highway 290 across I–35 about 5 miles, then turn south on U.S. Highway 183, traveling 30 miles to the burgh of *Lockhart,* seat of Caldwell County and home to just over 9,000 residents. *Kreuz* (pronounced krytes) *Market,* a veritable institution at its new location on U.S. Highway 183, is a cultural and gastronomical experience that will be long remembered.

Lines are long before the noon lunch hour, and steady streams of people file through the searing-hot, smoky pit room where your barbecue is cut to order by weight. They'll pile your request for smoked brisket, pork brisket, pork chops, or sausage onto brown butcher paper, along with a stack of white bread, which you then take over to a counter in the lunchroom to get "the fixins," such as sliced onion, tomato, cheese, avocados, jalapeños, and pickles. If you ask for barbecue sauce, be forewarned that you may insult the proprietors—the meat is so tender and flavorful none is needed. There are, however, bottles of hot pepper sauce on the tables for fire-eaters. Lunch is usually $5.00 to $10.00, plus cheap beer or soda pops. Kreuz's is open Monday through Friday 7:00 A.M. until 6:00 P.M. and Saturday 7:00 A.M. until 6:30 P.M. Call (512) 398–2361 for details.

> ### All Natural
>
> *Nature lovers will enjoy the McKinney Roughs, a blend of environmental laboratory and nature preserve found between Austin and Bastrop. The new park was developed by the Lower Colorado River Authority in 1998 and offers an Environmental Learning Center. Closed on Monday, it's found at 1884 Texas Highway 71, just 8 miles west of Bastrop. Call (512) 303–5073.*

If it's a typically pretty day, get that barbecue to go. Head east 26 miles on Farm Road 20 to Texas Highway 71 and follow 71 east 8 miles to *Bastrop,* where you can have a quiet picnic at *Bastrop State Park.* There, in 3,500 acres of rolling land studded with the mysterious "Lost Pines," is a tranquil and rich nature sanctuary along Lake Bastrop to be enjoyed for more than a mere day. Fishing, camping, hiking, golf, and nature study are big draws at the park, as are rustic but comfortable cabins. Find the park just a mile east of Texas Highway 71's junction with Texas Highway 21. Call (512) 321–2101.

The town of Bastrop is the Bastrop County seat and home to about 6,000 residents and several charming shops. The *Bastrop County Historical Museum* at 702 Main Street, Bastrop 78602, occupies the distinctive Cornelson-Fehr House, a Texas Historic Landmark and an 1850 structure resting on the site of a much older Spanish fort. Among miscellaneous and interesting manuscripts, pioneer collections, and Native American artifacts are silver spoons that are said to have been crafted from coins taken from Santa Anna at the Battle of San Jacinto. The museum is open Monday through Friday from noon until 4:00 P.M. and Saturday and Sunday from 1:00 until 5:00 P.M.; admission is just 50 cents. Call (512) 321–6177 for information.

If you decide to skip Bastrop, take U.S. Highway 183 south from Lockhart about 30 miles to *Gonzales,* appropriately nicknamed The Cradle of Texas Independence. Founded in 1825, Gonzales is the site where, a decade later, the first shot for Texas's independence was fired. The "Come and Take It" cannon, which fired that fateful shot on October 2, 1835, is displayed at Gonzales Memorial Museum, on East Street at Lawrence Street, a grand structure built for the Texas Centennial and given to Gonzales by the state.

Birders making the trek this way will want to stop at *Palmetto State Park* (north of Gonzales about 12 miles on U.S. Highway 183, 830–672–3266). Part of the Great Coastal Birders Trail, this 263-acre park is on the spring-fed San Marcos River and features natural artesian springs that have been thought for centuries to have healing powers. Numerous nature trails follow the steep banks of the river and wend through a palmetto swamp.

Bizarre Texas Stuff

*B*ASTROP: Sometimes people are not what they seem to be, even if they offer impeccable credentials. This was certainly the case with Baron de Bastrop, for whom the town 30 miles east of Austin was named. Claiming to be Felipe Enrique Neri, an important Dutch nobleman, the "baron" appeared in Texas in 1805; obtained a colony grant; established a freighting business; was named negotiator with the Mexican government for Stephen F. Austin's original Anglo-American colony; was elected representative to the Mexican state of Coahuila, which included Texas; and helped establish the port of Galveston. In reality, he was Philip Hendrik Nering Bogel, born in Dutch Guiana to ordinary Dutch parents. He moved to Holland, where he was a tax collector accused of embezzlement before fleeing to Texas for a life as an imposter. When he died in 1827, he didn't leave enough money to cover burial expenses, and there was still a reward offered in Holland for his capture. Interestingly, Bastrop was named for him a full decade after his death.

Gonzales's *Houston House Bed & Breakfast* (621 East Saint George Street, Gonzales 78629, 830–672–6940) is a Queen Anne Victorian mansion, built in 1895 with towers and wraparound porches, original parquet floors, fireplaces, and embossed ceiling. Hand-painted murals cover the parlor ceiling and dining room walls. Many of the antiques date to the Civil War. Four guest rooms include three with private baths. Breakfast often includes the host's Bavarian pancakes. Visit Houston House's Web site at www.houstonhouse.com.

From Gonzales, make a worthwhile detour via Alternate U.S. 90 east, driving about 20 miles to Shiner, a tiny town in Lavaca County and home to the *Spoetzl Brewery.* This is where Shiner Beer is "brewed with an attitude," as the slogan goes. Shiner Bock and Shiner Honey Wheat have become extremely popular beers in Texas, and demand across the country is growing. The brewery was founded by Kosmos Spoetzl, one of several German-Czech immigrants who came to this part of the state in 1909. Kosmos brought his Bavarian brewing recipes, and today the brewery produces Kosmos Reserve Lager in his honor.

Brewery tours, which end with complimentary tastings, are given on weekdays at 10:00 A.M., 11:00 A.M., 1:30 P.M., and 2:30 P.M. or by appointment by calling (361) 594–3383. There's also the Spoetzl Brewery Gift Shop/Museum, where a video offers the history of the brewery.

The Republic of Texas

To explore deep into Texas's past, begin your journey by driving east on Texas Highway 71, stopping just 32 miles down the road at the hamlet on the mighty Colorado River called *La Grange.* Seat of Fayette County and home to 4,000 residents, the establishment dates to 1831, when the road passing through was simply a buffalo trail. Historical markers abound—at the old railroad depot, the old county jail, the 1890s courthouse, the vintage Episcopal church—and the local historical route called Texas Pioneer Trail courses through town.

Of particular interest is *Kreische Brewery State Historical Site and Monument Hill,* 3 miles south of the town center on Spur 92. Vestiges of a stone brewery and home erected by stonemason Heinreich L. Kreische, a German immigrant who arrived in 1840, mark the first commercial brewery in Texas and one that produced more than 700 barrels a year in its prime. Tours of the brewery and ruins are conducted on Saturday and Sunday at 2:00 P.M. and 3:30 P.M. only and are included in the admission to Monument Hill, also part of the state park.

The latter is a resting place of the Battle of Salado martyrs and victims of the tragic Black Bean Episode of the Mier Expedition, all during the Mexican War. The dramatic monument is a 48-foot creation of stone, bronze, and polychrome. There's a visitors center, as well as an interpretive trail, nature trail, picnic sites, and playground. The monument park is open daily from 8:00 A.M. until 5:00 P.M. Admission is $2.00 for adults, $1.00 for children. For more details call (979) 968–5658.

The countryside is bound to make you yearn for home cooking, so look no further than *Bon Ton Restaurant* at 2359 Business Texas Highway 71, La Grange 78945. It may not look like much from the outside, but customers have counted for years on its wonderful fried chicken, sumptuous pies, and sweet cream butter. Bon Ton is open for breakfast, lunch, and dinner; call (979) 968–8875 for information.

If it's spring, endless *vistas of bluebonnets,* orange-and-yellow Indian paintbrushes, and pink primroses will be your vivid companions as you continue northeast on Texas Highway 159 just 15 miles to *Round Top.* This wide spot in the Fayette County road seems small, with fewer than one hundred residents, but it packs a cultural punch. The miniature town was once called Jones Post Office back in 1835, but its new name came from the Round Top Academy, which operated here from 1854 to 1867, with tuition costing $10 per semester.

Today, on what passes for a town square, there's *Klump's,* a country cafe serving cold beer and barbecued pork ribs, beef, roast, sausage, chicken, and trimmings on Saturday and Sunday. Come on Saturday morning and find fresh breads and coffee cakes. Open daily; call (979) 249–5696.

Bordering the square's east side, *Henkel Square* is an impressive, growing collection of homes and buildings dating from 1820 until 1870. Furnishings and artistic decor are examples of the period's Anglo and German influences. The collection is administered by the Texas Pioneer Arts Foundation. Open daily from noon until 5:00 P.M., there's a $3.00 admission for adults and $2.00 for children. Call (979) 249–3308 for more information.

Five blocks north, on Texas Highway 237, *Festival Hill* is the site of the International Festival-Institute. A concert weekend is scheduled monthly, and summer is devoted to popular performances by institute students with visiting orchestras and string quartets. Festival Hill is occupied by a marvelous array of restored period buildings; even if you're not planning to attend a concert, it's a gorgeous place to explore and photograph. For a schedule call (979) 249–3129.

It's only a 4-mile drive northeast of Round Top on Farm Roads 1457 and 2714 to the **Winedale Historical Center,** a picture seemingly realized from *An American Gothic.* Perfectly restored farms, ranch houses, plantation homes, log cabins, smokehouses, and barns represent more of the Anglo and German heritage prevalent in Texas. The center is an extension of the University of Texas, and it's open for weekday tours by appointment and all day on Saturday and Sunday.

Winedale's many events throughout the year include a summer Shakespeare Festival, Oktoberfest, Christmas open house, and spring craft exhibition. Some events cost $2.00 admission, but others are free. Call (979) 278–3530 for complete information and appointments.

An especially pleasant detour to make from Round Top is the one northwest 10 miles to **Ledbetter Bed & Breakfast,** Farm Road 1291 at U.S. Highway 290, (979) 249–3066. The farm spread is a great place to go for a family reunion or to meet fellow wanderers, as the B&B has fourteen rooms, eight with private baths and six with shared baths. A kitchenette is available, but you may not want to cook as the hosts provide a huge country breakfast buffet every morning. There's an indoor heated pool, volleyball court, trails for walking and cycling, plus a big living area, where the jukebox is loaded with golden oldies.

From Round Top, drive north on Texas Highway 237 about 8 miles to U.S. Highway 290 and turn east on Highway 290, continuing 16 miles to **Brenham.** Yum—you've reached the home of "the little creamery," **Blue Bell Ice Cream,** just 2 miles southeast on Loop Farm Road 577. *Time* magazine called it the best ice cream in the world, a small-town giant that now produces some twenty million gallons per year. Free tours and samples are given to visitors, who are also treated to a film and a look at production from an observation deck. For the seasonal tour schedule, call (979) 830–2197 or (800) 327–8135. Reservations are strongly recommended.

Brenham, seat of Washington County—birthplace of the Republic of Texas—and home to 12,000 residents and plenty of antiques shops, is known also for sweetness of an altogether different nature. Head 8 miles north of town on Farm Road 50 to **Antique Rose Emporium,** once strictly a wholesaler of antique rose varieties and now a beautiful nursery spread open to the public. You can buy rose bushes on site or pick up a hefty catalog for mail orders. Open Monday through Saturday 9:00 A.M. until 6:00 P.M. and Sunday 11:00 A.M. until 5:30 P.M. Call (979) 836–5548 for details.

For yet another rare scene, take Texas Highway 105 northeast from Brenham 9 miles to the **Monastery of Saint Clare,** where resident cloistered nuns breed, train, and sell gentle miniature horses. The ninety-eight-acre ranch is run by the sisters of the Order of Saint Clare, founded in the thirteenth century by a follower of Saint Francis of Assisi and now known as a top breeder of the tiny horses. The ranch unfolds along fertile slopes, shaded by ancient, spreading oaks. The horses are scaled-down duplicates of their full-size cousins, appaloosas, pintos, and Arabians, but these are a playful, endearing variety. A gift shop and ceramics studio is also on view. Visitors may come between 2:00 and 4:00 P.M. daily or by appointment. There's no admission, but donations are gratefully accepted. Call (979) 836–9652.

Nueces Canyon Ranch, just west of Brenham on U.S. Highway 290, is a working, eighty-acre horse ranch that accommodates visitors. If you choose, you can stay in a private, three-bedroom guest house alongside a trickling brook. There's horseback riding, volleyball, and horseshoe pitching. Breakfast is included, and it's hearty—eggs, hash browns, sausage, kolaches, and fruit. Overnight stays cost about $100; (979) 289–5600.

About 10 miles west of Brenham on U.S. 290, at the town of Burton, there's the exceptional **Long Point Inn,** (979) 289–3171, bearing wonderful resemblance to the romantic chalets of Europe, down to the window boxes overflowing with geraniums and flower arrangements made from the inn's seventy-plus rose bushes. The inn lies on Texas's only road to bear both Scenic Route and Historic Route designations, and the land is part of a 175-acre cattle ranch overlooking lovely Lake Somerville. Fish for bass, catfish, and bluegill in six stocked ponds and fill up on a ranch hands' breakfast of fruit compote, fruit juices, eggs, grits or potatoes, locally made German pork sausage, and homemade breads, jams, and jellies served at a formal table set with china, crystal, and silver.

Brenham has numerous bed-and-breakfast offerings and antiques shops. For more information contact the Washington County Convention & Visitors Bureau, 314 South Austin Street, Brenham, (979) 836–3695 or (888) BRE–NHAM.

A moving picture of Texas's past is seen in **Independence,** just an 11-mile drive north of Brenham on Farm Road 50. The Washington County settlement of 150 was founded in 1824 by one of Stephen F. Austin's original 300 families. A town square was designed for the Washington County seat, but Brenham won the hotly contested vote by just two.

Old Baylor Park, ¹/₂ mile west on flower-peppered Farm Road 390, holds the ruins of Old Baylor University and the restored home of John P. Coles, the founding settler. Also on Farm Road 390, you'll find the *Sam Houston Homesite,* noted by a granite marker. A few yards away, there's *Mrs. Sam Houston's Home*—one of the earliest surviving examples of Greek Revival architecture. Mrs. Houston bought it for herself and her eight children after her husband died in 1863. Sam Houston Jr., other Texas pioneers, and veterans of wars from the American Revolution to World War II are buried in the town cemetery.

It's but another 10 miles east on U.S. Highway 290 from Brenham to *Chappell Hill,* a charming Washington County township of 300 established in 1847. Set amid rolling pastures of horse farms, wildflowers, and twisting post oak trees, Chappell Hill boasts a bevy of historic structures, the most remarkable being the *Browning Plantation,* on Farm Road 1155 just south of town. Included on the National Register of Historic Places, the mansion dates to the 1850s and is a restoration masterpiece.

Fortunately for travelers, the Browning Plantation is also a bed-and-breakfast inn, where guests are spoiled with fine furnishings, scenery, 220 acres of natural trails, lake fishing, a swimming pool, and lavish breakfasts. Expect to pay between $85 and $110 for lodging; call (979) 836–6144 for reservations.

Another splendid B&B option in Chappell Hill is the *Mulberry House,* south of town off Farm Road 1155 and Farm Road 2447. The country house and renovated barn offer lodgings, all with private baths and phones. Good antique pieces are used throughout, and croquet is the game of choice in back. Breakfast lovers are in luck, as the hosts prepare extravagant spreads of casseroles and other baked dishes and myriad baked goodies. Rooms are $75 to $100; call (979) 836–1672 for reservations.

The inns are quiet places to stay after a trip to nearby *Washington-on-the-Brazos,* the legendary town where in 1836 the Texas Declaration of Independence was signed and where the constitution of the new Republic of Texas was drafted, also in 1836. From 1842 until 1846, Washington was also the capital of the Republic, and the town prospered as a commercial center for the cotton-rich Brazos Valley.

Today that heritage is memorialized at the *Star of Texas Museum at Washington-on-the-Brazos State Park,* on Farm Road 1155, 18 miles north of Chappell Hill. The museum is indeed star shaped, and its exhibits offer interpretation of Texas as a separate and exclusive nation as well as its journey to statehood. Seasonal exhibitions, audio-visual presentations, and demonstrations of early nineteenth-century life are often scheduled. The museum is open daily from 10:00 A.M. until 5:00 P.M. Call (979) 878–2461 for details.

The state historical park, which has just undergone an extensive $6 million expansion, contains a portion of the historic town site; a reconstruction of Independence Hall; the home of Anson Jones, Texas's last president; an outdoor amphitheater; and a pecan grove doubling as a picturesque picnic area. Hours vary for the different sites, and special events are held on the Sunday closest to March 2, Texas's independence day. For information call (979) 878–2461.

From Washington-on-the-Brazos, head north on Texas Highway 90 about 20 miles to the town of **Anderson,** a historic town of just 300, established in 1834 on La Bahia Road, the ancient Indian trail that stretched from Louisiana through Texas and was used by Spanish explorers. There are numerous charming buildings and homes from the post–Civil War and Victorian period, including the delightful 1891 Grimes County Courthouse. Don't miss an opportunity to see **Fanthorp Inn State Historic Park** in Anderson, (936) 873–2633, a pre–Republic of Texas log inn built in 1834. It's said that Texas notables such as Sam Houston, Anson Jones, Jefferson Davis (who became president of the Confederacy), and Gens. Stonewall Jackson and Robert E. Lee stayed here. There are stagecoach rides from 1:00 until 4:00 P.M. on the second Saturday of each month; tickets are $4.00 for adults and $2.50 for children twelve and under. The inn is open for tours from 9:00 A.M. until 4:00 P.M. Friday through Sunday. Admission is $3.00.

From Anderson take Farm Road 244 northwest about 10 miles to Texas Highway 30, then head west on Texas Highway 30 another 31 miles to **Bryan–College Station.** Always referred to in hyphenated form, the attached cities spread over the gentle hills of Brazos County and have long been mistaken as little more than a wide place in the road. Founded by Stephen F. Austin's colonists between 1821 and 1831, the duo has grown in leaps and bounds with Texas A&M University. Established in 1876 as the state's first public institution for higher education, Texas A&M became in 1996 the school with the nation's largest undergraduate enrollment, claiming more than 50,000 students.

If the university is College Station's heartbeat, the university's magnificent heart and soul is the **George Bush Presidential Library Center,** dominating the west campus. Opened in 1997, the $82 million facility includes the $42 million Presidential Library and Museum, which chronicles the history of the elder President Bush's time, including his presidency and his long public service career in the United Nations, China, the Central Intelligence Agency, Congress, and as vice president and world leader. As a part of the National Archives, the library is open to scholars and students from around the world. The center has offices and living quarters for President and Mrs. Bush, who make appearances for seminars and during special events. For more information and hours, call the center at (979) 260–9552.

Also of significant interest on the Texas A&M campus, the *Sam Houston Sanders Corps of Cadets Center,* (979) 862–2862, offers a look at the history and future of the illustrious Corps of Cadets. Bronzes of seven Aggie Medal of Honor Winners and the Metzger Sanders Gun Collection are on permanent display here. Open from 8:00 A.M. until 6:30 P.M. Monday through Friday and during certain hours on home football game weekends. Admission is free.

If you work up a hunger, stop across from the campus at *Wings 'N More* (1045 South Texas Avenue, College Station 77840, 979–693–6363), where Buffalo-style hot chicken wings have been the rage since 1989. The menu also includes tender baby-back ribs, grilled chicken breasts, fish and shrimp dishes, salads, soups, sandwich combinations, and desserts. Find daily lunch specials for under $5.00. Open from 11:00 A.M. until 10:00 P.M. Sunday through Thursday and until 11:00 P.M. Friday and Saturday.

In Bryan, which is immediately adjacent to College Station on the east, see the marvelous *Carnegie Library* (111 South Main Street, Bryan 77802, 979–361–3715). Built in 1903 with funds from the Carnegie foundation, it is the oldest existing Carnegie Library in Texas and has recently reopened as the Carnegie Center of Brazos Valley History.

For a look back to days before caller ID and call waiting, visit the *Brazos Valley Telephone Museum* (422 Dellwood, Bryan, 77802, 979–779–3414). The history of telephone service is explored in interesting detail. Open from 2:00 until 5:00 P.M. on Sunday only.

For a lazy afternoon, head to *Messina Hof Wine Cellar* (4545 Old Reliance Road, Bryan, 77802, 979–778–9463). One of the most awarded premium wineries in Texas, Messina Hof produces more than sixteen varietal wines at its state-of-the-art winemaking facility. The visitors center, which includes a tasting room and deli, is housed in part of the reconstructed former Bryan home of Ambassador Williamson S. Howell and is filled with antiques and memorabilia. Next door is the new Vintage House Sicilian Trattoria, which is open from 11:00 A.M.

until 2:00 P.M. Tuesday through Saturday. Call for the schedule of free tours and tastings daily at the winery. A lovely bed-and-breakfast is on site, too.

Here in the heartland of Texas, the best Mexican food is found at *Garcia's Mexican Cafe,* 1704 South Kyle Street, College Station 77840, (979) 696–5900. Regularly voted in local newspaper surveys as the area's most popular Tex-Mex, Garcia's is known for chimichangas, chicken enchiladas, quesadillas, and fajitas, as well as the festive happy-hour drink, the Sangrita. Open 11:00 A.M. until 9:30 P.M. Sunday through Wednesday, until 10:00 P.M. on Thursday, and until 11:00 P.M. on Friday and Saturday. Meals start at about $6.00.

The Grapevine Bistro & Restaurant, 201 Live Oak Street, College Station 77840, (979) 696–3411, is a longtime favorite for chicken broccoli, shrimp Alfredo, thick steaks, twice-baked potatoes, generous salads, excellent chocolate mousse, and California-style cheesecake. It's open for lunch and dinner.

For overnights in College Station, the B&B of choice is *The Flippen Place* (1199 Haywood Drive, 979–693–7660). Sitting on a heavily wooded, 35-acre spread with trails and two fishing ponds, this relocated, 170-plus-year-old Amish barn has three guest rooms, all with private baths. A full gourmet breakfast is served.

For more information contact the Convention and Visitors Bureau at (979) 260–9898 or (800) 777–8292. Visit the Internet site at www. bryan-collegestation.org.

OTHER PLACES TO STAY ON THE BRAZOS-REPUBLIC TRAIL

AUSTIN

Austin Motel, 1220 South Congress Avenue, Austin 78704, (512) 441–1157. Dating from the l0ate 1930s, this funky motel is pretty cheap ($65 and up) and has no two rooms alike in its rambling offerings. If possible, get one poolside with two double beds, Saltillo tile floors, and a tiny refrigerator.

Woodburn House Bed & Breakfast, 4401 Avenue D, Austin 78751, (512) 458–4335. A 1909 home with many design details typical of plantation homes of the Old South, along with ornamental Victorian architectural details, this Hyde Park neighborhood jewel has undergone extensive restoration. Five bedrooms with private baths, phones, and data ports are offered, and a full breakfast is included.

BASTROP

Pecan Street Inn, 1507 Pecan Street, Bastrop 78602, (512) 321–9504. This eclectic Queen Anne–gothic home is nearly a century old and is included on the National Register of Historic Places. Each of the five guest rooms, four of which have private baths, has a fireplace and a coffee-maker. The specialty breakfast dish is pecan waffles with Grand Marnier strawberries.

BRENHAM
Ant Street Inn, 107 West Commerce Street, Brenham 77833, (979) 836-7393 or (800) 481-1951. A sensational lodging that would impress even the most finicky traveler, this fourteen-room inn is owned by a former antiques dealer and a former teacher for *Southern Living* magazine's cooking school. Exquisite antiques, upholstery, bed linens, and attention to detail are matched only by the breakfasts of breakfast tacos, quiches, and blueberry popovers with lemon sauce.

COLLEGE STATION
Bayou on the Brazos, 1888 Bird Pond Road, College Station 78740, (979) 690-6643. Two guest rooms are offered, along with a New Orleans–style breakfast.

CORSICANA
The Ashmore Inn, 220 North Fourteenth Street, Corsicana 75110, (903) 872-7311. This renovated, four story mansion was built in 1898. Stays include a full breakfast.

GONZALES
St. James Inn, 723 Saint James Street, Gonzales 78629, (830) 672-7066.

This 1914 home with Greek Revival architecture has three floors, nine working fireplaces, five guest rooms, two suites, seven private baths, and period antiques. Guests are fed a full breakfast and can request candlelight dinners, too.

HILLSBORO
Countess Rose House 1910, 301 East Franklin Street, Hillsboro 76645, (254) 582-7673. A ninety-year-old, four-square, Prairie-style home completely restored and furnished with Victorian antiques and offering claw-footed tubs and a rose theme throughout. Surrounded by rose gardens with a lily pond, the house has a sun room, a wraparound front porch, and a balcony, as well as six guest rooms with private baths. High tea is available, and room rates include a gourmet country breakfast.

SALADO
Inn on the Creek, 602 Center Circle, Salado 76571, (254) 947-5554. An 1892 home that has been expanded, doubling the size to offer eleven bedrooms and eleven baths. There's also a cottage and a little restaurant for weekend dinners by reservation only.

SHINER
Shiner Country Inn, 1016 North Avenue E (Business U.S. 90), Shiner 77984,

(361) 594-3335. This updated country motel has a particularly friendly spirit as well as in-room phones and cable TV.

WACO
Judge Baylor House, 908 Speight Avenue, Waco 76706, (254) 756-0273. Five guest rooms are available.

OTHER PLACES TO EAT ON THE BRAZOS-REPUBLIC TRAIL

AUSTIN
El Sol Y La Luna, 1224 South Congress Avenue, Austin 78704, (512) 444-7770. Right next door to the Austin Motel, this colorful little cafe serves excellent breakfast, lunch, and dinner dishes from Mexico, Central America, and the Caribbean. It's a cheap and delicious place to spend a leisurely hour.

Mars, 1610 San Antonio Street, Austin 78703, (512) 472-3901. Almost always packed, this renovated house offers a series of little dining rooms where devoted diners tuck into plates of cassoulet, steamed dumplings, Greek salad, or Thai shrimp. Open for dinner daily.

Scholz Garten, 1607 San Jacinto Street, Austin 78701,

(512) 474–1958. Established in 1866, this beer garden calls itself the oldest tavern in Texas. Regardless, it's great fun.

Threadgill's, 6416 North Lamar Street, Corsicana 78734, (512) 451–5440 and 301 West Riverside Street, Austin 78704, (512) 472–9304. Need some comfort? Here's the place for rib-sticking pot roast, chicken-fried steak, meat loaf, mashed potatoes, and country vegetables. Meals start at about $6.00.

BRENHAM

Brazos Belle, on Main Street in Burton (16 miles west of Brenham via U.S. 290), (979) 289–3849. An 1870s-era general store is now occupied by a comfortable, casual restaurant whose owner-chef is a French native and a former chef at the Four Seasons in Houston. Excellent choices include steak Delmonico and cassoulet with duck and sausage.

CHAPPELL HILL

Bevers Kitchen, Main Street, (979) 836–4178. A cute, colorful country cafe, this great little find does good home cooking, from meat loaf to cobbler.

ELGIN

Southside Market and BBQ, U.S. 290 at Texas 95, (512) 285-3407. Located about 25 miles east of Austin, this smokehouse was founded in 1882 and has made "Elgin hot sausage" part of the Texas carnivore vernacular. Outstanding peppery beef sausage, brisket, ribs, mutton and much more keep diners coming back in droves.

ROUND TOP

Royer's Round Top Cafe, on the square, (800) 866–7437. An old grocery dating from around 1910, this adorable cafe serves everything from pasta to homemade pies for lunch and dinner. It stays pretty busy, so it's good to call ahead and get your name on the waiting list.

SALADO

The Range at the Barton House, 101 North Main Street, Salado 76571, (254) 947–3828. Sensational fare from husband-wife pair of graduates from the Culinary Institute of America in New York includes marinated chicken with roasted-garlic mashed potatoes, pan-seared salmon fillet in a mustard sauce, and creamy chocolate-pudding cake. The delightful setting is an 1866 limestone house. Open for lunch on Saturday and Sunday and for dinner Wednesday through Sunday.

WACO

Kitok's, 1815 North Eighteenth Street, Waco 76706 (254) 754–1801. This sixteen-table cafe draws crowds from Austin and Dallas for the Liplocker, a double-meat burger that goes well with Oriental fries, which are made tempura style in the batter-and-fry process. It's open daily from 11:00 A.M. until 8:00 P.M.

The Gulf Coast

The lengthy, shimmering curve of seashore known as the Gulf Coast of Texas has long been a place of fascination for visitors. The Spaniards arrived in 1528, when Cabeza de Vaca shipwrecked just off Galveston Island; he was followed by conquistadors looking for fabled treasures in cities of gold, and although none were discovered, the Spanish priests established missions as necessary for colonization.

The French came, too, led by the explorer La Salle, who landed in 1685 at Indianola, which became a thriving port—German colonists came through here in the 1840s—but it's now only a ghostly stretch of sand. French buccaneer Jean Lafitte enjoyed a lucrative stay at Galveston Island from 1817 until 1821, when the U.S. government ran him off for making moves on an American ship.

Significant milestones in American history came to pass on this shoreline: Texas's first oil well, the gusher Spindletop, blew in 1901 at Beaumont; NASA astronauts found a new home address in Houston's Lyndon B. Johnson Space Center in the early 1960s; and rock-and-roll legend Janis Joplin was raised in Port Arthur—if not for her, we might never have learned a great hum-along song, *Me and Bobby McGee,* written for her by fellow Texan Kris Kristofferson, who hails from the Gulf Coast town of Corpus Christi.

The 624 miles of coastline you find on Texas's Gulf offer everything from a Mardi Gras to symphony concerts, deep-sea fishing to whooping-crane watching, weekends whiled away in Victorian mansions to gambling the night away aboard a Mexico-bound cruise ship. You may never want to go home.

The Land of Spindletop

As the state's rich forests unwind en route to the Gulf, the land turns to that which has seen massive bursts of industry yet still languishes in woodsy radiance. **Beaumont,** a city of 118,200 connected to the Gulf by the Neches River, is a pulse point of this section, begun in

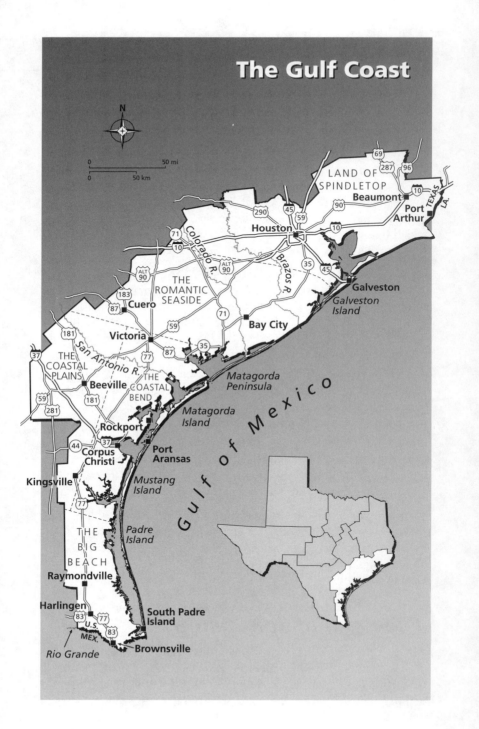

The Gulf Coast

N

0   50 mi
0   50 km

LAND OF SPINDLETOP

Beaumont
Port Arthur

TEXAS
LA.

Houston

Colorado R.

Brazos R.

Galveston
Galveston Island

THE ROMANTIC SEASIDE

Cuero

Victoria

Bay City

San Antonio R.

THE COASTAL PLAINS

Beeville

THE COASTAL BEND

Matagorda Peninsula

Matagorda Island

Rockport

Corpus Christi

Port Aransas

Gulf of Mexico

Kingsville

Mustang Island

Padre Island

THE BIG BEACH

Raymondville

Harlingen

U.S.
MEX.

South Padre Island

Rio Grande

Brownsville

THE GULF COAST

JUNE'S FAVORITE ATTRACTIONS ON THE GULF COAST

Bayou Bend Collection and Gardens, Houston

Big Thicket National Preserve

Channel Inn, Sabine Pass

Fulton Mansion State Historical Structure, Fulton

Padre Island National Seashore

Presidio La Bahia, Goliad

Rice University Village, Houston

San Jacinto Battleground State Historical Park

Tarpon Inn, Port Aransas

Tremont House, Galveston

1837 as a lumber center that literally exploded onto the energy map in 1901 when the world's first gusher, Spindletop, erupted here. The little settlement of a few hundred suddenly grew to a city of 30,000—literally overnight—and became the birthplace of oil companies such as Exxon, Texaco, and Mobil.

To see just what Beaumont looked like at its moment of glory, pay a visit to **Spindletop–Gladys City Boomtown** (University Drive at U.S. Highway 69, 409–835–0823). The whole place has been re-created, down to the post office, oil derricks made of wood, blacksmith shop, saloon, surveyor's office, photo studio, and so on. Here, too, is the 58-foot granite monument honoring Anthony F. Lucas's landmark well that blew in at 10:00 A.M. on January 10, 1901. The boomtown is open Tuesday through Sunday 1:00 until 5:00 P.M. A small admission fee is charged.

A modern look at the complex petroleum industry is found at the **Texas Energy Museum** (600 Main Street, Beaumont 77704, 409–833–5100), touted by the Smithsonian Institution as being one of the world's finest. A remarkable parade of exhibits includes multimedia displays that simulate rig functions, and robotics. Visit the museum Tuesday through Saturday 9:00 A.M. until 5:00 P.M. and Sunday 1:00 until 5:00 P.M. A small admission fee is charged.

Beaumont's other claim to fame is being home to Babe Didrikson Zaharias (1914–56), undoubtedly the world's greatest female athlete, some say the most gifted of all American athletes. The **Babe Didrikson Zaharias Museum** (1750 Interstate 10 East, Beaumont 77704, 409–833–4622) offers tourists a chance to learn more about the woman who was a three-time basketball All-American, double Olympic gold medal winner in track, and world-class golfer. A wealth of documents, awards, medals, and such chronicle her illustrious career and life. The museum is home also to a good visitors center, offering travelers a variety of information on the area. The museum and center are open daily from 9:00 A.M. until 5:00 P.M.

As you'll find throughout the state, early industrialists built extraordinary, lasting structures that we're fortunate enough to enjoy today. Beaumont is no exception, offering sensational vintage architecture.

One such place is the *McFaddin-Ward House* (1906 McFaddin Avenue, Beaumont 77704, 409–832–2134). The 1906 Beaux Arts home is filled with the finery of its day and is open for touring Tuesday through Saturday 10:00 A.M. until 3:00 P.M. and Sunday 1:00 until 3:00 P.M. A small admission fee is charged.

Visitors with an eye for history will also enjoy the nearby *Tyrrell Historical Library* (695 Pearl Street, Beaumont 77704, 409–833–2759). Listed on the National Register of Historic Places, the fine 1903 Romanesque-Gothic building, formerly a Baptist church, is a treasure chest of Texas history books, genealogical research materials, and art. It's open Tuesday 8:30 A.M. until 8:00 P.M. and Wednesday through Saturday 8:30 A.M. to 5:30 P.M.

Beaumont's *Fire Museum of Texas* (400 Walnut Street at Mulberry Street, Beaumont 77704, 409–880–3927) is housed within an early-twentieth-century fire hall. The history of firefighting since 1779 is detailed with equipment, machinery, and memorabilia. Open from 8:00 A.M. until 4:30 P.M. Monday through Friday. Admission is free.

A particular pride in Beaumont, understandably, is the *John Jay French Museum* (2975 French Road, Beaumont 77703, 409–898–3267), an exemplary 1845 home restored to its original Greek Revival grandeur. Inside, exhibits chronicle the lives of the French family. Open 10:00 A.M. until 4:00 P.M. Tuesday through Saturday. Admission is $3.00 for adults and $1.00 for children.

Texas Trivia

The proverbial six flags that have flown over Texas include that of Spain, 1519–1821; France, 1685–1690; Mexico, 1821–1836; the Republic of Texas, 1836–1845; the Confederacy, 1861–1865; and the United States, 1845–1861 and 1865 to the present.

You'll not find a better Cajun dinner than that at *Sartin's,* at 6725 Eastex Freeway, Beaumont 77706, (409) 892–6771. The seafood's super fresh—and frequently spicy—and the surroundings make you feel as though you're at a friend's cozy dining table. The restaurant is open for lunch and dinner daily.

For still more Cajun fare, check out *Swampee's Bayou* (4120 College Street, Beaumont 77706, 409–842–0500), where you'll get shrimp-stuffed jalapeños, grilled jumbo shrimp, and lots of fried goodies. Plan to watch lots of sports on the dozens of TVs spread around this bar and grill. Open for lunch and dinner daily.

The most popular Tex-Mex menu in town is found at *Elena's* (1865 College Street, Beaumont 77706, 409–832–1203), where the reigning appetizer is surely the *queso fundido,* a plate of bubbling-hot Mexican cheese

June's Favorite Annual Events on the Gulf Coast

Dickens on the Strand, Galveston, first weekend in December

Great Texas Birding Classic, entire coast, mid- to late April

Houston International Festival, Houston, mid-April

Houston Livestock Show and Rodeo, Houston, first two weeks of March

Mardi Gras, Galveston, weekend prior to Ash Wednesday

Oysterfest, Fulton, first weekend in March

Spring Artwalk, Galveston, first weekend in March

Spring Break, South Padre Island and Port Aransas, second and third weekends in March

plumped with sausage and bacon. Entree favorites include sizzling chicken, pork chops, and steaks, with the accompanying grilled onions and peppers, and rice and beans. Open daily for lunch and dinner.

Another good choice is **Esther's Seafood and Oyster Bar** (Rainbow Bridge in Port Arthur, 409–962–6268). Drive or boat to this seaside haunt, where Cajun-style seafood is unbeatable. Favorites are shrimp gumbo, rich étouffée, fried alligator tail, crawfish fritters, and voluminous platters of fried fish. Meals start at about $8.00. Open from 11:00 A.M. until 9:00 P.M. Sunday through Thursday and until 10:00 P.M. Friday; 5:00 until 10:00 P.M. Saturday.

In just a few minutes you can be out in the country enjoying an offbeat tour or two. It's a quick drive to **Plum Nearly Ranch** (409–722–2637 or 409–722–1192), a working Arabian horse ranch that offers tours by reservation. Or you could take in a tour at the **Alligator Island Gator Farm** (409–794–1995). A bit more on the tame side, drive east on I–10 about 25 miles to the town of Orange, where you can tour and taste the vintages of **Piney Woods Country Wines** (3408 Willow Drive, Orange 77630, 409–883–5408). The winery is open Monday through Saturday 9:00 A.M. until 5:00 P.M. and Sunday 12:30 until 4:00 P.M. Tours are by appointment and cost $2.00.

But if it's simply another fix of pure nature you need, drive north to the city limits, where the nation's biological crossroads—known best as **The Big Thicket National Preserve**—awaits. Spreading across seven counties, it's the only national preserve and the only place in the United States where eight ecosystems coexist. Established in 1974, the Big Thicket National Preserve is the focal point of a tranquil, woodsy region with a deep heritage and plenty of recreational opportunities. Once an ancient, 3 1/2-million-acre wild forest, it's now an inverted L–shaped, 84,000-acre ecological miracle struggling against the wrecking forces of human nature. The Big Thicket is a refuge for nature supporters who enjoy fishing, hiking, canoeing, and wildlife and wildflower watching. It's also a lab for naturalists and other scientists. The preserve is open daily, but hours vary by section and activity. For details contact the visitors center, 30 miles north of Beaumont via U.S. Highway 69 and Farm Road 420, (409) 246–2337.

One of the newest and more impressive distinctions related to Beaumont is its importance to the *Great Texas Coastal Birding Trail.* Conceived in 1993, the trail enables bird-watchers to get the best possible information about the millions of Neotropical migrant birds flying north to winter, most of them visiting the Texas coast from March through June. The evolving trail includes more than 200 good birding sites along the 500-mile reach of coastline extending from Beaumont to Brownsville. Detailed information on the Great Texas Coastal Birding Trail is obtained from the Texas Department of Transportation's Travel Information office, (800) 452–9292, and from the Texas Parks and Wildlife Department (c/o Great Texas Coastal Birding Trail, 4200 Smith School Road, Austin 78744).

It's but a 17-mile drive south of Beaumont via U.S. Highway 96 to the waterside town of *Port Arthur.* Originally called Aurora in 1840, the town on the shore of coastal Sabine Lake, on the Louisiana state line, changed its name to honor the financier responsible for bringing the railroad to town. Is it possible then, if he coaches teams to more Super Bowl titles, that Port Arthur would change its name to Jimmy Johnson City for its more famous son? That's more likely to happen than Port Arthur changing its name for its colorful daughter Janis Joplin— although her memory is honored each year in January with a birthday celebration of concerts, and she's the focus of an exhibit on rock-and-roll stars at the *Museum of the Gulf Coast,* 317 Stillwell Road, Port Arthur 77642, (409) 982–7000.

The oil boom brought prosperity to this town, which has served as one of the state's melting pots. French, Dutch, and early American heritage can be seen in Port Arthur's architecture and museums. A place with a particularly eclectic flair is *La Maison des Acadienne and Dutch Windmill Museum* (just north of town in Nederland, 409–722–0279), where the combined mix of exhibits includes a park dedicated to the memory of country singing star Tex Ritter; a 40-foot reproduction of a Dutch windmill; and a replica house of the French who were forced out of Nova Scotia by the British more than 200 years ago and wound up in Louisiana and Texas. From March until September the museum is open Tuesday through Sunday 1:00 until 5:00 P.M.; after early September it's open Thursday through Sunday 1:00 until 5:00 P.M.

In marked contrast there's the *Pompeiian Villa* (1953 Lakeshore Drive, Port Arthur 77642, 409–983–5977), a 1900 mansion nicknamed the

THE GULF COAST

Billion Dollar House for the owner who acquired the home in exchange for 10 percent in the newly formed Texas Company—which later became Texaco; the man's stock would be worth a billion dollars today. Look inside for its magnificent antiques. Tour hours are Monday through Friday 9:00 A.M. until 4:00 P.M. and by appointment. Admission is $2.00.

Another cultural twist is found at **Queen of Vietnam Church** (801 Ninth Avenue, Port Arthur 77642, 409–983–7676), where a *Hoa-Binh*—or shrine—was erected by Vietnamese Catholics grateful to the city that was a welcoming new home after their escape from Vietnam. Within the dedicated Area of Peace, there are exceptional gardens, a giant statue of the Virgin Mary, and at Christmas, biblical scenes decorated with 700,000 lights. The church and grounds are always open.

History lessons are fascinating at **Sabine Pass Battleground State Historical Park** (south of town 14 miles via Texas Highway 87 at Sabine Pass, 409–971–2451). The park is dedicated to the Confederate forces under Col. Dick Dowling, who managed a victory against staggering odds and much more powerful Union forces in an 1863 battle. In addition to a statue of Dowling, there are picnic areas and a boat ramp. The park is open daily 8:00 A.M. until 10:00 P.M.

> **ONE MAINSTREAM ATTRACTION WORTH SEEING ON THE GULF COAST**
>
> *With the Houston Astros's new stadium in place and the Oilers's move to Nashville, one wonders if the mighty Astrodome isn't destined to be known as just another white elephant. Nevertheless, the Harris County Domed Stadium (the official name) is a remarkable place in which an eighteen-story building would fit.*
>
> *It was the world's first air-conditioned domed stadium for baseball and football, and it accommodates basketball, boxing, conventions, and rodeos. Visitors can see a film called* Astrodome:
> The Original, *offering a historical perspective and putting you on the bench with the Astros, on the sidelines with the Oilers, backstage at a concert, and in the chutes with the bronco and bull riders. Find it at Kirby Drive at Loop 610 South. (713) 799–9544.*

While sailboarders and sailors are drawn to **Sabine Lake,** it's the camping, picnicking, nature study, and shell-collecting opportunities that make **Sea Rim State Park** a popular place. The state's only marshland park—spread over 15,109 acres—is 14 miles west of Sabine Pass on Texas Highway 87. Interestingly, the highway splits the park into two separate parts, the southern being the Beach Unit, with stretches of sandy beach and a biologically unique spot where the salt tidal marshlands join the Gulf; and the northern section being the Marshlands Unit, where canoe trails, observation platforms, and blinds are found. Bug repellant is a plus here, as mosquitoes can be vicious. Look for notices about airboat rides. For information call the park at (409) 972–2559.

While you're in the neighborhood—or even if you're not—make every effort to have lunch or dinner at *Channel Inn* (on Texas Highway 87 at the entrance to Sabine Pass, 409–971–2400). The no-frills place, an outgrowth of a commercial fishing business, simply serves up an astoundingly delicious platter of barbecued crabs—piles and piles of the wonderful things. Platters of frog legs, catfish, stuffed crab, fried shrimp, and oysters (in season) are also offered.

A trip to the nation's fourth-largest city, *Houston,* about 90 miles west of Port Arthur, can seem daunting; the key is to approach it simply by focusing on a handful of special places. Even though the entire metropolis sprawls across 500 square miles and is home to four million people, it is the city's individual elements that make it an intriguing whole.

Named, of course, for Sam Houston, the first president of the Republic of Texas, the town was founded in 1836, the year of the Republic's birth. A city that boomed with the development of both the oil and the space-exploration industries, Houston has a surprising number of historical and natural attractions.

The first of these, appropriately, is *Sam Houston Park* (1100 Bagby Street, Houston 77098, 713–655–1912), a twenty-acre spread immediately west of downtown Houston containing an array of the city's first buildings, dating from 1823 to 1905. There's a small church, a gazebo, and an early commercial building. On site there's the Museum of Texas History, with changing exhibits; and next door, the Long Row, a reconstructed office building, has a tearoom and gift store. Tours are offered Monday through Saturday 10:00 A.M. until 3:00 P.M. and Sunday 1:00 until 3:00 P.M. Admission is $6.00 for adults, $2.00 for children.

For another dose of history, head over to the *Bayou Bend Collection and Gardens* (One Westcott Place, Houston 77056, 713–639–7750),

Bizarre Texas Stuff

*H*OUSTON: *You'll find one of the state's better examples of weird folk art at The Beer Can House (222 Malone Street, 713–926–6368). More than 50,000 aluminum cans and pop-tops decorate this little bungalow in a quiet, modest neighborhood. The work was a* twenty-five-year effort by the late John Mikovisch, who cut, flattened, and reshaped the cans to cover his house and to make mobiles and sculptures. His widow still lives there and doesn't mind visitors looking at the exterior from the sidewalk.

Sam Houston Park

originally built as a residence in the 1920s for Will, Mike, and Ima Hogg, the children of former governor Jim Hogg. The paintings, furniture, ceramics, and silver housed here are among the finest collections of American decorative arts in the nation. Guided tours, lasting ninety minutes, are given from 10:00 A.M. until 2:45 P.M. Tuesday through Friday and 10:00 until 11:15 A.M. Saturday. Or visit at your own pace from 10:00 A.M. until 5:00 P.M. Tuesday through Saturday and 1:00 until 5:00 P.M. Sunday. Admission is $10.00 for adults, $8.50 for seniors, and $5.00 for children ages ten to eighteen. Children under ten are allowed during audio tours only. Tour reservations are required.

Make it a point to visit *The Orange Show* (2401 Munger Street, Houston 77056, 713–926–6368). Its late creator, Jeff McKissack, who hauled oranges during the Depression, began building this monument to the citrus fruit in 1954. Finally, in 1979, it was ready for folks to see. He was quoted as saying that he simply wanted "to encourage people to eat oranges, drink oranges, and be highly amused." What it is, is a patchwork, many-layered labyrinth of sculpture, wagon wheels, tractor seats, flags, tiles, wishing well, observation decks, and whirligigs. It must be seen to be believed. It's open from 9:00 A.M. until 1:00 P.M. Wednesday

Tee Up

The Texas Golf Hall of Fame, at 1800 South Mill-bend Drive in The Wood-lands, near Houston, shares all sorts of little-known Texas golf history. For instance, Texas had a 9-hole golf course in 1886, and an exhibition of the game was played in Texas in 1887. There's a museum and lending library, as well as an information and referral service for golfers who have questions about golf-related artifacts, people, and events.
(281) 364-7270.

through Friday and from noon until 5:00 P.M. Saturday and Sunday—usually. It's best to call first. Admission is $1.00.

See the final resting place of many who shaped the city of Houston. **Glenwood Cemetery** (2525 Washington Avenue, Houston 77056, 713–864–7886) is a sixty-five-acre, tree-covered expanse where remarkable headstones and monuments mark graves of local luminaries. Buried here are the bizarre billionaire Howard Hughes, former Texas governors Ross Sterling and William P. Hobby Sr., Astrodome founder Judge Roy Hofheinz, and Shamrock Hotel founder Glen McCarthy. Open daily from 8:00 A.M. until 5:00 P.M. Admission is free.

Newer than most Houston attractions is the **Holo-caust Museum** (5401 Caroline Street, Houston 77027, 713–942– 8000). Its exhibits and memorials provide testimonials of victims and survivors of one of the darkest eras in Western history. The museum also has an archives repository and an interactive learning center. Open from 9:00 A.M. until 5:00 P.M. during the week (until 9:00 P.M. Thursday) and from noon until 5:00 P.M. Saturday and Sunday. Admission is free.

The **Houston Fire Museum** (2403 Milam Street, Houston 77002, 713–524–2526) details the history of the Houston Fire Department and displays hats, badges, axes, photographs, and period uniforms from fire-fighting units all over the world. Also on display are a nineteenth-century steam engine and a water tower truck. Open from 10:00 A.M. until 4:00 P.M. Tuesday through Saturday. Admission is $2.00 for adults and $1.00 for seniors, students with identification, and children.

Among Houston's profound wealth of arts is the **Children's Museum of Houston** (1500 Binz Street, Houston 77027, 713–522–1138), housed inside a structure designed by Robert Venturi. This is a great place for kids to explore science and technology, archaeology, agriculture, and the environment. The KID-TV studio features real sound and video production equipment. The courtyard has a greenhouse, pirate's ship, and Victorian playhouse. Open from 9:00 A.M. until 5:00 P.M. Tuesday through Saturday and from noon until 5:00 P.M. Sunday. Admission is charged.

Other exceptional repositories of art are found at the **Menil Collection** (1515 Sul Ross Street, Houston 77098, 713–525–9400); and the **Museum** *of Fine Arts* (1001 Bissonnet Drive, Houston 77098, 713–639–7300). For more of the sciences, consider the Museum of Natural Science (in Hermann Park, 1 Hermann Circle Drive, Houston 77010, 713–639–4629) and the Museum of Health & Medical Science (1515 Hermann Drive, Houston 77010, 713–521–1515). Complete information on these and all attractions is available from the Houston Convention & Visitors Bureau, 801 Congress Street, Houston 77002, (713) 227–3100 or (800) 4–HOUSTON.

A nonmall shopping district well worth finding is **Rice University Village**, located southwest of downtown Houston. The district is bordered by Sunset Drive on the north, Kirby Drive on the west, University Boulevard on the south, and Morningside Drive on the east. Begun in 1932 in the shady area near beautiful Rice University, the 14-block center is populated by the original Rice Food Market (now the heart of an exclusive Houston chain), 70 cafes, and some 360 shops and galleries, of which at least three-fourths are individually owned. Among older businesses are the Variety Fair 5 & 10 (1948), G&G Model Shop (1954), and Jones Apothecary (1939). There's no rhyme or reason to the architecture, which evolved according to no special plan over the years, and this makes Rice Village all the more charming. For more information contact the University Village Association at (713) 526–4799.

When you're famished, **Berryhill Hot Tamales** (1717 Post Oak Road, Houston 77098, 713–871–8226) is a must-go for excellent enchiladas, fish tacos, and every sort of tamale for meat eaters and vegetarians. The margaritas and decor alone are worth a visit. Meals start at around $6.00. Open for lunch and dinner daily.

As Houston has become one of the nation's ethnically richest cities, you can count on an amazing variety of cuisine. Easily one of the most celebrated places in town is **Kim Son** (2001 Jefferson Street at Chartres Avenue, Houston 77003, 713–222–2461), with excellent Vietnamese dishes in gorgeous presentations. The egg rolls, noodle dishes, anything with shrimp, and soups are great. Meals are anywhere from $5.00 to $10.00. Open 11:00 A.M. until 11:00 P.M. Sunday through Thursday and until midnight Friday and Saturday.

The historic **Houston Heights** neighborhood is where you'll find **Sara's Bed & Breakfast Inn** (941 Heights Boulevard, Houston 77002, 713–868–1130 or 800–593–1130). Originally a one-story Victorian cottage, the home was later expanded and now contains fourteen guest rooms and suites. Choices range from rooms with twin, double, queen, or king beds, and one is a two-bedroom balcony suite with a kitchen. The breakfast, served in the garden room, consists of fruit, homemade breads, and juices.

The **Patrician Bed & Breakfast Inn** (1200 Southmore Boulevard, Houston 77004, 713–523–1114) is a lovely lodging in a quiet part of the museum district. With its cozy living room, airy dining room with hardwood floors, and backyard deck and gazebo, the inn is frequently used for weddings. Five guest rooms include two suites, and antique four-poster beds and clawfoot tubs are typical. A gourmet breakfast is included.

Another alternative to hotel stays is the historic **Lovett Inn** (501 Lovett Boulevard, Houston 77006, 713–522–5224 or 800–779–5224), the former home of a Houston mayor and federal court judge. Also found in Houston's museum district, the inn has rooms with private baths, phones, and remote-controlled color TV. Outside, lushly landscaped grounds and pool and spa are offered. Continental breakfasts are included with stays.

For a Texas experience with a conscientious spin on it, visit the **Taylor-Stevenson Ranch** (11822 Almeda Road, Houston 77045, 713–433–4441), where the roles of African-Americans, Hispanics, Native Americans, and women in western heritage are emphasized. That's the icing on top of the cake: Spend the day riding horses, going on a hayride or nature walk, and feeding ranch animals. Call for reservations.

Now, you can't have a true visit to such a prestigious Texan city without diving in headfirst to a real Lone Star meal, and the best in town is at **Goode Co. Barbecue** (5109 Kirby Street, Houston 77098, 713–522–2530, and 8911 Katy Freeway, Houston 77024, 713–464–1901). The mesquite-smoked ribs, brisket, chicken, and sausage links are outrageously succulent and richly flavored, and you'll rave over the homemade sauce, freshly baked bread, and other excellent fixins, such as potato salad and beans. You'll be back for more someday.

A visit to the site where Texas finally won its long, tragically difficult fight for independence from Mexico means driving 22 miles east from the city center to La Porte, where **San Jacinto Battleground State Historical Park** (3800 Park Road 1836, Houston 77571, 281–479–2421) is situated. Sam Houston and his army defeated the forces under Santa Anna in an eighteen-minute battle here in 1836, and markers on the battlefield detail positions and tactics of both armies. Rising from the park is the magnificent 570-foot **San Jacinto Monument,** honoring all who fought for Texas independence and

San Jacinto Monument

particularly those at this site. The observation floor allows a view of the Houston Ship Channel and permanent mooring slip for the **battleship Texas,** the sole surviving dreadnought dating to before World War I. The **San Jacinto Museum of History** has exhibits covering 400 years of area history, as well as a new theater showing *"Texas Forever!"* a multimedia presentation chronicling the events pertaining to the Texas Revolution and Battle of San Jacinto. You'll also find a gift boutique, picnic grounds, and concession stand in the park. It's open daily from 9:00 A.M. until 6:00 P.M. A small admission fee is charged only for the observation tower.

To gain deep, new appreciation for NASA and its work, pay a visit to **Space Center Houston** (1601 NASA Road 1, Houston 77058, 281–244–2100), situated 20 miles south of downtown Houston at Johnson Space Center. The sensational new attraction is essentially NASA's visitors center, but the effect is marvelous. Upon arrival, visitors are briefed via continuous NASA update videos and firsthand greetings by Johnson Space Center engineers, scientists, and astronauts. There's a Space Shuttle Mock-Up with flight deck and sleeping quarters to examine; Mission Status Center, where you can see space flight and training activities; The Feel of Space, an interactive area where visitors can use computer simulation to land the shuttle or launch a satellite; two theater presentations, including one IMAX show; and a guided tram tour going behind the scenes at Johnson Space Center. It's open daily from 9:00 A.M. until 7:00 P.M.; admission $10.95–$14.95.

Take time while you're in the NASA area to explore one of the more amazing tourist attractions to pop up in Texas. It's called **Kemah Boardwalk,** a creation on Galveston Bay in what was previously a quiet fishing village called Kemah, a Karankawa Indian word meaning "wind in the face."

Conceived and built by the owner of Landry's Seafood restaurants, Kemah Boardwalk is a sprawling arrangement of restaurants, amusement rides, landscaping with fountains and palms, as well as docks for visitors arriving by sailboat and yacht. The **Boardwalk Inn** is a fifty-two-room hotel with a rooftop patio, suites, kitchenettes, retail shops, and plenty of dining.

One of the restaurants at the boardwalk is called Aquarium, where dining areas are surrounded by giant aquariums filled with fish from the Caribbean, Hawaii, the South Pacific, and the Indian Ocean. Other dining spots include Landry's Seafood House; Joe's Crab Shack (you can't miss that EAT AT JOE'S sign); Cadillac Bar, a festive Mexican spot; and the Flying Dutchman, a favorite Kemah seafood spot for years.

Adjacent to Kemah Boardwalk is **Old Seabrook,** a cute cluster of antiques shops, seashell stores, a gourmet chocolate boutique, fine art galleries, and more. For details on Kemah Boardwalk and Old Seabrook, contact Clear Lake/NASA Chamber of Commerce, (281) 488–7676. To reach the Boardwalk Inn, call (281) 334–9880.

From Kemah or NASA it's a quick trip to **Armand Bayou Nature Center** (8500 Bay Area Boulevard, Houston 77058, 281–474–2551), an unusual 1,900-acre wildlife preserve encompassing forest, bayou, prairie, and marshland ecosystems. Choose one of several trails to hike or join up with a natural-history or boating tour. A re-created farmhouse recalls Victorian days and is designed to illustrate human-and-nature connections. Visit Wednesday from 9:00 A.M. until dusk; Thursday and Friday 9:00 A.M. until 4:00 P.M.; Saturday from dawn until 4:00 P.M.; or Sunday from noon until dusk. Call for tour times.

> ## Batter Up!
>
> *In Alvin, a town about 30 miles south of Houston at Texas Highways 6 and 35, you'll find a statue of native Nolan Ryan, retired pitcher from the Texas Rangers and new inductee to the Major League Baseball Hall of Fame in 1999. Find the statue at City Hall and watch for the Nolan Ryan Museum to open in late 1999.*

If this nature excursion leaves you inspired, you'll want to make time for an even greater communion with wildlife and the outdoors: This involves a journey west of Houston to the area of Eagle Lake, about an hour's drive west on I–10, then southwest on Farm Road 3013 to Colorado County, near the river of the same name. First you'll find the **Attwater Prairie Chicken National Wildlife Refuge** (Farm Road 3013, 979–234–2780). If you make your visit to the 8,000-acre reserve for the odd and endangered species between late February and early May, listen for the male's resounding mating call and watch the mates' ritualistic dance. It's open daily from dawn until dusk.

If you're of a mind to kick back for a day or two in this rolling countryside, you can hang around **Columbus,** just about 12 miles northwest of the Attwater Prairie Chicken National Wildlife Refuge. Settled in 1823 by members of the Stephen F. Austin Colony, and the seat of Colorado County, the town is home to a majestic live oak under which the first court of the Third Judicial District of the Republic of Texas convened in 1837. There are some inviting shops here, such as Atascosita Antiques & Friends (1124 Milam Street, Columbus 78934, 979–732–3864), offering excellent eighteenth- and nineteenth-century American and English antiques.

Columbus has beautiful old homes and buildings to tour, including the 1886 Stafford Opera House, where the local visitors office is located

(425 Spring Street, Columbus 78934, 979–732–8385). Pick up tour information as well as lodging details here. A nice bed-and-breakfast lodging to note is Magnolia Oaks (634 Spring Street, Columbus 78934, 979–732–2726), an 1890 Eastlake Victorian home. The local B&B registry is reached at (979) 732–5135.

The Romantic Seaside

The utterly Victorian island-city known as **Galveston,** population 72,000, is a one-hour drive from Houston via I–45. Plan to spend a few days here, because you'll be reluctant to leave.

Galvestonians lived lavishly in the mid-nineteenth century: In 1858 alone they bought 23 grand pianos, almost $2,500 worth of silverplate, more than 3,600 gallons of French wine, and nearly 800 gallons of brandy.

Galveston was the largest city in Texas, the second-wealthiest city in the nation, and the busiest port in the Southwest. Cotton was king, ships called from around the world to the deep natural harbor, and deals were made by the hundreds on **the Strand,** the waterfront banking center dubbed "the Wall Street of the Southwest" and today's tourism magnet.

Texas Trivia

From whence came the margarita? Published reports have credited a bar in Tijuana, Mexico, in 1930, and a hotel in Puebla, Mexico, in 1936. Another story says it came from a Galveston bartender named Santos Cruz, who made the drink in 1948 for singer Peggy Lee.

The opulent era of the island-city was characterized by full-scale mansions built by the local gentry; even an average family was housed quite comfortably in a pretty frame house, profuse with gingerbread trim. These are generally viewed on walking and driving tours in the **Silk Stocking and East End Historical Districts.** Several homes are showcased annually during the first two weekends of May during the **Historic Homes Tour.** Brochures from the Galveston Visitors Center (2016 Strand, Galveston 77550, 409–763–4311) have maps illustrating these neighborhoods.

An abrupt and terrifying end to the glamour came upon the dawn of the twentieth century: On September 8, 1900, a devastating hurricane claimed 6,000 lives and most of the city's structures, leaving Galveston in a deathly stillness. The event still ranks as the worst natural disaster in U.S. history.

To gain a deeper understanding of the devastation of the 1900 hurricane, see **"The Great Storm"** (Pier 21 Theater, Pier 21 at Harborside Drive, Galveston 77550, 409–763–8808). The multi-image documentary

THE GULF COAST

experience lasts about thirty minutes and provides actual accounts from diaries and letters of survivors of the storm.

In reconstruction, a 4½-mile seawall was built, and for seven years silt was pumped onto the land to raise the city's grading. The resilience of Galveston and its people was remarkable. Yet business moved in the meantime 50 miles north to Houston, and commerce on the Strand dwindled while countless stately Victorian homes lapsed into sickly states of disrepair. The Galveston Historic Foundation gathered its energy just in time, and wonderful vestiges of a golden era were saved from the wrecking ball in the 1970s.

Ashton Villa, a redbrick Italianate mansion at 2328 Broadway, Galveston 77550, was a primary salvage from threats of demolition in 1971. Built in 1859, the exceptional, antique-filled, three-story estate is open for tours daily; an excellent multimedia presentation on the hurricane and the rebuilt city is shown in Ashton Villa's carriage house. For tour information call (409) 762–3933; admission is charged.

The greatest of Galveston's historic structures, the **Bishop's Palace** (1402 Broadway, Galveston 77550, 409–762–2475), has a prestigious reputation among architectural experts, who compare its ornate design to the Biltmore House in Asheville, North Carolina. Crafted from Texas granite, limestone, and red sandstone, the Bishop's Palace is the only Texas creation included on the list of one hundred outstanding buildings in the United States by the American Institute of Architects. Completed in 1893, its great pitched roofs, cupolas, gables, and cast-iron balustrades bear the mark of famed architect Nicholas J. Clayton. It's open for tours Monday through Saturday 10:00 A.M. until 5:00 P.M. and Sunday noon until 5:00 P.M. from Memorial Day through Labor Day; closed Tuesday the remainder of the year. Admission is charged.

The spit-'n'-polish process continues on the Strand. This National Historic Landmark district, containing one of the nation's larger collections of restored Victorian buildings, is once again a vibrant and colorful mercantile center fixed within the old wharfside business zone. Great revelry invades during early spring for a massive **Mardi Gras** and again in December for a veddy British **Dickens on the Strand** celebration.

The **Mardi Gras Museum** (Twenty-third and Strand Streets, Third Floor, 409–763–1133) helps you see how Galveston's Mardi Gras has become the third largest in the nation, behind those in New Orleans, of course, and Lafayette, Louisiana. Costumes and historical memorabilia are displayed with models of the Arches created for Mardi Gras. There's a Mardi Gras gift shop here, too. Open from noon until 5:00 P.M. Wednesday through Friday and from noon until 6:00 P.M. Saturday and Sunday. Admission is free.

In the nineteenth-century banking buildings and cotton warehouses along the Strand is a trove of shopping and entertainment. Among the myriad stores are little galleries and boutiques such as Crabtree & Evelyn and Room With a View. Among wonderful antiques repositories are Somewhere in Time and the Antiques Mall.

Centerpiece for the Texas Seaport Museum is the **Elissa,** Texas's tall ship and another National Historic Landmark. The 1877 iron barque, built in Scotland, provides an exciting look at Galveston's seafaring past. The ship and adjacent museum, with superb exhibits and a dramatic film,

Elissa—Texas Seaport Museum

Rainforest Pyramid at Moody Gardens

are open daily 10:00 A.M. until 5:00 P.M. at Pier 21, near the Strand at the foot of Twenty-second Street. For information call (409) 763–1877.

Three blocks from the Strand, the *Grand 1894 Opera House* is a distinctive, lavishly decorated theater whose stage has been graced by dignitaries from Anna Pavlova and John Philip Sousa to Hal Holbrook and Ray Charles. Recently restored to the tune of $7 million, the Grand, at 2020 Post Office, Galveston 77550, continues to offer a full schedule of renowned entertainers. Self-guided tours are available Monday through Saturday 9:00 A.M. until 5:00 P.M. and Sunday noon until 5:00 P.M. For information call (409) 765–1894 or (800) 821–1894.

One of the most popular Galveston attractions is *Moody Gardens* (One Hope Boulevard, Galveston 77554, 800–582–4673). Here, a 10-story, 40,000-square-foot Rainforest Pyramid houses thousands of exotic plants, birds, butterflies, and fish in a rather fantastic tropical setting with waterfalls, cliffs, caverns, wetlands, and forests. The on-site 3-D IMAX theater offers a selection of three extraordinary multimedia films, while Palm Beach provides a white-sand beach with a blue lagoon, a 30-foot Yellow Submarine with octopus tentacle slides, a periscope, and water guns for kids. The newest attraction, the Bat Cave, is the largest bat exhibit in the Southwest. Open 10:00 A.M. until 6:00 P.M. Sunday through Thursday and 10:00 A.M. until 9:00 P.M. Friday and Saturday. Admission is $7.00 per attraction, but combination tickets are available.

The paddlewheeler *Colonel* now docks at Moody Gardens. The 800-passenger authentic reproduction of an 1800s paddlewheel offers day

Fort Travis Seashore Park

At Crystal Beach, Fort Travis Seashore Park still features battery sites of the military fortifications built in 1898 near the Port of Galveston and named for William B. Travis. Although heavily damaged in the huge 1900 storm, it was repaired and became a base where troops were stationed to defend U.S. shores during World Wars I and II. Picnic areas, cabanas, and campsites have since replaced the barracks.

and evening cruises on Offatt's Bayou. Call (409) 740–7797 for reservations and rates. You can also have a look around the heart of town on the cheery *Galveston Island Trolley,* from the Strand down to Seawall Boulevard. Or board one of the Galveston Harbour Tours at Pier 22, where a forty-five-minute narrated trip views the sugar, banana, cotton, and sulfur docks; the Grain Elevator; and the "Mosquito Fleet" shrimping boats along the wharf. Call (409) 765–1700 for rates and reservations.

Still another option is to see the island from above, via *Air Tours of Galveston Island* (2115 Terminal Drive, main terminal at Galveston's Municipal Airport, 409–740–IFLY). Aerial tours last thirty minutes to one hour and take in the beach to the ship channel, Bolivar Peninsula, Pelican Island, as well as the Bishops Palace, Sacred Heart Church, downtown Galveston, Galveston Bay, and Moody Gardens. Call for schedules and rates.

The island has 32 miles of beaches to explore, with *Stewart Beach* and *R. A. Apffel Park* among busy city areas with concessions, and *Galveston Island State Park,* Farm Road 3005 near 13 Mile Road, (409) 737–1222, where people go for bird watching, nature walks, and camping. Admission fees are charged at some beaches, and entry to the state park is $3.00 per person over twelve years of age. Be watchful on the sand at all beaches for tar deposits, generated by offshore oil rigs, and jellyfish, two sure vacation dampers.

Old-fashioned rest and relaxation are obtainable in Galveston's several historic hostelries. The *Hotel Galvez,* a Spanish-style stucco mansion built in 1911, faces the gulf at 2024 Seawall Boulevard, Galveston 77550 (409–765–7721). The sophisticated *Tremont House,* built in 1872 and located a block off the Strand at 2300 Ship's Mechanic Row, Galveston 77550, (800–874–2300 or 409–763–0300), has impressive appointments. Charming and genteel bed-and-breakfast lodgings are numerous; for information contact the Convention and Visitors Bureau (409–763–4311 or 800–351–4237), or try Bed and Breakfast Reservations (800–628–4644 or 409–762–1668).

Two bed-and-breakfast inns in Galveston are worth special mention. *The Victorian Inn* (511 Seventeenth Street, Galveston 77550,

409–762–3235) is a beautiful 1899 home filled with period antiques. It has a particularly appealing second-floor suite, with a private veranda, king-size brass bed, and private bath with stained-glass window. All rooms have private balconies, and the third floor features a two-bedroom suite with a living room. Guests frequently wind up the day over a cup of tea on the veranda, after strolling home from a day of shopping and gallery browsing on the Strand. Breakfasts usually consist of fresh baked goods, granola, juices, and fruits.

There's also *The Coppersmith Inn* (1914 Avenue M, Galveston 77550, 800–515–7444 or 409–763–7004), a Queen Anne mansion built in 1887 and outfitted with gingerbread trim; a double veranda; turret tower; winding staircase of teak, walnut, and curly pine; stained glass; fireplaces; and beautiful grounds with an herb garden. Among the guest rooms are Clara's Country Cottage, a private cottage nestled in the back garden, and three main-house rooms, each with shared baths. Guests enjoy afternoon wine and cheese, elaborate breakfasts, and the option of dinner catered in guest rooms.

Several other B&Bs are found in Galveston. For more information contact the Convention and Visitors Bureau at (409) 763–4311 or (800) 351–4237.

Dining has become a favorite reason to make escapes to Galveston. *Gaido's* (3828 Seawall Boulevard, Galveston 77550, 409–762–9625), founded in 1911, remains a place for divine fried blue crabs, five kinds of baked oysters, and homemade pepper cheese bread. It serves lunch and dinner daily.

More contemporary is the very popular *Saltwater Grill* (2017 Postoffice Street, Galveston 77550, 409–762–3474), with an open kitchen and chic decor. High marks go to Asian soba noodles cradling seared rare tuna and to the grilled red snapper draped in crabmeat. Prince Edward Island oysters are a big hit, too, at lunch and dinner. Very hip and casual is the *Mosquito Cafe* (628 Fourteenth Street, Galveston 77550, 409–763–1010), with a divine breakfast quiche of bacon and mushroom, and lunches of grilled shrimp salad. Weekend dinners are also a great idea.

Diners swoon over the Central American ambience and menu at *Rudy and Paco* (2028 Postoffice Street, Galveston 77550, 409–762–3696). Empanadas (Latin turnovers) stuffed with spicy meats, hearts of palm salad, and grilled vegetables are all huge hits at lunch and dinner.

The Coastal Bend

The tricky aspects of following Texas's jagged coastline southward are fully realized on wildly meandering drives from Galveston Island down to the Coastal Bend. Travelers making just this journey will pass through Brazoria, Matagorda, and Calhoun Counties, skirting the coast's series of inward jutting bays, driving 200 miles southwest on Texas Highway 35.

The first likely detour from this path is just past Lavaca Bay, where you can make a trip to the perfectly solitary beaches of *Matagorda Island State Park,* accessed via Texas Highway 316, Farm Road 1289, and Texas Highway 185—and then a passenger ferry from Port O'Connor. Sounds complicated, perhaps, but the diversion is well worth the trouble: The barrier island, which reaches almost 38 miles southwest beside the mainland, is an undeveloped wildland owned by the U.S. Department of the Interior and managed by the state parks department. Some 36,000 of the 45,000 acres are a wildlife management area; the remainder is a public park with 80 miles of immaculate beaches, bike and hike paths, and shoreline areas for bird watching (more than 300 species have been noted here), shell collecting, swimming, fishing, and picnicking. Be sure to bring your own water and food, as no concessions whatsoever are here.

The passenger ferry operates between the dock at Sixteenth and Maple Streets in Port O'Connor and the island three times daily on Saturday, Sunday, and holidays. Once on the island, you'll take a shuttle bus for a quick ride to the island's sandy gulf shore. The ferry ride

---

Bizarre Texas Stuff

*V*ICTORIA: *Unlike most of the windmills seen around Texas on farms and ranches, Victoria has a distinctive claim to a Dutch windmill. Located on Memorial Square in Victoria, it was built by two German immigrants, Fred Meiss Sr. and Otto Fiek, on a farm in the county around 1870. Made from hand-hewn logs and assembled with wooden pegs and homemade nails, it's thought that the windmill also con-tains machinery and millstones from a pre–Civil War windmill over in Goliad County. Interestingly, Henry Ford tried to buy the windmill in 1935 to exhibit at his Greenfield Village in Dearborn, Michigan, but the offer was declined. The Victoria Morning Study Club, a women's group, inherited the windmill and moved it to Memorial Square. See it at East Commercial and De Leon Streets, (361) 572–2767.*

June's Texas Anecdotes

GULF COAST: Every July from 1963 through 1973, my family spent a week or two vacationing in Port Aransas. Every year we would stay in the same inn, a two-story place with a rough cedar exterior; it was nice, but nothing fancy—certainly not by today's standards. My sisters and I always had such a wonderful time there, playing in the waves all day until our skin was burnished and our eyes stung from the salt. I clearly remember the texture of the straw-mat floor covering in our rooms, the creak of the boardwalk leading down to the dunes, the feel of the cool, cobblestone floor of the inn's restaurant against my bare feet, and the scent of the cedar, sea oats, and salt air that surrounded the inn. Not too long ago, when I was staying in a large condo complex in Port A, I looked off the balcony and saw our old inn next door. It had gone to seed in the years since we stayed there, but I had to go look anyway. As I walked up the drive toward the main building, I was overcome by an old familiar scent that brought back some of my fondest family memories.

costs $10.00 for adults and $5.00 for children; the shuttle is $2.00 for adults and $1.00 for children; reservations should be made by calling (361) 983–2215.

A pair of slightly simpler detours en route south are found together just shy of the LBJ Causeway, the portion of Texas Highway 35 spanning **Copano Bay.** At the tiny community of Lamar—it's too small even to be listed on the state highway map—you'll find Park Road 13, which leads to **Goose Island State Park** (361–729–2858), a 314-acre recreation area covering a little peninsula and an assortment of islands in the waters where Aransas, Copano, and St. Charles Bays meet. You can fish from a 1,620-foot lighted pier, bird-watch, take nature and wildlife walks, swim, and camp, and you'll have a chance to see a historical Karankawa Indian meeting site, **The Big Tree of Lamar.** This coastal live oak is possibly 2,000 years old and measures more than 35 feet around, 44 feet tall, and 89 feet at its crown span.

About 50 miles northwest of Port O'Connor, via Texas Highway 185, the town of **Victoria** has some interesting diversions. One of the first three towns incorporated by the Republic of Texas, Victoria's history dates to its 1824 founding by forty-one Spanish families. Among the sites and sights is the Texas Zoo (110 Memorial Drive in Riverside Park, 361–573–7681), a six-acre spread with 200-plus animals indigenous to this area. In September the zoo hosts an annual South Texas Beautiful Burro Pageant, awarding prizes to the most beautiful, most congenial, best-dressed, and most obstinate burro. Open 10:00 A.M. until 5:00 P.M. daily. Admission is $2.50.

There's also the **Nave Museum** (306 West Commercial Street, Victoria 77902, 361–575– 8227), a Graeco-Roman–style building erected by the widow of artist Royston Nave to exhibit his Texas landscape and portrait paintings. Open from 1:00 until 5:00 P.M. Tuesday through Sunday. Admission is charged.

The Victoria Convention & Visitors Bureau (700 Main Center, Victoria 77902, 361–573–5277) provides a good visitors' guide and map to point you toward other interesting area attractions.

When you decide to head on down to the Corpus Christi area, you'll stay on Texas Highway 35, cross the LBJ Causeway, and find yourself at the other end in the adjoining towns of **Rockport** and **Fulton.** Rockport, the Aransas County seat and home to a seaside art colony of about 4,700, is a quiet community fostering its cultural growth in places like the **Rockport Art Center** (at the point, Rockport Harbor, 361–729– 5519), which occupies the restored nineteenth-century Bruhl–O'Connor home. Studios, classrooms, and four galleries are inside; the center is open Tuesday through Saturday 10:00 A.M. until 4:00 P.M. and Sunday 1:00 to 4:00 P.M.

Also at Rockport Harbor, the **Texas Maritime Museum** (1202 Navigation Circle, Rockport 78381, 361–729–1271) showcases the state's seafaring heritage from the arrival of early Spanish explorers and Texas's battle for independence to the development of a dozen deep-water business ports and offshore oil exploration. Exhibits include shipwreck relics nearly 450 years old, portraits of every ship that sailed in the Texas Navy, and a new collection of watercolors of Texas lighthouses. The museum is open Wednesday through Saturday 10:00 A.M. until 4:00 P.M. and Sunday 1:00 until 4:00 P.M. Admission is charged.

Barely 5 miles away in Fulton—also on Texas Highway 35 and not far from the exotic-looking windswept leaning trees, twisted by constant winds—is the **Fulton Mansion State Historical Structure** (Fulton Beach Road at Henderson Street, 361–729–0386). A four-story showpiece dating to 1876, the innovative home was uniquely outfitted with central air and hot and cold running water at its beginning. A French Second Empire design surrounds the thirty-room mansion, which was restored by the state parks department. Visitors are asked to wear soft-soled shoes to protect the floors, and you're advised to call ahead in summer to find out if touring lines are long. The home is open Wednesday through Sunday 9:00 A.M. until noon and 1:00 until 4:00 P.M.; a small admission fee is charged.

Rockport and Fulton most often host nature enthusiasts visiting *Aransas National Wildlife Refuge* between November and March, prime months for viewing the rare whooping cranes, which numbered only fourteen in 1941. The United States and Canada have joined together in a sensational effort for almost fifty years to save these remarkable migratory birds, who journey annually from Canada in October and November to spend winter in these nesting grounds. The 55,000-acre asylum, home now to some 140 whooping cranes, is operated by the U.S. Fish and Wildlife Service for protection and management of around 300 species of birds, including Canada geese, sandhill cranes, and pintail and baldpate ducks, as well as white-tailed deer, javelina, and raccoon. You can view the birds from an observation point or from one of several boat tours along the intracoastal canal from Rockport.

Information on the refuge, situated 37 miles north of Rockport and reached by car via Texas Highway 35, Farm Road 774, and Farm Road 2040, is available by calling the visitors center at (361) 286–3559; the refuge is open daily from dawn until dusk, and the visitors center is open daily from 8:30 A.M. until 4:30 P.M. Boat tours departing Rockport cost about $20 to $25 per person; for a list of skippers, contact the Rockport-Fulton Chamber of Commerce at (361) 729–6445 or (800) 242–0071.

One of the oldest and most popular tour outfits is *Captain Ted's Whooping Crane Tours* (at Sandollar Pavilion in Rockport, 361–729–9589 or 800–338–4551), offering close-up views of the endangered whooping cranes in the MV *Skimmer* on a trip covering 60 miles of wetlands and bays including St. Joseph Island, Matagorda Island, Blackjack Peninsula, and, of course, the Aransas National Wildlife Refuge. The narrated tour includes complete wildlife identification, complimentary use of binoculars, and a continental breakfast. Call for schedules and rates.

Fourteen miles southeast of Rockport via Texas Highway 35, Port Aransas can be reached via *free ferry*—which departs from a huge dock in Aransas Pass—operated twenty-four hours daily by the state highway department. For decades the little beach community fondly called Port A, at the northern tip of Mustang Island, has been a vacation spot where families spend days or weeks deep-sea fishing and body surfing in the gulf and shell collecting on the hot sand. While it was once known as a lazy town, better access spurred the growth of multistory condos, beachwear boutiques, and nightspots.

Now as then, however, Port A, population 2,200, is a place meant for dawdling—if not feasting on fresh shrimp and crab, taking long walks on the shore, horseback riding, or Jet-Skiing. Children and grownups get a kick out of clinging to the rail and watching for porpoise acrobatics during the five-minute ferry trip to the island. The other island access is at the southern end, where a highway connects Corpus Christi on the mainland to Mustang and to Padre Island, adjacent to the south.

At either end of the ferry run are several brightly painted shacks selling fresh seafood. These bear come-on banners: BEST LITTLE SHRIMP HOUSE IN TEXAS and MAKE A COW HAPPY—EAT SHRIMP. Here people buy five pounds of shrimp for as little as $15 for bargain suppers in their rented cottages or for icing down in a take-home cooler or for fish bait.

New to Port Aransas is a *free trolley system* to cart you around town. The cute, vintage trolleys run continuously each day from 10:00 A.M. until 5:00 P.M., with pick-up points including the Beach Access Road, the Birding Facility, the Marina, the Jetties, and Horace Caldwell Pier.

Mustang Island was one of Texas's barrier islands frequented by Jean Lafitte and his buccaneer buddies in the 1820s. Now and then, island romantics, perhaps with the help of a little grog, set out in search of a legendary Spanish dagger that is said to mark the spot of a buried pirate treasure. The most common booty, however, is a wealth of sand dollars and varied seashells found just after high tide on the light brown sand. The island's 18 miles of beach are cleaned daily, and the tar deposits are significantly fewer than those at Galveston. Cars are no longer allowed free rein of the beaches as they were until the 1980s but are limited to a narrow path alongside the dunes.

Crowds are naturally drawn to **Mustang Island State Park** (on Texas 361, 361–749–5246), almost 3,500 acres decorated with sand dunes, sea oats, and morning glory. The park, just 14 miles south of the town of Port A, has 5 miles of gulf-front beach, and it offers camping, picnicking under arbors, a nature trail, a fish-cleaning station, and showers. The park is open daily from 8:00 A.M. until 10:00 P.M. for day use and at all times for campers. Admission is $3.00 per person. For a more private, open expanse of white sands, hop the Jetty Boat at Woody's Boat Basin for a fifteen-minute ride to **San Jose Island** (Woody's Boat Basin at Cotter Street, 361–749–5252)—or, as the locals call it, St. Jo. The uninhabited beach reserve is known for excellent shelling, and it's an ideal place to take a picnic, fresh water, and some fishing gear for a real getaway.

The passenger-only ferry operates from 6:30 A.M. until 6:00 P.M.; fares are $9.95 for adults and $4.95 for children.

Mostly, though, people come to Port A to see what they can find in the water. The town calls itself the place "where they bite every day," and fishing for redfish, speckled trout, flounder, and drum is free in the surf from the south jetty and the Station Street Pier. Group fishing aboard party boats such as the *Island Queen* gives anglers a chance to reel in bigger game fish for just $20 per person, which includes rod, reel, and tackle. Private charters, which can cost in the hundreds, go in search of tarpon, sailfish, marlin, kingfish, mackerel, bonito, red snapper, amberjack, barracuda, yellow-fin tuna, wahoo, and shark. For charter companies, ask at the chamber of commerce, (361) 749–5919 or (800) 452–6278.

People who just want to look at sea life can go to the ***University of Texas Marine Science Institute*** (Cotter Street, opposite Port Aransas Park, 361–749–6806). The research facility has seven habitat aquariums as well as impressive shell displays. It's open from 8:00 A.M. until 5:00 P.M. daily during summer months and Monday through Friday only from September through May.

Because travelers want to simply stay and stay once they've arrived in Port A, comfortable condos have become plentiful without being congestive—and most are reasonably priced. Some of the high-rises are a bit south of town, while many of the two-story complexes are close to the commercial area, and everything's on the beach. Generally, condos are individually owned and well maintained and have large pools, tennis courts, cable TV, and landscaped boardwalks reaching across the dunes to the beach. For something a little on the funky side, check out the ***Tarpon Inn*** (200 East Cotter Street, Port Aransas 78373, 361–749–5555), now in its fourth incarnation. Originally built in 1886 by a boat pilot and lighthouse keeper who used surplus lumber from nearby Civil War barracks, the inn burned down and then its replacement was destroyed in a hurricane. Today's version is a renovation of the 1920 structure, and it remains popular with anglers. A list of noted guests includes Franklin D. Roosevelt, and the inn is included on the National Register of Historic Places.

> ### Texas Trivia
>
> *Texas is second only to Alaska in volume of inland water, with more than 5,175 square miles of lakes and streams.*

Other accommodations to consider are Sandollar Sity (3038 On the Beach, Port Aransas 78373, 361–749–5000), a bed-and-breakfast with three rooms and five beach houses near the beach, plus sauna and whirlpool; and Sunrise Villa Condominiums (1505 South Eleventh

Street, Port Aransas 78373, 361–749–6409 or 800–722–6409), with twenty units on the beach, roof-top decks, pool, and TVs. For a complete listing of lodgings, contact the Port Aransas Chamber of Commerce Tourist & Convention Bureau, (800) 45–COAST. Visit the Internet site at www.portaransas.org.

The *Crazy Cajun restaurant* on Alister Street Square offers a Louisiana-style shrimp and crawfish boil: hot fresh shrimp, crawfish, stone crab claws, new potatoes, corn on the cob, and smoked sausage. The gumbo and sourdough bread are good, too. It's open for dinner only, Tuesday through Friday, and lunch and dinner Saturday and Sunday; closed Monday; call (361) 749–5069.

Other worthy Port A eating spots include Shell's Pasta and Seafood (522 East Avenue G, Port Aransas 78373, 361–749–7621), serving blue crab ravioli in red bell pepper cream sauce, open for lunch and dinner Wednesday through Sunday; and Pelican's Landing (337 North Alister Street, Port Aransas 78373, 361–749–6405), specializing in locally caught fresh fish, fresh-cut steaks, and music on the patio.

Just across Corpus Christi Bay, which laps at Mustang Island's western shore, is the same-name city with almost 300,000 residents. The Nueces County seat, *Corpus Christi* is reached on a half-hour drive inland from Mustang Island and is the most common arrival spot for travelers flying to Texas's Coastal Bend area.

Corpus is thought to have first hosted a European in 1519, when explorer Alonzo de Pineda made a visit. Today the city is separated from the Gulf by a lengthy *seawall,* which was designed by sculptor Gutzon Borglum of Mount Rushmore fame. Just a few years ago eight gazebolike *miradors*—Spanish for "lookouts"—were added to the seawall; the brilliant white miradors, capped by pointed, barrel-tile roofs and complemented by Victorian-style street lamps, function as both resting spots and wedding sites.

Corpus is a magnet for sailing and sailboarding fans, as well as a new breed of tourists interested in ecology. *The Dolphin Connection,* a small business run by a husband-wife team conducting dolphin research, illustrates the ecotourism premise that things educational can be fun, with dolphin-feeding tours departing twice every morning. Guides provide dolphin data throughout the expedition, which begins with a five-minute trip into the bay's shrimping zone. As soon as a tour boat arrives, nearly a dozen dolphins appear, flipping and jumping and practically begging for attention. During the next hour, the Judge, Mary, Whistler, Fritz, June Bug, and several other family members pop up out of the water, much to everyone's amusement, and the audience of ten tourists gets to know the entertainers, feeding long, stringy ribbon fish to the dolphins, petting their necks, and calling them by name. The dolphins respond, showing their pleasure by changing their undersides from dull gray to a distinctive pink. The tours are offered daily, weather permitting. Reservations are required; call (361) 776–2887. Call for rates and schedules.

The shining star in Corpus remains the *Texas State Aquarium* (2710 North Shoreline Drive, Corpus Christi 78403, 361–881–1200 or 800–477–4853, www.txstateaq.com), an outstanding aquarium featuring 250 species of aquatic plants and animals. Within you'll see that more than 350,000-plus gallons of sea water are required to support all the Gulf of Mexico life on exhibit, as well as an artificial reef created by the legs of an oil derrick, providing a home for rays, sharks, and tropical fish. Turtle Bend is a pool and beach area where several rare species live, including the endangered Kemp's turtle. Open Memorial Day through Labor Day weekend, 9:00 A.M. until 6:00 P.M. Monday through Saturday and until 8:00 P.M. on Tuesday, and 10:00 A.M. until 6:00 P.M. Sunday. The rest of the year it's open from 9:00 A.M. until 5:00 P.M. Monday through Saturday and from 10:00 A.M. until 5:00 P.M. Sunday. An admission fee is charged.

Nearby is the newer *World of Discovery* (1900 North Chaparral Street, Corpus Christi 78403, 361–883–2862). Home to the ships of Christopher Columbus, this is where today's discoverers can explore exact replicas of the *Nina, Pinta,* and *Santa Maria,* built by the government of Spain for the 500th anniversary of the great voyage. Explore a working shipyard, see Columbus's quarters, and go below the decks on the *Santa Maria.* Adjacent you'll find the Corpus Christi Museum of Science and History, where an armada of interactive exhibits includes the Smithsonian's "Seeds of Change," commemorating the impact of Christopher Columbus's voyages as well as science and natural history displays focusing on energy, birds, gems and minerals, and shells. The hands-on children's area has a shrimp boat, bird costumes, video phones, etc., while "Reptiles of South Texas" features a live alligator, and *Shipwreck!* is the award-winning story of the 1554 Spanish shipwreck off of Padre Island. Open from 10:00 A.M. until 5:00 P.M. Monday through Saturday and noon to 5:00 P.M. Sunday. Admission is charged; call for rates and packages.

Since 1992, when the World War II aircraft carrier *USS* **Lexington** opened as a museum in the port near the aquarium, naval history has been observed as never before on the Texas coast. Only the fourth carrier to make such a conversion, the *Lexington*—nicknamed the *Lady Lex*—was commissioned in 1943, participated in all major Pacific battles from Tarawa to Tokyo, collected eleven battle stars, and was the first to enter Tokyo Bay in September 1945. Among sixteen decks to explore are the cavernous hangar area, where immense elevators carried fighters and attack planes from the landing deck for maintenance; and the landing deck, where volunteer guides—mostly retired naval officers—show center lines and arrest and catapult areas and explain the complications that go into running a small oceantop landing strip where planes land as often as every thirty seconds. The USS *Lexington* is open Monday through Saturday 9:00 A.M. until 5:00 P.M. and Sunday 11:00 A.M. until 5:00 P.M. An admission fee is charged, and military discounts are offered. Call (361) 888–4873 or (800) LADY–LEX.

The soaring white Harbor Bridge stretches south over the busy port to the **Bayfront Arts and Sciences Park** (north end of Shoreline Boulevard) and downtown. At Bayfront kids get a kick out of summer melodramas at **Harbor Playhouse** (361–888–7469). Don't miss the **South Texas Institute for the Arts** (361–884–3844), an austere white building whose interior is acclaimed for its huge picture window looking over the water. Traveling exhibits have included such varied works as those of Remington and Warhol. Open Tuesday through Saturday 10:00 A.M. until 5:00 P.M. and Sunday 1:00 until 5:00 P.M.; the museum also charges a small admission.

Heritage Park (361–883–0639), still within the Bayfront complex, provides an opportunity to look at various historic homes all conveniently situated on 1 block. The structures are among the best of old Corpus Christi, dating back to 1851. Among them are elaborate designs, such as the Colonial Revival Victorian Lichtenstein House and the ornate Queen Anne Sidbury House, as well as simpler cottages. The homes have been painstakingly restored and are open for tours. Stop in the Merriman-Bobys House—the second-oldest house in the city—home now to Olde Tyme Deli, for a BLT, a bowl of chili, a piece of apple pie, or a lemonade.

Texas's oldest federal military cemetery is Corpus Christi's **Old Bayview Cemetery** (Ramirez Street at Waco Street), laid out by U.S. army engineers while Gen. Zachary Taylor was encamped in Corpus Christi in 1815. Seven of Taylor's soldiers are buried there, as are many pioneer settlers, veterans of the American War of Independence, the Mexican War, Indian campaigns, and the Civil War. You'll find a Texas Historical Marker.

Learn still more about the city's early history at **Centennial House** (411 Upper North Broadway Street, Corpus Christi 78403, 361–882–8691), the oldest existing structure in Corpus Christi. Built 1849–1850,

THE GULF COAST

the spectacular building and Texas Historical Landmark served as a Confederate hospital, a hospital and officer's mess for the federal army, and a citizen's refuge during desperado and Indian raids during the 1870s. Open from 2:00 until 5:00 P.M. on Wednesday.

For a change of pace there's *The Asian Cultures Museum* (1809 North Chaparral Street, Corpus Christi 78403, 361–882–2641), focusing primarily on Japanese history, religion, and art. Exhibits feature Kabuki masks, shrine replicas, a large collection of costumed Hakata dolls, and a wonderful Buddha statue dating to the 1700s. Open from 10:00 A.M. to 5:00 P.M. Tuesday through Saturday. Admission is free, but donations are welcome.

Thrusting seaward from the huge seawall is the *city marina,* bustling within the shadows of tall downtown buildings. Watery diversions found in the marina vary from sailboat and sailboard rentals to fishing excursions. People arrive in droves in the afternoon to make cheap buys from fishermen of live shrimp and blue crabs. The marina is home, too, to the reproduction paddlewheeler **Flagship,** which makes daily morning, afternoon, and evening sightseeing cruises. The triple-decked white ship plies water from the bay to the port and back, with interesting detailed narration of the city, past and present. In the port, huge tankers from distant places around the world—Moravia is just one spotted on a recent trip—are passed. Nighttime cruises often offer live jazz music. Cruise times and prices vary according to the season; for details call (361) 884–8306.

Corpus Christi's status as one of the breeziest cities in the nation makes it a hot spot for those sailing and sailboarding fans. Sailboat regattas are held each Wednesday evening on Corpus Christi Bay. The variety of waterways, from open Gulf beaches to protected coves, including the Laguna Madre, Gulf of Mexico, Corpus Christi Bay, and Bird Island Basin, make this appealing to beginners and experts alike. Rentals and lessons are readily available.

Some places to consult are the Corpus Christi International School of Sailing (at the marina on Cooper's Alley L-head, 361–881–8503), with services for the beginner, intermediate, and advanced sailor by captains licensed by the U.S. Coast Guard; Wind & Wave Water Sports (10721 South Padre Island Drive, Corpus Christi 78418, 361–937–9283), offering sailboarding lessons for beginner and advanced, individual or group instruction, as well as sailboard, surfboard, and boogie board rentals and kayak rentals available; and World Winds (14225 South Padre Island Drive at Bird Island Basin, Corpus Christi 78403, 361–949–7472 or 800–793–7471), with lessons and equipment rental.

Fishing enthusiasts are well served in Corpus by companies such as Boat Star Trek (Peoples Street T-head, 361–883–5031); and Clark's Guide Service (361–854–4461 or 800–487–2312), which offers fishing charters as well as seasonal duck hunting/fishing trips. For other companies call the Corpus Christi Visitors Office at (361) 561–2000.

At the south end of town, Corpus Christi Bay meets Laguna Madre at the JFK Causeway, the connection to *Padre Island National Seashore.* The legendary narrow island extends 113 miles southward nearly to Mexico and is the longest of all barrier islands on the Texas coast. No commercial development is allowed on the 80-mile midisland stretch, but National Park Service rangers provide information on camping and four-wheel-driving areas. Beachcombing and shell collecting are the national seashore's primary attractions, but federal law forbids taking flint points, coins, or anything that might be considered historical. Daily programs offered in summer by National Park Service rangers at *Malaquite Beach* include a 1:00 P.M. walk and study of the sea's natural flotsam and jetsam and a 2:00 P.M. in-water look at marine animals in Laguna Madre. Rangers also conduct fireside talks at dusk on Friday and Saturday on a variety of island topics. For information call the National Park Service's Padre Island office on the mainland at (361) 937–2621. At Malaquite Beach, the ranger office number is (361) 949–8068.

The Corpus Christi area also features sites on the *Great Texas Coastal Birding Trail,* a $1.4 million effort with more than 300 marked spots along nearly 700 miles of coastline reaching from Beaumont to Brownsville. Some 500 species of birds have been documented on the Isles of Texas, including sightings of brown pelicans, the rare masked duck, and the endangered whooping crane. Birding assistance can be provided by guides available through the Corpus Christi Guides Association, which offers a Bird Hotline, (361) 364–3634. Other good birding information sources are the Coastal Bend Audubon Society, (361) 882–7232; the Coastal Bend Sierra Club Group, P.O. Box 3512, Corpus Christi 78404; and the state birding information center, (888) TXBIRDS, www.tpwd.state.tx.us.

Memories of fantastic fresh fish will linger if you dine downtown at *Water Street Seafood Company* (309 North Water Street, Corpus Christi 78401, 361–882–8683), open daily for lunch and dinner. The food is every bit as good, but the view is better at *The Lighthouse* (444 North Shoreline Boulevard at the Lawrence Street T-head, Corpus Christi 78403, 361–883–3982), which has an ideal location looking out over the marina. U-peel-em shrimp, fried oyster sandwiches, grilled fresh shrimp, and steaks are served at lunch and dinner daily.

Catfish Charlie's (5830 McArdle Street, Corpus Christi 78412, 361–993–0363) offers a treat called the SOB, or shrimp stuffed with oysters, wrapped in bacon, then grilled. Other good choices are fried catfish with peppery hush puppies. The food, served for lunch and dinner, is cheap. A favorite for many years, *Snoopy's Pier* (13313 South Padre Island Drive, Corpus Christi 78412, 361–949–8815), is a waterside joint on Laguna Madre with excellent fried shrimp, oysters on the half shell, cheeseburgers, and ice cream. It's also cheap and open for lunch and dinner daily.

For more information contact the Convention and Visitor Department of the Greater Corpus Christi Business Alliance at (800) 678–6232, or visit the Internet site at www.corpuschristi-tx-cvb.org.

The Coastal Plains

An excursion from Corpus that won't easily be forgotten is the one to *Goliad,* a deeply historic spot northwest about 78 miles via U.S. Highway 181, U.S. Highway 77, and U.S. Highway 183. There you'll find the most fought-over and exemplary Spanish fort in Texas and the state's true birthplace. A metal plaque outside the heavy chapel doors at *Presidio La Bahía* seems to glow with the poignancy of the words it bears:

HERE FELL THE MEN IN MARTYRED DEATH TO GAIN THE FREEDOM AND INDEPENDENCE OF TEXAS; AND HERE FOR CENTURIES TO COME GENERATIONS OF MEN WILL GATHER IN REVERENCE AND APPRECIATION OF LA BAHIA'S GLORIOUS PAST.

The rough-hewn building dates to 1749 and is the nation's only completely restored inland fort. Among several important roles the presidio played is one from the Republic of Texas, one wrought with utter tragedy: The stillness of the tiny chapel here continues to emanate the desolation of Palm Sunday morning, 1836, when Col. James Walker Fannin and 352 Texas volunteers were held captive there before being marched out and shot under orders of Mexican dictator Santa Anna. The death toll was twice that of the Alamo's.

The first flag of Texas independence, emblazoned with a bloody arm wielding a saber, is still flown here in remembrance of La Bahía's stature as the place where independence was first planned and where the Declaration of Texas Independence was signed December 20, 1835. A museum in soldiers' quarters and officers' barracks details nine levels of civilization uncovered in artifacts, as well as artifacts from the revolution. Behind the presidio you'll find the Fannin Monument and Grave. The presidio, on U.S. Highway 183 about 2 miles south of Goliad, is open daily from 9:00 A.M. until 4:45 P.M. Admission is charged; call (361) 645–3752 for more information.

Across the San Antonio River from La Bahía rises the white-walled majesty of *Mission Espiritu Santo de Zuñiga,* once New Spain's finest outpost north of the Rio Grande. The mission is now contained within *Goliad State Historical Park,* also on U.S. Highway 183, just a quarter mile south of modern Goliad. Espiritu Santo functioned as a mission for 110 years and was the home of Texas's first large cattle ranch. Within the old mission building is a superb if small museum detailing Spain's attempt to colonize the New World.

The surrounding 2,200-acre park has wonderfully scenic shaded picnic and camping areas, interpretive nature trails, and river fishing. Across the highway, a junior-Olympic swimming pool is operated by the city of Goliad. Park admission is $2.00 per person; for information call (361) 645–3405.

Mission Espiritu Santo de Zuñiga

The *Goliad town square* surrounds a grand limestone courthouse, built in 1894, and an enormous live oak known as the *Hanging Tree.* Court was held here during the mid-nineteenth century, and the guilty were hanged, as many as five men at a time. Wonderful old Victorian and Texas pioneer buildings line the square. Nearby, at Franklin and Market Streets, *Fannin Park Plaza* contains a cannon from the revolution and a memorial to Fannin and his men. In June the town square is the site of the *Goliad Longhorn Stampede,* a festival celebrating the "Fastest Parade in History," which occurred in a 1976 Bicentennial party when a reenactment of a big cattle drive got out of hand and the one hundred longhorn steers created the last stampede in an incorporated city. For information on the town square and the annual stampede party, call the Goliad County Chamber of Commerce, (361) 645–3563.

It's only an hour's drive back to the beach, but you can find a restful sleepover in Goliad at the *Dial House* (306 West Oak Street, Goliad 77963, 361–645–3366). Lovely gardens surround an old family place, wherein wait five guest rooms, including a bridal suite. Breakfasts are bountiful, and the hostess is known for her crepes, pastries, and sweets.

If it's springtime, and especially in March, you'll want to make a detour from Goliad southwest on U.S. Highway 59 to *Beeville,* seat of Bee County, where *wildflowers* create a great big buzz in spring. A favorite route outlined in *Southern Living* magazine follows U.S. 181 south from Beeville about 10 miles to the town of Skidmore, where you'll turn right on Farm Road 797 and then loop into Farm Road 1349 back to Beeville. Your drive's reward will be stunning vistas of tall, crimson Indian paint-brush next to purple-topped thistles, lemony blooms on prickly pear cactus, pink primrose and white prairie larkspur, burgundy-colored wine cups, and delicate crochet blankets of Queen Anne's lace.

From Goliad it's an easy, 95-mile path south via U.S. Highway 183 and U.S. Highway 77 to *Kingsville,* home of still more pure Lone Star her-itage. Former riverboat captain Richard King established the leg-endary *King Ranch* in 1853 in the southeast Texas coastal plains by purchasing 75,000 acres of a Spanish land grant for $300, originally naming it the Santa Gertrudis Ranch for the rare creek running through it. That the ranch succeeded in such an uninhabited place and time is as profound as the modern accomplishments that would come in the next dozen decades.

Ranch workers and King's family fought off armed attacks by Mexican bandits on at least two dozen occasions; the towers from which guards kept watch remain the most notable design element on the ranch's oldest structure, a big white commissary built in the 1850s. Visitors straggled through the area without much regularity, but King and his wife, Henrietta, took in overnighters. One guest is said to have been Jesse James, who gave a gray stallion to King after the captain admired it; today, ranch lore holds that all gray stallions are descendants of James's horse.

King brought longhorn cattle to Texas from Mexico, luring entire Mexican villages to come along and work the livestock for room and board. The offspring of these *kiñeos*, or king's men, work today with King's own kin.

By the early twentieth century, 1.175 million acres with departmentalized operations formed an empire that would be known worldwide as innovative in the cattle and horse industries. Today, the spread measures 825,000 acres and reaches over Nueces, Kenedy, Kleberg, and Willacy Counties. Its fences, if placed in a straight line, would reach from the plains near Corpus Christi to Boston. The ranch is larger than the state of Rhode Island and home to 50,000 head of cattle, 1,000 head of horses, and 300 artesian wells reaching 600 feet into the earth.

Tours aboard minibuses take travelers through the brushy landscape, and guides point out the romantically named vegetation that characterizes this challenging corner of the world. The anaqua, or sandpaper tree, often grows up to 50 feet high, guides explain, and the sprawling, low-lying lantana brightens the terrain with a rainbow of colored flowers. In addition to live oak, persimmon, yucca, hackberry, and prickly pear, you'll find fragrant purple sage at home on the King Ranch range. Mesquite, that most defiant of Texas trees, gave the Kings plenty of problems, so a massive root-digging plow was invented expressly to clear mesquite from the King Ranch. One of the hostile, fanged machines is displayed with other model equipment near a cattle pen.

During the 12-mile tour, travelers can see where Santa Gertrudis cattle— the first beef breed developed in the United States—are worked, as well as the horse areas, famous for having contributed to American quarter horse development.

A much photographed building is the 1909 livery stable, a classic blend of western and Victorian influences. The only real disappointment is not being able to see the fabulous main house. It's open to tour groups of twenty or more–if there's no official ranch business being conducted at the time by any of the one hundred King descendants. Birding tours are becoming more popular here. The scissortail flycatcher, whose males sport beautiful orange breasts, is one of 350 species living on the ranch. Call for tour rates and schedules. For details contact the King Ranch, (361) 592–8055 or (800) 282–KING.

The adjacent town of Kingsville was created in 1903 when King's widow, Henrietta, deeded 853 acres of the ranch for a town to be built. An interesting stop after ranch exploration, it's home to the **Connor Museum**. Situated on the campus of Texas A&M–Kingsville, the Connor has a unique collection once belonging to Graves Peeler, a rustler and hunter whose assemblage of horns, arrowheads, game trophies, spurs, and such is strange and almost creepy, but a collection that's worth a stop. Also at the Connor, "The Living Mosaic" is a polished educational TV production illustrating the Texas coastal plain and its natural resources and history. The photography of plant and animal life, especially wildflowers, is nothing but stunning. Open Tuesday through Saturday, 9:00 A.M. until 5:00 P.M.; call (361) 595–2810 for more information.

The **King Ranch Museum** (405 North Sixth Street, Kingsville 78364, 361–595–1881), housed in a renovated 1907 icehouse, exhibits a wonderful, award-winning photographic essay by Toni Frissell depicting life on the King Ranch in the early 1940s. Also of interest are fabulous collections of antique coaches, vintage cars, and saddles. Open Monday through Saturday noon until 4:00 P.M. and Sunday 1:00 until 5:00 P.M. Admission is $4.00.

The **Running W Saddle Shop** (Sixth and Kleberg Streets, Kingsville 78364, 361–595– 5761 or 800–282–KING) is the place to spend big dollars in a short time, although it takes a few hours to really see the spectacular inventory. A very sophisticated boutique, its pale hardwood floors and rough wood walls are adorned with artfully composed displays and beautiful Indian saddle blankets and rugs. Custom-made goods include leather backpacks, "gunpowder" shoulder or belt bags, antler candlesticks, Running W collector's china, a gift crate of mesquite, cactus and jalapeño jellies, and jewelry, including sterling-silver cufflinks bearing the King Ranch's Running W brand against prickly-pear cactus.

The Big Beach

From Kingsville it's a little more than a two-hour shot straight south to Texas's most famous spread of sand. To reach **South Padre Island,** just follow U.S. Highway 77 down to Los Fresnos, then turn east on Texas Highway 100, which ends at the state's southernmost beachfront.

The only reason to pause even for a moment before hitting the beach is to stock up on supplies in **Port Isabel.** Certainly there are legions of stores on the island, but you'll save money by shopping for groceries and fresh-caught fish in the placid little fishing village.

While you're at it, take note that the smallest state park in Texas is right here—the **Port Isabel Lighthouse State Historic Park** (Texas Highway 100 and Tarvana Street at the Causeway, 956–943–1172). It's the only lighthouse on the coast open to the public, casting its light 16 miles out on the Gulf from its erection in 1853 until it was closed in 1905. Those in shape can scale the winding seventy-plus steps to the top to gain a view of Port Isabel, the Causeway, South Padre Island, and on to the Gulf of Mexico.

Can't wait to get to the waves? Then head east, crossing the great blue Laguna Madre Bay on the **Queen Isabella Causeway,** Texas's longest bridge, stretching just over 2¹/₂ miles. The center span rises 73 feet above the mean high tide, allowing ships heading to sea to pass below; its strength will withstand threefold hurricane-force winds.

The lower end of long, skinny Padre Island gained its name, South Padre, when the Mansfield Cut—about 35 miles north of this developed tip—was created by state engineers in 1964, severing the island in two. Padre Island National Seashore (profiled in the Corpus Christi section) is north, and this mega resort area is south.

Texas Trivia

The largest county in Texas is Brewster, in west Texas, measuring 6,233 square miles, an area larger than the state of Connecticut. The smallest of the 254 counties is Rockwall, in north Texas, at 154 square miles.

From a scattering of simple beachy bungalows in the 1960s grew a city of high-rise hotels and condominiums in the 1980s known for its powerful tourism magnetism. South Padre's 34 miles of coastline and beaches, music, volleyball, and dance clubs bring 125,000 college kids to the beach from more than 125 colleges and universities in the United States and Canada during spring break, which occurs between early March and early April. Unless you're among this notorious crowd, it's best to visit South Padre Island any other time of the year.

Things are a bit more sane during other periods of celebration, including the big **Windsurfing Blowout** in May; the **Windjammer Regatta** in June; the **Texas International Fishing Tournament** in late July; and **Christmas by the Seas** and **Island of Lights Festival** throughout December.

State and world **fishing** records are frequently set in South Padre's bay and Gulf waters—and no wonder, with the bounty of whiting, drum, flounder, trout, redfish, kingfish, wahoo, tuna, marlin, and sailfish here. Half-day and full-day trips in the Laguna Madre Bay and the Gulf of Mexico cost as little as $14 or as much as $1,000, depending on skill, budget, and how far offshore you venture. Find out more about conditions and booking a trip at Jim's Pier, (956) 761–2865; Fisherman's Wharf, (956) 761–7818; or the Sea Ranch Marina, (956) 761–7777.

Fly-fishing in the clear, pale aqua Laguna Madre has become possibly the favorite pastime of all. Check into kayak and fly-gear rentals, as well as lessons, at the Fly Shop in Port Isabel (318 Queen Isabella Boulevard, Port Isabel 78578, 956–943–1785). For a fly-fishing experience that includes lodging, contact the Kingfisher Inn and Guide Service (36901 Marshall Hutts Road, Rio Hondo 78583, 956–748–4350), which offers guided fishing trips and bed-and-breakfast stays on the Arroyo Colorado, about forty-five minutes from South Padre Island.

The Laguna Madre Bay also is recognized as one of the world's top **sailboarding** destinations. The sailing season off South Padre runs from September through May. Water depth varies from 3 to 5 feet; daytime winds average 18 miles per hour. Novices and pros come to sail the bay, the Jetties, Boca Chica, and the Ditch. For complete information on conditions, accommodations, equipment, and rentals, contact the South Padre Island Visitors Office, (800) 767–2373.

Horseback riding has become a great way to enjoy the beach. Island Equestrian Center (at Andy Bowie County Park, north of the city limits, 956–761–HOSS) offers horse and pony rides on the beach daily, as well as guides and instruction.

Kids get their due on South Padre at places such as Ben's Fun & Sun (at the north end of Padre Boulevard, 956–761–5429), with go-carts and four-wheeler rentals. Jeremiah's (in Isla Blanca Park, 956–761–2131) has water slides for big kids as well as tots, miniature golf, a driving range, a video arcade, a Skycoaster, a snack bar, and a full-service bar. Three Flags over Padre (1201 Padre Boulevard, South Padre Island 78597, 956–761–1947) has go-carts, miniature golf, spaceball, a Ferris wheel, and a video arcade.

Golfers visiting South Padre tee up twelve months a year at courses in Brownsville (twenty-five minutes away) and Harlingen (forty minutes away). Choose from Brownsville's Country Club (1800 West San Marcelo, 956–541–2582), 18 holes, par 70, green fees $10; and Harlingen's Tony

Butler Municipal Golf Course ($^1/_2$ mile south of M Street, 956–430–6685), 27 holes, par 71/35, green fees $11.

An unforgettable experience is a dolphin tour with an outfit called **Colleys Fin to Feathers** (at Sea Ranch Marina, South Padre Island, 956-943-BIRD). Guides Scarlett and George Colley have spent years cultivating a respectful relationship with several families of bottlenose dolphins in the Laguna Madre, and they'll share their friends with you in a most eco-conscious manner. The Colleys are also expert birders and can customize birding tours to suit all interests.

Nature lovers will enjoy visiting **Sea Turtle, Inc.,** an endeavor begun years ago by the Turtle Lady, the late, beloved Ila Loetscher. Her successors continue to present shows on Tuesday and Saturday to raise money for the preservation of the nearly extinct Kemp's ridley sea turtle and other endangered turtles. Several of the rehabilitating specimens are observed, and the staff offers information about these marine creatures. Visit Sea Turtle, Inc. at 5805 Gulf Boulevard, South Padre Island 78597; call (956) 761–1720 for schedule or visit their Web site at www.seaturtleinc.com. A small admission fee is charged.

The internationally acclaimed environmental artist simply known as **Wyland** picked the South Padre Island Convention Centre as his canvas for Whaling Wall No. 53. The giant mural, featuring a pod of orcas (commonly known as killer whales), covers three walls of the Convention Centre. The life-size whales are illustrated in full color and are accompanied by other local sea life. Wyland's purpose for painting giant murals—he plans one hundred during his career—is to raise awareness of the dangers facing these wonderful creatures. In addition to his Whaling Walls, Wyland is recognized for his outstanding ability as a fine-arts painter and sculptor.

Next to the Convention Centre and Whaling Wall No. 53, the **Laguna Madre Nature Trail** is a 1,500-foot boardwalk that extends across four acres of wetlands. Containing informative signs about dune systems and bird species that frequent the area, the nature trail provides visitors with the opportunity to observe many species of birds and other wildlife in their natural habitat. Both the Whaling Wall and the nature trail are always open to the public free of charge and can be accessed through the circle driveway leading up to the Convention Centre, located at 7355 Padre Boulevard at the north end of town.

The **University of Texas Pan American Coastal Studies Lab** (in Isla Blanca Park at the south end of the island, 956–761–2644) has aquarium displays of fish and other marine life indigenous to the area as well as an extensive shell collection. It's open from 1:30 until 4:30 P.M. Sunday through Friday. Admission is free.

The area's largest nature exhibit is found at the **Laguna Atascosa National Wildlife Refuge,** a 45,000-acre federal preserve for wildlife and bird watching, located about fifteen minutes away on the mainland across the Laguna Madre from South Padre Island. The largest protected area of natural habitat left in the Rio Grande Valley, it's home to redhead ducks, snow geese, sandhill cranes, and white-tailed hawks, as well as ocelot, white-tailed deer, mountain lion, javalina, ground squirrel, long-tailed weasel, coyote, various snakes, and other animals and reptiles. The refuge is open daily from sunrise to sunset. The visitors center at the refuge is open from 10:00 A.M. until 4:00 P.M. A small admission fee is charged. For more information and detailed driving directions, contact the refuge at (956) 748–3607 or (956) 748–3608.

Birders are flocking to a lovely retreat called the **Inn at Chachalaca Bend,** a small bed-and-breakfast lodge in the town of Los Fresnos, which is about twenty minutes from South Padre Island and convenient to Laguna Atascosa. Guests wake to the call of the wild chachalacas, native to south Texas and the nearby reaches of Mexico, which live on the grounds and wander between aged Texas ebony and honey mesquite trees. Nature lovers roam the walking trails to viewing platforms and towers and to butterfly gardens, or sit by the outdoor fire pit to watch the soothing resaca, or oxbow that feeds a nearby river flowing to the Gulf of Mexico. The renovated home features beautifully used mahogany and teak and holds six lavishly decorated bedrooms, all with beautiful private baths. Elaborate breakfasts include salmon-ricotta frittata and apple soufflé. The inn is located at 20 Chachalaca Bend Drive, Los Fresnos 78566, (956) 233–1180 or (888) 612–6800, www. chachalaca.com.

There's so much good food on South Padre Island that it seems a shame to only mention a few restaurants. For excellent grilled shrimp and

The Aplomado Falcons' Comeback

*T*hanks to the Peregrine Fund's 1986 breeding program, Aplomado falcons are making a promising comeback at the Laguna Atascosa National Wildlife Refuge. Almost extinct since the end of World War II, the Aplomado are nesting at the refuge after being captured in Mexico and released in the south Texas sanctuary where they are safe from the pesticides and loss of habitat that threatened their existence.

snapper, try Amberjack's Bayside Bar and Grill (209 West Amberjack Street, South Padre Island 78597, 956–761–6500), open for lunch and dinner. For the island's own home brew, check out Padre Island Brewing Company (3400 Padre Boulevard, South Padre Island 78597, 956–761–9585), where the hot-hot chicken wings, beer-battered shrimp, snapper, and other fish are super. For a special evening, consider The Grill Room at the Pantry (708 Padre Boulevard at Franke Plaza, South Padre Island 78597, 956–761–9331), where you'll pay handsomely for gourmet versions of seafood, beef, lamb, quail, and shrimp "Bubba." This one's open for lunch and dinner, Tuesday through Sunday.

As South Padre has boomed, so has its nightlife. Some of the most happening places include Black Marlin Tavern (2301 Padre Boulevard, 956–761–1997); Kelly's Irish Pub (101 East Morningside Street, 956–761–7571); Boomerang Billy's (2612 Gulf Boulevard at the Surf Motel, 956–761–2420); Coconuts (2301 Laguna Boulevard at Marlin Street, 956–761–4218); and Wahoo's Saloon (201 West Pike Street, South Padre 78597, 956–761–5344). All, by the way, are open during the day, too, if you need to rest that sunburn.

Finding a place to stay on South Padre Island can be an overwhelming task, with more than 5,000 condo and hotel rooms to consider. For help with finding the condo or beach house you'd like, there are several reservation agencies on South Padre Island. These include (all are in the 956 area code) Island Services, 1700 Padre Boulevard, 761–2649, (800) 426–6530; Padre Island Rentals/Island Reservation Service, 3100 Padre Boulevard, 761–5512 or (800) 926–6926 (United States and Canada); Tropical Condominium Services, 200 West Kingfish Street, 761–1323 or (800) 221–5218; and Island Time Vacations, 100 Padre Boulevard, Suite 3309, 761–5242. (All South Padre Island establishments use the zip code 78597.)

For more information contact the South Padre Island Convention & Visitors Bureau at (800) SO–PADRE. Visit the Internet site at www.sopadre. com; when the home page is loaded, you'll hear the ocean's roar—literally.

OTHER PLACES TO STAY ON THE GULF COAST

CORPUS CHRISTI

Villa del Sol, 3938 Surfside Boulevard, Corpus Christi 78402, (800) 242-3291. One-bedroom condos facing the surf have complete kitchens, barbecue grills, swimming pools, and private balconies.

George Blucher House, 211 North Carrizo Street, Corpus Christi 78401, (361) 884-4884. This stately 1904 home, one of the oldest in the city, is an elegant bed-and-breakfast with six guest rooms and private baths, and private phones, voice mail, TV/VCR, individual climate control, fine linens, and toiletries in each room. A full gourmet breakfast is included.

GALVESTON

Casa del Mar Beachfront Suites, 6102 Seawall Boulevard, Galveston 77551, (409) 740-2431 or (800) 392-1205. This beachfront offering has condo suites, in-room movies, two pools, and rates starting at $69.

Martha's Vineyard Guest House, in Gilchrist on the Bolivar Peninsula, reached by ferry from Galveston, (409) 286-5441. Right on the beach, it's perfect for birders and anglers.

Mermaid & Dolphin Bed & Breakfast, 1103 Thirty-third Street, Galveston 77550, (409) 762-1561. An impressive 1866 home underwent extensive renovation to become this luxurious inn with six rooms and private baths, video and book libraries, bicycles, hot tub, spa massage therapy, happy hour in pub, and full breakfast. Rates are about $125 and up.

HOUSTON

Houstonian Hotel, Club & Spa, 111 North Post Oak Lane, Houston 77024, (713) 680-2626. Sprawling over a woodsy setting near the Galleria and Memorial Park, this exquisite lodging offers weekend golf packages and health club facilities. About $200-$350.

KINGSVILLE

B Bar B Ranch Inn, Route 1, Box 457, Kingsville 78363, (361) 296-3331. A bed-and-breakfast retreat on an eighty-acre, working ranch, this remote escape offers six bedrooms in the ranch house—all with private baths—and a pool house that can accommodate a large family. Breakfast is included with stay, and other meals are available. There's plenty of land for nature walks, and depending on the season, you can hunt for quail, deer, doves, wild hogs, and turkeys. The innkeepers

can also arrange fishing in nearby Baffin Bay and golf games. Rates start at $75.

PALACIOS

Moonlight Bay and Paper Moon Bed & Breakfast, 506 South Bay Boulevard, Palacios 77465, (361) 972-2232 or (800) 714-1997, ext. 51. In the Matagorda Bay area, Moonlight Bay is a B&B tucked inside a 1910 prairie-style home reminiscent of Frank Lloyd Wright's designs; four guest rooms with private baths are offered. Next door is Paper Moon Guest House, offering three guest rooms (with private baths) named for the owner's favorite literary works, such as Fitzgerald's *The Great Gatsby*. Afternoon tea is served on Friday and Saturday for guests, and an elaborate breakfast spread is included with stay. Fixed-price dinners are available with advance notice. Rates are $65 to $140.

PORT ARANSAS

Gulf Beach Cottages, 506 East Avenue G, Port Aransas 78373, (361) 749-5416. Inexpensive complex offers seventeen cottages near the beach.

SEABROOK

The Pelican House Bed & Breakfast, 1302 First Street, Seabrook 77586, (281) 474-5295. A ninety-year-old home shaded by live oak and pecan trees next to Galveston Bay, located about 3 miles from NASA and Space Center Houston. The B&B offers four guest rooms with private baths; one has a private entrance and one opens onto a deck overlooking the water. Rates start at $65.

SOUTH PADRE ISLAND

The Brown Pelican Inn, 207 West Aries Street, South Padre Island 78597, (956) 761-2722. Eight guest rooms are filled with European and American antiques and knickknacks. There are private baths for each room, and most rooms have covered porches and a view of Laguna Madre.

Casa de Siesta, 4610 Padre Boulevard, South Padre Island 78597, (956) 761-5656. New and very comfortable, this bed-and-breakfast offers a Mexican stucco design, twelve oversize rooms with lovely, tiled private baths, Mexican antique decor, and hand-carved New Mexican furniture, continental breakfast, and a large, pretty pool in the central courtyard. Walking distance to the beach.

OTHER PLACES TO EAT ON THE GULF COAST

CORPUS CHRISTI

Rosita's, 5253 South Staples Street, Corpus Christi 78411, (361) 906-1007. This busy cafe serves no-frills Mexican breakfast, lunch, and dinner at prices starting at $5.00.

Taqueria Garibaldi, 200 North Staples Street, Corpus Christi 78401, (361) 884-5456. Hearty, authentic Mexican breakfasts and lunches start at about $4.00.

GALVESTON

Cafe Michael Burger, 8826 Seawall Boulevard, Galveston 77550, (409) 740-3639. This madly popular burger joint offers the Michael Burger, a third-pounder with the usual trimmings; the Campeche, with jalapeños and picante sauce; the Jamaica Beach, with pineapple, jalapeños, and Swiss; and the Lichtenfeldt, with sauerkraut and Swiss. Open for lunch and dinner Wednesday through Sunday.

Leon's World's Finest In & Out BBQ House, 101 Fourteenth Street, Galveston 77550, (409) 763-5651. This old house serves well as a great bar

becue joint, where you can have brisket or sausage sandwich, or ribs, chicken, and other smoked meats by the pound or with turnip greens (this is the South, you know) cole slaw, potato salad, Leon's "rice stepped up," beans, green beans, and pies. Rum cake and sweet-potato pie are super desserts. Open for lunch daily and for dinner (until 8:00 P.M.) Friday through Sunday.

The Original Mexican Cafe, 1401 Market Street, Galveston 77550, (409) 762-6001. Billed as the oldest continuously operating restaurant on the island, the Original takes a healthful approach to Tex-Mex by using olive oil, skinless chicken, 90 percent lean meat, and cholesterol-free oil for frying. Mexican breakfasts are a big hit on weekends, and tacos and fajitas, grilled chicken, and vegetarian tamales are popular otherwise. Open for lunch and dinner Sunday through Friday and for breakfast on Sunday.

Phoenix Bakery and Coffee House, Twenty-third Street at Ship's Mechanic Row, Galveston 77550, (409) 763-4611. A picturesque setting with a menu of breakfast burritos, pancakes, waffles, sandwiches, soups, and salads. Open for breakfast, lunch, and dinner daily; meals start at $5.00.

HOUSTON

Backstreet Café, 1103 South Shepherd Drive, Houston 77019, (713) 521–2239. Balancing acts include meat loaf with garlic mashed potatoes and roasted beet–goat cheese salad. Setting is a pretty, old house with a shady patio and overall comfort. Lunch and dinner are offered; reservations are advised.

Cafe Annie, 1728 Post Oak Boulevard, Houston 77056, (713) 840–1111. This long-revered bastion of fine dining is known for its haute Southwestern fare, including chicken, beef, and seafood. Open for lunch and dinner, the average meal is about $20.

Churrascos, in Shepherd Square at 2055 Westheimer Road, Houston 77098, (713) 527–8300. Updated, stylish Latin dishes ranges from empanadas (savory turnovers) and quesadillas to yucca pancakes to grilled tenderloin with shrimp, jacketed with fried plantain. Open for lunch and dinner, Monday through Saturday; reservations are recommended.

Gugenheim's Delicatessen, 1708 Post Oak Boulevard, Houston 77056, (713) 622–2773. You couldn't want for better homemade food, Kosher and otherwise. The menu is overwhelming with its hundreds of offerings, but regulars swear by the chicken soup, cold borsch with sour cream, and corned beef hash. Of course, the sandwiches are to die for–particularly the 5-inch-tall triple deckers, like the Grand Central Station, piled with turkey, roast beef, salami, cole slaw, Muenster cheese, and Russian dressing. Open daily for breakfast, lunch, and dinner.

Picnic, 1928 Bissonnet Street, Houston 77005, (713) 524–0201. Light, casual lunch fare includes spinach salad, tuna salad with basil mayonnaise on fresh sourdough, as well as lovely soups and desserts. Open daily for breakfast and lunch.

PORT ARANSAS

Beulah's at Tarpon Inn, 200 East Cotter Street, Port Aransas 78373, (361) 749–4888. Elegant versions of tuna steak, red snapper, shrimp, and other fish are served at dinner Wednesday through Sunday; prices start at around $10.

ROCKPORT

Chandler House Tea Room, 801 South Church Street, Rockport 78382, (361) 729–2285 or (800) 843–1808. Inside a turn-of-the-twentieth-century mansion that's been converted to a B&B, this antiques-filled dining room offers lunches of cream soups, fruit salads, turkey sandwiches, and fresh fruit cobblers Tuesday through Saturday.

SOUTH PADRE ISLAND

Blackbeard's, 103 East Saturn Street, South Padre Island 78597, (956) 761–2962. Stuffed shrimp, crab, and shrimp fajitas are unbeatable; it's open for lunch and dinner.

Blue Rays Diner, 410 Padre Boulevard, South Padre Island 78597, (956) 761–7297. In addition to great sandwiches and salads, the cafe offers Harley-Davidson decor. Open for lunch and dinner.

The Hill Country

Visualize two-lane roads, twisting and climbing, leading to an antique borough here, a pioneer settlement there. Imagine hills, soft and scrubby, green valleys, limestone cliffs. Conjure up ranches and communities of German heritage, wineries and fields of wildflowers, sparkling rivers lined with cypress and oak.

Ah, the Hill Country realized. To some it's the state's greatest natural resource. No big cities, no bustle. Just cafes with country cooking, water for fishing and inner tubing, and old places with timeworn comfort.

Raised by the Edwards Plateau, the hilly region extends west from I–35, which follows the edge of the Balcones Fault. You can find this land of escape below U.S. 190 and above U.S. 90. Wander alone or take the whole family. But don't venture too far west of U.S. 83, where the hills—and the Hill Country—taper off. Just go armed with plenty of film.

Spring—when Texas is blanketed in glorious wildflowers—is by far the most popular time to wander through the Hill Country. Experts at the Lady Bird Johnson Wildflower Center in Austin are deluged with calls every year in early March, when travelers are begging for information as to when the bluebonnets, the state flower, will sprout their colorful hats.

These experts manage to patiently explain time and time again that everything depends on whether fall and winter rains reached the wild-flower seeds after germination, whether sunshine followed, and whether Mother Nature decides to cooperate. In other words, blooming is just too hard to predict.

While there's no guarantee for abundant *Lupinus texensis* (the blue-bonnet's proper name), you'll usually find plenty of opportunities to pose children amid the colored country fields for an Easter portrait. What the country's wildflower authorities will promise is that they'll pass along to you whatever bluebonnet and other flower information they have. Call the center at (512) 292–4200 or the highway department's hotline at (800) 452–9292 for information about the best highway routes in Texas for wildflower watching.

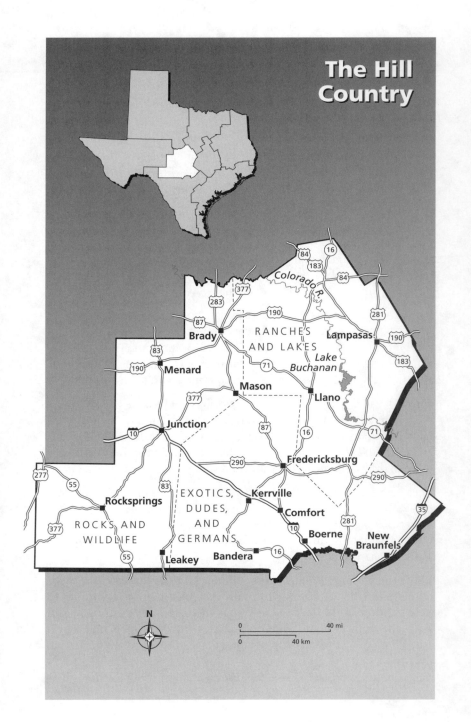

The Hill Country

June's Favorite Attractions in the Hill Country

Badu House, Llano

Comfort Common, Comfort

Enchanted Rock State Park, near Fredericksburg

Farm Road 337, Vanderpool

Guadalupe River Ranch, Boerne

Luckenbach

Pedernales Falls State Park, near Johnson City

Vanishing Texas River Cruise, Lake Buchanan

Wimberley Pie Co., Wimberley

Y.O. Ranch, near Kerrville

As the deeply blue carpet spreads northward from south Texas, we cross our fingers in hopes that the sapphire blooms—mixed in with the palette of Mexican hat, Indian paintbrush, black-eyed Susans, primroses, and hundreds of others—will make a timely appearance in the Hill Country for a scattering of festivals. The Hill Country's upper reaches, called the Highland Lakes for the 150-mile, sparkly string of seven lakes formed by the Colorado River, are particularly vibrant for two weeks in spring when the Highland Lakes communities throw out floral welcome mats during the annual Bluebonnet Arts & Crafts Trail.

Here it's easy to spend a day or a weekend at a medley of arts and crafts fairs, featuring works by more than 500 artists in all, as well as related musical events, street parties, cook-offs, and fishing tournaments. Waterside pastimes—golf, tennis, and hiking among them—are handy, too, on cliff-lined lakes that offer more total shoreline than even the whole Texas coast. Stay the night at a lakefront resort, waterfront cabin, or bed-and-breakfast inn. Just pick your pace and do the self-guided tour, aided by a free Bluebonnet Trail brochure and map. Call the Highland Lakes bluebonnet hot line at (512) 793–2803 between 9:00 A.M. and 5:00 P.M. daily, from mid-March through the end of April.

Before you begin touring, you may want to note on your map the Hill Country's best lanes for spring wildflowers and year-round scenery. They include U.S. 281 from Lampasas south to San Antonio; Texas 16 from Llano south to Medina; U.S. 290 from Austin to west of Fredericksburg; Texas 71 from Austin northwest to Llano; Texas 29 from Burnet west to Llano; and Texas 46 from New Braunfels to just east of Bandera.

Ranches and Lakes

There's no better place to begin the Hill Country tour than in *Johnson City,* found about 50 miles west of Austin at the junction of U.S. 290 and U.S. 281. The seat of Blanco County, the town of only 932 residents and its nearby neighbor, *Stonewall* (just across the Gillespie County line, 16 miles west on U.S. 290), lay in relative obscurity a hundred peaceful years before one of the most colorful men in political history became president suddenly in 1963. Lyndon Baines Johnson was

A Taste of the Grape

The tiny town of Stonewall, just outside of Fredericksburg, is home to two wineries. Becker Vineyards features a reproduction, nineteenth-century German stone barn and more than twenty-four acres of grapevines producing chardonnay, cabernet sauvignon, ruby cabernet, and others. Located on Jenschke Lane, about 1 mile off U.S. 290,

(830) 644–2681. Grape Creek Vineyard is known for its antique roses, gift shop, tasting room and the only fully underground wine cellar in Texas, where bottles of cabernet sauvignon, chardonnay, fume blanc, and cabernet blanc are stored. Find it on South Grape Creek, just west of Stonewall on U.S. 290, (830) 644–2710.

profoundly attached to his roots and made his family ranch in Stonewall, just 14 miles west of his Johnson City birthplace, the Texas White House.

The **Lyndon B. Johnson National Historic Park,** with units on U.S. 281 in both Johnson City and Stonewall, and adjacent **Lyndon B. Johnson State Park** do a fine job of detailing the heavy heritage of this bigger-than-life figure and his land. The national park visitors center has a multimedia program on the illustrious LBJ and Johnson City history as well as a gift shop. There's also the president's boyhood home, a humble 1886 frame house where LBJ's parents moved in 1914; it's been restored and furnished to 1920s style.

The park's ranch unit spreads along the serene **Pedernales River** and is where LBJ retired (some say as a lonely and fractured man). National Park Service buses take groups through the grounds to view the ranch house, cattle, family cemetery where LBJ is buried, and a reconstruction of the president's birthplace. A living historical farm; small church cemetery; two furnished, pioneer dogtrot-style houses; swimming pool; and tennis court are spread about the parks, but it's riverside picnic areas shaded by ancient live oaks that provide unparalleled peace. From here you can look across the water at cattle grazing on the Johnson Ranch and at the white ranch house where Lady Bird Johnson still spends time.

For details on the state park, contact park headquarters at (830) 644–2252 or (830) 644–2241. For national park information call (830) 868–7128.

There's plenty to do in Johnson City, otherwise. Browsing around **The Feed Mill compound** (U.S. Highway 290 at Nugent Street, 830–868–7299) will entertain a while. There's the Feed Mill Mart on the first floor, with a good collection of Texas books as well as unusual antiques. Texas

THE HILL COUNTRY

JUNE'S FAVORITE ANNUAL EVENTS IN THE HILL COUNTRY

Bluebonnet tours; Burnet, Llano, Buchanan Dam, Lampasas, Marble Falls, and Kingsland; early April

Easter Fires Pageant, Fredericksburg, day before Easter

Folk Festival, Kerrville, late May and early June

Founders' Day Sidewalk Sale, Wimberley, first weekend in March

Oktoberfest, Fredericksburg, early October

Wurstfest, New Braunfels, first two weekends in November

Vintage Wines offers tastings of Texas wines and specialty foods. For imported goods try Amaru Ka, on the second and third floors, for Latin American gift items; and Kiya's Ethnic Shop for imported jewelry and clothes from Africa, India, and Indonesia. And The Enchanted Olive sells a variety of olive oils, olives, Texas gourmet products, and espresso. The Feed Mill Cafe offers lunch and dinner, with chicken-fried steak, burgers, sandwiches, and salads among favorites.

Overnight stays in Johnson City are coziest at *Carolyne's Cottage* (103 Avenue D, Johnson City 78636, 830–868–4548 or 830–868–4374), a bed-and-breakfast nestled in a native-stone house outfitted with English and Texas antiques and lace curtains. Breakfast goodies are stocked in the refrigerator.

Other bed-and-breakfast choices include *Hoppe's Guest House* (404 Avenue N, Johnson City 78636, 830–868–4548), with an herb garden and white picket fence; and *Smith's Tin House* (204 Avenue G, Johnson City 78636, 830–868–4548), furnished with local antiques. For all bed-and-breakfasts in Johnson City, try the central booking agency at (830) 868–4548.

Pedernales Falls State Park, about 10 miles east of Johnson City via Farm Road 2766, (830) 868–7304, is a stunning spread of nearly 5,000 acres of former ranch land with 6 miles of spectacular riverfront for tubing, swimming, fishing, hiking, and camping. The park is open daily and charges a small admission.

Another detour for naturalists is to *Westcave Preserve,* a thirty-acre nature reserve northeast of Johnson City, near the Pedernales River. A Lower Colorado River Authority property, Westcave is first seen as upland savannah, replete with wildflower meadows, before it descends to a verdant canyon formed hundreds of centuries ago when a huge limestone cave collapsed. As you hike along, you'll find an amazing development: A spring-fed creek meanders for a while before sharply turning into a 40-foot waterfall spilling into a radiantly green pool. Sensational bird watching and wildflower spotting can be had in the preserve. Tours are given Saturday and Sunday at 10:00 A.M., noon, 2:00 P.M., and 4:00 P.M., weather permitting. No admission is charged, but contributions are welcome. You can reach Westcave by driving north on U.S. 281 from Johnson City about 12 miles, turning east on Ranch Road 962, and continuing another 12 miles. For information call (830) 825–3442.

From Johnson City it's also easy to make a side trip to **Blanco,** south just 14 miles on U.S. 281. A bucolic burg of the first order, this is the place to go to spend idle hours on the Blanco River banks. Named the Blanco County seat upon organization in 1858, the town of 1,200 lies about 45 miles north of San Antonio.

The town's pride is the old **Blanco County courthouse,** a Second Empire design built in 1886 but then abandoned when the county seat moved to Johnson City in 1890. After a recent impressive restoration effort, it is open to the public. For tour information contact the Blanco Chamber of Commerce at (830) 833–5101.

Throughout the town, century-old limestone buildings are a testament to the German colony that settled in the river valley, and some of the best historic buildings line the **courthouse square.** Businesses here now include Lindeman's Grocery, a general store in business since 1870; a covey of antiques shops with some funky collectibles; a tiny library; and a handful of cafes.

One of the shops to seek out on Blanco's square is **Wagner & Chabot** (830–833–4350), selling antiques, imported knickknacks from India, Japan, and Guatemala, candles and jewelry, and picture frames and potpourri. Within the shop is **Hard Scrabble Cafe,** serving lunches of homemade soups and sandwiches and dinners of steak, quail, and pork loin.

After your Blanco diversion, it's time to journey from Johnson City north on U.S. Highway 281 to the **Highland Lakes.** You'll first reach **Lake Marble Falls** in Burnet County, about 25 miles north of Johnson City. Overlooking the lake is a town of the same name, at U.S. 281's junction with Ranch Road 1431, one of the Hill Country's most scenic highways. **Marble Falls,** with 4,000 residents, is home to **Granite Mountain,** situated just west on Ranch Road 1431, an 860-foot-tall dome of rusty-red granite sprawling across 186 acres. It's this rock source from which the spectacular state capitol in Austin was built more than a century ago. You can see it from the highway, but the quarry isn't open to the public.

A good reason to stop in Marble Falls is to eat at the **Bluebonnet Cafe** (211 U.S. Highway 281, Marble Falls 78654, 830–693–2344), a delightful country diner serving Texas and southern specialties, such as chicken and dumplings, cobbler, catfish, chicken-fried steak, steaks, and all-day breakfasts. It's open for breakfast, lunch, and dinner daily.

Just 8 miles west of Marble Falls is a little hideout in the town of Granite Shoals called *Island View Bed & Breakfast* (1710 Lakecrest Drive, Granite Shoals 78654, 512–244–7126). The hosts own this two-story lakeside retreat and offer a guest room on the ground floor. Bicycles are available for riding the hilly terrain, but you'll need to be back from riding in time to see the heart-stopping sunsets over Packsaddle Mountain.

During the spring bluebonnet season, the *Highland Arts Guild,* at 318 Main Street, Granite Shoals 78654 in this tiny but historic downtown, exhibits original paintings, sculpture, and crafts. For details contact the Marble Falls Chamber of Commerce, (830) 693–4449.

The best scenic drives from Marble Falls can easily fill a morning or afternoon. Try heading northwest on Texas Highway 71 for a 32-mile jaunt to Texas Highway 16; or go west on Ranch Road 1431, which unwinds 18 miles through the tiny towns of *Granite Shoals* and *Kingsland* before its intersection with Texas Highway 29. This latter route follows the lakes trail, as the Colorado River meanders past dams creating Lake LBJ and then Inks Lake and Lake Buchanan Dam.

If you reach Kingsland during bluebonnet weekends, hand-crafted items are exhibited and sold at the *Kingsland House of Arts and Crafts,* on Ranch Road 1431.

A turn-of-the-twentieth-century railroad hotel has been renovated and reopened as *The Antlers* (Ranch Road 1431 at Kingsland, 915–388– 4411 or 800–383–0007). First opened in 1901 by the Austin & Northwestern Railroad, the inn now offers five suites, each accommodating up to three people; one room for two people; and four cabins equipped with kitchens and porches. All lodgings have private baths; rates are $120 to $150. The fifteen acres of wooded grounds have nature trails, a fruit orchard, and 1,500 feet of waterfront on Lake LBJ.

> ## Texas Trivia
>
> *Guadalupe Peak, at 8,749 feet, is the state's highest mountain. That's more than 2,000 feet higher than North Carolina's Mount Mitchell, the highest point east of the Mississippi River.*

Lake LBJ, immediately west of Lake Marble Falls, lies on the line shared by Burnet and Llano Counties and is probably the best liked of the Highland Lakes in terms of recreation and scenery. The 6,300-acre impoundment of the Colorado River is shielded from winds by tree-cloaked bluffs and granite cliffs and is consequently a big lake for waterskiing, sailing, Jet-Skiing, and fishing.

Some travelers who make Lake LBJ their destination settle in at *Horseshoe Bay Country Club and Resort* (Ranch Road 2147 just west of U.S. 281, 800–531–5105, 800–252–9363, or 830–598–2511). Guests stay in hotel-style rooms, condos, or townhouses and spend time playing golf on three 18-hole courses spread around the lake. There's also a beach, marina, indoor and outdoor tennis, and stables.

Your traveling path will likely take you from Marble Falls 12 miles north on U.S. Highway 281 to *Burnet* (pronounced BURN-it), seat of Burnet County and home to 3,423 residents. Frontier Fort Croghan was established here in 1849, and the town grew up around it. Today, Burnet— known as one of the most interesting geologic spots in the world—is a magnet for rock hounds as well as professional and amateur geologists.

Longhorn Caverns State Park (south on U.S. 281, 5 miles to Park Road 4, 512–756–6976) is a remarkable, 11-mile underground maze of caves and passages a million years in the making. What's odd about this cavern is that it was the site of big speakeasy parties during Prohibition. On the first and second Saturday of each month, naturalists lead a program called Wild Cave Tours, which take you on a three-hour adventure, crawling and climbing and squeezing through small passageways where outlaw Sam Bass was said to have stashed $2 million. Other guided tours are offered daily, too. The snack bar and souvenir shop are better than some. Tour hours vary; admission is charged.

Another Burnet stop is the *Fort Croghan Museum* (703 Buchanan Drive, Burnet 78611, 512–765–8281). The museum offers more than 1,200 items pertaining to early central Texas history plus six pioneer cabins. Open from 10:00 A.M. until 5:00 P.M. Thursday through Saturday and from 1:00 until 5:00 P.M. Sunday from April through October. There's no admission, but donations are welcome.

Burnet's Bluebonnet Trail offerings include a show from the *Burnet Creative Arts,* which includes original work by creators of ceramics, china paintings, oils, jewelry, stained glass, woodwork, weavings, and porcelain dolls. You'll find the show on Texas Highway 29 at the Catholic Educational Building. Call the Burnet Chamber of Commerce for details, (512) 756–4297.

Just west of Burnet, head along Texas 29 to Lake Buchanan and the new Canyon of the Eagles Lodge, found at the northern tip of the lake at the end of Ranch Road 2341, which you'll follow north from Texas 29. This nature lovers' retreat is perfect if your interests include hiking, canoeing, kayaking, fishing, and birding. The long-popular *Vanishing Texas River Cruise* is based at the lodge; regularly scheduled tours take you on Lake Buchanan in fall and winter to look for great blue herons, osprey, red-tailed hawks, American white pelicans, and, with any luck at all, a bald eagle, roosting in trees along the shoreline or gliding overhead. In spring and summer the cruises give you a chance to see wildflowers, deer, and other samples of Mother Nature's gifts. To book cruises call (800) 728–8735 or log onto www.vtrc.com.

The lodge also schedules programs such as guided nature hikes, arts-and-crafts classes, cowboy poetry readings, and hayrides. Lodgings are very attractive wood-and-stone cottages with tin roofs, rocking chairs on the porches, and quilts and Texas- and Mexican-made furniture in the rooms. The lodge serves inexpensive meals, as well as beer and wine. Call (800) 977–0081 to reserve or log onto www.canyonoftheeagles.com.

After the cruise continue on Texas 29 west to *Inks Lake State Park,* just an 8-mile reach from Burnet, (512) 793–2223. This 1,200-acre spread—one of the smaller but prettier lakes in Texas—is perfect for anybody who wants beautiful surroundings in which to read, sketch, or

Vanishing Texas River Cruise

Joy to the Fishes in the Deep Blue . . . Lake

Inks Dam National Fish Hatchery features scientific ponds in which thousands of fish are bred for stocking lakes across the nation. It's open week-days and until noon on weekends and is located at Farm Road 2342 at Park Road 4; look for signs. (830) 793–2474.

write postcards, and it affords camping, picnicking, fishing, and hiking. The park is open daily and charges a small admission. Inquire about canoe tours to the Devil's Waterhole.

Just 5 miles west of Inks Lake via Texas Highway 29, across the line into Llano County, is the town of **Buchanan Dam** (pronounced buck-ANN'n), sitting on the lovely Lake Buchanan. Only 1,100 people call it home, but it's a busy place in mild weather and spring flower time. The 2-mile-long dam is a work of arches and is likely the largest multi-arch dam in the nation. Built in the 1930s, it holds the Colorado River and forms the highest and largest of the Highland Lakes. One of the better places to view the lake and dam is at the Lake Buchanan Chamber of Commerce office, on Texas Highway 29 in the observation building at the dam, (512) 793–2803.

From the town and lake, it's an easy, 14-mile side trip up to the town of **Tow,** on the lake's northwestern shore, to visit **Fall Creek Vineyards** (west on Texas 29, north on Texas 261, north on Ranch Road 2241; 512–476–4477). One of the more successful wineries in the state, Fall Creek offers an impressive visitors center, guided tours, tasting room, and gift shop. Admission is free, but hours vary.

From Buchanan Dam the Hill Country tour continues 17 miles west again on Texas Highway 29 to **Llano,** seat of Llano County. Nearly 3,000 folks find Llano a comfortable place to live, and it's largely due to an undisturbed array of historic buildings. You'll want to explore the town one afternoon—it's easy to see on foot—to have a look at places such as the **Llano County Courthouse** (Main and Ford Streets), built in 1892; **Acme Dry Goods** (109 West Main Street, Llano 78643), dating to the same time; the **Southern Hotel** (201 West Main Street, Llano 78643), built in 1881 and housing a century-old hardware business; and the **Old Llano County Jail** (Oatman Street, northeast of the courthouse), today occupied by a museum. All details are available from the Llano Chamber of Commerce, (915) 247–5354.

The town is extremely popular with deer hunters in late fall and with rock hounds year-round. As the county is on the 1½-billion-acre *Llano Uplift,* described as a geological phenomenon, the ground is riddled with sensational finds of amethyst, azurite, dolomite, galena, garnet, quartz, serpentine, gold, and llanite, a brown granite with blue crystals and pink feldspar unique to this area.

People have been known to drive quite a way to eat Llano's barbecue. *Cooper's,* just west of Texas 16 on Texas 29 (604 West Young Street, Llano 78643, 915–247–5713), produces outstanding smoked ribs, brisket, pork, chicken, sausage, and cabrito (baby goat), with a fine pot of beans and savory barbecue sauce. It's open for lunch and dinner daily.

A delightful place to overnight in Llano is the *Badu House,* a two-story bed-and-breakfast inn (601 Bessemer Street, Llano 78643, 915–247–4304). A converted bank, the building dates to the town's iron boom in 1891 and is included on the National Register of Historic Places. Antiques are used throughout the inn, and the downstairs bar is covered by the world's largest piece of polished llanite, discovered by N. J. Badu, who transformed the bank into a home years ago.

The wildflower period in spring signals a show and sale of paintings, sculpture, drawings, weavings, pottery, and more at *Llano Fine Arts Guild Gallery* (503 Bessemer Avenue, Llano 78643, 915–247–5354).

Llano is the best place to strike out for a side trip to *Colorado Bend State Park.* Reach it by driving north on Texas 16 for 16 miles, then, inside San Saba County, turn east on Ranch Road 501 for 15 miles. A relatively new park, it's not yet well known and is sometimes a private Eden for travelers. Beautiful scenery unwinds along the banks of the Colorado River, where primitive camping sites, hiking trails, and picnicking areas are scattered. Anglers say the fishing is unsurpassed, and cave tours are offered on weekends. One is a walking tour through *Gorman Cave,* while the crawling tour explores smaller caves suited to the most dedicated spelunkers. Call for tour fees and times. The park is open daily and charges a small admission. For information call (915) 628–3240.

Rocks and Wildlife

*F*rom Llano, point your car northwest on Texas Highway 71 to *Brady.* It's a 54-mile drive to the seat of McCulloch County, home to 7,000 residents, and the town closest to the geographic center of Texas—hence the nickname, the Heart of Texas.

Any Texan who holds Lone Star foods near and dear to the heart can tell you Brady is the site of the **World Championship Barbecue Goat Cook-Off,** held annually on the Friday and Saturday before Labor Day. Don't laugh—the competition draws more than one hundred teams from around the United States and from abroad. The weekend brings plenty of entertainment and unique contests, all held at Richards Park on Commerce Street, just west of downtown. Admission is free; for details call (915) 597–3491.

For a look into the past, check out the **Heart of Texas Historical Museum** (High and Main Streets, 915–597–3491), a converted old jail (1910–74) that rises three stories into the sky and resembles a castle. You'll see exhibits on area history and the background of the jail cells and gallows. Open Saturday through Monday, 1:00 until 5:00 P.M.; admission is free.

In case you miss the cook-off and want to sample some barbecued goat before heading out of town, stop in at **Charlie's Barbecue and Steakhouse** (U.S. Highway 87 at the railroad tracks, 915–597–0603). Besides goat, there's tender beef brisket and mammoth steaks. Open for lunch and dinner daily.

Anyone who finds romance in history—and has a soft spot for animals—will want to stop in **Mason,** 28 miles south of Brady via U.S. Highway 377. The seat of Mason County—home to just 2,000—took its name from Fort Mason, built in the early 1850s as one in a chain of army posts established to protect against Indian attacks between the Red River and the Rio Grande.

Mason was unusual among Texas towns in that it endured an internal war in the 1870s when cattle rustlings and prejudices between German and Anglo settlers stirred up angry emotions; the upshot is that more than ten men were killed in ambushes and lynchings before the Texas Rangers were summoned to reestablish peace in the community.

You can explore the fort and town history at **Fort Mason Officers Quarters** (Rainey and Post Hill Streets, 915–347–5758). Among the illustrious soldiers who were once stationed at the fort were George Armstrong Custer, Albert Sidney Johnston, and Robert E. Lee. Today's fort is a reconstruction on the original foundation, and a miniature of the fort is among the exhibits. The museum is open daily, but it's best to call ahead for hours.

If you read the book or saw the film *Old Yeller,* you probably never stopped crying long enough to wonder where its author, Fred Gipson, was from; Mason, it turns out, was his hometown. Gipson and other local notables are detailed in the local library, found at Post Hill and Schmidt Streets.

Rather unexpectedly you'll come upon the **Reynolds-Seaquist Home** (400 Broad Street, Mason 76856, 915–347–5413), a sensational three-story, Queen Anne Victorian mansion. Remarkable are its twenty-two rooms, fifteen fireplaces, beautiful wooden staircase constructed without nails, galleries wrapping around two stories on the exterior, and third-floor ballroom. The house was started in 1891, then renovated in 1919 by a Swede who made his fortune in boots. Tours are scheduled by appointment, and at least four people are required for a tour; admission is $5.00 per person.

There's no shortage of down-home, country stays in the Mason area: There's **Bridges House Bed & Breakfast** (305 Broad Street, Mason 76856, 915–347–6440 or 800–776–3519), an 1884 home in a historic area with porches and lovely antiques; **Hasse House** (east from town square 6 miles on Texas Highway 29, 915–347–6463), a spacious place on a 300-acre working ranch; and **Martin Guest Ranch** (south 9 miles on Farm Road 1723, 915–347–6852), a 5,000-acre ranch on the Llano River with modern cabins, big lodge, game room, hiking, fishing, swimming, and inner tubing.

Finally, rock hounds will be thrilled at the area's fantastic variety of minerals and rocks located in the geologic outcroppings. Specifically, blue topaz, the state gem—a rarity in North America—is found here. The public can hunt topaz at the **Seaquist Ranch** (915–347–5413) and the **Hofmann Ranch** (915–347–6415); both are situated just northwest of Mason, charge fees, and permit camping.

Continuing along the Hill Country trail, turn southwest on U.S. Highway 377 and go 39 miles through big deer-hunting country to **Junction,** the seat of Kimble County, home to about 2,600 people and more flowing streams than any other Texas county.

Most people citing Junction as a destination do so for its wildlife watching and other outdoorsy pursuits. **South Llano River State Park** (4 miles south of town on U.S. 377, 915–446–3994) is just the right place for these, as animals often seen here include white-tailed deer, wood ducks, fox squirrels, rock squirrels, javelina, and the Rio Grande turkey. The turkey roost in bottomlands, and this site is closed to visitors from October through March. At the park enjoy camping, hiking, picnicking, canoeing, and inner tubing between wildlife sightings. The spring-fed river is simple pleasure itself. Admission is $2.00 per person.

Historians are wise to make two detours from Junction before exploring the remainder of the Hill Country. Thirty miles due north of Junction is the town of *Menard,* seat of Menard County, with a population of about 1,600. Established during the pioneer and cattle-driving days near the ruins of the eighteenth-century Spanish mission *Santa Cruz de San Saba,* Menard tells its story in a little county museum in the old train depot at 100 Frisco Avenue (915–396–2365).

Rather intriguing is the sight of ruins on the city golf course. There, by the eighth hole, are the ancient walls of the Spanish presidio built to protect the mission. The mission was attacked in 1758 by Comanche and other Native Americans; the presidio soldiers weren't numerous enough, and the presidio was abandoned in 1769. Learn details about the town and its annual outdoor musical drama in June by calling the local chamber of commerce at (915) 396–2365.

About 20 miles west of Menard, in the southwestern corner of Menard County, *Fort McKavett State Historic Site* (Ranch Road 864, 915–396–2358) presents yet another portrait of rugged Texas history. Established as Camp San Saba in 1852, the fort was one of the most important in west Texas pioneer history; fifteen restored buildings include an officers' quarters, barracks, hospital, and a cluster of interpretive exhibits pertaining to military history and historic archaeology. From Memorial Day through Labor Day, the park is open daily 9:00 A.M. until 6:00 P.M.; the balance of the year, it's open 8:00 A.M. until 5:00 P.M., Wednesday through Sunday.

On the road again, prepare yourself for spectacular scenery. From Junction, take U.S. Highway 83 south, making a 57-mile journey to *Leakey* (LAY-kee), the Real County seat and a town of 400 tucked into an especially picturesque corner of the Edwards Plateau. About 12 miles shy of town, you'll be happy if you packed a picnic lunch, because there's a particularly good roadside park with superb scenery right there.

Although you won't see Comanches and Apaches living in the area around Leakey as did the Spanish explorers, you will find flocks of registered Angora goats, from which area ranchers harvest mohair. This, too, is a popular hunting ground for white-tailed deer, mourning dove, quail, wild turkey, and javelina.

Consider taking a day or two to revel in the surroundings, putting your feet up at places such as *Rio Frio Bed and Breakfast* (Farm Road 1120 and Farm Road 2748, 830–966–2320), with cabins and homes on the river; and *River Haven Cabins* (Farm Road 1120, 830–232–5400), with log cabins and fireplaces.

An appealing park in the area is *Garner State Park* on the Frio River, just inside Uvalde County, a 9-mile drive south of Leakey via U.S. Highway 83. Here the fun in warm weather is all about settling into a big inner tube and floating down the clear, cold Frio, surrounded by limestone shelves and shady cypress lining the way. Stone-and-timber cabins at the park offer a comfortable night's rest; call (830) 232–6132 for reservations. Other diversions include pedal boats, miniature golf, camping, hiking, fishing, and grocery facilities. (Note: Spring break crowds tend to be wild.) The park is open daily and a small admission is charged.

If the park is full, check out *Neal's Vacation Lodges,* right on the Frio River near the park, (830) 232–6118; rustic cabins are available, and Neal's cafe serves country breakfast, lunch, and dinner.

From Garner State Park, your next destination is east on Farm Road 1050—one you'll always remember for climbing views of bluffs and valleys and blooming cacti—15 miles to *Utopia,* an appropriately named town if ever one existed. The farming-ranching hamlet—population just 360—in Uvalde County was established on Sabinal Creek in 1852 and is a second home to hunters and campers; spring wildflowers and fall foliage bring plenty of fans, too.

Sparkling spring water drinkers have likely heard of Utopia by now—the crystal liquid is bottled here and shipped around the world. Notice how at the post office, the general store, and the cafe, all those friendly people seem unusually happy? It must be the water.

Unbeatable country cooking is the pride at *Lost Maples Cafe* (in the middle of town on Ranch Market 187, 830–966–2221). Chat with the local game warden, park rangers, neighboring farmers, and outgoing staffers over Frisbee-size pancakes or fresh-fresh chicken-fried steak, enormous baked potatoes, and barbecue.

Another great place to stay is at the *Texas Stagecoach Inn,* north and slightly east of Concan on Ranch Road 187 (830–966–6272). Surrounded by three acres of sensational scenery, this 1885 mansion has been remade into an inn with two suites and two guest rooms, all with private baths. The owners have decorated the place with original landscapes and custom-made furniture, and they've provided guests with Texana literature. The countryside here is perfect for hiking and mountain biking, and there's good horseback riding nearby. Breakfasts are hearty, homemade affairs.

People who want the restoration found in long, breathtaking drives come to the Leakey-Utopia area to see where the Frio, Nueces, and

Sabinal Rivers etched vividly shaded canyons, from which hills and mesas rise between 1,500 and 2,400 feet. The specific drives from Leakey that attract photographers, painters, and other artists of the soul are Farm Road 337 west to Camp Wood, past wooded rises and lonely, green valleys colored purple in spring with mountain laurel; and Farm Road 337 east into Bandera County to *Vanderpool,* then north on Ranch Market 187.

Lost Maples State Natural Area is on every Texas fall foliage fan's list as a must-see, but be assured the park is roaring with beauty in all seasons. These bigtooth maples are said to be lost because they're far from any other stands of their kind, which are scattered over the western United States and northern Mexico. The brilliant orange, red, and gold peak is usually in early November, and crowds tend to be staggering.

There are more than 90 plant families in the park, represented by more than 350 species. Bird population is healthy, as well, with the golden-cheeked warbler among uncommon finds. Camping and hiking are the park's other big draws, and reservations are a good idea; call (830) 966–3413. The park is open daily, and admission is charged.

The town of Vanderpool, population twenty, is 4 miles south of the park on Ranch Market 187. You'll find accommodations here, including *Fox-fire Cabins* (1 mile south of the park facing the Sabinal River, 830–966–2200), offering log cabins.

Exotics, Dudes, and Germans

From Vanderpool journey north on Farm Road 187 for 19 miles to Texas Highway 39, then eastward on Texas 39 for 26 miles, through the town of *Ingram* to the intersection of Texas Highway 27; take this highway just another 7 miles east into *Kerrville,* the seat of Kerr County, largest city in the Hill Country, and home to more than 17,000 people.

Easily the spiritual center of the Hill Country, Kerrville straddles the peaceful *Guadalupe River* and captures all that Texans treasure about this agreeable region—clean air, clear water, limestone bluffs, and pure repose. Kerrville owes its success to developer Charles Schreiner, who became a Texas Ranger at age sixteen and later served as a captain in the Civil War, and whose grandson brought the Texas longhorn breed back from the brink of extinction.

The Texas Longhorn

An enduring foundation of the area, Schreiner's *Y.O. Ranch,* 26 miles west on I–10 and Texas Highway 41, is a top working ranch and a top attraction in the state. Forty thousand acres remain of Schreiner's 550,000 acquired in 1880, and a Longhorn Trail Drive is still held annually one weekend in early May. There are herds and herds of longhorn, sheep, and goats, plus free-ranging animals from around the globe; this is considered North America's largest collection of exotic wildlife.

In all, there are some 10,000 of 55 species, including wildebeest, oryx, addax, Japanese sika, aoudad, black buck antelope, ostrich, giraffe, zebra, and Watusi cattle, to name a few. The owner-family's conservation efforts are visible in the ranch's programs for children. Most day-trippers come for a tour and chuckwagon lunch, while springtime brings photo safaris and an annual cattle drive. Summer afternoons are whiled away in a pretty swimming pool, and horseback rides can be arranged. Century-old log cabins and a former ranch home accommodate thirty-five overnight guests. For details and reservations call the ranch at (830) 640–3222.

You may spend a day seeing the Y.O.'s animals, but you won't want to miss a weekend in town, where culture and cowboys prevail. Kerrville's a bastion of artistic diversity, with folk music and folk art festivals in May. For details contact the chamber of commerce at (830) 896–1155.

Kerrville is also home to possibly the nation's only museum dedicated to the work of a single group of living artists. The *Cowboy Artists of America Museum* features the paintings and sculptures of about thirty members, some of whom are considered the country's foremost artists of Western American Realism. The building itself is wonderfully artful, incorporating light Mexican brick in *bóveda* domes that need no supporting forms or wiring. The museum charges admission and is just south of downtown on Texas 173; call (830) 896–2553 for more information. The museum is open Monday through Saturday 9:00 A.M. until 5:00 P.M. and Sunday 1:00 until 5:00 P.M. It's closed Monday, September through May.

Don't wander off before poking through some of the shops in Kerrville. *The Water Street Antique Company and Tea Room* and *Artesian Accents* are good for finding an assortment of old furniture and the odd collectible.

For a lovely sunset drive, head west from Kerrville on *Ranch Road 1340,* which winds its way through the scenic communities of Ingram and Hunt. The ribbon of road twists and turns, repeatedly crossing the Guadalupe River, passing a scattering of summer cottages, boys' and girls' summer camps, and deer-hunting country. In the middle of one field, you'll see a Stonehenge replica, of all things.

There are three good places to find rest in Kerrville, starting with the *Inn of the Hills River Resort* (1001 Junction Highway, Kerrville 78028, 830–895–5000), a spreading complex with motel rooms, suites, and condo-apartments. Four pools, pretty landscaping, games and activities for kids in summer, three restaurants, an exercise facility with sauna and whirlpool, bowling lanes, putting green, bike and boat rentals, fishing in a stocked lake, and lighted tennis courts make this a full-service resort.

The *Y.O. Ranch Holiday Inn* (2033 Sidney Baker Boulevard, Kerrville 78028, 830–257–4440) is a charming hotel accented with western design. The huge lobby is lighted with chandeliers crafted from branding irons and is dominated by a bronze of a mounted cowboy working to bring a longhorn back to the herd. Room furnishings continue the theme.

Lazy Hills Guest Ranch (west on Texas Highway 27, just past Ingram, 830–367–5600) offers horseback riding, tennis, swimming, fishing, hot tubbing, and family-style dining in a beautiful hilly setting.

A newer and excellent lodging in Kerrville is *River Run B&B Inn* (120 Francisco Lemos Street, Kerrville 78028, 830–896–8353), a four-room, two-suite lodging crafted of native limestone and a high-pitched tin roof characteristic of the German-influenced corners of the Hill Country. All rooms have queen-size beds and private baths with whirlpool tubs and showers, and there are generous common areas and plenty of books for guests to read. A bounteous breakfast is included with stay.

Next stop after Kerrville is found north on Texas 16, 24 miles away in *Fredericksburg,* seat of Gillespie County. Texas's cache of German heritage is a miniature Bavarian treat with a proliferation of bed-and-breakfast lodgings, the backbone of Old World touring. In Fredericksburg, guests have the state's largest selection of places to spend rest periods off the road in quaint historic homes and inns, much more appealing to some than sleeping in cookie-cutter hotels. Here you'll make new friends along the way, sharing a cup of tea, a glass of wine, or breakfast with hosts and fellow guests.

Fredericksburg's bed-and-breakfast industry continues to boom. Where there were some one hundred B&Bs a few years ago, there are now nearly 300 B&B inns, cottages, guest houses, ranches, and farms—remarkable for a town of fewer than 10,000 people. Descriptions vary widely from tiny, cute places to larger, rambling Victorian homes in town, to remote cabins and historic stone buildings in the countryside. Some are luxuriously decorated and command higher prices. All include breakfast, of course, which can mean breads, fruits, and juices left for guests to have when they choose, to formal feasts served at a

June's Texas Anecdotes

*H*ILL COUNTRY: One gorgeous spring weekend I went with my childhood friend Cary to shop and stay in a little bed-and-breakfast in Fredericksburg. We ate fabulous food, found plenty of things in the stores that we couldn't live without, and caught up on the reading we never had time for at home. My favorite part of the trip, however, was our visit to Enchanted Rock early on Saturday morning. The last time I had tried to go to Enchanted Rock, it was 2:00 P.M. and the park was packed. (Because of erosion problems, the state park has since put a limit on the number of visitors that can be accommodated each day.) Cary and I arrived just as the sun was coming up, and we made quick work of the hike 600 feet up to the top of this glorious granite mound. There we stood for a long time, not saying a word, just reveling in the first light of day as it fell across the most phenomenal panorama in all the Hill Country.

large dining room table. There are three reservation services to consult: Bed & Breakfast of Fredericksburg (240 West Main Street, Fredericksburg 78624, 830– 997–4712); Be My Guest (402 West Main Street, Fredericksburg 78624, 830–997–7227); and Gastehaus Schmidt (501 West Main Street, Fredericksburg 78624, 830–997–5612).

One of the superb listings through Gastehaus Schmidt is *Schmidt Barn* (no relation), one of the town's original B&B offerings. The 1860s rock barn has been carefully restored to offer a queen-size bed and a sleeper sofa, accommodating four people in all; antique furnishings and quilts; a sunken tub for bubble-bath relaxation; a microwave, coffee maker, CD and tape player; a phone; and oak-covered grounds.

Still another rustic but choice lodging available through Gastehaus Schmidt is the *Schildknecht-Weidenfeller House,* a charming, 1870s rock structure with thick stone walls, pine flooring, deep-set windows, full bath, kitchen and dining room, and utter privacy. Guests are welcomed with a plate of German meats and cheeses upon arrival, and a plentiful continental breakfast is provided for you to enjoy on your own.

Fredericksburg guests looking for lodging that incorporates exceptional food should check out *Patsy's Guest Cottage, Elizabeth's on Austin Street,* or *The Cook's Cottage,* three B&Bs owned by San Antonio–based culinary arts teacher, Patsy Swendson. Her guest houses are terribly romantic, and she's always ready to make special arrangements—i.e., champagne, flowers, candy, candlelight dinners—with advance notice. Reach Patsy at (210) 493–5101 or e-mail her at patsy@aisi.net.

While in Fredericksburg take time to explore history a bit. The town was the 1885 birthplace of Adm. Chester W. Nimitz, commander-in-chief of

The George Bush Gallery

*J*une 11, 1999, marked the opening of the George Bush Gallery at the Museum of the Pacific War in the Admiral Nimitz Museum in Fredericksburg. This $3 million addition offers high-tech, highly interactive exhibits, such as those on a Japanese midget sub preparing for its attack on Pearl Harbor and a B–25 bomber preparing to take off from an aircraft carrier. The project is named for former president Bush, whose plane was shot from the sky over Chi Chi Jima in 1944 and who was awarded a Distinguished Flying Cross for completing his bombing mission before parachuting into the sea. Call (830) 997–4379 for more information.

the Pacific fleet during World War II. A tribute to him is the *Admiral Nimitz State Historical Park,* a collection of attractions at 340 East Main Street, including the restored Nimitz Steamboat Hotel, a renowned frontier inn that hosted U. S. Grant, Robert E. Lee, and Jesse James and now is home to the Museum of the Pacific War. Behind the building is the Garden of Peace, a gift from Japan, and across the street a history walk winds through an array of rare aircraft, tanks, and guns. The park is open daily, 8:00 A.M. until 5:00 P.M., and a small admission is charged; (830) 997–4379.

Shoppers can spend considerable time (and money) at the one-hundred–plus boutiques and stores along *Fredericksburg's Main Street,* offering everything from books, candles, quilts, primitive antiques, bath goods, and herbal remedies to peach jam, wine, pewter mugs, dulcimers, jewelry, clothing, and fine art and folk art. It's not unusual to bump into Hollywood types such as Tommy Lee Jones or Madeleine Stowe—who live on ranches nearby—at *The Homestead,* 223 Main Street, where an exceptional collection of European, American, and Texas antiques and handmade furniture are sold.

At the *Fredericksburg Brewing Company* (245 East Main Street, Fredericksburg 78624, 830–997–1646), visitors tour the area's largest brew facility, housed in an 1890s rock building. There's a restaurant and beer garden, too.

If you happen upon Fredericksburg just before the Christmas holidays, see if you're in time for *Kristkindl Market,* an Old World–style affair staged at Market Square in the center of town. The Fredericksburg Shopkeepers Guild creates a Christmas village featuring music, German foods, hand-crafted toys and gifts, art, and sweets. Admission is $4.00 for adults, $1.00 for children. For details call the guild at (830) 997–8515.

Among the favorite Hill Country eateries is the *Hill Top Cafe,* 11 miles northwest of Fredericksburg via U.S. 87. Specialties include crawfish étouffée, frog legs, Greek salads, chicken-fried steak, and fresh fish with deluxe herb-and-spice treatments, as well as spectacular desserts; reservations are advised, (830) 997–8922. Open from 6:00 P.M., Wednesday through Saturday.

Crowds are as likely found at the lovely *Oak House* restaurant, which occupies a beautifully restored 1903 native-rock home at 755 South Washington Street, Fredericksburg 78624 (830–997–6223). A perfect light lunch or dinner spot where you'll linger for at least a couple of hours over an excellent bottle of wine, the Oak House specializes in such pleasures as pan-seared shrimp and scallops, pecan-crusted trout, grilled filet mignon topped with fried onions and Maytag blue cheese sauce, and smoked prime rib.

For burgers, nachos, fresh vegetable plates, and traditional German fare, try the *Plateau Cafe* (312 West Main Street; Fredericksburg 78624, 830–997–1853). In pretty weather, its beer garden is hard to beat.

Extensive, helpful information is available from the Fredericksburg Convention & Visitors office, found at 106 North Adams Street, (830) 997–6523. Or visit the Internet site at www.fredericksburg-texas.com.

Side trips from Fredericksburg are abundant, and the first to consider is the jaunt to *Enchanted Rock State Park,* 18 miles north of town on Ranch Road 965. The park surrounds an otherworldly, huge, monolithic dome of pink granite, rising 600 feet into the sky—a challenge perfect for ambitious hikers. Climb it if you have stamina, good athletic shoes, and the foresight to have arrived early enough to find a parking space inside the park, as the annual visitor count is now 350,000. The surprising vegetation up top is as impressive as the views, particularly in the first light of day. On summer nights the huge rock creaks and moans as it cools down, an occurrence the Comanches understandably found to be of a powerfully spiritual nature. The park is open daily and charges a small admission; get details by calling (915) 247–3903.

If you tackle Enchanted Rock in the morning, leave the afternoon free to take what's possibly the most unusual scenic drive in Texas, the *Willow City Loop.* To begin this adventure, head north from town on Texas Highway 16 about 12 miles, then turn east on Farm Road 1323, and you'll go just 3 miles before picking up one of Texas's more fiercely beautiful roads at the town of Willow City. Watch for a little wooden sign indicating the Willow City Loop and get ready for a sensory trip: Drive a ridge the first few of the 13 miles, then prepare to swoop down into Coal Creek Valley, also called the Devil's Kitchen, the Dungeon, and even Hell's Half-Acre. Centuries ago, heavenly bodies crashed into the ground here, leaving a massive depression filled with sleek meteoric rocks. The valley vistas of bluebonnets in spring go on forever, giving rise to Cedar Mountain, whose blooming yuccas crown the picture. Here, 8 miles into the drive, find Texas's sole serpentine quarry, where the stone with a luminous polish is mined for terrazzo floors. Oh, and watch for wandering cattle on the road.

Another diversion out of Fredericksburg is found at *Bell Mountain Vineyards* (Texas 16 north about 14 miles, 830–685–3297), one of several Hill Country vineyards. This winery scales the side of Bell Mountain

Texas Trivia

Texas Hill Country native Lyndon B. Johnson was the first American president to host a barbecue on the White House lawn. He usually served Texas-style barbecued ribs at official parties and receptions.

and offers its products—including chardonnays, Rieslings, and pinot noirs—for tasting on tour day, Saturday, Easter to Christmas.

Bell Mountain is one of several wineries in the region, many of which joined forces to create the *Texas Hill Country Wine Trail.* The group hosts regular celebrations, such as fall touring events and holiday celebrations. To find out what's in store at Fredericksburg-area wineries such as Becker Vineyards, Grape Creek Vineyard, Sister Creek Vineyards, and Fredericksburg Winery, as well as others in the Hill Country, log onto www.texaswinetrail.com.

For an explosion of color at any time of year, head to *Wildseed Farms,* 7 miles east of Fredericksburg on U.S. Highway 290; (830) 990–1393. Recently relocated from the Houston area, Wildseed Farms harvests up to 400,000 pounds of wildflower seeds annually. There are some 600 acres blooming in the Fredericksburg area, and the farm center allows visitors to see planting, harvesting, and flowers in various stages. The market complex, crafted from handcut Texas cedar and native stone, sells fresh-cut flowers, dried flowers, herbs, and hundreds of gifts pertaining to herbs and flowers. Plans call for peach orchards, a winery, restaurant, and bed-and-breakfast.

The most famous detour of all is *Luckenbach,* population twenty-five, reached by driving 6 miles east of town on U.S. 290, then turning south (right) on Ranch Road 1376; continue on this little road about 5 miles till you see signs. If you cross the creek, you've gone too far—maybe it's time to stop and ask directions, as signs to Luckenbach just don't last long, thanks to souvenir hunters.

Bizarre Texas Stuff

*L*UCKENBACH: When Jerry Jeff Walker sang, "Let's go to Luckenbach, Texas, with Willie an' Waylon an' the boys," he knew instinctively how to get there. He had to, because there's no sign indicating where it is. The tiny burgh of twenty-five people became so famous for its spontaneous concerts and parties in the 1970s that souvenir hunters kept swiping the signs. The highway department dutifully replaced them for years, just to have them stolen again and again. It gave up, deciding visitors who really wanted to find the place would do so. And they do.

"In Luckenbach, Texas, ain't nobody feelin' no pain," is how the Willie Nelson–Waylon Jennings song goes, and, honestly, everybody feels fine when they're in Luckenbach because it's mostly a state of mind. It isn't even a town, but a little pocket of peace where the population is really just the number of people sitting around drinking longnecks on the porch of the eternally unpainted general store, playing dominoes, or pitching horseshoes. Some Saturday nights you'll find the dance hall overflowing with folks two-steppin' to the likes of Gary P. Nunn, who stops in occasionally to entertain the idea of going "home with the armadillo" in his song "London Homesick Blues."

An 1850 German settlement, Luckenbach was unremarkable for more than a century, with the exception of Jacob Brodbeck, who—twenty-five years before the Wright Brothers—invented an airplane powered with coiled springs. He abandoned the project after a discouraging crash in 1865.

Then in the 1970s humorist-writer and legendary Texas character Hondo Crouch invited like souls to share in Luckenbach's bucolic remoteness, laced with bluebonnets and pioneer flavor. This made it a place where "everybody's somebody," as prescribed by Waylon Jennings and Jerry Jeff Walker, whose song propelled the tiny spot in the road into fame.

The Hell-Hath-No-Fury-Like-A-Woman-Scorned Chili Society found a friend in Hondo, and Luckenbach's lazy pace would forever be radically altered one weekend each year. The group—formed when a woman was turned down as an entrant in a Texas chili cook-off—hosts its *Ladies' State Championship Chili Cook-Off* in Luckenbach annually on the first weekend in October.

You can find great T-shirts, postcards (stamped with a Luckenbach postmark), jewelry, snacks, beer, and plenty of conversation in the general store, and a barbecue stand next to the dance hall is generally open on weekends. For information call the general store at (830) 997–3224.

From Fredericksburg the tour continues south on U.S. Highway 87 to *Comfort,* a 23-mile drive. Barely inside the Kendall County line, the borough of almost 1,800 was settled in 1854 by free-thinking German intellectuals, some of whom later joined Union forces in the Civil War; you'll see the Treue Der Union Monument, a tribute to them, on High Street between Third and Fourth Streets.

Comfort is also known for being batty: The *Hygieostatic Bat Roost,* 1 1/2 miles east on Farm Road 473, was a 1918 experiment; seventy-five years later, the bats still use it. Sunset is the time to watch for them here and at the Old Railroad Tunnel, 14 miles north via Farm Road 473 and Old Highway 9, where several thousand bats live in a tunnel abandoned in 1942.

Take a stroll down **High Street,** particularly the 800 block, to have a close-up look at one of the state's more complete nineteenth-century business districts still intact. The Chamber of Commerce office, at Seventh and High Streets, (830) 995–3131, has free, helpful guides. Of particular interest to shoppers is **Comfort Common** (717 High Street, Comfort 78013, 830–995–3030), a bevy of antiques and gift boutiques in the old Ingenhuett-Faust Hotel.

Within the lovely, 1880 building remarkable for wide verandas that open onto a shady, rear courtyard are ten gorgeous suites and rooms, all with private baths and exquisite antique furnishings. Rates average $100. Through Comfort Common, you can also stay at **Storyville,** a Victorian cottage 1 block from the hotel; and the two-story **Gladys Krauter Log Cabin.** Note that the Common doubles as a bed-and-breakfast inn.

Cozy sleepovers can be had, too, at **Meyer Bed & Breakfast** (952 High Street, Comfort 78013, 830–995–2304 or 800–364–2138), a historic little hostelry with a swimming pool and fishing behind the complex in Cypress Creek. The main building was a stage stop in Comfort's earliest days.

Do arrive in Comfort with an appetite, as the home cooking at **Cypress Creek Inn** (Texas Highway 27 at the Cypress Creek Bridge, 830–995–3977) aims to fill you up with chicken-fried steak, sausage, liver and onions, fried chicken, or meat loaf. And please leave room for dessert—the pies are super.

Camp Verde, west of Comfort 17 miles via Texas 27 and then Ranch Road 480, is barely a wide spot in the road. The community has only forty residents but a Texas-size heritage. At its heart is Camp Verde General Store, in continuous operation since 1857 (intersection of Texas 173 and Ranch Road 480, 830–634–7722). Inside you'll find great souvenirs such as camel bells, T-shirts, gift baskets, Hill Country jams and jellies, wood carvings, books, and home decor items. Don't forget to ask about (and buy for yourself) the store's lucky pigs—the stories you'll hear are memorable. For a snack pick up some homemade tamales, fried pies, jelly beans, or hard candies.

If you're ready to be a dude, head south on Texas 173, about 15 miles to **Bandera,** the Bandera County seat and home to a population of nearly 900, and growing fast. It claims the title "Cowboy Capital of the

Bizarre Texas Stuff

*C*AMP VERDE: It is known as the great failed camel experiment. In 1856 the U.S. Cavalry placed an outpost at Camp Verde, where Texas Rangers had already fought off Comanches in what was known as the Bandera Pass. Secretary of War Jefferson Davis chose the site for an Army experiment, using camels as pack animals. The idea was that the camel corps would be useful in communication and transportation through the arduous west to Fort Yuma, California. While there was some success, Confederate troops took over the fort in 1861, and many of the camels were allowed to wander off or simply die. At least one of the descendants of the camel corps lives at a ranch near Camp Verde, but visitors can see a camel theme in the Camp Verde General Store in the form of camel wind chimes and a camel topiary at the rear of the store.

World" not just for its cattle-drive and ranching heritage but also for the record number of National Rodeo Champions who lived there or still do. And, what travelers most like to find, Bandera is home to seven terrific dude ranches.

Long before dudes began showing up, about forty Texas Rangers were ambushed by several hundred Comanches in Bandera in 1841. Peace eventually prevailed, and settlers arrived in 1852, finding the cypress-and-live-oak–laden banks of the Medina River a good place to put down roots. The primitive countryside about 45 miles west of San Antonio still holds that appeal, and vacationing cowboys and cowgirls have all the western-style fun they want.

The dude ranches each offer family lodging in bunkhouses or cabins, horseback and hay rides, trick-roping and snake-handling (!) demonstrations, rodeos, country-western dancing, chuck-wagon meals on the trail, golfing, swimming, fishing, and inner tubing on the river.

Dixie Dude Ranch (9 miles south of town on Ranch Road 1077, 830–796–7771 or 800–375–9255) has been in the family for more than fifty years, and now the fourth generation is running the 800-acre spread. The place is nothing if not homey, and guests find themselves making friends from all over the globe during fried-chicken suppers, poolside cookouts, and Saturday-night barbecues. The ranch hands—especially good at matching riders with mounts—lead trail rides through a wild terrain, pointing out historic sites along the way.

Mayan Dude Ranch (1½ miles northwest of town via Main and Pecan Streets, 830–796–3312) is more like summer camp; it's an all-year affair for one hundred or more guests of all ages. Days begin with cowboy-made breakfast on a trail beside the Medina River and usually continue in the saddle or in the Olympic-size pool. Nights are never dull—each one brings a different theme and activity, such as a Mexican fiesta, a ghost-town trip and steak fry, or a cocktails-barbecue-and-ice-cream party. The *Flying L Ranch* (1^1/$_2$ miles south on Texas 173, 830–796–3001 or 800–292–5134) has cabins and condos, golf and tennis facilities, and horseback riding.

If you're on your own for meals, the *OST*—named for the Old Spanish Trail on which Bandera lies—(305 Main Street, 830–796–3836) will do you right with its chicken-fried steak, biscuits and gravy, Mexican food, and grilled steaks.

Even people just passing through Bandera should take just thirty minutes or so to have a peek at one of the funkier collections ever assembled: The *Frontier Times Museum* (506 Thirteenth Street, Bandera 78003, 830–796–3864) exhibits more than 40,000 items, including bottles from Judge Roy Bean's saloon; 500 bells from around the world; antique firearms and saddles; and spear- and arrowheads.

Don't miss an evening at Bandera's *Cabaret Cafe,* where the Lone Star State's best music makers often fill the bill. The stage at this 1936 dance hall has hosted Jimmie Dale Gilmore, Dana Cooper, Charlie Robison, Terri Hendrix, Pat Green, and many more. Call (830) 796–8166 for ticket prices and schedule.

Immediately southwest of Bandera is *Hill Country State Natural Area,* reached by driving south of Texas 173 to Ranch Road 1077, which you'll follow to the west for 10 miles (830–796–4413). This 5,370-acre spread—once the Bar-O Ranch—is cloaked with oak and juniper and offers 32 miles of trails shared by hikers, mountain bikers, and equestrians. The twenty-three marked trails are often used by trail-riding guests at the nearby dude ranches, as these pathways take in sensational springs, waterfalls, creeks, and hilly vistas. The park is absolutely primitive, so backcountry camping is the only option. The park is closed on Tuesday and Wednesday; entry is $3.00 per person over twelve years of age.

One of the more appealing places to open in the Bandera area in recent years is the *Hill Country Equestrian Lodge,* about 10 miles outside of town just off Ranch Road 1077 (830–796–7950). Unlike the other guest ranches around, this one gives you a chance to take private riding lessons or even bring your own horse. Guests who don't want to ride can amuse themselves by hiking, birding, fossil hunting, mountain biking (bring your own wheels), or spending the day fishing, inner-tubing, or kayaking on the nearby Medina River.

The lodge offers new cabins crafted from native limestone and rough cedar, with fireplaces, sleeping spaces for four or six guests, one or two bathrooms, full kitchens, and great decks from which to watch the sun rise or set. Breakfast goodies are supplied for you to fix your own.

If you drive about 15 miles northwest from Bandera on Texas Highway 16 to the town of Medina, you'll be in the Apple Capital of Texas. *The Texas International Apple Festival* is held here on the last weekend in July. Any time of the year, however, is fine for visiting the Love Creek Orchard Cider Mill and Country Store, where you'll find delicious bakery goods, ice cream, coffee with apple strudel flavoring, as well as apple jelly, cider, and saplings.

After living the ranch life, it may be time to search for more of that German Hill Country; you can do that by driving east on Texas Highway 46, 23 miles from Bandera to Boerne (BURN-ee), seat of Kendall County, with a population of about 5,000. The cerebral Germans who settled the town in 1851 named it for Ludwig Boerne, one of their fellow countrymen who was a political satirist, journalist, and refugee. You may run into day-trippers from San Antonio, just 30 miles southeast, while out browsing through the creaky old antiques shops—packed with great little finds—or at one of the pleasant restaurants in town.

You can't go hungry in Boerne, that's certain. A favorite is *Po Po Family Restaurant* (at I–10, 7 miles west of Boerne, at the Welfare exit, 830–537–4194), in an old stone house and former dance hall decorated with an array of at least 1,000 china plates on the wall, serving solid American and southern fare. It's open daily for lunch and dinner.

Also, consider *Cafe Ye Kendall Inn* (128 West Blanco Street, Boerne 78006, 830–249–7992 or 800–364–2138), where steaks, seafood, and salads are good choices. It's in an 1859 two-story inn, facing the town square.

A special place to visit in Boerne is the *Kuhlmann–King Historical House* (402 East Blanco Street, Boerne 78006, 830–249–8000). Built in the late 1880s by German physicist William Kuhlmann, the two-story house offers a look into life in that period. The separate Archives Building houses historical documents of the area. Call for tour times. A $2.00 donation is welcomed.

Boerne's *Guadalupe River Ranch* (605 Farm Road 474, Boerne 78006, 800–460–2005 or 830–537–4837) has become one of the Hill Country's premier lodgings in recent years. The main lodge (owned at one time by actress Olivia de Havilland) was built in 1929 and has been carefully restored. There are forty-three rooms and three suites in the attractive stone cottages on the 360-acre ranch. Breakfast and dinner are included. Guests are welcome to play pool, Ping-Pong, and tennis; go horseback riding, hiking, and canoeing; or just relax in the sauna and hot tub.

Spelunkers will be happy to know that two caves open to the public are nearby. The larger is **Cascade Caverns** (3 miles south on I–10 to Cascade Caverns Road, 830–755–8080), fascinating for its 90-foot interior waterfall, crashing from an underground stream. Tours last forty-five minutes; a nice park with campsites, picnic areas, dance pavilion, swimming pool, snack bar, and bunkhouses is outside the cave. Admission is $8.50 for adults, $5.50 for children; open Wednesday through Monday 9:00 A.M. until 5:00 P.M.

The smaller, far less commercial cave is simply known as **Cave Without a Name** (Farm Road 474 east 6 miles to Kruetzberg Road, 5 miles along this road to the cave, 830–537–4212), so called because the 1939 contest held to give it a title was won by a local boy who declared the cave "too pretty to name." It isn't easy to find, as the directional signs are greatly faded, but it's worth the effort. The cave, 98 percent still active, is enormous—it takes from about an hour to ninety minutes to tour—and is filled with stalagmites and stalactites, "soda straws," "strips of bacon," "gnomes," and all sorts of mushrooming formations. Call ahead for tour schedules, which change without much notice; admission is $7.00 for adults, $4.00 for children.

Guadalupe River State Park (Texas 46 and Park Road 31, 16 miles east of Boerne, 830–438–2656) occupies 1,900 acres where cypress, limestone bluffs, and natural rapids blend to make a place of beauty on the gracious Guadalupe River. Canoeing, fishing, hiking, camping, and nature study are all available. Open daily; admission is $3.00 per vehicle on weekdays, $5.00 weekends.

Just in case you haven't had enough of Texas's rich German heritage, more awaits in **New Braunfels,** a 43-mile drive east of Boerne on Texas 46. The seat of Comal County, New Braunfels has more than 27,000 citizens and a history that was almost very romantic.

The story goes that the town was settled in 1845 by a German prince and 200 immigrants; the prince named his establishment for the town in Germany where his castle stood. He was to build a new castle for his

Conserve History

*C*onservation Plaza is where you'll go in New Braunfels to see priceless historic structures, including the Lindheimer Home, the Rose Conservatory, the Church Hill School, the Jahn Cabinet Shop, the Buckhorn Barber Shop, and the Wagenfuehr Home. The local conservation society's work is also seen in the Baetge House, built 26 miles from town but dismantled and relocated in the downtown plaza to display its fine example of fachwerk construction, done in 1852 by a German engineer.

fiancée, Princess Sophie, but she refused to come to this rough, unknown land, so he returned home to marry her and never saw Texas again. This and the remaining history of New Braunfels are told at the *Sophienburg Museum*—named for her anyway—at 401 West Coll Street, New Braunfels 78130, (830) 629–1572.

The newest addition to New Braunfels is the *Hummel Museum* (199 Main Plaza, New Braunfels 78130, 800–572–2626 or 830–625–2385), featuring the art of a German nun, M. I. Hummel. Hummels, as they're known, are the famous figurines of children who have a certain Alps-and-Black-Forest appeal. These and the Hummel plates are collector's items, and they're costly. Sister Hummel was the creator of more than 500 drawings prior to and throughout World War II; the New Braunfels collection, which for the moment contains 300-plus, is the world's largest Hummel exhibit. Usually the display contains about eighty drawings, and some extremely valuable illustrations will be visiting exhibits from time to time.

One of the state's lovelier places to rest is the *Prince Solms Inn* (295 East San Antonio Street, New Braunfels 78130, 830–625–9169), a luxury bed-and-breakfast hotel filled with antiques and housing a fine restaurant, Wolfgang's Keller. The historic *Hotel Faust* (240 South Seguin Street, New Braunfels 78130, 830–625–7791) is restored and filled with antiques.

If you happen upon New Braunfels in the fall, plan to dance a polka and drink a stein or two to the oompah-pah in Wursthalle, as the town hosts well over 100,000 people each year at *Wurstfest,* an enormous German party held over the first two weekends in November. A generous schedule of events is always offered, as is food and drink. For details call (830) 625–9167.

If you miss the celebration, there's always good German food ready at *Krause's Cafe* (148 South Castell Street, New Braunfels 78130,

THE HILL COUNTRY

830–625–7581), a 1938 establishment with the basics, plus chili, chicken, steaks, and sinful pies.

For anyone looking for a little watery excitement, head north a couple of miles to the restored town of **Gruene** (north on I–35 to Farm Road 306, west about 1¹/₂ miles to Hunter Road, then follow the signs). There, on the Guadalupe River, several river outfitters (call 830–625–2385 for a list) offer trips lasting anywhere from three to five hours. If it's late spring or early summer, the river will probably run high and fast, so do as the instructors say and paddle like crazy through the little rapids. If it's late in summer and there hasn't been much rain, you're likely to have a slow trip. For a lonely, peaceful trip, tackle the river on a weekday, when high-spirited rafters and tubers won't be clogging the waters.

> **ONE MAINSTREAM ATTRACTION WORTH SEEING IN THE HILL COUNTRY**
>
> An oldie but goodie, Schlitterbahn is a splashy, sixty-five acre spread in New Braunfels, which celebrated its twentieth anniversary in 1999. Known for German-like castles, waterslides, hot tubs, uphill water coasters, inner-tube chutes, and six water playgrounds, the park's newest attraction is Hans's Hideout, a 5-story water funhouse with a pirate theme. Yo-ho-ho and a stein of beer. Open all summer, Schlitterbahn is located at 400 North Liberty Street, (830) 625–2351.

While in Gruene plan to spend time poking around **Gruene Historic District,** a quaint 1870s cotton-gin town containing what is now the oldest dance hall in Texas; restored buildings housing antiques shops, clothing boutiques, woodwork, leather goods, and pottery shops; a winery tasting room; and good restaurants, starting with the **Gristmill** (1287 Gruene Road, 830–625–0684), purveyors of excellent fried catfish, grilled chicken, steaks, burgers, and frosty margaritas. Weekend nights there's live music on the patio under the stars.

Next door to the Gristmill, **Gruene Mansion Inn** (1275 Gruene Road, Gruene 78130, 830–629–2641) is a gorgeous Victorian home overlooking the Guadalupe River and operating as a bed-and-breakfast inn.

From New Braunfels head north on I–35 just 16 miles to reach **San Marcos,** seat of Hays County and home to nearly 29,000 residents. The headwaters of the San Marcos River are here, where Indians are thought to have lived some 12,000 years ago, making this one of the oldest continuously inhabited places on the continent. Springs forming the river come from the Edwards Underground Reservoir, pushing up through the Balcones Escarpment limestone at a rate of at least a million gallons daily.

Aquarena Springs (512–245–7575) was long the primary reason folks visited San Marcos. In 1994, however, Southwest Texas State University in San Marcos—whose wonderful, red-topped spires are seen on a hill above town—purchased Aquarena Springs and closed the resort. Today it's a center for the study of endangered species and archaeological finds on this site. Visitors can still enjoy the beautiful springs, feeding ducks, walking the scenic grounds, touring an 1846 log home, and riding the famous glass-bottom boats. Admission to the grounds is free, but a small fee is charged for boat rides. Hours vary, so call ahead.

To see another set of Hill Country caverns, head to **Wonder World** (1000 Prospect Street, San Marcos, 78667, 512–392–3760). There's a 120-foot-tall observation tower and tour of the million-year-old limestone cave. Hours and fees vary according to season.

Canoeing is a hugely popular activity on the fabulous San Marcos River. Outfitters include **T.G. Canoe Livery,** (512) 353–3946. Floating the river on inner tubes is another great way to pass a warm day; call **Lions Club Tube Rental** in summer, (512) 396–LION.

While it's not the typical, off-the-beaten-path sort of place, it's hard to resist shopping at the **San Marcos Factory Shops** center (on I–35 at exit 200 in San Marcos, 512–396–7183). Possibly the state's top outlet mall (and that's saying something), this is *the* place to find great deals on clothes, shoes, housewares, gifts, lingerie, and more. Stores with deep discounts here include Casual Corner, Nine West, Sharif Collection, Guess?, Umbro, Napier, Duck Head, Brooks Brothers, American Tourister, and Vitamin World.

There's plenty more good shopping and dining in San Marcos, as well as three historic districts to tour. For information contact the San Marcos Convention and Visitors Bureau at (800) 782–7653, extension 177. Or stop at the tourist information center at 1811 I–35, open daily.

From San Marcos you're in for a day in shopping heaven and a charming bed-and-breakfast night at **Wimberley,** a 15-mile drive west of San Marcos via Ranch Road 12. It's a small town—population 3,000—but its stature is large, indeed, among the enlightened.

Here's a miniresort town that happens to rest between two of the prettiest little streams in Texas—the Cypress Creek and the Blanco River. It's a hub of shopping activity on weekends, when dozens of pottery studios, art galleries, antiques shops, and boutiques are open for business. The Blue Hole, on Cypress Creek, is one of the state's primo swimming holes, and most guests at resorts, ranches, and B&Bs spend a few lazy hours floating under the clouds.

If you're in the humor for shopping, Wimberley is a great place to exercise those credit cards. On the square, which isn't square shaped at all, you'll find **Rancho Deluxe** (512–847–9570), selling curios and imports from Mexico and Guatemala; the **Broken Arrow Rock Shop** (512–847–2282) for gems and minerals; and **Gypsy Piddler** (512–847–5647), a place selling all manner of old collectibles, from tins to books. Around the corner at Olde Towne Plaza, shop for cowboy boots, hats, jewelry, blankets, and spurs at **The Wild West Store** (512–847–1219).

Wimberley has become a prime place to unwind with expert help. **Touched by Angels** is a relaxation spa (River Road Landing, 512–847–7568) where you can enjoy a facial, aromatherapy massage, manicure, and pedicure. At **Serenity** (1 mile north of the square on Ranch Road 12, 512–847–8985), you can enjoy nature trails, a Japanese bathhouse, massage, mask and facial, body scrub, hot tub, and peppermint foot treatment.

Sweet tooths will have a heyday at **Wimberley Pie Co.** (on Ranch Road 12 just south of the square, 512–847–9462), where you'll be wowed by aromas of seventy or so pies baking at once. Pie varieties include buttermilk, black bottom cherry cheesecake, Key lime, and pecan. It's open from 8:00 A.M. until 5:00 P.M. Monday through Friday, 10:00 A.M. until 5:00 P.M. Saturday, and noon until 4:00 P.M. Sunday.

7A Ranch Resort (1 mile west on River Road from Ranch Road 12, 830–847–2517) has rustic cottages and lodges, river frontage, and a reconstructed pioneer village–amusement park.

For something more luxurious, but not in the least bit fussy, a great new choice is the **Wimberley Lodge at Lone Man Creek,** just a short drive from the square in Wimberley (512–847–0544). Surrounded by thirty-three wooded, hilly acres, the lodge was built for hunters in the 1960s by a wealthy Galveston family. The current owners found it in sorry shape but recognized great potential in the beautiful stonework and the stunning view from the porch.

What has resulted are three huge suites, furnished in chic Texana style, with hefty, handcarved Mexican tables and chairs, plus giant couches and more chairs covered in mellow leather and heavy upholstery. Bedding is sumptuous, as are the bath linens and expensive hair and body products. The most popular suite is the one with the biggest kitchen, which is stocked with continental breakfast goodies. Suites also come equipped with TV/VCR and movies, as well as telephones. An Olympic-size swimming pool is just a few yards away from the suites, as is a wonderful hot tub.

A good night's rest is needed to prepare you for a drive on the **Devil's Backbone,** the wildly twisting Ranch Road 32, reaching from Ranch

Road 12 immediately south of Wimberley almost 25 miles toward Blanco. This, a dramatically nicknamed route, is easily a contender for the state's most scenic drive, cutting a winding path along a sharp ridge through the hills; be on the watch early or late in the day for white-tailed deer. It's spectacular at any time, but with spring wildflowers or autumn foliage, it's the ultimate.

OTHER PLACES TO STAY IN THE HILL COUNTRY

BOERNE

Borgman's Sunday House B&B Inn, 911 South Main Street, Boerne 78006, (800) 633–7339.

Lone Star Palace at Fair Oaks Ranch, c/o Bed & Breakfast Texas Style, (972) 298–8586, (800) 899–4538, or, on the Internet, www. bnbtexasstyle.com.

BRADY

Brady House, 704 South Bridge Street, Brady 76825, (915) 597–5265 or (888) 272–3901.

FREDERICKSBURG

Creekside Inn, 304 South Washington Street, Fredericksburg 78624, (830) 997–6316. A quick walk from Main Street, this inn was built onto a historic home and offers seven large, modern suites with TV/VCR, phone, kitchenettes, and large bathrooms.

Austin Street Retreat, c/o Gastehaus Schmidt, (830) 997–5612. Just a block off Main Street, this elegant compound of five cottage suites features king- or queen-size beds, phones, central heat and air, kitchenettes with coffeemakers, refrigerators, and microwaves, as well as fabulously designed, two-person whirlpool tubs. Some suites have fireplaces. Book well in advance; about $135 and up.

LLANO

Ford Street Inn, 1119 Ford Street, Llano 78643, (915) 247–1127.

LUCKENBACH

The Luckenbach Inn, Old Luckenbach Road, Luckenbach 78624, (830) 997–2205.

NEW BRAUNFELS

Karbach Haus B&B, 487 West San Antonio Street, New Braunfels 78130, (800) 972–5941.

Kuebler-Waldrip Haus B&B, 1620 Hueco Springs Loop, New Braunfels 78130, (800) 299–8372.

SAN MARCOS

Crystal River Inn, 326 West Hopkins Street, San Marcos 78667, (512) 396–3739.

WIMBERLEY

The Homestead Bed & Breakfast, Ranch Road 12 at Scudder Lane, Wimberley 78676, (512) 847–8788. Eight cottages on Cypress Creek in town are available.

Old Oaks Ranch Bed and Breakfast, P.O. Box 912, Wimberley 78676, (512) 847–9374.

Rancho Cama Bed & Breakfast, 2595 Flite Acres Road, Wimberley 78676, (800) 594–4501 or (512) 847–2596.

Southwind Bed & Breakfast, 2701 Farm Road 3237, Wimberley 78676, (512) 847–5277 or (800) 508–5277. Cottages with hot tub are offered.

OTHER PLACES TO EAT IN THE HILL COUNTRY

COMFORT

Arlene's Cafe, 426 Seventh Street, Comfort 78013, (830) 995–3330.

FREDERICKSBURG

Ernie's Mediterranean Grill, 423 East Main Street, Fredericksburg 78624, (830) 997–7478. Former Four Seasons chef serves grilled vegetable-pesto sandwiches, baked calamari, pork tenderloin with peaches, and inspired pastas at lunch and dinner in smart shopping compound.

Fredericksburg Brewery, 245 East Main Street, Fredericksburg 78624, (830) 997-1646.

Navajo Grill, 209 East Main Street, Fredericksburg 78624, (830) 990-8289. Charming spot attracting visitors such as John Travolta, Sharon Stone, and George Strait offers goodies such as crawfish enchiladas, grilled shrimp and grapefruit salad, and smoked salmon cakes. Open for lunch and dinner.

The Nest Restaurant, 607 South Washington Street, Fredericksburg 78624, (830) 990-8383.

The Oak House Restaurant, 755 South Washington Street, Fredericksburg 78624, (830) 997-6223.

The Peach Tree Tea Room, 210 South Adams Street, Fredericksburg 78624, (830) 997-9527. This lovely shop offers lunches of salads, soups, sandwiches, pasta, and desserts Monday through Saturday and more elaborate fare Friday and Saturday.

GRUENE

Guadalupe Smoked Meat Company, 1299 Gruene Road, Gruene 78130, (830) 629-6121. Barbecue, burgers, desserts, Texas wines, and beer provide rib-sticking pleasure at lunch and dinner.

JOHNSON CITY

The Hill Country Cupboard, at the junction of U.S. Highways 290 and 281, (830) 868-4625. Specialties are plate lunches and dinners, plus fresh bakery goods.

KERRVILLE

Cypress Grill, 433 Water Street, Kerrville 78028, (830) 896-5577.

Joe's Jefferson Street Cafe, 1001 Jefferson Street, Kerrville 78028, (830) 257-2929.

SAN MARCOS

Texas Reds Steakhouse, 120 Grove Street, San Marcos 78667, (512) 754-8808.

SPICEWOOD

R.O.'s Outpost, Texas 71 near the community of Briarcliff, (512) 264-1169. An offshoot of the popular Clark's Outpost near Denton in north Texas, with good eats such as smoked brisket, ribs, sausage, pork loin, pan-fried steak, and quail. Terrific desserts, too.

WIMBERLEY

Cypress Creek Cafe, 320 Ranch Road 12, Wimberley 78676, (512) 847-2515.

South Texas

R esting beneath the Hill Country's lower reaches, San Antonio is undisputably the gateway to vast south Texas—often a lonely, wide open region. Long, unhurried drives impart views that must have been overwhelming to early settlers, so endless is the fiercely blue sky, the ferocious and scrubby land.

The Spaniards came to colonize the new land, doing so mightily in the San Antonio area with their missions, and other Europeans eventually followed. Fanning southward from the great Alamo City are settlements reflecting varied origins, from Alsatian to Polish and, of course, Hispanic.

Only a few communities in south Texas are heavily populated, but most towns have surprising depth of character. In between are protracted stretches of road, ranch land, and thickets of mesquite—a tough tree if ever one lived. For an hour or more you'll see nothing piercing the horizon other than clumps of cacti, fence posts, an occasional telephone pole, a very rare windmill, and that tenacious mesquite. For anyone who appreciates truly raw beauty, this might be heaven.

Along the Mexican border various small settlements still simmer with Texas's Old West heritage, and all are permeated by a binational spirit that flows alongside the Rio Grande as it continues quietly and at length to the Gulf of Mexico. It's easy to picture, right there in your mind's eye, pioneer ranchmen of a century ago surveying the border, hoping somehow to tame a hopelessly wild land.

Missions and Europeans

K aleidoscopic vistas of bluebonnets, Indian paintbrush, and other wildflowers frame U.S. Highway 281, Texas Highway 16, and I–35 as you approach San Antonio in spring and summer, a subtle prelude to the year-round symphony of sights waiting in this cultural paradise. Get ready, because this vast storehouse of heritage and diversion knows how to entertain.

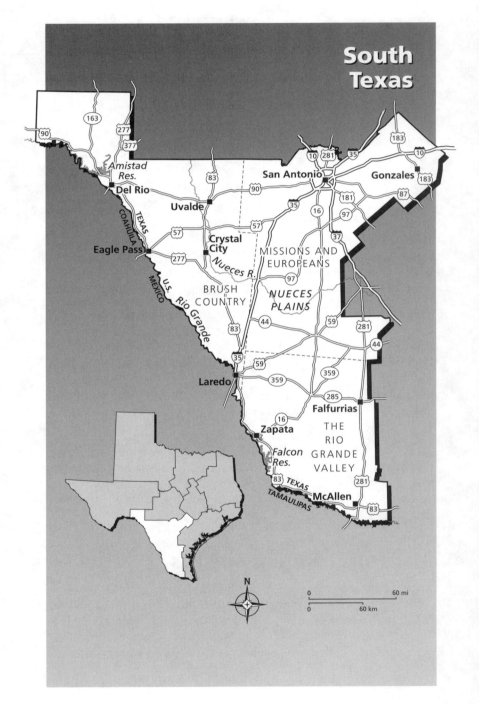

163

90
277
377

Amistad
Res.
Del Rio

Uvalde

83

90

San Antonio

10 281 35

183

10

Gonzales 183

87

COAHUILA
TEXAS

MEXICO
U.S. Rio Grande

57

Crystal
City

57

35

16

181

97

37

MISSIONS AND
EUROPEANS

Eagle Pass

277

Nueces R.

97

BRUSH
COUNTRY

NUECES
PLAINS

83

44

59

281

44

35

59

Laredo

359

359

285

Falfurrias

16

Zapata

THE
RIO
GRANDE
VALLEY

281

Falcon
Res.

83 TEXAS
TAMAULIPAS

McAllen

281

83

N

0   60 mi
0   60 km

JUNE'S FAVORITE ATTRACTIONS
IN SOUTH TEXAS

San Antonio, now the nation's tenth largest city, boasts a healthy German and Native American influence, but Hispanic culture dominates San Antonio. This Mexican-American accord will always be part of San Antonio, as the city was part of colonial or independent Mexico for nearly 150 years.

No written records tell us much of the area's early Native American period, but writings show that in the late 1690s resourceful Spaniards camped on the San Antonio River, then called Rio San Antonio de Padua. Six Spanish missions were established in the early 1700s, but only five were successful. The first was Mission San Antonio de Valero in 1718, best known later under its nickname, *The Alamo.*

The Alamo mission doubled as a fort, where Davy Crockett, Jim Bowie, and William B. Travis were among the patriots who gave their lives for the Texas Revolution. For thirteen days in late February and early March 1836, 187 men were surrounded and then crushed by the Mexican

Fort Clark Springs,
Brackettville

Institute of Texan Cultures,
San Antonio

La Borde House,
Rio Grande City

La Posada Hotel, Laredo

Lake Amistad, near Del Rio

Los Barrios, San Antonio

*Santa Ana National
Wildlife Refuge,* McAllen

*Seminole Canyon State
Historical Park,* Comstock

Spanish Governor's Palace,
San Antonio

*Texas Iwo Jima
War Memorial,* Harlingen

The Alamo

Army. The would-be liberators managed to deplete Santa Anna's forces considerably before falling, enabling the Texans to win the Battle of San Jacinto and the revolution.

Heavy doors bearing bullet holes still front the Alamo, which sits before one of four Spanish plazas downtown, all connected by winding streets. Some people are disappointed to find the landmark to be such a small place, but its size doesn't diminish its significance. The Alamo, at 300 Alamo Plaza downtown, is open Monday through Saturday 9:00 A.M. until 5:30 P.M. and Sunday 10:00 A.M. until 5:30 P.M.; (210) 225–1391.

Behind the Alamo, in the elaborate RiverCenter Mall, there's an *IMAX Theatre* presenting an excellent docudrama entitled *Alamo: The Price of Freedom* on a six-story-tall film screen. Historians double as actors in this production, telling a more factual story than the John Wayne movie version. For show schedule and ticket information, call (210) 247–4629; an admission fee is charged.

Mission San Jose (6539 Mission San Jose Drive at Mission Road, San Antonio 78210), founded two years after the Alamo, is the most interesting of the four still functioning as churches. The mission, noted for its rare and opulent hand-sculpted Rose Window, is home each Sunday to a lively mariachi mass at noon. Today San Antonio is the only U.S. city with as many missions within its city limits, and the five erected here comprise the *San Antonio Mission National Historic Park* (2202 Roosevelt Avenue, San Antonio 78210, 210–534–8833); missions are open daily from 9:00 A.M. until 6:00 P.M. in summer and 8:00 A.M. until 5:00 P.M. in winter.

Certainly San Antonio has always been a bastion of military history. *Fort Sam Houston* (North New Braunfels Avenue at Grayson Street, 210–221–1886) dates from 1876, making it the city's oldest fort. Continuing as a working army base, Fort Sam is engaging, with its Victorian officers' quarters and Quadrangle, where special events include period reenactments and dress parade drills. Two museums include one with military artifacts and one with medical exhibits. Open Wednesday through Sunday from 10:00 A.M. until 4:00 P.M.

The history of manned flight and the evolution of aerospace medicine is explored at Hangar 9/Edward H. White Museum at Brooks Air Force Base (Southeast Military Drive at I–37, 210–531–9767). Hangar 9, the oldest wooden aircraft hangar in the Air Force, houses the Museum of Flight Medicine and the Flight Nursing Annex, which is dedicated to the history of flight nurses. Hangar 9 is open only by special appointment;

SOUTH TEXAS

JUNE'S FAVORITE ANNUAL EVENTS IN SOUTH TEXAS

Alamo Irish Festival, San Antonio, second weekend in March

Borderfest, Laredo, near Fourth of July

Charro Days, Brownsville, mid- to end of February

Cinco de Mayo, Laredo, May 5

Fiesta, San Antonio, mid-April

Texas Citrus Festival, Mission, late January

Washington's Birthday, Laredo, second or third weekend in February

the Annex is open Monday through Friday, 9:00 A.M. until 4:00 P.M. Admission is free.

Aviation history is also the focus, naturally, at the *Air Force History and Traditions Museum* (Orville Wright Drive, San Antonio 78227, 210–671–3055) on Lackland Air Force Base. Find a collection of rare airplanes and components dating from World War II. The museum and gift shop are open from 8:00 A.M. until 4:30 P.M. Monday through Friday. Admission is free.

The biggest of Texas's parties is *Fiesta San Antonio,* begun as a festival honoring visiting president Benjamin Harrison. Everyone had such a good time they didn't notice that the prez was a no-show, and the bash—now in its second century—is repeated annually. Fiesta, put on by some 50,000 residents, covers a nine-day period in the latter part of April and includes 150 events. Among the flashier are the Battle of Flowers Parade, the King's River Parade, Fiesta Night Parade, and A Night in Old San Antonio. There's also a king's coronation, Alamo pilgrimage, arts fair, and *charreada,* or Mexican rodeo. For information call the Fiesta office at (210) 227–5191.

A rather bizarre cultural assemblage is that found at the *Buckhorn Saloon and Museum,* at 318 East Houston Street, San Antonio 78205 (210–247–4000). See the museum's 118-year-old gallery of animal horns and antlers, plus hundreds of fish, bird, and large mammal trophies, combining to deliver visual overload. There's also a remarkable collection of antique and custom-made firearms, plus a wax museum that chronicles Texas history in figures from Cabeza de Vaca to Teddy Roosevelt. And finally, there's the preserved San Antonio home of the writer O. Henry. Open daily at least 10:00 A.M. until 6:00 P.M., some days until 8:00 P.M. (per manager's discretion). The museum charges admission.

Kids will find plenty to entertain them in San Antonio. For starters there's the *San Antonio Children's Museum* (305 East Houston Street, San Antonio 78205, 210–21–CHILD). This entertaining hands-on museum appeals to kids ages two to ten and makes learning fun with all kinds of interactive educational exhibits. Open from 9:00 A.M. to noon Monday, 9:00 A.M. until 5:00 P.M. Tuesday through Friday, 9:00 A.M. until 6:00 P.M. Saturday, and from noon until 4:00 P.M. Sunday. Admission is charged.

The Cowboy Museum (209 Alamo Plaza, San Antonio 78205, 210–229–1257) lets you visit a Western town replica and see how the people of the Old West lived. Plenty of artifacts help tell the story, and, of course, there's a gift shop so you can take home some cowboy souvenirs. Open from 9:00 A.M. until 6:30 P.M. daily. A small admission fee is charged.

Young and old will get a kick out of the *Hertzberg Circus Museum* (210 Market Street, San Antonio, 78205, 210–207–7810 or 210–207–7819), an unusual place with more than 20,000 items of Big Top memorabilia, including a priceless collection of antique circus posters, Tom Thumb's carriage, and an intricately detailed scale model of the three-ring circus. On weekends special events may include a classic film series, jugglers, mimes and magicians, and face painting/mask making workshops. Open from 10:00 A.M. until 5:00 P.M. Monday through Saturday. A small admission fee is charged.

HemisFair Park (Alamo Street, I–37, Durango, and Market Streets) is home to the 750-foot Tower of the Americas, the symbol built for the 1968 World's Fair. A glass elevator whisks you to the top in less than a minute, and the sky-high restaurant makes one revolution per hour. On the ground there's a pleasant configuration of walkways, ponds, and waterfalls.

The park is home to the *Institute of Texan Cultures,* by far one of the nation's superior ethnic history museums. Exhibits focus on the people of twenty-six ethnic and cultural groups of Texas; the multi-media show and museum store are also superb. Open Tuesday through Sunday 9:00 A.M. until 5:00 P.M.; admission is charged. Call (210) 458–2300 for information.

Bizarre Texas Stuff

*H*ELENA: *About an hour southeast of San Antonio in Karnes County lies the ghost town of Helena, population thirty-five. Established in 1852 near the famed Chihuahua Trail and the Indianola–San Antonio Road, the rowdy frontier town saw plenty of shoot-outs—one too many, it seems. When twenty-year-old Emmett Butler, an area resident, was killed during a* saloon gunfight in 1884, his wealthy rancher-father, Col. William Butler, vowed to kill the town that killed his son. By donating free land miles away, he persuaded the railroad being built across south Texas to bypass Helena. Helena lost its county seat status, and the townsfolk moved away. The old courthouse, a post office, and a jail can still be seen.

SOUTH TEXAS

For 50 cents you can hop aboard a renovated, motorized trolley and ride from the Alamo–HemisFair Plaza area to **Market Square,** a re-created Mexican mercado (514 West Commerce Street, San Antonio 78205, 210–207–8600). Time and money easily disappear among the bustle of mariachis, whir of margarita machines, and come-ons from vendors in hundreds of booths packed with arts, crafts, jewelry, and produce and other foods. While you're there, **Mi Tierra** (210–225–1262) is the place to find good Tex-Mex eats twenty-four hours daily—and the bakery case is where you'll satisfy that sweet tooth.

Sunset Station is San Antonio's newest showplace, a 30,000-square-foot music and entertainment center inside the 1903 Southern Pacific Depot. Through the station, which served the famous Sunset Limited that ran from New Orleans to Los Angeles, passed such luminaries as Mary Astor, Calvin Coolidge, Cecil B. DeMille, Judy Garland, and Dizzy Dean. The 1998 renovation cost about $52 million. Find it near the River Walk at St. Paul Square.

Near Market Square see what the National Geographic Society once called one of San Antonio's most beautiful buildings. **The Spanish Governor's Palace** (105 Plaza De Armas, San Antonio 78205, 210–224–0601) was the former home of officials who governed the Spanish Province of Texas; over its entrance is the original keystone on which is carved the double-headed eagle of the Hapsburg coat-of-arms and the inscription in Spanish, "finished in 1749." Distinguishing features include the period furnishings and a spacious cobblestone patio with fountain and luxurious foliage. Open Monday through Saturday 9:00 A.M. until 5:00 P.M. and Sunday 10:00 A.M. until 5:00 P.M. Admission is $1.00 for adults and 50 cents for children under fourteen.

An extraordinary source of pride for more than seventy years is the **Witte Museum** (3801 Broadway Street, San Antonio 78212, 210–357–1900). The exciting regional museum features history; science; the humanities; hands-on exhibits of Texas history, natural science and anthropology; changing exhibits; and family programs. Permanent exhibitions include "Texas Wild: Ecology Illustrated," focusing on the ecological diversity of the state's seven natural areas. Recent additions to the Witte include the H-E-B Science Treehouse, a four-story building full of multiple-level hands-on exhibits that make all kinds of scientific stuff a real treat for kids to explore. You'll also want them to have a look around Ancient Texans, a place to see pictographs from Native Americans of the Lower Pecos region, and Unwrapping the Past, an archaeological display that includes an Egyptian mummy. A walk-through diorama re-creates the south Texas thornbrush and its wildlife, including javelina, armadillo, and the endangered jaguar. The

Have a Seat

Texas has everything else, so why not a Toilet Seat Art Museum? It's in San Antonio and contains the work of Barney Smith, who has painted more than 400 toilet seats for display in his garage. Inspired by his various journeys throughout the world, the artist opens his exhibit space when he's home. Call for directions and hours, (210) 824–7791.

museum also includes an EcoLab of live Texas animals, an outdoor Butterfly and Hummingbird Garden, and five restored historic homes. The museum is open Monday through Saturday from 10:00 A.M. until 5:00 P.M. (9:00 P.M. on Tuesday) and Sunday noon until 5:00 P.M. Admission is charged for visitors ages four and older.

Next door to the Witte, the **Pioneer, Trail Drivers and Texas Rangers Memorial Museum** (3805 Broadway, San Antonio 78212, 210– 822–9011) houses nineteenth- and twentieth-century artifacts such as guns, saddles, badges, and pictures of the men who used them. One of the trail-driver statues in front of the museum was sculpted by Gutzon Borglum of Mount Rushmore fame. Open daily 10:00 A.M. until 5:00 P.M. Admission is minimal.

History buffs will enjoy the **Texas Transportation Museum** (11731 Wetmore Road in McAllister Park, 210–490–3554), filled with antique pedicabs, horse-drawn and gas-powered vehicles, three model railroads, and technology and physics displays. Train rides are offered on Sunday afternoon from 1:00 until 3:00 P.M. with donation. The museum is open from 9:00 A.M. until 4:00 P.M. Thursday, Saturday, and Sunday. Admission is $4.00 for adults and $2.00 for children twelve and under.

Art is another of San Antonio's considerable strengths. The **McNay Art Museum** (6000 North New Braunfels at U.S. Highway 81, San Antonio 78212, 210–824–5368) is the former estate home of Marian Koogler McNay and now repository of postimpressionist paintings (van Gogh, Monet, Picasso, Matisse, O'Keeffe, Goya, Renoir, and Bourdelle), early New Mexican arts and crafts, plus gothic and medieval collections and one of the nation's largest theater-arts collections. A highlight of the McNay is its charming patio and gardens and the excellent museum store. Open from 10:00 A.M. until 5:00 P.M. Tuesday through Saturday and noon until 5:00 P.M. Sunday. Donations are accepted.

The **San Antonio Museum of Art** (200 West Jones Avenue, San Antonio 78205, 210–978–8100) is housed inside the remarkable former Lone Star Brewery's castlelike building. Art collections range from ancient art to the most contemporary, including magnificent Greek and Roman sculpture and Latin American folk art. The Asian section has been expanded to include Asian sculpture as well as Chinese, Japanese, and Korean art. The museum is listed in the National Register of Historic

Places. Open Tuesday 10:00 A.M. until 9:00 P.M., Wednesday through Saturday 10:00 A.M. until 5:00 P.M., and Sunday noon until 5:00 P.M. Admission is $5.00 for adults, $4.00 for senior citizens and college students with I.D., and $1.75 for children four to eleven.

Two galleries worth seeking out are the *Blue Star Art Space* (116 Blue Star Street, San Antonio 78204, 210–227–6960) and *ArtPace* (445 North Main Street, San Antonio 78205, 210-212-4900). Blue Star is a very stylish, contemporary gallery in a fashionably renovated warehouse area, featuring such works as mixed-media paintings, papier-mâché sculptures, and videos. It's open from noon until 6:00 P.M. Wednesday through Sunday. Housed inside a renovated 1920s auto dealership, ArtPace features contemporary art that ranges from hand-tinted photos to mixed media from international artists. This gallery is open from noon until 5:00 P.M. Wednesday through Sunday.

The *Southwest Craft Center* (300 Augusta Street, San Antonio 78205, 210–224–1848) occupies a former girls' school established by the Ursuline Order. The old convent and beautiful courtyard are the settings for classes, workshops, exhibitions, special events, and a restaurant. Artistic craftpersons create, exhibit, and sell a variety of items on-site, from weaving and macramé to pottery and wood carvings. Gallery hours are 10:00 A.M. until 5:00 P.M. Monday through Saturday. Admission is free.

Just south of downtown, the *King William Historic District* (on and around King William Street) is a trove of wonderful mansions built by

June's Texas Anecdotes

*S*OUTH TEXAS: *In the dozens of times I've visited San Antonio, I've always encountered genuine hospitality. Probably the finest example was a few short years ago when a group of writers chartered a bus to make a Memorial Day weekend trip to Alamo City with thirty of our closest friends. After months of planning, we made our way south, stopping first to spend a day rafting on the Guadalupe River. Finally, this motley bunch—sunburned, wearing T-shirts over our wet river clothes, full of beer and revelry—*

arrived at the lovely Crockett Hotel in San Antonio. Two of us went to the desk to get our keys and room assignments, only to find out we had arrived a day early. We were shown our signed contracts, and sure enough, we goofed. A reservations manager took one look at our pitiful group and made some calls to other hotels. Within an hour, she had us booked into the beautiful Gunther Hotel, a block from the River Walk, at the same rate we had arranged at the Crockett months earlier. That's Texas hospitality.

the city's German gentry. Walking and cycling this area on spring or fall days is a pleasure that will be long remembered, but you can have a look inside, too. The **Steves Homestead** (509 King William Street, San Antonio 78204, 210–225–5924) is a century-old Gothic Revival mansion on the San Antonio River containing period antiques owned and maintained by the San Antonio Conservation Society; a small admission fee is charged, and the home is open daily from 10:00 A.M. until 4:15 P.M.

Make it a point to visit **Guenther House** (205 East Guenther Street, San Antonio 78204, 210–227–1061) in the King William Historic District. Inside you'll find historic items related to the development of Pioneer Flour Mills, an impressive collection of Dresden plates, a gift shop, and a restaurant. Museum and gift shop hours are from 9:00 A.M. until 5:00 P.M. Monday through Saturday and from 8:00 A.M. until 2:00 P.M. Sunday. Restaurant hours are 7:00 A.M. until 3:00 P.M. Monday through Saturday and 8:00 A.M. until 2:00 P.M. Sunday. Admission is free.

The city is chock-full of art galleries, clothing boutiques, gift shops, craft markets, and the like. Those accessible on foot are found on the flagstone banks lining the **River Walk,** or *Paseo del Rio,* sitting beneath street level downtown and following the river's twisting contours. Arbors of palms, olive trees, cottonwoods, cypress, and willows shade sidewalk cafes, and pots of flowers are set between doors to shops, galleries, boutiques, hotels, bistros, and watering holes. Beware that crowds on weekends can be crushing.

River barges cruise the Paseo's 21 blocks, allowing visitors to review the retreats, unique retail shops, restaurants, and nightclubs. This thirty-five to forty-minute historical tour can be reserved by calling the Yanaguana Reservation Line at (210) 244–5700 or (800) 417–4139. Special breakfast, lunch, or dinner cruises can be arranged, as well.

La Villita (418 Villita, facing the Convention Center, San Antonio 78205, 210–207–8610) is an unusual arts-and-crafts community adjacent to the River Walk. Working artists in twenty-six shops as well as three restaurants and a post office are within. You're likely to find irresistible creations such as Oaxacan rugs and Peruvian tapestries at Village Weavers; mixed-media paintings at Artistic Endeavors; stoneware and porcelain pottery at the Village Gallery; colorful Oaxacan animal sculptures at Casa Manos Allegres; and all manner of supplies at Bonsai Arbor. You'll also find the Old San Antonio Exhibit (located in Bolivar Hall), housing a small collection of art objects and artifacts relevant to San Antonio's earliest days. Open daily; admission is free.

San Antonio's sightseeing and shopping are nothing if not exhausting, so it's probably time to check into the *Menger Hotel,* outfitted recently with the new Alamo Plaza Spa, where an old-fashioned two-hour treatment includes steam bath, sauna, and herbal scrub. The Menger, next door to the Alamo, was a splendid hotel at its 1859 opening, and its claim to fame is that Teddy Roosevelt came to this wild and raucous city and this very hotel in 1898 to recruit his Rough Riders—or so the story goes. It's still a good hotel with choice rooms in the older section, and the bar has a friendly, comfortable feel. It's located at 204 Alamo Plaza, San Antonio 78205, (210) 223–4361 or (800) 345–9285.

Travelers will have to look long and hard to find better Mexican food anywhere else. The first of two favorites is *Los Barrios* (4223 Blanco Street, San Antonio 78205, 210–732–6017), a delightful family operation with hearty Mexican and South American dishes of beef, chicken, and soups. Open for lunch and dinner daily, prices start at about $8.00. More elaborate in decor and menu, *La Fogata* (2427 Vance Jackson at Addax Street, San Antonio 78213, 210–340–1337) continues to pull people in droves to its rambling patios and its unbeatable chiles rellenos, flaming cheese, enchiladas, and possibly the best salsa anywhere. Open for lunch and dinner daily, meals average about $10 to $12.

Keep in mind that the Alamo City grows ever more popular: Recent polls conducted by a national travel magazine show San Antonio ranking consistently in the top ten favorite U.S. destinations. Between ten and eleven million people visit annually, so don't think you can just show up and get a room in the central area without a reservation.

Easily one of the most beautiful lodgings in all of San Antonio—and there are plenty of them—is *Beckmann Inn and Carriage House* (222 East Guenther Street, San Antonio 78204, 210–229–1449 or 800–945–1449). Right in the heart of the King William Historic District and listed among the city's historic landmarks, the home was built in 1886 by Albert Beckmann for his bride, Marie Dorothea, daughter of the Guenther Flour Mill family, on the mill grounds. Immediately winning is the wraparound porch, where wicker furniture is perfect for enjoying a cup of tea or coffee. Design includes a rare burl pine front door, wood mosaic floor imported from Paris, and beveled glass windows. One of three guest rooms in the main house has a fireplace, and all have private baths. The Carriage House features two private suites, each with sitting room and private bath. Gourmet breakfasts typically include juices, hot entrees, fresh fruit, and coffee cake. There is a two-night minimum stay on weekends.

Simply Batty

Although everyone expects Austin to hold this honor, it's actually a spot about 20 miles north of San Antonio that is home to the world's largest bat colony. The Bracken Cave Colony is a population of some twenty to forty million bats, thought to be the largest congregation of mammals anywhere, eating some 250,000 pounds of insects nightly.

Just as luxurious is **The Oge House** on the River Walk (209 Washington Street, San Antonio 78204, 210–223–2353 or 800–242–2770). Located in the King William Historic District, this gorgeous and extensively refurbished 1857 home is packed with period antiques and offers nine rooms, many with fireplaces.

Complete information is offered by the San Antonio Convention & Visitors Bureau, (210) 207–6748; a handy visitors center is situated steps from the Alamo at 317 Alamo Plaza, San Antonio 78205, (210) 207–6748, open daily from 8:30 A.M. until 6:00 P.M. Visit the Internet site at www. sanantoniocvb.com.

Head to **Castroville,** 20 miles west on U.S. 90, a town of just more than 2,000 in Medina County. It became the "Little Alsace of Texas" after founder Henri Castro brought a band of Alsatian settlers with him from that region of France. It's the only Alsatian community in the country, and it has clung tightly to its heritage; it's a lucky visitor who comes across descendants of those settlers, especially those who can speak the original, unwritten dialect, which is more German than French.

For a look into Alsatian history, visit **Mount Gentilz Cemetery** (U.S. Highway 90 and Alsace Street), also called Cross Hill. Here you'll have a far-reaching view of the Medina Valley, and you can see the burial spot of Amelia Castro, Henri's wife. Also see **St. Louis Catholic Church** (U.S. Highway 90 and Angelo Street), built in 1868–70 next to the colonists' original chapel, built in 1846. The big, three-story building is the **Moye Center,** a convent erected in 1873 for the Sisters of Divine Providence.

Travelers will be pleased to find the Alsatian community's **Landmark Inn State Historic Site** (Florence and Florella Streets, 830–931–2133), a hotel on the San Antonio–El Paso road when built in 1863; it's said that Robert E. Lee was among its guests. Now it's the only historic inn run by the state, which restored it to a 1940s look. A visitors center and an old gristmill are here, too.

A surprising number of visitors make special trips from San Antonio to Castroville specifically to eat at **La Normandie** (1302 Fiorella Street, Castroville 78009, 830–538–3070), a modest but excellent restaurant turning out fine French fare. High marks go to the veal in a cream-shallot-mushroom sauce, rack of lamb, and crepes filled with gently sautéed, fresh apples. Lunch is served daily, and dinner is served Wednesday through Sunday. Note that credit cards are not accepted, but personal checks are.

Continue west from Castroville on U.S. Highway 90, traveling another 20 miles to *Hondo,* which became the seat of Medina County after the Southern Pacific Railroad bypassed Castroville in the 1880s. Today it's a community of 6,000 known best for attractions of the four-legged kind.

Much older and far more exotic, *dinosaur tracks* cast in stone are easily viewed in Hondo Creek's bed, almost 24 miles north of town via Farm Road 462. Scientists speculate these were made by 15-ton, 40-foot herbivores called trachodons.

Forty-two miles farther west on U.S. Highway 90, *Uvalde,* seat of the same-named county and home to 15,000 residents, is known as the crossroads of two roads spanning the whole country—U.S. Highway 90 and U.S. Highway 83—and a fat little pocket of Old West and U.S. history.

In the 1880s, *J. K. King Fisher and Pat Garrett*—two unforgettable lawmen of their day—lived in Uvalde. Fisher was an outlaw who became a deputy, though some said he was both at the same time, and Garrett was the man who killed Billy the Kid in nearby New Mexico in 1881.

And Uvalde's John Nance Garner served as vice president of the United States from 1933 to 1941; his life is chronicled in detail at the *Garner Museum* (333 North Park Row, Uvalde 78801, 830–278–5018). Garner went to Congress in 1903 during Teddy Roosevelt's administration, served as Speaker of the House, and stayed in Washington, serving as the number-two man under FDR. It's said that his signature Texan candidness earned him the nickname "Cactus Jack." The museum is housed in his former home, a beautiful building, and he was buried shortly before his ninety-ninth birthday at the west end of City Cemetery (on U.S. Highway 90 West). The museum is open Monday through Saturday 9:00 A.M. until noon and 1:00 until 5:00 P.M. Admission is $1.00 for adults, 50 cents for children.

Take time to look at *Uvalde Grand Opera House* (104 West North Street at North Getty Street, 830–278–4184). A building befitting its name, this two-story creation seated 370 patrons and is now partially occupied by a museum. Open Monday through Friday 9:00 A.M. until noon and 1:00 until 5:00 P.M.; Saturday 10:00 A.M. until 3:00 P.M. Admission is free.

With big skies and pretty rivers nearby, Uvalde's fine for hanging around for a couple of days. Check into *Casa de Leona Bed & Breakfast* (Farm

Road 140, 830–278–8550), a Spanish hacienda-style place with five guest rooms with fireplaces, an art studio, and gift shop. Several options are available, too, just 24 miles north via U.S. Highway 83 in Concan; check with the Uvalde Convention & Visitors Bureau at 300 East Main Avenue, (830) 278–4115 or (800) 588–2533, for details.

Brush Country

From Uvalde, proceed 40 miles west on U.S. Highway 90 to reach *Brackettville,* seat of Kinney County. Be assured that this is the epitome of isolation: There's only one other town in the county, which is more than twenty times the size of Rhode Island.

You'll see a familiar sight here, and maybe it will seem like a mirage: The Alamo right here in Brackettville's *Alamo Village* is the one in the 1959 John Wayne movie, not the one in San Antonio. That's because an entire set had to be built for the epic film—it's still one of the larger and more thorough sets ever built in this country—and this lonesome land provided ideal scenery. Adobe craftsmen from Mexico created the Alamo replica, which continues to overlook a complete frontier village straight out of the nineteenth century. Rounding out the village are a cantina and restaurant, stage depot, jail, bank, livery, and trading post. In summer there are musical shows and melodramas, often interrupted by Old West gunfights. To reach the village, drive 7 miles north from town on Ranch Road 674; admission is charged, and it's open daily 9:00 A.M. until 5:00 P.M. except December 21–26. Call (830) 563–2580 for details.

Texas Trivia
The Dallas Morning News *reports that armadillos—seen in the mid-nineteenth century in the United States only along the Rio Grande—are now migrating north and east from Texas at a rate of about 6 miles per year. The armadillo became the State Small Mammal in 1995.*

On the town's eastern edge on U.S. 90, find *Fort Clark Springs,* a resort resting on old Fort Clark, one of the country's best preserved cavalry posts. Built in 1852 to protect western settlers against Indians and banditos, the fort is famous for having been the training ground for ninety years for several infantry units, including the Ninth and Tenth Infantry's black Buffalo Soldiers and almost all of the army cavalry units. Others stationed at Fort Clark included generals George S. Patton Jr. and George C. Marshall. Historic buildings remain, some of which have been restored. The Old Guardhouse contains a small museum, and the resort offerings include a motel in old limestone barracks; two restaurants; a large, spring-fed pool; tennis courts and golf courses; and a fitness center. Call (800) 937–1590 or (830) 563–2493 for details.

At *Seminole Indian Scout Cemetery,* 3 miles south of town on Farm Road 3348, you'll find the burial sites of several scouts hired by the army to help in campaigns against the warring Apaches. These Seminoles were descended from escaped Georgia slaves who intermarried with Florida Native Americans and moved west. Four of those buried here received the prestigious Congressional Medal of Honor, and some of the Seminole offspring still reside in Brackettville, working at ranching or farming.

From Brackettville, keep steady on U.S. Highway 90 another 32 miles to *Del Rio,* the seat of Val Verde County and nicknamed Queen of the Rio Grande. In this corner of dry, hot south Texas, Del Rio is a blessing, as it rests atop bubbling San Felipe Springs, the outlet of an underground river pouring forth ninety million gallons of crystal water daily. *That's* why you see so many ranches around–the irrigation opportunity is abundant for those prospering in sheep and Angora goat ranching nearby.

One look at the ornate, gothic 1887 *Val Verde County Courthouse* is to understand the wealth and depth of history in this town. Stop by the Del Rio Chamber of Commerce (1915 Avenue F, Del Rio 78840, 830–775–3551) and pick up the detailed walking guide and map of thirty-four historic homes, buildings, and sites, many dating to a romantic, if tumultuous, time in Texas history.

Two of the homes on the historical tour have been converted to bed-and-breakfast inns. One is The Price-Woods Home, now called *The 1890 House* (609 Griner Street, Del Rio 78840, 800–282–1360 or 830–775–8061), found right in downtown Del Rio. Furnished with period antiques, there are four-poster beds, baths with Jacuzzi tubs, TVs, gourmet breakfasts, and gracious service; three rooms and one suite are offered. The other home is noted as the Mason-Foster House on the tour, but it's the B&B called *Villa del Rio* (123 Hudson Street, Del Rio 78840, 830–768–1100). Surrounded by twenty-two centurion pecan trees and fifteen century-old palms and magnolias, the 4,600-square-foot mansion offers two guest rooms and two suites and a heavy continental breakfast.

Another gaping surprise out here is *Lake Amistad,* home of *Amistad National Recreation Area,* northwest of town 10 miles via U.S. 90. This 67,000-acre, vividly blue impoundment on the Rio Grande is a perfect example of the unity enjoyed today between Mexico and the United States, and particularly Texas. As the United States shares the river with

Mexico, it also shares the dam creating the mesmerizing, binational lake, which stretches 75 miles upriver and offers 1,000 miles of shoreline. Fishing permits are offered by both countries, and there are dozens of other diversions, including camping, boat rentals, picnicking, and bow hunting. The dam is topped by a 6-mile road, offering access between the lake's two sides. For information contact the National Park Service office on U.S. Highway 90 West, just at the Del Rio city limits, (830) 775–7491.

Texas Trivia

In 1900 Texas had twenty-six wineries; only one of those remains operational today: Val Verde Winery in Del Rio outlasted the Prohibition era.

For true international flavor, plan a day a few yards away, crossing over the border into **Ciudad Acuna, Mexico,** Del Rio's Mexican twin—to miss such a treat is to neglect the legacy created between Texas and Mexico through generations. Along **Avenida Hidalgo** you'll find shops stocked with baskets, pottery, leather goods, silver jewelry, glassware, tiles, and other hand-crafted items—and you can bet the prices are low even on items of very high quality. Be sure to find **La Paloma Curios,** No. 190 Hidalgo, for nice pottery, jewelry, and picture frames; and **Casa Uxmal,** No. 125 Hidalgo, for great rustic furniture, pewter frames, malachite chess sets, beautiful mirrors, blown glass, table linens, and leather goods. Don't hesitate to bargain with shopkeepers, many of whom speak English and accept American dollars, as it's an expected practice. Cafes and bakeries offer good snacks, too. You can drive across the border, but it's better not to hassle with the insurance necessities; just park on the U.S. side of the river and walk across the bridge. To reach it follow Garfield Avenue, also called Spur 239, west about 3 miles to the river.

Another look into history is discovered at **Val Verde Winery** (100 Qualia Street, Del Rio 78840, 830–775–9714), Texas's oldest winery, begun in 1883 by Italian immigrant Frank Qualia. It's still in the same family, whose members offer free tours of the vineyards, storage vats, aging room, and bottling processors. Among eight wines made here, one is the Lenoir, the first wine produced more than 110 years ago. Tasting and buying opportunities follow the tour. It's open Monday through Saturday from 9:00 A.M. until 5:00 P.M.

Set aside ample time for two outstanding side trips from Del Rio, which can be done on the same drive northwest of the city along U.S. Highway 90. The first stop is **Seminole Canyon State Historical Park,** 45 miles from Del Rio and about 9 miles past the village called Comstock. The rugged setting of desert and canyons showcases a collection of Indian paintings and pictographs thought to be more than 8,000 years old.

Look in Fate Bell Shelter, just below the park's interpretive center, for the most brilliant pictographs. Discoveries of other human artifacts—possibly 12,000 years old—and the drawings have combined to give scientists some ideas of daily life all those millennia past, which are illustrated in a life-size diorama at the visitors center. Call to inquire about ranger-led tours, usually offered on weekends. The park is open daily 8:00 A.M. until 10:00 P.M. and at all times for campers. Admission is $2.00 per adult thirteen and older; call (915) 292-4464.

The second side trip from Del Rio is *Langtry*, only 20 miles beyond Seminole Canyon on U.S. Highway 90, still in Val Verde County. The desperately lonely Wild West outpost was founded in 1881, when the railroad came through, representing the junction of eastbound and westbound construction. How the town's name came about is still up for debate: Some historians believe that the civil engineer, a man called Langtry, who directed a crew of Chinese railroad laborers, is the source, but romantics stick with the story of Judge Roy Bean, who says he named the town for his favorite actress, the Jersey Lily, Englishwoman Lillie Langtry.

Worth the trip alone, the recently updated and remodeled *Judge Roy Bean Visitor Center* is the preserved site of the infamous, unforgettable "Law West of the Pecos," whose 1880s rule was a masterful blend of wit and bravery. Travelers find the rustic saloon, courtroom, and pool hall that was Bean's, along with a full-scale state visitors' travel center, staffed by counselors and stocked with loads of free brochures, maps, guides, and varied information. Outside there's a cactus garden with indigenous southwestern plant life. Open daily from 8:00 A.M. until 5:00 P.M., the center's phone number is (915) 291-3340.

Notice on your way to Langtry, about 18 miles east of town, there's a terrific *Pecos River Canyon scenic overlook*, offering a stunning view of the formidable canyon. This is an ideal place to stretch your legs, and a picnic area is right there if you've brought lunch along.

From Del Rio, you can begin making tracks to the southeast along the Rio Grande, traveling 56 miles on U.S. Highway 277 to *Eagle Pass*, the seat of Maverick County and home to 20,650 residents. An early U.S. settlement during the Mexican War, it's where the government founded Fort Duncan in 1849 and remains a gateway to Mexico today.

Have a look into that window of history at *Fort Duncan Museum*, housed in the old headquarters. There are archaeological exhibits, as well as details on the Kickapoo tribe nearby, and eleven surviving buildings. The history told here is of the post's closing in 1900, then reopening in 1916 during the Mexican Revolution, and its use as a

Judge Roy Bean Visitor Center

World War I training base. Among famous officers who spent time here were Phil Sheridan, James Doolittle, and Matthew Ridgeway. Open Monday through Saturday 1:00 until 5:00 P.M., the museum is found on Bliss Street between Monroe and Adams Streets, (830) 773–1217.

Eagle Pass extends across the border in the form of *Piedras Negras,* a Mexican sister and home to 265,000. To truly experience your border vacation, you have to find the wonderful deals to be made in the market downtown on glassware, wood carvings, woven blankets and rugs, silver jewelry, and colorful smocks and blouses. Bullfights are held in summer, and restaurants offer good, cheap Mexican dishes. You can gain access across an international bridge via Garrison Street, also known as U.S. Highway 57. Parking on the U.S. side of the bridge and walking across saves you from having to buy the required Mexican auto insurance.

From Eagle Pass, travel 50 miles east on U.S. Highway 277 and east on Farm Road 191 to *Crystal City,* seat of Zavala County. It may seem odd, but this seat of Zavala County and town of 8,000 is home to a big *statue of Popeye the Sailor,* found in front of city hall on the square. Well, it's not so strange after all—as this town calls itself The Spinach Capital of the World for its huge production of spinach. Look also for farmers selling enormous watermelons, tomatoes, onions, carrots, and peppers from their pickup trucks.

Now it's 92 miles straight south on U.S. Highway 83 to **Laredo,** seat of Webb County, with nearly 150,000 residents. Rich in history and culture, Laredo is the place for more of that beloved binational experience. Since its founding by Don Tomás Sánchez, a captain in the Spanish colonial army, on May 15, 1755, Villa San Agustín de Laredo has served as everything from a raiding site for Lipan Apaches and Comanches, a cattle and sheep ranching community, and an outpost for the expanding New Spain to capital of the Republic of the Rio Grande and an international commerce center.

The city's chamber of commerce (2310 San Bernardo Street, Laredo 78040, 956–722–2200) offers an excellent walking-tour guide, with details on numerous historic neighborhoods and buildings; shopping districts in both Laredo and **Nuevo Laredo,** the Mexican twin across the Rio Grande; and dining and hotel offerings. While you're looking around downtown, be sure to pay attention to **San Agustín Plaza,** bordered by Grant, Zaragoza, Flores, and San Agustín Streets; here you'll see the beautiful **St. Agustín Church,** a Gothic Revival masterpiece, and several remarkable buildings in designs ranging from Mexican colonial and Mexican vernacular to Victorian and neoclassical revival, dating from the 1700s.

Facing the plaza, **La Posada Hotel** (1000 Zaragoza, Laredo 78040, 956–722–1701) occupies the former Laredo High School, built in 1916. The hotel is nothing short of lovely, with an exquisitely blue-tiled pool surrounded by a lush courtyard. The food is fair to good in the hotel's restaurants, the best being the **Tack Room,** upstairs in an adjacent building that was once the town's telephone exchange. You'll find big steaks, spareribs, chicken, and fish on the menu.

Laredo's supply of Mexican food will keep your motor running. Start your day with a blast at **Las Cazuelas** (303 Market Street, Laredo 78040, 956–723–3693). Be bold and have a breakfast taco packed with stewed meat, potato and eggs, or avocado. Soups are excellent at lunch. Open daily 6:30 A.M. until 2:30 P.M.

If you happen upon Laredo in February, you may be in for a real treat during **George Washington's Birthday Celebration,** a two-week party held annually since 1898. The fiesta includes parades, pageants, fireworks, dances, a jalapeño festival (one contest challenges brave souls to gobble as many jalapeños as possible in fifteen minutes!), carnival, *charreada* rodeo, and an occasional bullfight.

The **Laredo Children's Museum** (at the west end of Washington Street, 956–725–2299) sits on the Laredo Community College campus inside two restored buildings, relocated from old Fort McIntosh. Children are offered exhibits on science and technology. Open from 1:00 until 5:00 P.M. Wednesday through Friday and Sunday and from 10:00 A.M. until 5:00 P.M. Saturday. Admission is $2.00 per adult and $1.00 per child three and older.

For a selection of superb food and shopping, make the requisite walk across one of two international bridges to Nuevo Laredo, a busy city with a population of a quarter million. International Bridge #1 is reached via Convent Street, and International Bridge #2 is accessed from I–35. Again, it's a good idea to park on the U.S. side and walk across; auto insurance for Mexico is a bother, and parking is tough in Nuevo Laredo.

One of the more popular spots to dine in Nuevo Laredo is *Las Jarritas* (2002 Heroes de Nacataz, 011–52–87–12–88–90), a terrific gathering spot for feasting on grilled steak and sweetbreads, as well as smoked meats and all the trimmings. Strolling musicians and a bar keep things energized. It's open daily from noon until midnight.

Another worthwhile choice is *Restaurant El Rancho* (2134 Guerrero, 011–52–87–14–80–18) a giant party place specializing in tacos, soups, and revelry until the wee hours each night. For a selection of more than one hundred tequilas, head over to *Sombreros Tequila Bar and Grill* (2813 Belden, 011–52–87–12–20–20), a friendly watering hole with plates of sour cream enchiladas and grilled chicken platters. This one is open daily until 2:00 A.M.

Nuevo Laredo's *El Mercado,* at the intersection of Guerrero Avenue and Belden Street, is a two-story, square-block retail center where vendors sell goods that range from jewelry, sandals, leather bags, and saddles to barware, clothing, baskets, pastries, and pottery. Prices are low to begin with, but you can bargain to the basement. A gorgeous department store, *Marti's,* at Guerrero Avenue and Victorian Street, stocks fancy gold and silver jewelry, china, crystal, antiques, designer dresses, expensive tapestries and rugs, and furniture. To call from Laredo, dial 52–87–12–31–37.

The Rio Grande Valley

ack on the road, it's another 49 miles south on U.S. 83 to *Zapata,* seat of Zapata County and home to 3,500 Texans. Named in honor of Antonio Zapata, the renowned Mexican pioneer and tough Indian fighter, the town is mostly a supply point for outdoor enthusiasts embarking on an adventure at *Falcon State Park,* 28 miles south on U.S. 83, Farm Road 2098, and Park Road 46, (956) 848–5327. The shores of the enormous international lake, impounded on the Rio Grande, offer more than 500 acres for camping, picnicking, fishing, and swimming. There are groceries at the park, too, as well as a snack bar. Admission is $2.00 per person; the park is open daily.

Just across the southern end of International Falcon Reservoir from Falcon State Park is the near-ghost town of **Ciudad Guerrero Viejo,** just off Mexico's Highway 2. Designated a National Historic Site by the government of Mexico, it's to become a park. Reach it along dirt roads to see traces of another civilization. Information is available from the Texas Historical Commission in Austin, (512) 463–6100. Ask specifically about the Los Caminos del Rio project.

From Zapata, it's 51 miles south on U.S. 83 till you reach **Rio Grande City,** seat of Starr County, with a population of 5,700. The town came about in 1848 when Gen. Zachary Taylor established Fort Ringgold, which was named for Maj. David Ringgold, the first army officer killed in the Battle of Palo Alto, opening the Mexican War. The fort remained active until 1944 and was home to Col. Robert E. Lee when he commanded the Department of Texas prior to the Civil War.

Travelers will want to pause in Rio Grande City just to stay at **La Borde House** (601 East Main Street, Rio Grande City 78582, 956–487–5101), the 1899 home and border mercantile built by a French merchant and riverboat trader who had the house designed in Paris, then refined by San Antonio architects. Totally renovated, the home was made into a hotel years ago and contains sublime Victorian furniture and antiques. With shaded verandas, courtyard, patio, parlor, guest rooms, and restaurant, it's a showplace on the Rio Grande.

Continuing south on U.S. 83 just 12 miles, watch for Farm Road 886, which you'll turn right onto for 2 miles until you reach the Rio Grande and a sight found nowhere else on a U.S. border. The **Los Ebaños Ferry** is a wooden, two-car ferry hand-pulled by a Mexican staff using ropes and is possibly in numbered days, as plans call for its eventual replacement by a bridge. For the moment, vehicle ferry is $1.00 and people are 25 cents each.

Another 14 miles south on U.S. 83, **Mission** is an 1824 settlement where the Rio Grande Valley's famous citrus industry was begun, possibly by the original priests. Today the town of 28,000 in Hidalgo County is Home of the Grapefruit, specifically the famous Texas ruby red. Mission is not only the citrus center but also the state's **poinsettia center** and home of the nation's only all-poinsettia show, held annually in December. Most Texans—and all Rio Grande Valley residents—will also proudly tell you that Mission is the birthplace of Tom Landry, the first (and thirty-year) coach of the World Football Championship Dallas Cowboys.

Should you join other winter Texans for a January stay in the Valley, rest up for the seventy-year-old *Texas Citrus Fiesta,* held the last week of the month all over the area. The bash consists of a grand parade, barbecue cook-off, carnival, dances, citrus judging, arts and crafts show, sporting events, and a spectacular citrus products costume style show. For information call the Mission Chamber of Commerce at (956) 585–9724 or (956) 585–2727.

La Lomita Chapel (on Farm Road 1016, 3 miles south of town) was first an adobe waystation dating to 1865 for Oblate padres traveling on horseback upriver from Brownsville. The present, rebuilt version, erected in sandstone in 1889, is a tiny structure with original floors, rough beamed ceilings, and outdoor beehive oven. It sits in a seven-acre park with picnic areas, barbecue grills, rest rooms, walkways, and historic site signs.

For still more outdoors, head for *Bentsen–Rio Grande Valley State Park* (6 miles southwest on U.S. 83, Farm Road 2062, and Park Road 43, 956–585–1107), nearly 600 acres of land along the Rio Grande with excellent bird watching, especially for the Audubon's oriole, hooded oriole, zone-tailed hawk, and redeye cowbird. At the park office, pick up lists and booklets on these, as well as mammals, herbs, plants, butterflies, and other flora and fauna to be seen on nature trails. Camping, picnicking, and boating are options, too. The park is open daily; admission is $2.00 for adults, children twelve and under and seniors sixty-eight and older get in free.

McAllen, 10 miles east along U.S. 83, also lies in Hidalgo County and is home to 95,000 residents. The hub of activity in the lower Rio Grande Valley, McAllen appeals to retirees from the Midwest and Canada who spend entire winters here in the subtropical environs.

McAllen International Museum (1900 Nolana Street, McAllen 78502, 956–682–1564) has a wonderful Mexican folk-art mask and textile collection, as well as contemporary American and regional prints, sculptures, and oils from sixteenth- to nineteenth-century Europe. Open Tuesday, Wednesday, Friday, and Saturday 9:00 A.M. until 5:00 P.M.; Thursday noon until 8:00 P.M.; and Sunday 1:00 until 5:00 P.M. A small admission fee is charged.

The citrus season lasts from October through April, so to pick some citrus for yourself or buy your own crates, head over to *Cherry Acres* (immediately west on Farm Road 494, 956–581–7783), a great place to buy fruits to be shipped home. Gift packs are sold, and an adjacent garden center offers exquisite tropical foliage. A similar business is *Klement's Grove* (Farm Road 1924 and Taylor Road, 956–682–2980), which offers you-pick-'em fruit off the trees, fruit selection in baskets, and gift packs, as well as mesquite and wildflower honey, pecans, fresh pies, and fruit cake.

You could spend all your time eating in McAllen. Keeping with the local flavor, you'll do well to have lunch or dinner at *Guacamaya Grill* (400 Nolana Loop, McAllen 78504, 956–668–7229), a hugely festive spot featuring *ceviche* (a lime-drenched fish salad), grilled steak, and pan-fried, buttery red snapper. It's open daily.

Republic of the Rio Grande (1411 South Tenth Street, McAllen 78501, 956–994–8385) is a trendy bistro showing spaghetti westerns on a giant screen and serving quesadillas packed with smoked chicken and pizzas topped with smoked salmon. Open for lunch and dinner daily.

Right down the street is *Santa Fe Steakhouse* (1918 South Tenth Street, McAllen 78504, 956–630–2331), a beautiful yet casual restaurant known for its exquisite steaks, seafood, and salsa made from black beans and corn. Open only for dinner Monday through Saturday.

Texas Trivia
Country-western musician and singer Freddie Fender was born Baldemar G. Huerta in San Benito.

For a real change of pace, there's *Sushi Unagui* (4500 North Tenth Street, Suite 50, McAllen 78504, 956–618–4996), where chefs combine the best of two worlds in sushi with chipotle chiles and fried shrimp. It's open for lunch and dinner Thursday through Saturday until 3:00 A.M.

A side trip to take if you have a free morning or afternoon—and if it's not too awfully hot—is to *Santa Ana National Wildlife Refuge* (U.S. 83 east to Alamo, south on Farm Road 907, 7 miles to U.S. 281, and east to the entrance, 956–787–3079). Here, 2,000 acres of subtropical foliage provide a habitat for an astounding variety of bird species, some of which aren't found elsewhere in the United States. The species list of nearly 400 can be picked up at the visitors center, and three nature trails are offered. In the winter a tram tour is available. Trails are open daily from sunrise until sunset, and the visitors center is open daily 9:00 A.M. until 4:30 P.M. Admission is free, but tram tours, which run Thursday through Monday, cost $3.00 for adults and $1.00 for children. Note: Use insect repellent before going out on trails.

Head north of McAllen 8 miles on U.S. Highway 281 to **Edinburg,** the Hidalgo County seat, on Saturday night to see a proud Texas tradition, the rodeo. The **Sheriff's Posse Rodeo** is a weekly offering, with cowboys demonstrating calf roping, bull riding, and quarter horse racing. The rodeo arena is 2 miles south of town on U.S. 281. Admission is free.

Just a couple of miles east of McAllen via U.S. 83, the San Juan exit delivers you to the doors of the **Shrine of La Virgen de San Juan del Valle** (U.S. 83 and Raul Longoria Road, 956–787–0033). This impressive church was built to the tune of $5 million—mostly paid for by small contributions—after the elaborate, 1954 original was destroyed when a plane deliberately crashed into it. The wooden La Virgen statue wasn't harmed, and now it has a special place at the center of a 100-foot wall. Open daily from 6:00 A.M. until 7:00 P.M.

The next south-of-the-border experience is just a walk across the International Bridge to **Reynosa,** reached by driving 10 miles south on Tenth Street, also known as Texas Highway 336. The city, founded in 1749, is home now to more than half a million residents, and it's a great place for travelers to shop, eat, and see a bullfight or a baseball game in the Mexican League. It's best to park on the U.S. side of the bridge and walk across.

You can also head into Reynosa via buses leaving every twenty minutes from the bus station at 120 South Sixteenth Street in downtown McAllen, delivering riders to the bridge or to the Reynosa bus station. The final bus of the evening leaves at 10:15 P.M.; call (956) 686–5479 for more information.

The **Zaragoza Market,** Hidalgo and Matamoros Streets, is a standard market with brass, glass, wood, silver, leather, straw, and pottery gifts. Don't forget to bargain. Go to **Gabii's,** 1097 Avenida Los Virreyes, Reynosa, for pretty Mexican designer dresses, folk arts and crafts from Mexico and Central America, and finer giftwares.

The best food is at **La Cucaracha,** at Aldama and Ocampo Streets, serving chateaubriand, lobster thermidor, and flaming desserts and offering live music for dancing. Also try **Sam's,** Allende at Ocampo Streets, for cheap, reliable eats popular with tourists since 1932.

Another good dining room is **La Fogata** at 750 Matamoros, Reynosa, a recently expanded restaurant and piano bar. The menu is known for tender *cabrito*, steaks, and frosty margaritas. And there's **Cafe Paris** at Emilio Portes Gil No. 701 in Colonia del Prado, which is anything but French. Open for breakfast, lunch, and dinner, there are very good pastries as well as well-seasoned beef and chicken dishes.

It's but 30 miles south from McAllen on U.S. 83 to *Harlingen,* a town of nearly 50,000 in Cameron County named for a city in the Netherlands. Called Sixshooter Junction for a wild time around 1910 and the Mexican Revolution, when frequent bandit raids necessitated the peacekeeping efforts of the Texas Rangers and mounted patrols from U.S. Customs. The National Guard was eventually brought in to help the Rangers when, it's said, there were more firearms than citizens in town.

Things have calmed down considerably since then, but visitors can become better acquainted with history at the *Rio Grande Valley Historical Museum Complex,* off Loop 499, at Boxwood and Raintree Streets, (956) 430–8500. The four museums here are the Historical Museum, detailing the culture of the lower Valley; a restored nineteenth-century stagecoach inn; a medical museum, with 1920s equipment; and the Lon C. Hill Home, a 1905 house built by the city founder, who hosted dignitaries such as William Jennings Bryan. The complex is open Wednesday through Saturday 10:00 A.M. until 4:00 P.M. and Sunday 1:00 until 4:00 P.M. Admission is $2.00 for adults, $1.00 for senior citizens fifty-five and older, and $1.00 for children five to eighteen.

A somewhat unexpected treat is found at Harlingen's *Marine Military Academy and Texas Iwo Jima War Memorial,* 320 Iwo Jima Boulevard, Harlingen 78550, (956) 423–6006. The Public Affairs Office will tell you if any parades or activities are scheduled, which offer the chance to see a U.S. Marines–style private academy at work. On the campus is the original working model for the Iwo Jima Memorial bronze statue at Arlington National Cemetery, donated to the academy by sculptor Dr. Felix W. de Weldon in 1981. The figures are 32 feet high, the M-1 rifle is 16 feet long, the flagpole is 78 feet long, and the canteen could hold 32 quarts of water. The pole flies a cloth flag. The Marine placing the flagpole in the ground was Corp. Harlon Block from nearby Weslaco, who was later killed in battle.

Visit also the *Texas Air Museum* in Rio Hondo, 10 miles east of Harlingen via Farm Road 106, (956) 748–2112. More than fifty vintage aircraft from the first era of flight through the Vietnam war are displayed, and visitors can see the process of current restorations. Open from 9:00 A.M. until 4:00 P.M. daily. A small admission fee is charged.

Good Harlingen eats, such as hearty dishes of smoked pork, beef ribs, hot Polish sausage, chicken, and turkey, are served at *Lone Star* (4201 Business Highway 83, Harlingen 78552, 956–423–8002). It's open for lunch and dinner daily, and prices start at about $8.00. If your mouth waters for huge platters of fajitas, however, head to *Los Asados* (210

Bizarre Texas Stuff

*B*OCA CHICA: Texas Highway 4 leads east from Brownsville in a slightly curving path 24 miles to the Gulf of Mexico. Boca Chica is the name given to the end of the road, where motorists will find a stop sign at the point that the road ends, meeting the sand. There's the beach, period. Apparently the stop sign is meant to keep you from driving straight into the ocean.

North U.S. Highway 77/Sunshine Strip, Harlingen 78552, 956–421–3074). Just south of Harlingen in San Benito, try **Longhorn Cattle Company** (3055 West U.S. Highway 83, San Benito 78559, 956–399–4400). Smoked beef brisket, sweet pork ribs, and all the fixins are served while you watch longhorn cattle graze out in the pastures. Open for lunch and dinner Tuesday through Sunday; prices start at about $8.00.

The final leg of the Valley tour is a 26-mile stint south from Harlingen on U.S. 83/U.S. 77 to **Brownsville,** seat of Cameron County and city of 115,000 Texans. While it's a pleasant place near the ocean and a popular gateway to Mexico, Brownsville's past is tumultuous.

In 1846 President Polk ordered Gen. Zachary Taylor to build a fort at this spot, and the Mexicans understood this to be an act of veiled aggression. Soon the Mexicans invaded Texas here, igniting the Mexican-American War, which counted among early casualties a Maj. Jacob Brown, for whom the fort and city were eventually named. Two important battlefields are found near town, the first being the **Palo Alto Battlefield,** north of town at Farm Road 1847 and Farm Road 511, marked by a historical marker. The other is **Resaca de la Palma Battlefield** on Farm Road 1847 between Price and Coffeeport Streets; a leader in this battle was 2d Lt. Ulysses S. Grant.

Another significant battle site—this in the Civil War—is **Palmitto Ranch Battlefield,** about 14 miles east of downtown via Texas Highway 4. The fight was won by Confederate forces who hadn't heard that Lee had surrendered at Appomattox a month earlier. When the Rebels learned of the South's concession, the victors were taken prisoner by the prisoners.

For a much more modern and nature-oriented attraction, look no further than the **Gladys Porter Zoo,** at Ringgold and Sixth Streets, (956) 546–2177. Widely considered one of the top ten zoos in the nation, this one is special for having no bars or cages. Animals in the thirty-one-acre spread are kept separated by moats and waterways and have room to roam. There are some 1,800 birds, mammals, and reptiles representing five continents. A children's zoo offers petting opportunities and an animal nursery. There's a half-hour, narrated tour aboard a miniature train on Sunday. Open Monday through Friday 9:00 A.M. until 5:30 P.M. and Saturday and Sunday 9:00 A.M. until 6:00 P.M. Admission is charged.

A favorite for Philly cheese-steak sandwiches is *Cobbleheads Bar and Grill* (3154 Central Drive, Brownsville 78521, 956–546–6224), open for lunch and dinner daily. For the most authentic tacos anywhere, check out *El Pato* (1631 Price Road, Brownsville 78520, 956–541–0241), where fillings inside soft tortillas include spicy, stewed beef; potatoes; chicken; cheese; avocado; beans; and *chorizo,* a spicy Mexican sausage.

If you've a hankering for some crashing waves, head just 22 miles east of town on Texas Highway 4 till you find *Brazos Island State Park,* also known as Boca Chica. There's nothing but ocean and a little swatch of sand—it's completely undeveloped, and no facilities are available, so take your own water, drinks, ice chest, snacks, towels, and sunblock. If you're so inclined, feel free to swim, camp, surf, picnic, hunt for seashells and sand dollars, or just stroll the dunes. For Gulf fishing, there's a 1/2-mile-long stone jetty at the northern end of the beach.

Finally, there's one more Tex-Mex adventure to be had: *Matamoros* is a city of a half million and Brownsville's sister across the border, reached by two international bridges. One—Gateway International Bridge—is at the end of International Boulevard, and the other is south at Perl Boulevard, also called East Twelfth Street. Both come out at Avenida Alvaro Obregon, a major thoroughfare in Matamoros. Most gringos find it's better to park on the U.S. side and walk across, then hop aboard a maxicab or minivan, which are cheap and go to all the popular tourist places.

Once there, as in all the Tex-Mex border towns, you'll find the shopkeepers and restaurant servers speak plenty of English, and they'll happily take American dollars. Mexican border towns like this one extend sunny personalities and the *mañana* attitude you've become familiar with all over south Texas. Shopping is a primary reason for making a Matamoros trip, with stores such as *Barbara de Matamoros,* 37 Avenida Alvaro Obregon, Matamoros, heading the list of good ones. Beautiful gifts, bearing appropriate price tags, are the specialty here. Find mammoth, colorful papier-mâché parrots and macaws on brass perches; life-size brass animals; ceramic tableware; jewelry; paintings; weavings; and other crafts from deeper Mexico.

The less pricey goods are sold at *Mercado Juarez,* Matamoros at Nueve/Ninth Streets. All the standard items are here, including silver jewelry, embroidered cotton blouses and dresses, baskets of every description, pottery and glassware, leather crafts, and wood carvings. You'll find the pushiest salespeople here, so bargain like crazy to get the prices you want.

After all that shopping, take a load off and have a ball over drinks and dinner. For something rather elegant, head for *Garcia's,* on Obregon near the bridge, where pretty linens and regal service are part of the pleasures, as are excellent steaks, frog legs, lobster, quail, and Mexican dishes. No less fancy and long popular with Americans is the *Drive-In,* Sexta/Sixth and Hidalgo Streets. Here the crystal chandeliers and red upholstery, bird-filled aviary, and continental dishes—including shrimp, steaks, and lobster—keep crowds coming back.

OTHER PLACES TO STAY IN SOUTH TEXAS

BROWNSVILLE
Holiday Inn Fort Brown Resort, 1900 East Elizabeth Street, Brownsville 78520, (956) 546–2201. Situated right next to the International Bridge, this two-story hotel has two swimming pools, golf privileges, dining room, nightclub, and 168 rooms.

DEL RIO
Amistad Lodge, on U.S. Highway 90 West, Del Rio 78840, (830) 775–8591. It has a look left over from the sixties but suits anyone who wants to be on the water. There's a restaurant, bar, and swimming pool on-site, and some of the forty rooms have kitchenettes.

HARLINGEN
Palmetto Inn, 1524 West Jackson Road, Harlingen 78550, (956) 428–2711.

LAREDO
Howard Johnson, 1 South Main Avenue, Laredo 78040, (956) 722–2411. Just west of the International Bridge and adjacent to River Drive Mall, this hotel has a pool, exercise room, 207 guest rooms, and accepts small pets.

MCALLEN
Rose Garden Inn & Suites, 300 East Expressway 83, McAllen 78503, (956) 630–3333. All ninety-two rooms have coffeemakers and cable TV, and the on-site cafeteria is open for breakfast and dinner.

REYNOSA
La Mansion del Prado, Mendez at Emilio Portes Gil Street, 011–52–89–22–10–25.

SAN ANTONIO
Chabot Reed House, 403 Madison Street, San Antonio 78204, (210) 223–8697. This 1876 Victorian made from local limestone in King William District offers several rooms in the main house with balconies and fireplaces, and two suites in the carriage house open onto gardens. A full breakfast is served.

The Columns on the Alamo, 1037 South Alamo Street, San Antonio 78204, (800) 233–3364 or (210) 271–3245. An 1892 Greek Revival home and adjacent 1901 guest house in King William District offer eleven guest rooms with Victorian antiques and reproductions. Full breakfast is included.

St. Anthony Hotel, 300 East Travis Street, San Antonio 78205, (210) 227–4392. Since 1909, one of the more elegant places to stay downtown; rooftop pool especially appealing. Convenient to the River Walk.

OTHER PLACES TO EAT IN SOUTH TEXAS

BROWNSVILLE

Miguel's, 2474 Boca Chica Boulevard, Brownsville 78521, (956) 541-8641.

LAREDO

Cotulla's Pit BBQ, 4502 McPherson Street, Laredo 78041, (956) 724-5747. Breakfast tacos, soups, barbecue, and Tex-Mex combo plates are offered at this old favorite. Open for breakfast and lunch daily; prices start at about $5.00.

Koto Sushi and Sea Bar, 1010 East Hillside Road, Laredo 78041, (956) 712-2550.

La Roca, 6102 McPherson Road, Laredo 78041, (956) 726-6027.

MATAMOROS

Blanca White's Bar, Grill, and Clothesline, at Avenida Alvaro Obregón No. 49. The local version of the crazy Carlos 'n' Charlie's restaurants in Cancun, Los Cabos, and other big Mexican resort towns, this party-mood place has tacos, enchiladas, fajitas, nachos, as well as excellent grilled fish, plus deadly but delicious margaritas. Open daily from 1:00 P.M. until late at night; plates start at about $5.00.

MCALLEN

Espana, 701 North Main Street, McAllen 78501, (956) 618-1178.

Jalapeño's Bar and Grill, 2013 Nolana Loop, McAllen 78504, (956) 630-2466.

Pecos Red's Roadhouse, 601 Nolana Loop, McAllen 78504, (956) 664-9458.

SAN ANTONIO

Biga, 203 South St. Mary's Street, San Antonio 78205, (210) 225-0722, has made dedicated fans of its upscale fusion (Asian–Southwestern–New American) dishes. Steaks, fish, chops, vegetables, salads, and soups receive any number of treatments in smoking, roasting, poaching, and pan-frying, and it commands medium to high prices for dinner, Monday through Saturday.

Boudro's, 421 East Commerce Street, San Antonio 78205, (210) 224-8484. Possibly the very best restaurant along the River Walk, this one does wonderful blends of Southwestern and Cajun influences in seafood, beef, soups, salads, and fowl. Open for lunch and dinner; the average meal costs $10.

Josephine Street Cafe, 400 East Josephine Street, San Antonio 78205, (210) 224-6169. An unpretentious favorite for years, this restaurant's menu offers great steaks, shrimp, and chicken, while the bar is legendary. Open for lunch and dinner Monday through Saturday; meals average $10.

Liberty Bar, 328 East Josephine Street, San Antonio 78205, (210) 227-1187. Longtime favorite for salads, soups, steaks, seafood, pasta, and fowl. Open daily for lunch and dinner; prices start at about $7.00.

Rudy's Country Store and Bar-B-Q, 24152 I-10 West, San Antonio 78257, (210) 698-0418. Open daily for lunch and dinner, this favorite on the outskirts does good smoked barbecue. Meals average $5.00 to $7.00.

UVALDE

Evett's Barbecue, 301 East Main Avenue, Uvalde 78801. (830) 278-6204, is a local favorite for smoked brisket and barbecue sandwiches. Open for lunch and dinner Tuesday through Saturday.

Rexall Drug and Soda Fountain, 201 North Getty Street, Uvalde 78801, (830) 278-2589, is the place for old-fashioned burgers, shakes, and malts. Open for lunch only.

WESLACO

Cafe Picasso, 702 South Texas Boulevard, Weslaco 78596, (956) 969–8455. Surprisingly upscale for this part of the valley, this cafe is a pretty adobe place where shrimp in white wine, red snapper in a light tomato treatment, and sumptuous desserts are served. Open only for lunch on Sunday and for lunch and dinner Tuesday through Saturday. Meals are typically $9.00 or $10.00.

The Piney Woods

East Texas's Piney Woods region defies so many myths held by those who don't truly know Texas: It's generously green, frequently hilly, and always lush. There are majestic millions of acres of forest—four national forests, to be exact. Rich in ancient pines, cypress, and plenty of hardwoods, this is where Texans make annual pilgrimages in autumn to see fall blazing in its radiant glory. And in spring, country paths in and out of the forest lands are sensational with brilliant explosions of magenta azaleas, frilly pink and white dogwoods, and evening primroses blooming across wild fields in lavender profusion. Amidst the legions of trees pushing skyward are lakes and more lakes, small places and big spreads of water, where lifelong lake residents share space and stories of honey holes with anglers hoping to catch even a little one—shimmering lakes where sailing and waterskiing and watching sunrises are the most important events that will occur in a day, places where timeless Native American legends tell of the Great Creator's work in watery, woodsy artistry.

Everything in the Piney Woods seems fresh and new, though the area has history dating to Texas's origins as a Republic and as a state. Vestiges of the life of Sam Houston—whose later years were spent serving his beloved Texas—are found here, and the state university in Nacogdoches, a wonderful Piney Woods town, is named for the "Father of Texas," Stephen F. Austin. A healthy

> ### Texas Trivia
>
> *The east Texas town of Noonday hosts the annual Onion Festival on the second Saturday in June.*

population of Native Americans, the people of the united Alabama and Coushatta nations, live on a reservation near one of the state's great pioneer living-history museums. Travelers to the Piney Woods can ride restored nineteenth-century railroads or buy baskets that have been made here for more than one hundred years and pottery that has been crafted by generations of the same families, families that helped settle the region. There are no amusement parks or major league athletic teams or four-story shopping malls in the Piney Woods, but you will find a rose garden with 500 varieties that supplies a third of the nation

The Piney Woods

with its commercial roses; the state's antiques capital; Victorian mansions made over into bed-and-breakfast homes, some rumored to be staffed by resident ghosts; and towns offering the World's Richest Acre, the nation's first drill team, a biblical airplane, and some of the best fried alligator tail you could ever hope to savor. That's just a small taste of the Piney Woods.

Deepest East Texas

Begin this journey in **Huntsville,** an hour north of Houston, the Walker County seat and home to 33,000 east Texans. Settled in a very pretty setting of rolling, forested terrain at I–45 and U.S. Highway 190, Huntsville was founded as a trading post in 1836, the same year Texas won its independence from Mexico. Now the home to Sam Houston State University (SHSU), the city is better known as the place to learn more about the life of Sam Houston himself. The **Sam Houston Memorial Museum Complex,** on the SHSU campus at 1836 Sam Houston Avenue, Huntsville 77340 (936–294–1832), is a fifteen-acre spread that belonged to the Texas hero and now holds two of his homes, the furnished Woodland Home and the Steamboat House, the latter of which was the site of his death in 1863. Other buildings there include a law office, kitchen, and blacksmith shop displaying, among other things, some of Houston's possessions, as well as Mexican items taken at the defeat of Santa Anna at San Jacinto. Pack a lunch for this visit, as the grounds have a spring-fed pond with picnic facilities. Open Tuesday through Sunday 9:00 A.M. until 4:30 P.M. Free admission.

There's no better testimony to Houston's huge bearing on Texas than the enormous, 67-foot-tall statue of Big Sam, dedicated in October 1994. Called *A Tribute to Courage,* it's the world's tallest statue of an American hero. Made from thirty tons of concrete and steel, artist David Adickes created the monument from his life-size (6-foot, 6-inch) model, which is seen in the library at Sam Houston State University. See Big Sam at 34000 U.S. Highway 75, off I–45 at exit 109. There's a visitors center with a gift shop; it's open from 10:00 A.M. to 5:00 P.M. Monday through Friday, 10:00 A.M. until 6:00 P.M. Saturday, and 11:00 A.M. until 6:00 P.M. Sunday. Call (936) 291–9SAM for more details.

You can visit Houston's burial site at Oakwood Cemetery, Avenue I and Ninth Street. *Sam Houston's Grave and National Monument* is marked by a tomb bearing Andrew Jackson's sentiment, "The world will take care of Houston's fame." Open always, there is no admission charge.

An entirely different kind of attraction is found at the *Texas Prison Museum* (1113 Twelfth Street, Huntsville 77340, 936–295–2155), where exhibits include the history of the Texas prison, with Bonnie and Clyde's rifle collection; Old Sparky, the electric chair; relics from the Carrasco prison siege; and memorabilia from the famous, defunct Texas Prison Rodeo; plus music and art projects by inmates. Open Tuesday through Friday and Sunday from noon until 5:00 P.M. and Saturday from 9:00 A.M. until 5:00 P.M. A small admission fee is charged.

In warm weather, Huntsville's *Blue Lagoon* (north 6 miles on Farm Road 247, then left on Pinedale Road, 936–291–6111) is the place to go for dips and dives in a quarry filled with sparkling artesian water providing 40-foot visibility. There's an underwater platform at 20 feet and a submerged yacht for divers, and other splashy appeal is found on beach areas. Open Monday through Friday from 10:00 A.M. until 6:00 P.M. and Saturday and Sunday from 8:00 A.M. until dark in spring, summer, and fall. Admission is $15.00 for divers and $5.00 otherwise. Note that non-divers are allowed only with a diver.

To begin your tour of Texas's thick forest country, drive east on U.S. Highway 190 just 2 miles from Huntsville, and you're in *Sam Houston National Forest* (936–344–6205). Covering 160,000 acres in Montgomery, San Jacinto, and Walker counties, this forest contains 27 miles of the 140-mile Lone Star Hiking Trail. To reach this National Recreation Trail, find the trailhead off Farm Road 1725 just northwest of the town of Cleveland on the forest's southern edge. For a map see the forest ranger's offices either at Cleveland or at New Waverly, 13 miles south of Huntsville. There is a $2.00 parking fee per vehicle. Also in the forest, Stubblefield Lake is on the West Fork of the San Jacinto River about 12 miles north and west of New Waverly; there you can go camping ($9.00 per night) and picnicking.

From the forest head east on U.S. Highway 190; you'll immediately see *Lake Livingston,* 52 miles long and lined with 452 miles of wooded shoreline with every sort of recreation. The 640-acre state park on the east shore of the lake offers campsites, screened shelters, group trailers, boat ramps, a store, floating docks and gas docks, showers, and hiking-nature trails. Fishing, swimming, and waterskiing are the most popular pastimes on the lake. For details call the state park at (936) 365–2201.

THE PINEY WOODS

Admission is $3.00 per person for day users; $2.00 per person for overnight users thirteen and older. Groceries, restaurants, and all supplies are available in the town of Livingston, the Polk County seat, 7 miles east of the park.

Two side trips worth your time are directly east from the lake. The first is the **Alabama and Coushatta Indian Reservation** (33 miles east of the lake on U.S. Highway 190, 936–563–4391), home to two Native American tribes that have lived in these woods for a century and a half. Some of their ancestors fought with Sam Houston, and others were Confederates in the Civil War. The 500 people living here offer visitors a chance to observe tribal customs, such as dances and traditional craft work. You can ride a miniature train to tour a traditional village, then visit a museum, gift store, and restaurant. Open in summer Monday through Saturday from 10:00 A.M. until 6:00 P.M. and Sunday from noon until 6:00 P.M. In fall and spring hours are reduced, so please call ahead. Admission is $12 for adults and $10 for children four to twelve; admission is free for children under four.

JUNE'S FAVORITE ANNUAL EVENTS IN THE PINEY WOODS

Azalea and Spring Flower Trail, Tyler, *first weekend in April*

Dogwood Trails Festival, *Palestine, third and fourth weekends in March and first weekend in April*

First Monday Trade Days, *Canton, weekend prior to first Monday of each month*

Helen Lee Daffodil Gardens Tour, Gladewater, *first weekend in March*

Heritage Festival, **Nacogdoches,** *third weekend in March*

Historic Pilgrimage, Jefferson, last weekend in April and first weekend in May

Tour de Palestine Bike Tour, Palestine, *second weekend in March*

About 12 miles east of the reservation, watch for **Heritage Village Museum** (right on U.S. Highway 190, 936–283–2272). This reconstructed pioneer village contains old shops, homes, and vehicles, while photographs, documents, maps, and other aids show the difficult lives of early settlers. A log cabin built on this site in 1866 still has its peg windows and wooden door hinges. Also on the site is a rebuilt 1911 Cherokee church, which was moved from the Cherokee Dies community, northwest of Woodville, in 1990. Open from 9:00 A.M. until 5:00 P.M. daily, admission is $4.00 for adults, $3.00 for seniors sixty and older, and $2.00 for children under twelve.

Don't miss the chance to eat at the nearby **Pickett House** (936–283–3371), a re-created boarding house with family-style offerings including fried chicken, chicken and dumplings, homegrown veggies, stone-ground cornbread, and homemade preserves. Hours vary according to season, so call ahead.

If that's not enough food for you, take note that you're in superior home-cooking country. Just another 2 miles from the Pickett House east on

Pickett House

U.S. Highway 190 is the community of Woodville, where you can pick up U.S. Highway 69 and follow it 8 miles south to the village of Hillister and its superb restaurant, *The Homestead* (936–283–7324). This restored 1912 house behind a white picket fence has a certain rustic charm, with its hardwood floors and walls, and rugs, wallpaper, and furniture from the period—but atmosphere isn't the main appeal of The Homestead. The cornucopia of country cooking is nothing short of outstanding, including smothered or baked chicken, steaks and roast beef, fish and ham, plus irresistible desserts. Be advised that reservations are a good idea at this small place, which serves Friday and Saturday from 5:00 until 10:00 P.M. and Sunday from 11:00 A.M. until 3:00 P.M.

Spend a little time moseying around *Woodville,* a town of 2,000 residents and the Tyler County seat, 90 percent of which is covered in forest. This is another good jumping-off place to explore the Big Thicket National Preserve (see Gulf Coast chapter) and a pleasant place to hunt for antiques. One shop, for starters, is *Another Time Antiques* (112 South Charlton Street, Woodville 75979, 936–283–2119), with furniture, old linens, glassware, kitchen collectibles, primitives, quilts, candles, and homemade jellies.

Back on Lake Livingston, *Davy Crockett National Forest* is 11 miles west from the lake on U.S. 190, then north on Farm Road 356, 12 miles northwest to Sebastopol, where you'll pick up Farm Road 355 and go 14 miles north. This forest, like the other three national forests in Texas, was ravaged early in this century yet has made remarkable recovery in its hardwood and pine populations. The Davy Crockett is 161,000 acres in Houston and Trinity Counties, containing the Big Slough Canoe Trail and Wilderness Area on the Neches River, and the Four C Hiking Trail, a 19-mile path linking the Neches Bluff and Ratcliff Lake. That lake has camping, picnicking, and swimming areas, plus screened shelters and canoe rentals. For maps and facilities go to the ranger station at Ratcliff (936–655–2299) on Farm Road 227 just off Texas Highway 7, or Apple Springs (936–831–2246), in the forest on Texas Highway 94.

While you're in the neighborhood, make a detour to the town of *Crockett,* about 10 miles west of Davy Crockett Forest via Texas Highway 7. Naturally the town—the Houston County seat—was also named for the Alamo hero, and it's said he stopped en route to the Alamo to camp at the springs found at the intersection of Texas Highways 7 and 21, now marked by a historical plaque. Spend some time poking around the quaint town, filled with antiques shops.

At the *Texas Forestry Museum* (1905 Atkinson Drive, Crockett 75901. 936–632–9535), in Lufkin, 12 miles east of the forest on Texas Highway 94, the state's lumber industry is detailed, as well as the impact the forestry-products business has had on the region. Also there's a moonshiner's still, a fire lookout tower, a blacksmith's forge, and a logging train. Open 10:00 A.M. to 5:00 P.M. Monday through Saturday and 1:00 to 5:00 P.M. on Sunday. Admission is free, but donations are welcome.

From Lufkin head 22 miles southeast on U.S. Highway 69 to the *Angelina National Forest,* a 152,000-acre preserve spreading across Angelina, Jasper, Nacogdoches, and San Augustine Counties and wrapping itself

Bizarre Texas Stuff

*M*OSCOW: *Several years before Hollywood reveled in the dinosaur creations of Steven Spielberg, an industrious creator in heavily forested Polk County put together his own Jurassic Park. In the town of Moscow (population 170), on U.S. Highway 59 between Lufkin and Houston, Dinosaur Gardens offers several life-size replicas of prehistoric beasts, such as the triceratops and the Smilodon (saber-toothed tiger). Visitors wandering down a 1,000-foot path in the thick forest hear the roars of the creatures they're seeing.*

around vast **Lake Sam Rayburn.** The lake, exceptionally popular with bass and catfish anglers, has 560 miles of shoreline with numerous marinas and campgrounds. The pine-and-hardwood land gives shelter to deer, squirrel, and turkey, some of which can be seen on the Sawmill Hiking Trail, a 5^1/$_2$-mile path following the Neches River and stretching from Bouton Lake Park to the Old Aldrich Sawmill and Boykin Springs. Along the way you'll find ruins of an old tram line, logging camps, and bridges. Several parks line the lake, offering various concessions. For maps and information, as well as ranger-led activities, check at the ranger office next door to the Texas Forestry Museum in Lufkin (listed earlier); call (936) 639–8620.

After a day on Lake Sam Rayburn, you can rest easy at a pleasant little inn in Jasper, 15 miles south of Angelina National Forest via Texas Highway 63. The seat of Jasper County, Jasper's courthouse square is lined by antiques shops. The **Belle-Jim Hotel** (160 North Austin Street, Jasper 75951, 936–384–6923) is right there, too; the 1910 structure offers private baths and homemade breads for breakfast. There's a cafe on-site, too, that offers weekday lunches of soups, salads, and sandwiches.

From the Angelina forest, head for the **Sabine National Forest** by following Texas Highway 147 to its intersection with Texas Highway 103, which leads east to this last of Texas's four national forests. At nearly 158,000 acres, covering ground in Jasper, Sabine, San Augustine, Newton, and Shelby Counties, the Sabine hugs the 65-mile-long **Toledo Bend Reservoir,** which Texas shares with Louisiana. Along the lake, in the shade of southern pines and hardwoods, are seven different parks, with offerings ranging from picnicking, camping, and swimming to boating areas and nature trails.

Fishing on Toledo Bend is a big attraction to anglers in search of bass, catfish, bluegill, and crappie. Check at the ranger offices for maps, concessions, and activities in Hemphill, in the forest on Texas Highway 87 (936–787–2791).

San Augustine is conveniently found just 8 miles west on Texas Highway 21. A town of nearly 3,000, San Augustine is known as "The Cradle of Texas" and was settled officially in 1832, although it was a community on the Spaniards' Old Road to San Antonio, also called El Camino Real, even earlier. Because a mission was established here in 1716 (and abandoned just twenty years later), San Augustine claims to be the oldest town in Texas. Important historical residents included Sam Houston, who was a San Augustine resident while seeking the Republic presidency, and J. Pinckney Henderson, Texas's first governor.

Although much of the town burned in 1890, there are some good sites still standing, such as the **Ezekiel Cullen House** (207 Congress Street, San Augustine 75972, 936–275–5110). The home belonged to a judge and Texas House of Representatives member who fought for public school lands funding. This Greek Revival house was built in 1839, given to the Daughters of the Republic of Texas by Cullen's family, and is headquarters for an annual tour of homes in April. At press time, the house was undergoing reconstruction to repair damage suffered in high winds. Call ahead for hours and admission fees.

San Augustine's quiet, shady environs are likely to lull you into taking time out from the journey. Maybe it's time to check into **The Wade House** (202 East Livingston Street, San Augustine 75972, 936–275–5489 or 936–275–2553), within walking distance of the historic downtown area. The house sleeps seventeen in six rooms with three private baths and one shared bath, and continental breakfast is offered, as is use of the kitchen.

From San Augustine, continue your tour for 36 miles on Texas Highway 21 to **Nacogdoches** (NACK-ah-DOE-chez), the town generally credited with being the oldest in Texas. The settlement is historically believed to have had hospitable Native Americans—the Caddo people—when the Spaniards came through en route to Mexico, probably around 1541 or 1542. The first permanent European settlement, however, is dated at 1716, when Father Margil founded the Mission of Our Lady of the Guadalupe of Nacogdoches; it was abandoned in 1773, when the settlers were ordered to move to San Antonio.

Several weren't happy and moved back with Antonio Gil Ybarbo to Nacogdoches; in 1779 he laid out the town and built a stone house and trading post there, which survives as **The Old Stone Fort,** the town's most heritage-packed site. An exact replica of Ybarbo's structure sits today on the Stephen F. Austin State University Campus, at Griffith and Clark Streets (936–468–2408). Its long and colorful history includes its service as a fort and a prison, as well as government headquarters during many attempts to establish the Republic of Texas; its function as offices for the first two newspapers published in Texas; and the place that Bowie, Thomas Rusk, Sam Houston, and Davy Crockett were administered the oath of allegiance to Mexico. Nine different flags have flown over the fort, including those from three failed revolutions. Now a museum, the Old Stone Fort offers exhibits detailing this tumultuous past and the people who left an indelible mark on the republic and the state. Open Tuesday through Saturday from 9:00 A.M. until 5:00 P.M. and Sunday from 1:00 until 5:00 P.M. Admission is free, but the museum welcomes donations.

Nacogdoches is fairly flooded with historic sites directly related to the Republic of Texas. One that must not be missed is the **Sterne-Hoya House** (211 South Lanana Street, Nacogdoches 75961, 936–560–5426), built in 1828 by Adolphus Sterne, a prominent landowner who raised $10,000 to outfit a volunteer company to serve in San Antonio. Sam Houston was baptized there in the Roman Catholic faith in 1833 as Mexican law required at the time to become a Texas citizen. Today the home is a memorial library and museum of Texas history since colonization. Open Monday through Saturday from 9:00 A.M. until noon and 2:00 until 5:00 P.M. Admission is free.

Nearby **Oak Grove Cemetery,** Lanana and Hospital Streets, is where four of the signers of the Texas Declaration of Independence are buried. One is Thomas Rusk, secretary of war in the republic, San Jacinto hero, commander-in-chief in Sam Houston's army, and one of the first U.S. senators from Austin. Another is William Clark, the great-grandfather of this author's maternal grandmother. The cemetery is always open, and there is no admission.

Today Nacogdoches—seat of the same-named county—is home to nearly 29,000 residents, some of whom have worked to make a success of several worthy downtown antiques shops, as well as the showplace known as **Millard's Crossing,** at the north end of town (6020 North Street, also U.S. Highway 59 North, Nacogdoches 75964, 936–564–6631). Numerous nineteenth-century homes and commercial buildings have been relocated here in a village setting. Among them is the first Methodist parsonage (1900) and its chapel (1843); a rustic stone-and-log cabin (1830); and the Millard-Burrows House (1840), graced with enormous holly bushes and an iron fence with fleur-de-lys detail. Tours are given Monday through Saturday from 9:00 A.M. until 4:00 P.M. and Sunday from 1:00 until 4:00 P.M. Admission is charged.

Take time out to have a good Mexican lunch or dinner at **La Hacienda** (1411 North Street, Nacogdoches 75961, 936–564–6450). Situated in a lovely home built in 1913, the restaurant has a long reputation for hearty Tex-Mex plates, as well as steaks, chicken, and seafood. It's open daily for lunch and dinner.

Do plan to relax for a few days at the **Llano Grande Plantation Bed and Breakfast,** a complex of three historic homes sheltered deep in the woods immediately south of town. The centerpiece is the Tol Barrett house, a pioneer farmhouse dating to 1840, named for its original owner, the oilman credited as being the first to drill a producing well west of the Mississippi. It's rustic, but most guests find it comfortable.

Its front is framed by myriad wildflowers, and the interior is filled with period pieces. Guests cook their own breakfasts of venison sausage and homemade breads (in the stocked kitchen, of course) in this private house; other guests stay in one of the two other lovingly restored houses, within walking distance of the Tol Barrett. Guests find their hosts to be hospitable and friendly historians. Reservations and directions must be obtained in advance by calling (936) 569–1249. Visit the Web site at www.llanogrande.com.

Another countryside retreat is **Pine Creek Lodge,** 8 miles west of Nacogdoches via Farm Road 225 and Farm Road 2782 (936–560–6282 or 888– 714–1414). The Pitts family has owned the hilly, 140-acre farm near Lake Nacogdoches off and on since before World War II and developed it into a bed-and-breakfast in 1995. Rustic buildings contain a total of fourteen guest rooms filled with handmade furniture, and each has a king bed, sitting area, small refrigerator, private bath, and a basket of candies and fruit. There are terry robes for guests to wear to the hot tub, and a swimming pool is on-site. A full breakfast buffet is offered daily in the main lodge, where guests are welcome to borrow videos and help themselves to popcorn, coffee, tea, and hot chocolate. Weekend steak dinners are available, too.

> ### Texas Trivia
>
> *The first oil well was drilled in Texas in 1886 near Nacogdoches. By 1928 Texas was the leading oil-producing state in the United States, a position that's never been relinquished.*

The Nineteenth-Century Trail

From Nacogdoches head east on the very scenic Texas Highway 21— once the famed El Camino Real—25 miles to the town of Alto, where you'll head north on U.S. Highway 69 for 12 miles to reach **Rusk.** Just under 4,400 people live in the Cherokee County seat, cited for having the nation's longest footbridge, measuring 546 feet, located in Footbridge Garden Park, 1 block east of the town square on East Fifth Street. The town was also the birthplace of Jim Hogg and Thomas Mitchell Campbell, the first and second native-born Texans to serve as governor.

Most visitors come to Rusk with a single purpose, that of riding the **Texas State Railroad,** which has one of its two depots here. **Rusk State Park** is spread with one hundred acres of pines and hardwoods surrounding the train terminal. Not only can you catch the scenic train ride here, but you can camp, hike on trails, picnic, rent paddleboats and rowboats, turn the kids loose in a playground, play tennis, and cast for catfish, bass, and perch in the fifteen-acre stocked lake. The park is 2 miles west of town on U.S. Highway 84, (903) 683–5126; it's open at all times, and admission is charged.

The Texas State Railroad is said to be the longest and skinniest state park in the entire nation, as it offers travelers the chance to ride just under 26 miles between Rusk and *Palestine,* a town directly west. Passengers ride in vintage coaches powered by antique steam engines through gorgeous forest lands, decorated with pink-and-white dogwood blooms in spring and rust-scarlet-gold tapestries in fall. There's a snack bar aboard the train and short-order restaurants at both terminals. The train trip is exceptionally popular, and reservations are a must. In service on weekends from March through May and in October, and Thursday through Sunday in June and July and the first three Saturdays in November. For reservations, schedules, and fares, call (903) 683–2561 or (800) 442–8951 (in Texas only) for reservations.

In Palestine, the Anderson County seat and home to 18,000 Texans, your sightseeing opportunities are varied. The *Howard House Museum* (1011 North Perry Street, Palestine 75802, 903–729–5094) has been established in an 1851 home and offers a doll collection, an array of antique photos depicting early residents and events, and good period furniture. The home is shown by appointment but is usually open during Palestine's *Dogwood Trails,* a popular event among Texans from around the state, as it is a prime opportunity to see the delicate pink-white blooms cover the forests in a dainty blanket. The event is usually held in late March and early April and features tours of historic homes, a parade in historic downtown, an arts and crafts festival, a chili cook-off, a community theater play, trolley tours, and a car show. Contact the festival headquarters at (903) 729–7275.

A great reason to hang around Palestine a little while longer is to dig into one of the choice black angus steaks served at the Ranch House (305 East Crawford Street, Palestine 75801, 903–723–8778). A rustic, upbeat place where you can toss your peanut shells on the floor, the Ranch House also does a good job with grilled chicken and fish. Find it opposite the wonderful Shelton Gin Antiques complex.

Once back in Rusk via the Texas State Railroad, you can continue your journey by driving north on U.S. Highway 69, 14 miles to *Jacksonville,* another Cherokee County town. Known fifty years ago for its abundant tomato crop, the modest city of 12,000 residents today is known for baskets. *The Texas Basket Company* (100 Myrtle Drive, Jacksonville 75766, 903–586–8014) is one of a handful of such companies still in operation in the nation. Established in 1924, this outfit still uses original equipment to make baskets crafted entirely from wood cut within 200 miles of town, including sweet gum, black gum, birch, hackberry, elm, cottonwood, and sweet bay. Between 6,000 and 10,000 baskets are produced daily for shipment to all fifty states, as well as to Canada, Germany, and Puerto Rico. Visitors can watch craftspeople at work, and most will want to spend some shopping time in the large store, stocked with thousands of baskets in every imaginable shape and size. Open Monday through Saturday from 8:00 A.M. until 5:00 P.M. Admission is free.

Look also at *Jackson Street Mercantile* (1201 South Jackson Street, 903–586–0282), a restored turn-of-the-twentieth-century home where antiques and collectibles are sold. Or look in *Smith-Barrett Antiques* (531 North Bolton Street, 903–586–5123), where the inventory includes eighteenth- and nineteenth-century American, French, English, and Oriental furniture, and home accessories, rugs, antique bamboo boxes, brass and copper pieces, designer lamps, and nineteenth-century porcelains.

While you're in Jacksonville be sure to eat at *Sadler's Kitchen* (221 South Main Street, 903–589–0866), which by day is a good place to have anything from deluxe sandwiches and salads to pot roast and grilled chicken. But on Friday and Saturday nights it's open for lovely dinners of pecan-crusted rainbow trout and shrimp with spinach fettuccine. The restaurant doubles as an antiques shop, too. Closed on Monday.

Travelers who enjoy a leisurely drive filled with exquisite scenery will rejoice in the countryside surrounding Jacksonville. Take a picnic to *Love's Lookout Park,* on the roadside 5 miles north of town on U.S. Highway 69. Or just take a few soft drinks and soak in the hilly vistas of forest and water on Farm Roads 747 and 2138 wrapping around Lake Jacksonville.

For a lake of greater import, follow U.S. Highway 175 from Jacksonville 17 miles west to Frankston and catch Texas Highway 155 north, which crosses *Lake Palestine,* a 25,500-acre impoundment on the Neches River in this rolling timberland. Anglers especially will want to spend time here, as the lake is known for record catches, such as a twelve-pound striper bass and a twelve-pound largemouth bass. Waterskiing is popular here, as well. Marinas and campgrounds surround the lake, as do numerous catfish restaurants serving up the freshest local catches.

From the east side of Lake Palestine, continue north on Texas Highway 155 another 13 miles to *Tyler,* the Rose City of Texas. The Smith County seat, Tyler has more than 75,000 residents. After the Civil War, nurserymen found the sandy soil and rainfall ideal for growing fruit trees and roses.

ONE MAINSTREAM ATTRACTION WORTH SEEING IN THE PINEY WOODS

In Tyler, your kids will enjoy seeing Brookshire's World of Wildlife Museum and Country Store (1600 West Southwest Loop 323 at the Old Jacksonville Highway, 903–534–2169). One section features stuffed and mounted critters from Africa and North America, including some 250 specimens of animals, reptiles, and fish. The Country Store illustrates the kind of marketplace found in east Texas in the late 1920s, complete with products and fixtures. A 1926 Model T Ford delivery truck and an antique fire truck are on-site, too. Closed Sunday and Monday.

The fruit trees became diseased before the turn of the twentieth century, however, and the rose business carried these growers happily into the 1900s. Today more than a third of the nation's commercially grown rose bushes are raised within a 50-mile radius of Tyler.

Visitors revel in the glory found at Tyler's **Municipal Rose Garden** (1900 West Front Street, Tyler 75701, 903–531–1212), where more than 30,000 rose bushes in 500 varieties fill a fourteen-acre park—making it the country's largest municipal rose garden. The blooming season peaks in mid-May and continues through November. The garden is open daily from 6:00 A.M. until 10:00 P.M. Admission is free.

This huge rose business gives rise to the **Texas Rose Festival,** a giant celebration held every October, complete with the crowning of a Rose Queen, a rose show featuring more than 100,000 roses, and parades, balls, antiques shows, crafts fairs, and more. Call the chamber of commerce at (903) 592–1661 for details.

Tyler is well known for its **Caldwell Zoo** (2203 Martin Luther King Drive, Tyler 75701, 903–593–0121), begun in 1938 as a backyard menagerie. Today it's a thirty-five-acre spread with wonderful, lush settings for elephants and giraffes, birds, bears, alligators, flamingos, and numerous ducks from around the world. There's a monkey island, an aquarium, and a native Texas exhibit. Open daily from 9:30 A.M. until 6:00 P.M. April through September and until 4:30 P.M. the rest of the year. Admission is free.

Should you find yourself in Tyler and starving for performing arts, check out the schedule at the **Cowan Center on the University of Texas/Tyler campus** (3900 University Drive, Tyler 75703, 903–592–1427). Typical playbills include the Vienna Boys' Choir, the Russian National Ballet, and Hal Holbrook in his Mark Twain show.

You also might consider a visit to the **Tyler Museum of Art** (1300 South Mahon Street, Tyler 75701, 903–595–1001). Exhibits featured here have included one on Latin American textiles and another entitled Self-Taught Artists of the Twentieth Century. Open from 10:00 A.M. until 5:00 P.M. Tuesday through Saturday and from 1:00 until 5:00 P.M. Sunday. Admission is free.

The sweetest place to stay in Tyler is the *Rosevine Inn* (415 South Vine Avenue, Tyler 75701, 903–592–2221). A 1930s-style home in a bricked-street area becoming well known for good antiques shops, the inn is surrounded by a white picket fence with well-manicured grounds. The interior is thoughtfully decorated as an inn, its cozy corners and comfortable rooms scattered with antiques and country decor. All six rooms have a private bath, and there's a hot tub on the patio. Breakfasts are gourmet affairs.

Another excellent choice is the *Woldert-Spence Manor* (611 West Woldert Street, Tyler 75701, 903–533–9057 or 800–WOLDERT), an 1859 home built by a German immigrant and civil engineer. The home has been added on to over the years, and today it's an elegant inn with original stained glass windows, chandeliers, several porches and fireplaces, and five guest rooms. A full breakfast is served on antique china. (You can tour the house on the Internet by clicking onto www.woldert-spence.com).

Also luxurious is *Charnwood Hill* (223 East Charnwood Street, Tyler 75701, 903–597–3980). An 1855 Greek Revival mansion, it was home to oil baron H. L. Hunt and continues to be a showplace in Tyler's oldest neighborhood, spreading over two acres with gardens often used for weddings. The main house has five elaborately decorated rooms and suites, while a guest house—once the kitchen and servants' quarters— has another room. A full breakfast is served in one of two downstairs dining rooms in the main house.

Tyler's selection of good eating places has grown at a surprising rate. For traditional Southern breakfasts and juicy burgers, try *Cox's Grill* (706 West Front Street, Tyler 75701, 903–593–8940). A longtime favorite for lasagna, veal, shrimp, pastas, and cozy dinners is *Mario's* (6701 South Broadway, Tyler 75703, 903–581–2309). For excellent Cajun and Southern seafood dishes, you can't beat *Cace's* (7011 South Broadway, Tyler 75703, 903–581–0744), where service, oysters Rockefeller, shrimp remoulade, and shrimp and scallops Diane are superb.

> ## The War Between the States
>
> *In the spring of 1864, a place called Camp Ford had a stockade holding some 6,000 Union troops, making it the largest prisoner-of-war compound west of the Mississippi. You can see a historical marker noting the place in a rest area on U.S. 271, about 2 miles northeast of Tyler.*

Tyler is a central location for various east Texas side trips. One to keep in mind is a jaunt to *Edom,* 15 miles west of Tyler via Texas Highway 31 and Farm Road 279. A tiny artists' enclave, Edom has become known for its extraordinary annual arts and crafts show held in September, with juried works drawing artists from around the nation. Several artists—mostly crafters of pottery, leather, and brass—keep shops in town right on the main street, which is Farm Road 279. These shops don't keep regular hours, so you have to take your chances. Next to a row of shops on the road is *The Shed,* a simple country cafe serving huge lunches and dinners, with specialties including pork chops, chicken-fried steak, catfish, and enormous coconut, banana cream, and chocolate pies. The cafe's phone number is (903) 852–7791.

Most travelers come to Edom, however, to stay at *Wild Briar,* a pretty, modern home on twenty-three acres in the country operating as a bed-and-breakfast inn. A large den serves as a parlor, where guests gather by the fireplace before dinner or breakfast: The hosts have hosted more than a dozen weddings there. Dinners are an event, with cheese vegetable soup, eye-of-round roast beef, three fresh vegetables brought from the Farmers' Market in Dallas, grilled potatoes, and black-bottom pie or peach cobbler composing a typical meal. Breakfast is nearly as elaborate. A British theme is carried throughout the inn, as the hosts have spent years traveling in England, Scotland, and Wales. For reservations call (903) 852–3975.

Another option is an excursion to *Kilgore,* 25 miles east of Tyler via Texas Highway 31. Crude, classics, and kicks aren't what most people expect in an east Texas town of 11,000: Home to the *World's Richest Acre,* Kilgore has the mammoth success of the Great Texas Oil Field discovery in 1930 to thank for its prosperity, but the community is best known as giving the world its most famous classical pianist, Van Cliburn, who now resides in Fort Worth; it's also responsible for the phenomenon known as the drill team.

First the oil business: Head to the corner of Main and Commerce Streets, a small area with one life-size derrick and twenty-three miniderricks representing the oil boom days when more than a thousand wells were jammed into the downtown area and twenty-four wells, claimed by six different operators, were crowded onto a one-acre site, creating the World's Richest Acre, which produced more than two and a half million barrels of crude oil.

To see the industry explained in an interesting manner, visit the *East Texas Oil Museum,* Henderson Boulevard at Ross Street on the Kilgore College campus (903–983–8295), and see how a town grew from 800 to 8,000 residents in twenty-four hours. There's a working oil rig out front, with a 70-foot wooden derrick, steam boiler, rotary table, and draw works. A realistic model of a 1930s street is created inside, complete with a car stuck in the mud, board sidewalks, post office, barbershop, general store, sounds of a thunderstorm building overhead, and music from a period radio. Firsthand accounts of boom-town existence can be heard through headphones; a fifteen-minute film of actual footage is shown in a "town theater," with the theater rumbling during a gusher; and an elevator takes riders to the center of the Earth. This just scratches the surface of the museum's offerings; see for yourself Tuesday through Saturday from 9:00 A.M. until 4:00 P.M. (9:00 A.M. until 5:00 P.M. Tuesday through Saturday from April through September) and Sunday from 2:00 until 5:00 P.M. Admission is $4.00 for adults and $2.00 for children three to eleven years of age.

For something radically different, and certainly more frivolous, walk down the street a block to the *Rangerette Showcase,* also on the Kilgore College campus, at Broadway and Ross Streets (903–984–8531). In this little corner of east Texas is yet another worldwide attention getter, born ten years after the oil boom began. The Kilgore Rangerettes formed their first high-kick line in 1940, and the showcase tells the story of this famous precision-and-drill dance team of Kilgore College. Some may say it is sexist, but many will argue it's just Texas camp. The first of their kind, Red Grange called them the "sweethearts of the nation's gridiron," and they perform annually on New Year's Day at the Cotton Bowl halftime, their painted red lips matching their shirts, contrasting with little blue skirts and white boots and cowgirl hats. The group responsible for putting showbiz on the football field is chronicled through an assemblage of displays with historical films and videos and decades of newspaper clippings illustrating the team's global reach. The showcase is open Monday through Friday from 9:00 A.M. to 4:00 P.M. and Saturday from 10:00 A.M. to 4:00 P.M. Admission is free.

Even if these attractions don't draw you to Kilgore, probably *The Country Tavern,* on Texas Highway 31 just on the western outskirts of town, will. Most patrons are from all over Texas, and many will argue that this unassuming beer joint serves the best pork ribs in the state. A juke box and dance floor are good for dancing the Texas two-step, and blue-jeaned waitresses are good for friendly local color. For more than thirty years, this place has served up the biggest platter of ribs in memory, with sides of tasty potato salad, onions, and pickles. Open Monday through Saturday for lunch and dinner, the tavern's phone number is (903) 984–9954.

Still another side trip from Tyler is *Mineola* (minny-OH-lah), north 27 miles on U.S. Highway 69. An impressive collection of antiques shops brings folks to Mineola, but it's the *Munzesheimer Manor* (202 North

Newsom Street, Mineola 75773, 903–569–6634) that makes them stay. The remarkable 1906 home—with stained-glass windows, seven fireplaces, wraparound porch, and footed tubs—has been thoroughly restored and decorated with English and American antiques. It's a huge, comfortable home, perfect for settling in with a cup of tea and a good novel. Breakfasts during the week are continental, while weekends are full affairs with such treats as fresh berries and German pancakes.

Munzesheimer Manor isn't the only B&B to note in Mineola, however. Another wonderful place is **The Noble Manor** (411 East Kilpatrick Street, Mineola 75773, 903–569–5720). A stately, white Greek Revival home built from 1910 to 1913, it has original hardwood floors, vintage chandeliers, fireplaces in the dining and living rooms, as well as five rooms in the main house. The adjacent **Brooks House** has three guest suites, each with private entrances, and there's a lover's hideout called Cupid's Cottage, once the servants' quarters. Just a block away, The Lott Home Cottages (311 East Kilpatrick, Mineola 75773, 903–569–0341) is a 1918, two-story Southern home with suites in cottages, private baths, porches with rocking chairs, antiques, bicycles, and TVs.

Amidst Mineola's antiques shops, a wonderful find is **Kitchen's Hardware & Deli,** at the corner of Pacific and Broad Streets. Part museum and part retailer, the vintage store has old auger bits and ancient tools on display, as well as new stuff, ranging from plumbing supplies and Case knives to American flags and Marshall pottery. In front there are some picnic tables where you can lunch on the deli's roast beef sandwiches,

June's Texas Anecdotes

*P*INEY WOODS: When I visited a farm/bed-and-breakfast, I was very curious as to why there was electrical wiring on the cow pen behind the barn. Owner Susie Joiner, who lives in the home between the guest houses and the barn, explained that one of the cows in the pen had discovered how easily the gate to the pen opens, and because the cow is so fond of her owners, she wanted to spend more time closer to them. Susie would awake at night to hear a slurping noise coming from the French doors of her bedroom, which open onto a deck on the back of the house. The cow—after climbing up the steps to the deck— was trying to turn the knob on one of the doors with her mouth. After several nights of this, Susie told her husband, Brad, to do something about it fast, or they'd be eating a lot more beef at supper. Brad finally wired the pen with electrical charges, and the cow has chosen to stay in her pen rather than endure the shock.

German sausage plate, homemade chili, or specials such as cornbread, beans, and greens. Or, get an old-fashioned root beer float to go. Another stop might be Miss Scarlett's Tea Room (408 South Pacific Street, 903–569–5316). Lunch is served Monday through Saturday.

While you're in the area, drive 10 miles north from Mineola on Texas Highway 37 to the town of Quitman, home to **Governor Hogg Shrine State Historical Park** (903–763–2701). The only park in the state with three museum buildings, it's named for Rusk-born James Stephen Hogg, who served as governor of Texas from 1891 to 1895. The honeymoon cottage of Hogg and his bride, Sallie Stinson, is on-site, as is the Miss Ima Hogg Museum, named for their daughter.

Fishing enthusiasts will want to linger in this area, as 27,000-acre **Lake Fork** (fewer than 10 miles west of Quitman, via Texas Highway 182) is where record-setting bass are caught annually. The lake is surrounded by marinas where you'll find good fishing guides, while Lake Fork Lodge offers everything from comfortable rooms, hot tubs, a game room, bass boats, licensed guides, dog kennels, fishing pier, and full breakfasts with your stay. Find the lodge on the southern end of the lake at the intersection of Texas Highways 17 and 515 at the town of Alba, (903) 473–7236.

Your next destination is Canton; head west of Tyler 40 miles on Texas Highway 64, and you'll wind up directly at the Van Zandt County Courthouse Square, just a few yards beyond your actual destination, **First Monday Trade Days.** If you arrive early and are lucky, you may be able to find a parking spot on the square or nearby, then just walk the block east to the one-hundred-acre fairgrounds, where some 5,000 vendors are spread out with their goods for sale. This, of course, occurs the Friday, Saturday, and Sunday preceding the first Monday of each month. Since the middle of the nineteenth century, country folks have been traveling here to buy and sell everything from kitchen wares, clothes, farm equipment, furniture, and toys to baby carriages, jewelry, homemade jellies and jams, and books. Collectors of Depression glass, quilts, iron beds, and china find this a great place to hunt bargains. Food booths are set up everywhere, too, selling burgers, barbecue, pastries, and cold drinks. It's a colorful experience well worth taking in, even for visitors who aren't in the market to buy anything. Trade Days gates open at 7:00 A.M. and close at dark; for information call the chamber of commerce at (903) 567–2991.

From Canton head south on Texas Highway 19 almost 30 miles to the town of **Athens,** a celebrity in east Texas on two counts. First, it's known as the Black-Eyed Pea Capital of the World, and its citizens celebrate the

Southern legume on the third weekend in July with the Black-Eyed Pea Jamboree. Athens is known, too, as the birthplace of the hamburger. Look on the north side of the Henderson County Courthouse Square, next to the 1927 First National Bank Building, and find a historical marker. It explains that on this site in the late 1880s, a cafe owner named Fletcher Davis (1864–1944) created the first hamburger sandwich. He took his invention for exhibit at the 1904 St. Louis World's Fair, in fact. Family members and local friends, as well as the resources of the McDonald's Hamburger Univeristy, support this story.

In more recent years Athens has become a terrific place to find good antiques at reasonable prices. A row of great shops called **Athens Alley** lines North Prairieville Street, just north of the Henderson County Courthouse square. You'll enjoy spending time and money at the Alley Antique Mall (400 North Prairieville, Athens 75751, 903–675–9292), where numerous dealers are located.

Athens has become nationally famous in the past couple of years for its proximity to **Black Beauty Ranch** (18 miles east of town off Texas Highway 31, via Farm Road 1803 and County Road 3806, 903–469–3811). Open to the public only on Saturday from 9:00 A.M. until 4:00 P.M., the ranch is a setting for modern-day miracles in the form of a 1,150-acre refuge for abandoned and abused animals of all sorts, from chimpanzees, burros, and elephants to dogs, cats, and horses. Founded in 1979 by the late author Cleveland Amory and the Fund for Animals, the ranch is operated as a nonprofit facility supported primarily by donations. Today several hundred animals are guaranteed a healthy, safe home for their lifetimes at this extraordinary sanctuary. Call ahead to have a guide show you some of these wonderful, living stories.

In town, be sure to take the kids to visit the **Texas Freshwater Fisheries Center** (5550 Flat Creek Road, Athens 75751, 903–676–BASS), a 106-acre operation of the Inland Fisheries Division of the Texas Parks and Wildlife Department. Here you'll learn about the "sharelunker" program, designed to increase the production, size, and quality of Florida largemouth bass in Texas waters.

The massive visitors center—named for Athens native Edwin L. Cox Jr., a former chairman of the Parks and Wildlife Foundation of Texas, rancher, and conservationist—presents an introduction to this intriguing aquarium and hatchery complex, which houses some 300,000 gallons of more than forty fishy representatives from the state's freshwater streams, ponds, and lakes. Among hundreds of things to see (and often, to catch) are some of the heftiest largemouth bass in the world and the American alligator. The fisheries center is open from 9:00 A.M. to 4:00 P.M., Tuesday through Saturday and from 1:00 to 4:00 P.M. Sunday. Admission is charged.

Two bed-and-breakfast lodgings worth noting are found in the Athens area. Oak Meadow (Farm Road 2495, 903–675–3407 or 877–675–3407) was built in 1983 as a quarter horse breeding ranch and serves as a real escape to the countryside today. Three guest rooms have private baths and one has a television. Pine Cone Country Inn is a renovated 1960s Athens home with four bedrooms and private baths; call (800) 449–PINE or (903) 479–3807.

This last side trip done, you'll want to head on from Tyler to *Big Sandy,* 30 miles north on Texas Highway 155. A burg of just 1,100 in Upshur County, Big Sandy is home to the *Victorian Village,* an unusually busy complex for such a tiny town. What started as a kitchen-table business of mail-order sales of needlework patterns in the 1970s has exploded into a retailing and hospitality industry spread over several buildings splashed with pastel paints and endearing Victorian appeal. First there's The Village Tea Room, at U.S. Highway 80 and Texas Highway 155, a sweet place to have breakfast, lunch, or tea; offerings typically include cold strawberry soup, cream-cheese-stuffed French toast, chicken salad, and orange muffins. It's open daily from 11:00 A.M. until 3:00 P.M. Call (903) 636–4952 for information. Next door there's a gift shop and needlework-catalog publishing business. Directly across the street is *Annie Potter's Victorian Village Bed and Breakfast,* a house with thirteen rooms. It's all lacy and frilled, with small but comfortable rooms. The parlor downstairs usually winds up being a good place to meet fellow travelers over a cup of tea or a glass of wine. For reservations call (903) 636–4355 or (800) BB–ANNIE.

If you're looking for more rib-sticking fare, drive west from Big Sandy just 7 miles on U.S. Highway 80 to *Petty's Cafe* (903–769–4806), in the tiny town of Hawkins, right on the highway. Here you'll find comfort in thick chicken-fried steaks; fat burgers in little paper wrappers; meaty BLTs; the biggest, crustiest onion rings anywhere; and great homemade apricot fried pies.

From Big Sandy it's only 10 miles east on U.S. Highway 80 to the *Antique Capital of East Texas,* seen on the map as Gladewater, a town of 6,000 Texans in Gregg County with more than 250 antiques dealers scattered around in sixteen antiques malls and sixteen individual shops. Most of the shopping is concentrated in Gladewater's vintage downtown area, all within easy walking distance from one point to another.

Slow down long enough to enjoy lunch at *Glory Bee Baking Co.* (111 North Main Street, Gladewater 75647, 903–845–2448), a good place for soups, salads, sandwiches, and rich desserts; it's also open for dinner on Saturday. There's a bed-and-breakfast upstairs if you're too full to go on. Call Honey Comb Suites at (800) 594–2253.

Before you leave Gladewater, be sure to check out *One Horse Gallery* (207 West Commerce Street, Gladewater 75647, 903–845–6621), a gallery featuring original western and equine art by noted artist and author Monty Graham.

From Gladewater continue east to *Longview,* 13 miles east on U.S. Highway 80. The unassuming town of 70,000 is the Gregg County seat and has a heritage of railroad, agriculture, lumber, and oil businesses that left it somewhat undistinguished. This has changed, however, in recent years, as the popularity of the *Great Texas Balloon Race* has skyrocketed. For a three-day weekend in mid-July, hundreds of brightly colored hot air balloons can be seen scattered throughout the sky in early morning or evening as pilots from around the nation compete in tests of skill. The contest involves a pilot's ability to maneuver the balloon between points and drop a marker on a designated target—all of which is determined by the winds. Besides the flights, there are on-ground events during the festival, such as arts and crafts fairs, aircraft exhibits, evening concerts, and other fun for spectators. The party is held at the Gregg County Airport; information is available from the chamber of commerce, (903) 753–3281. Admission is free, but parking fees are charged.

Two other diversions are worth investigating in Longview. First, the *Gregg County Historical Museum* is a modest but interesting collection of area memorabilia detailing the growth of the county from the late nineteenth century through World War II. The bank building, built in 1910, makes a handsome home for the museum, lending itself to exhibits such as a period bank president's office and vault. A hands-on area is good for children. Find the museum at 214 North Fredonia Street (903–753–5840). Admission is charged; the museum is open Tuesday through Saturday from 10:00 A.M. until 4:00 P.M.

If you've worked up an appetite, head for *Bodacious Barbecue,* 227 South Mobberly, Longview 75602, (903–753–8409), an east Texas institution famous for its chopped-beef sandwiches as well as sliced beef brisket, ribs, and spicy links. Open Monday through Saturday 10:00 A.M. until 7:00 P.M.

With bellies full, try to find the strength to push on to *Marshall*, 23 miles east on U.S. Highway 80. The Harrison County seat, with almost 24,000 residents, has a deep Southern heritage imbued with plantations and Civil War history—in fact, more than 150 historical markers are found throughout Harrison County. So strong is its legacy that newsman Bill Moyers, Marshall's favorite son, hosted a PBS broadcast titled "Marshall, Texas, Marshall, Texas" in his *A Walk Through the 20th Century with Bill Moyers.*

People whose artistic tendencies run toward throwing clay may have already heard about Marshall's famous retailer, *Marshall Pottery,* an old-fashioned business that celebrated its centennial in 1995. Found at 4901 Elysian Street, Marshall 75671, the pottery is the largest manufacturer of red clay pots in the nation, but it retains every bit of its friendly country charm. Master potters—some of whom are third- and fourth-generation potters—can be observed at their craft, some painting the cobalt-blue decoration commonly seen on the glazed bowls, pitchers, mugs, and dinnerware. These items are all for sale and are always reasonably priced. Under the same roof are twenty shops with savings on baskets, silk flowers, linens, candles, and other decorative housewares. Outside, a "seconds" yard is filled with slightly misshapen or barely chipped pottery—look for real steals here on many things that don't appear to be damaged at all. Next to the main building, a Victorian cottage houses the Hungry Potter, a cafe open for lunch daily. Soups, salads, and sandwiches are better than average, but the pies, cobblers, and other sweets are worth a long look. Open Monday through Saturday from 9:00 A.M. until 6:00 P.M. and Sunday from 10:00 A.M. until 6:00 P.M. Admission is free; the phone number is (903) 938–9201.

Artistic expression of a different nature is in the *Michelson Museum of Art* (216 North Bolivar Street, Marshall 75671, 903–935–9480), a small treasure house of works by French impressionist Leo Michelson (1887–1978). His work is also displayed in museums in Baltimore, Jerusalem, Paris, San Diego, and Tel Aviv, among others. Traveling exhibits fill the gallery, as well. Open Tuesday through Friday from noon until 5:00 P.M. and Saturday and Sunday from 1:00 until 4:00 P.M. Admission is free.

The folks in Marshall are big on celebrations, and the *Fire Ant Festival,* held annually on the second weekend in October, is a fine example. Some 50,000 people have been known to pour into town for a party dedicated to a truly aggravating insect, so you know this is a place with a sense of humor. Costume contests, fire ant calling contests, a chili cook-off, the World Championship Pizza Crust Fling, and a parade are among the wild and woolly events. Things calm down a bit in time for the holidays, and Marshall lights up like a Christmas tree—literally. The Wonderland of Lights is focused on the historic county courthouse, which is covered with four and a half million tiny white lights, and area businesses and homes are aglow, as well, from Thanksgiving until New Year's Day. For information on special events, call the chamber of commerce at (903) 935–7868 or (800) 953–7868.

The first of two lovely lodgings to consider in Marshall is Heart's Hill (512 East Austin Street, Marshall 75670; 903–935–6628 or 888–797–7685), a fancy 1900 Queen Anne design that was built by a local doctor. Prepare to prop your feet up on the wraparound veranda and watch the world go by. Four guest rooms have private baths, and breakfast is a large, lavish spread. And on the grounds of the beautiful Starr Family Home State Historical Park, find Rosemont Cottage (407 West Travis Street, Marshall 75670, 903–935–3044), offering one bedroom, private bath, TV, and telephone.

Music fans will find a worthwhile detour 31 miles south of Marshall, via U.S. Highway 59, in the town of Carthage. In the summer of 1998, Panola County residents welcomed the new *Texas Country Music Hall of Fame at the Tex Ritter Museum* (300 West Panola, Carthage 75633, 903–693–6634). The first inductees were the late Jim Reeves, whose nearby grave is noted with a Texas Historical Marker, as well as Gene Autry and Tex Ritter. The museum is filled with honorees' guitars, stage clothing, gold records, and photographs. Hours vary according to season, so call ahead.

Bayous, Lakes, and Legends

From Marshall you need travel only 14 miles northeast on Texas Highway 43 to find one of the state's greatest natural assets, *Caddo Lake.* The only lake in Texas not created artificially, the 35,400-acre lake is characterized by seven-century-old cypress trees draped in an ethereal manner with heavy curtains of Spanish moss. The effect nature has wrought is one of a haunting beauty, appropriate for a place whose creation is a mystery. One legend holds that the reservoir was formed when a resident Caddo Indian chief was warned by the Great Spirits to move his people to a higher ground or watch them die in a terrible earthquake and flood. It seems he ignored them and chose to take his warriors hunting, as they returned to find that a mighty shake had occurred and their village had been replaced by a huge lake. Some part of the story could be true, as recorded history shows that an earthquake in 1811 in New Madrid, Missouri, is estimated to have had a force that would register 8.9 on today's Richter scale—and it's possible that that tremor created a logjam in the Red River that dammed Caddo Lake, lapping a bit across the Louisiana state line.

Naturally, photographers and painters are captured by Caddo's ancient beauty, best seen on boat tours led by lake experts. These sloughs and canals are terribly confusing to anyone unfamiliar with its shrouded paths, but the fishing and wildlife watching are far too wonderful to pass up. Inquire about guides at **Caddo Lake State Park** on Texas Highway 43, (903) 679–3351.

At the state park, on Farm Road 2198, just 1 mile east of Texas Highway 43 (903–679–3351), several rock cabins—which have been completely remodeled and updated—are available for rental, but they are reserved for weekend stays up to ninety days ahead, so call early or try for a weeknight stay. Shaded by towering pines near the water, these are nice places to kick back for a while. Canoe rentals are offered in the park, as is camping, fishing, hiking, picnicking, and nature study. One of the canoe outfitters to try is **Caddo Canoe Rentals & Boat Tours** (in Caddo Lake State Park, 903–679–3743). Note that it is closed on Wednesday.

Caddo Lake

Adjacent to the park is the tiny community of *Uncertain*—and no one's certain how the name came about. One theory is that when the hamlet was contemplating incorporation, a poll was taken to choose a town name, and "Uncertain" was frequently listed on the third-choice line. Of one thing you can be sure, there is a cluster of little businesses offering rustic accommodations, marina and fishing guide services (helpful in navigation and landing big catfish and bass), cafes, and good humor. Among these multiservice places are Shady Glade (903–789–3295) and Hodge Podge Cottages (903–789–3901). More lodging is available at the Mossy Brake Lodge (903–789–3440); and at Uncertain Inn (Farm Road 2189, on the lake, 903–789–3292).

If you don't sign up for a fishing tour, be sure to book a ride with Caddo Lake's Steamboat Company (888–325–5459, 903–789–3978, or 903–665–1665), a Southern-style paddlewheel boat operating from Uncertain. Tickets are $15; call well in advance for a schedule and reservations.

One of the most delightful lodgings to open in east Texas in years is the very simple but mighty comfortable *Cypress Moon Cottage,* near the town of Uncertain on Caddo Lake (903–679–3154). A charming house on stilts, just a few yards from the water, the cottage has two bedrooms, one bath, a big living area, and a full, roomy, completely outfitted kitchen. It's perfect for a family or for friends traveling together; you can sit on the deck and watch the dawn arrive or the night fall, and you can canoe beneath the moss-draped trees from your own little dock.

A little side trip into history from Caddo is a short drive away at *T. C. Lindsey and Company General Store,* found by following Farm Road 134, 13 miles east in the town of Jonesville. In business since 1847, it's still a family-owned, no-frills country store. With high ceilings and creaky wooden floors, this general store is obviously the real McCoy. Shelves are stacked with groceries, fabrics, and feed, while a room off to the side is now a makeshift museum. You'll find farm tools, ancient hunting traps, horseshoes, massive iron skillets, and other relics from another time. Glass cases in front hold antique eyeglasses, glass bottles, toiletries, and household items used by our grandparents and great-grandparents. Snacks, candies, cold drinks, and slices from a massive wheel of cheese will tide you over until supper. The store is open Tuesday through Saturday from 8:00 A.M. until 4:00 P.M. Admission is free; call the store at (903) 687–3382.

From Caddo Lake your next destination could be the old bayou town of *Jefferson,* a town packed with charm and romance, reached west from the lake 13 miles on Farm Road 134. The Marion County community of 2,200 is rapidly growing in stature around the state for its perfect balance of historical preservation and hospitality.

A good place to call home during a few days of relaxation and exploration is *The Excelsior House* (211 West Austin Street, Jefferson 75657, 903–665–2513). The second-oldest hotel in Texas, the Excelsior has been in continuous operation since 1858 and has hosted dignitaries such as Ulysses S. Grant, Rutherford B. Hayes, W. H. Vanderbilt, Oscar Wilde, and Lyndon B. and Lady Bird Johnson. A beautiful place with ornate furniture and heavy, baroque French frames around paintings; crystal chandeliers; Oriental carpets; a grand piano; Italian marble mantels; and pressed-tin ceiling; it's a showplace as well as a delightful setting in which to have a plantation breakfast—by reservation, of course. The fourteen rooms and suites are in demand on weekends, so call ahead or try for a midweek visit.

The Excelsior's 1961 restoration spurred revitalization throughout the town, which had fallen into a quiet decline after its riverboat days were

Jefferson

long past. In the nineteenth century steamboats churned the waters of the Big Cypress Bayou from Jefferson, via Caddo Lake and the Red River, all the way south to New Orleans. Today's visitors can still tour the bayou aboard the *Turning Basin River Boat tour,* an open-air boat departing Jefferson Landing four times daily in spring, summer, and fall for one-hour, narrated tours. Call (903) 665–2222 for hours and rates.

Another way to see the water and woodsy environs is aboard the *Jefferson and Cypress Bayou Railroad,* a narrow-gauge railroad powered by an antique steam locomotive winding along the bayou on a scenic, 5-mile route; this is another great way to gain an overview of the town. Tours are offered on weekends. Call (903) 665–7454 for details and schedule updates.

You can also take a steamboat tour aboard the *Graceful Ghost,* which plies the Caddo Lake waters. Contact the *Caddo Lake Steamboat Company* in Jefferson, (903) 789–3978, for rates and schedules.

For more background on the town and area, head for *Jefferson Historical Society Museum* (223 West Austin Street, Jefferson 75657, 903–665–2775), where history lessons are made fun. Housed in a former federal courthouse and post office (1888), this big red gem of the past contains three floors of the historical society's collected memories. More than 30,000 visitors come annually to see the dress Lady Bird Johnson (from nearby Karnack) wore to a State dinner for the West German chancellor; sterling silver flatware that belonged to Whistler's mother; and personal belongings of Sam Houston and Annie Oakley. Open daily. Admission is charged.

For a great, fresh lemonade or scoop of ice cream, visit *City Drug & Old Fashioned Soda Fountain* (109 West Lafayette Street, Jefferson 75657, 800–287–0378), where books and all sorts of souvenirs and gifts are sold.

A Blast from the Past

*T**he Texas Heritage Archives and Library opened in Jefferson in late 1997, to offer visitors a treasury of more than 600 rare and historic maps of Texas, the Southwest, and the New World. Inside, the research library has the largest existing collection of Texas bank notes, as well as land grants dating from the first Anglo settlements. The museum is found within the 1865 Haywood House Hotel. (903) 665–1101.*

Dozens of antiques shops are found along the brick streets of downtown in historic commercial buildings. Some beautiful nineteenth-century homes are open for tours year-round, while eight designated homes are chosen annually to be on show during the *Jefferson Pilgrimage*, always held the first weekend in May. The weekend features not only the homes but also the **Diamond Bessie Murder Trial**, a wonderful melodrama based on the story of a former prostitute who was thought to have been murdered by her rich diamond-merchant husband. For pilgrimage information contact the chamber of commerce, (903) 665–2672, or the Jessie Allen Wise Garden Club, event hosts, at the Excelsior Hotel, (903) 665–2513.

Jefferson is said to be the birthplace of Texas bed-and-breakfast offerings. The very first is thought to be *Pride House* (409 East Broadway Street, Jefferson 75657, 903–665–2675), a gabled Victorian home built in 1888 and noted with a Texas Historical Marker. There are original stained-glass windows in each room and elegant period furnishings throughout. The downstairs parlor is frequently used as a setting for small weddings. A guest cottage in back, called The Dependency, offers accommodations for up to twelve guests. Breakfasts are usually something elaborate, with baked fruit, egg casseroles, and any number of breads.

Also among the finer B&Bs in the state is *McKay House* (306 East Delta Street, Jefferson 75657, 800–468–2627 or 903–665–7322). An antebellum home built in 1851 bearing state and national historical markers, this home has hosted guests such as Lady Bird Johnson, Alex Haley, Martin Jurow, and George Bush's staff. Each of the seven guest rooms has a private bath, Victorian nightgowns and sleep shirts, and bath goodies. The "gentleman's breakfast" is always something special. Featured in *Vacation* magazine as "One of the Ten Most Romantic Inns in America," McKay House is extremely popular, so make reservations early.

Jefferson's dining options are numerous. Lunch at the *Hamburger Store* (203 Market Street, Jefferson 75657, 903–665–3251) means good burgers, taco salads, fries, and homemade fruit pies. For lunch and dinner try *The Galley Pub* (121 West Austin Street, Jefferson 75657, 903–665–3641), a series of parlors where salmon, shrimp, and steaks are served. A lively spot for nachos and beer is *Auntie Skinner's River Boat Club* (107 West Austin Street, Jefferson 75657, 903–665–7121), while the town's most elegant dinners of grilled veal chop, red snapper, and dessert soufflés are served at *Stillwater Inn* (203 East Broadway Street, Jefferson 75657, 903–665–8415).

For complete details on Jefferson, call the Marion County Convention & Visitors Bureau at (888) 467–3529.

For a detour into curiosity, take an hour's drive north from Jefferson on U.S. Highway 59 to **Texarkana,** sometimes called the State Line Cities, as it's part Texas, part Arkansas—hence, the name. Of particular interest here is **The Perot Theatre** (at 221 Main Street, Texarkana 75501, 903–792–4992), an Italian Renaissance theater opened as The Saenger in 1924. Seating 1,600 patrons, it was among the most famous showplaces in a four-state area in its heyday. In the late 1970s, Texarkana native, now Dallas billionaire, Ross Perot donated two million dollars to restore the theater to its former magnificence with glistening chandeliers, royal-blue and gold interiors, and marble floors. A symphony series, plays, musicals, and pop music concerts are staged here from September through May. Tours are by reservation, depending on scheduled events.

Most unusual in Texarkana is the **Bi-State Justice Center** (100 North State Line Avenue, Texarkana 75501, 903–798–3000), a building straddling the Texas-Arkansas line and, therefore, shared by two cities, two counties, and two states. It is thought to be the world's only post office and federal building with a state line bisecting it. As was appropriate, the building was crafted from both Texas pink granite and Arkansas limestone. The building is open Monday through Friday from 8:00 A.M. until 5:00 P.M.; tours are free and by appointment.

Texarkana hosts the annual Scott Joplin Multi-Cultural Music Festival in late November to honor the ragtime master who came from this town. The two-day, outdoor festival is held downtown; call (903) 792–7191 for schedule of events.

Once you've laid eyes on the **Mansion on Main** (802 Main Street, Texarkana 75501, 903–792–1835), you won't want to leave Texarkana any time soon. Built in 1895, the inn is found in the downtown historic area and bears a state historical marker. The front exterior is noteworthy for fourteen, two-story columns that came from the Mississippi Exhibit at the St. Louis World's Fair in 1904. There are six guest quarters, including the Butler's Garret and the Governor's Suite, all with private baths and antique furnishings. Snacks usually include Scottish shortbread or bread pudding, and the lavish breakfast often features orange French toast, Chicken à la Mansion, shirred eggs with ham, blueberry pancakes, or homemade breads.

From Jefferson there is still much to be seen in the way of outdoor beauty. To sample this bounty drive west from Jefferson on Farm

THE PINEY WOODS

Road 729 for 17 miles and you'll find yourself at the shores of shimmering *Lake o' the Pines,* surrounded by lush hardwoods and pines, a scene that's splendid in autumn, as the leaves make quite a show of changing to crimson, burnt orange, and amber. The lake is 18,000 acres, with excellent fishing for large-mouth, white, and spotted bass; swimming, waterskiing, and sailing are favorites here, too. Campsites abound, as do picnic areas and nature trails. The Army Corps of Engineers, (903) 665–2336, offers more information.

About 10 miles north of the lake via U.S. Highway 259, the town of *Daingerfield,* Morris County seat and home to 2,500 Texans, offers supplies, groceries, lodging, and an excellent array of cheesecakes and other sweets at Main Street Bakery. Check out the offerings available at the chamber of commerce, 208 Jefferson Street, (903) 645–2646.

At *Daingerfield State Park,* immediately east of town on Texas Highway 11, 550 acres of pine-blanketed land surround a lovely, eighty-acre, spring-fed lake. Photographers have traveled from around the state to capture the color riot in autumn, and spring's demonstration is just as dramatic, as redbuds, dogwoods, and wisteria explode in shades of pink and purple. Hiking trails, fishing, camping, cabins, playgrounds, and picnic areas make this a place to stay for more than a day. For information and reservations call the park office at (903) 645–2921.

From Daingerfield, travel west 16 miles on Texas Highway 11 to *Pittsburg,* the Camp County seat and home to 4,000 residents. Its economy is based on a significant poultry business—Pilgrims Pride alone produces more than 600 million pounds of chicken yearly.

The chicken business may be big here, and there is a Spring Chick Festival held in Pittsburg in late April, but the primary food found here is the *Pittsburg Hot Link.* The not-too-spicy sausage made from beef and pork is, appropriately, served up hot at the Pittsburg Hot Links Restaurant (136 Marshall Street, 903–856–5765). Patrons place their orders at the counter in back, ordering links by the link or choosing from other specialties, such as beef stew, chili, burgers, or chicken-fried steak. The restaurant is open Monday through Saturday from 8:00 A.M. until 6:00 P.M.

Like so many other towns in east Texas, Pittsburg has a growing antiques industry. One shop worth finding is *Pittsburg Victorian Furniture & Antiques,* 106 Jefferson Street, Pittsburg 75686 (903–856–6848).

Bizarre Texas Stuff

*P*ITTSBURG: *This modest town is regionally famous for possessing the Ezekiel Airship, a replica of a 1902 flying craft that, while undocumented, is said to have been airborne a year before the Wright Brothers made their first flight. Its inventor was an inspired, sometime Baptist preacher who took his idea of an airship from the prophet Ezekiel, who described in the Bible an apparatus* *that flew. The preacher raised $20,000, sold stock in his company, and built his ship. Unfortunately it was destroyed during shipment to the St. Louis World's Fair in 1904. The 26-by-23-foot replica was for many years displayed at a restaurant in Pittsburg. Now it's on view at the Northeast Texas Rural Heritage Center and Museum, 200 West Marshall Street, (903) 856–0463.*

There's been substantial growth in the bed-and-breakfast business, as well. Try **Carson House Inn & Grill** (302 Mount Pleasant Street, Pittsburg 75686, 903–856–2468), a century-old home with gorgeous woodwork, gothic windows, chandeliers, and an elegant restaurant. There's also **Mrs. B's Cottage Guest House** (512 Quitman Street, Pittsburg 75686, 903–856–6232).

Before heading back to your cabin at Daingerfield, your campsite at Lake o' the Pines, or your cozy corner in Jefferson, consider another detour, this time to **Winnsboro,** a pleasant hamlet just 22 miles west of Pittsburg on Texas Highway 11. There's another pretty lake here for a dip in summer, but the primary attractions come after the weather begins changing. Fall foliage is a cause for big celebrations, hence the **Autumn Trails Festival,** held every weekend in October. The chamber of commerce hosts an antique car show and a homes tour; driving maps to see the best in fall's color parade are offered, too. And the Christmas season brings folks from all over east and north Texas to choose a special tree from one of the several area Christmas-tree farms; hot apple cider is a bonus offered by the farmers while customers find the prettiest evergreen. For details contact the chamber of commerce, 201 West Broadway Avenue, Winnsboro 75494, (903) 342–3666.

One of the finest, most praised bed-and-breakfast inns in the state happens to be in Winnsboro. **The Hubbell House** (307 West Elm Street, Winnsboro 75494, 903–342–5629) is an 1888, two-acre plantation estate containing a mansion, where there are five luxurious guest rooms and suites and a wonderful carriage house with six guest rooms. All have private baths, and all stays include a full plantation breakfast in the mansion.

OTHER PLACES TO STAY IN THE PINEY WOODS

ATHENS

Avonlea Bed & Breakfast, 410 East Corsicana Street, Athens 75751, (903) 675–5770.

Carriage House Bed & Breakfast, Route 2, Box 2153, Athens 75751, (800) 808–2337.

Oak Meadow Farm Bed & Breakfast, 2781 Farm Road 2495, Athens 75751, (903) 675–3407.

CANTON

Pine Cone Bed & Breakfast Country Inn, on Texas Highway 19, 15 miles south of Canton and 12 miles north of Athens, (903) 479–3807 or (800) 449–PINE. Situated on sixty wooded acres, this B&B's four guest rooms are named Juniper, Spruce, Cedar, and Ponderosa, and all have private baths. Guests share a sunroom with a fireplace; a full country breakfast is included.

CROCKETT

Warfield House, 712 East Houston Avenue, Crockett 75835, (888) 988–8800 or (409) 544–4037.

JEFFERSON

Breckenridge House, 502 Houston Street, Jefferson 75657, (903) 665–7738.

Small garden cottages with kitchenettes afford lots of privacy.

Falling Leaves Bed & Breakfast, 304 Jefferson Street, Jefferson 75657, (903) 665–8803. Antiques fill four guest rooms.

Old Mulberry Inn Bed & Breakfast, 209 Jefferson Street, Jefferson 75657, (903) 665–1945 or (800) 263–5319.

The Claiborne House, 312 South Alley Street, Jefferson 75657, (903) 665–8800 or (877) 385–9236. This restored 1872 home has rooms with private baths named for poets Browning, Yeats, Tennyson, Wilde, Dickenson, and Keats. Ask about the Jacuzzi tubs and king-size beds.

Clarksville Street Inn, 107 East Clarksville Street, Jefferson 75657, (903) 665–6659 or (877) 665–6659. An updated 1860s home that offers an elegant guest room with a king-size bed and private bath with Jacuzzi in the main house and two romantic queen suites with Jacuzzis and showers in the Carriage House. Breakfast is included.

The Daniel House, 502 East Taylor Street, Jefferson 75657, (903) 665–7840. Surrounded by giant trees and wrapped by a massive veranda, this pretty, old home has a bedroom and bath in the main house, as well as a guest house and a carriage house.

Hale House, 702 South Line Street, Jefferson 75657, (903) 665–8877. A renovated nineteenth-century Greek Revival home in easy walking distance of downtown, offering six lovely rooms with private baths, enclosed sun porch, gazebo, antiques, and a big, gourmet breakfast.

NACOGDOCHES

Anderson Point, 29 East Lake Estates, Nacogdoches 75964, (936) 569–7445.

Haden Edwards Inn, 106 North Lanana Street, Nacogdoches 75964, (936) 559–5595.

Hardeman Guest House, 316 North Church Street, Nacogdoches 75964, (936) 569–1947.

Stag Leap Retreat, Route 3, Box 1267, Nacogdoches 75964, (936) 560–0766.

QUITMAN

Fall Farm, Farm Road 779, 3 miles west of town, (903) 768–2449. This country retreat is on ten pine-covered acres. Five guest rooms include three suites, and guests are treated to tea cakes, pies, cookies, a breakfast buffet, and a swimming pool.

UNCERTAIN

Blue Heron Inn Bed and Breakfast, Big Oak Road, Uncertain 75661, (903) 679-4183.

Caddo Cottage, Route 2, Box 66, Uncertain 75661, (903) 789-3988. A secluded, two-story cottage with two bedrooms and two bathrooms, A/C, color TV, deck, patio, gas grill, full kitchen, and boathouse.

Hodge Podge Cottages, Route 2, Box 55B, Uncertain 75661, (903) 789-3901.

Mossy Brake Lodge, P.O. Box 473, Karnack 75661, (903) 789-3440. One bedroom and bath with living room, TV, kitchenette, continental breakfast, picnic area, hammock, and waterside setting. Fishing guide available.

Spatterdock, Route 2, Box 66B, Uncertain 75661, (903) 789-3268. Three guest houses, one with three bedrooms and two baths, one with four bedrooms and three baths, and one with one bedroom and bathroom. All have fully equipped kitchens. The hosts offer fishing and hunting guide services, too.

WOODVILLE

The Antique Rose, 612 Nellius Street, Woodville 75979, (409) 283-8926. A bed-and-breakfast tucked inside a southern plantation Federal-style house.

**OTHER PLACES TO EAT
IN THE PINEY WOODS**

JEFFERSON

The Bakery and Restaurant, 201 West Austin Street, Jefferson 75657, (903) 665-2253. Draws a great breakfast crowd for raisin bread done French toast-style, coffee, and chat.

NACOGDOCHES

Aubrey's Café, 1523 East Main Street, Nacogdoches 75964, (936) 560-9557. Old-fashioned meat loaf, smothered chicken, chicken-fried steak, veggies, and desserts.

Mike's BBQ House, 1622 South Street, Nacogdoches 75964, (409) 560-1676.

Smoke House Meat and BBQ, 2709 Westward Drive, Nacogdoches 75964, (409) 560-6714.

TYLER

Allen's Steak House, 4111 Troup Highway, Tyler 75703, (903) 509-2535. A former bicycle store now houses a lovely place for grilled steaks, lamb, pork chops, and fried frog legs. Open for dinner Monday through Saturday.

Mansion on the Hill, Texas Highway 64 East at Spur 124, Tyler 75703, (903) 533-1628. A 1936 mansion is now a restaurant serving wild game, shellfish, steaks, lamb, and pasta. Open for lunch 11:00 A.M. to 2:00 P.M. Tuesday through Friday and for dinner at 5:00 P.M. Monday through Saturday. Dinner averages $12 to $15.

North Texas

orth Texas mirrors the Lone Star State's uncanny ability to wear a vast number of different hats. Denying any one classification or description, the region exhibits a broad range of personalities. Big D, as Dallas is proudly called in the Southwest, was built largely from the fruits of the oil and cattle industries and is known as well as a major fashion, electronics, and motion pictures center. Further, Dallas boasts having more restaurants per capita than any city in the nation, and the city joins Fort Worth in being home to teams competing in every professional sport. Together the two are called the Metroplex. Fort Worth, 30 miles east, is also called Cowtown, and it is famous for a curious mix of Wild West and world-class fine arts. In addition, Fort Worth has a restored stockyards area where Butch and Sundance hid out and where today you can "scoot a boot" in the world's largest honky-tonk.

Travelers to the north Texas region find that in perfect balance to this unusual cosmopolitan–Wild West mix are the small towns where a simpler way of life is still valued. Communities that gave the world such dignitaries as Sam Rayburn and Dwight D. Eisenhower are special places that continue to live in yesteryear, where historic houses and pretty lakes—instead of shopping malls and symphonies—are the draws. Exotic wildlife ranches, a quiet Norse community, a rustic ranch where city folks can play cowpoke for a day, an ancient riverbed where dinosaur tracks are plainly visible—these are the places where people go to escape fax machines and voice mail.

Red River Country

ldest town in the Red River Valley and home to more than 6,600 residents, the Fannin County seat of **Bonham** was settled in 1837 by a former Arkansas sheriff who brought settlers to a land grant he received from the Republic of Texas. The community was eventually named for James Butler Bonham, the Alamo's courageous messenger, whose statue stands before the courthouse.

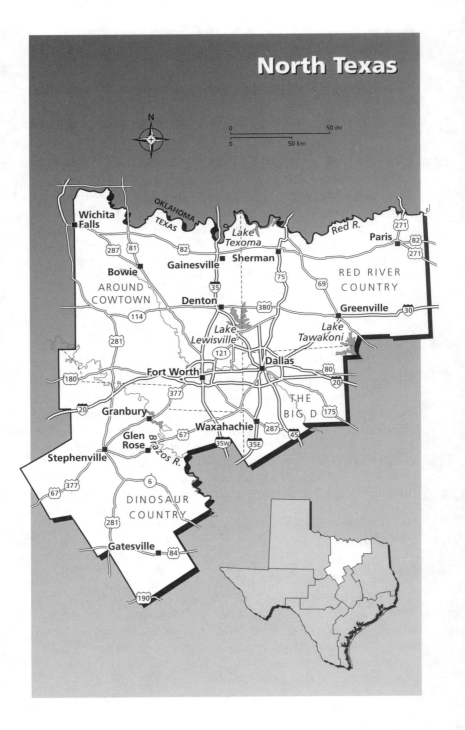

North Texas

JUNE'S FAVORITE ATTRACTIONS
IN NORTH TEXAS

Acton State Historic Site,
Acton

Ballpark in Arlington,
Arlington

Hall of State, Dallas

Kimbell Art Museum,
Fort Worth

Mineral Wells State Park,
Mineral Wells

Ranchman's Cafe, Ponder

Sam Rayburn Library,
Bonham

Sixth Floor Museum,
Dallas

The Dove's Nest,
Waxahachie

White Elephant Saloon,
Fort Worth

But Bonham's greatest claim to fame is Sam Rayburn, the political legend who spent forty-nine consecutive years, or twenty-five terms, in the U.S. House of Representatives—seventeen of those as Speaker of the House. Mr. Sam, as he was fondly called, is remembered at the **Sam Rayburn Library** (800 West Sam Rayburn Drive, Bonham 75418, 903–583–2455), which holds a perfect replica of his Capitol Hill office, with all furnishings. A host of his memorabilia is displayed here, including a gorgeous white marble rostrum that was used by every House speaker from 1857 until 1950. Other interesting artifacts are a collection of political cartoons, gavels, and a 2,500-year-old Grecian urn Rayburn received from the Athens Palace Guard. The library was donated to the University of Texas, whose students come to use it for research. It's open Monday through Friday 10:00 A.M. until 5:00 P.M., Saturday 1:00 until 5:00 P.M., and Sunday 2:00 until 5:00 P.M. Admission is free.

Rayburn, who was born in Tennessee in 1882, moved to Texas with his parents in 1887. The **Sam Rayburn House,** 1 mile west of town on U.S. Highway 82 (903–583–5558), is a fourteen-room home he built for his parents in 1916. Modest but comfortable, it's been restored, along with the grounds, to the look it had upon his death in 1961. It's open Tuesday through Friday 10:00 A.M. until 5:00 P.M., Saturday 1:00 until 5:00 P.M., and Sunday 2:00 until 5:00 P.M. Admission is free. Rayburn's funeral was attended by President Kennedy, Vice President Johnson, and former presidents Truman and Eisenhower; Rayburn is buried in Bonham's **Willow Wild Cemetery,** on West Seventh Street at Texas Highway 121. The large monument there bears the impression of a gavel and the simple epitaph, MR. SAM, 1882–1961. The cemetery is never closed, and no admission is charged.

If you happen onto Bonham in October, see if you're in time for the **Fannin County Fair,** a wonderful tradition more than a hundred years old, with livestock shows, baking and other homemaker contests, a carnival, and entertainment. Call the chamber of commerce at (903) 583–4811.

Also in Bonham, see the **Fannin County Museum of History** (1 Main Street, Bonham 75418, 903–583–8042), housing pioneer furniture, tools, vintage clothing, toys, Native American artifacts, and photographs depicting life in one of the counties of the Republic of Texas. A genealogical and historical library and the Red River Valley Art Gallery are also located here. Open from 10:00 A.M. until 4:00 P.M. Tuesday through Saturday between April 1 and September 1. Open from noon until 4:00 P.M. Tuesday through Saturday the remainder of the year. Admission is free.

From Bonham follow U.S. Highway 82 west 15 miles, then head north on U.S. Highway 69 another 13 miles to *Denison,* a town of 21,000 in Grayson County. It's best known for being the gateway to *Lake Texoma,* created from the mighty Red River by the building of Denison Dam, the nation's largest rolled earth-fill dam upon its completion in 1944. The enormous reservoir on the Texas-Oklahoma line covers 89,000 acres and has fifty parks, more than one hundred picnic areas, and plenty of recreation facilities along 580 miles of shoreline. Travelers come from a three-state area to the resort hotels and motels and marinas surrounding these waters, and anglers spend time on the lake catching record black bass, striper bass, crappie, and lunker catfish. Many of today's vacationers head for the 14-mile Cross Timber Hiking Trail that hugs the water. See the Denison Chamber of Commerce at 313 West Woodward Street for specific information (903–465–1551).

Lake Texoma has dozens of places to stay right at the water's edge. The nicest of all is *Tanglewood Resort* (903–786–2968), where accommodations range from hotel rooms to master suites complete with kitchens. Rates are about $100 to $250. Options include *Lake Texoma Lodging,* 236 Paradise Cove Road in Pottsboro 75076, (903) 786–9037; houseboat rentals at *Willow Springs* (580–924–6240); and motel-style lodging at *Lake Texoma Resort* (580–564–2311).

Interesting that the same year the dam was completed, Denison's most famous son became an all-time American hero. Five-star general and two-term U.S. president Dwight D. Eisenhower is remembered at the *Eisenhower Birthplace* at 208 East Day. The two-story frame house saw the birth of the great soldier and leader on October 14, 1890, and it's been restored to that period. The family moved a short time later to Abilene, Kansas, but there is an Eisenhower family quilt displayed in the bedroom where Ike was born. His large bronze statue makes a great place for souvenir photos of the family. People interested in taking the "Ike Hike" on the ten-acre reserve should make reservations. Open daily from 10:00 A.M. until 5:00 P.M. A small admission fee is charged; for information call (903) 465–8908.

Don't miss Denison's charming *Red River Railroad Museum* (101 East Main Street, Suite 120, Denison 75021, 903–463–6238). The small

JUNE'S FAVORITE ANNUAL EVENTS IN NORTH TEXAS

Chisholm Trail Round-Up, Fort Worth, mid-June

Hoop it Up, Dallas, last weekend in June

Irish Festival, Dallas, first weekend in March

Main Street Arts Festival, Fort Worth, third weekend in April

Mayfest, Fort Worth, first weekend in May

New Vintage Wine and Art Festival, Grapevine, mid-April

Pioneer Days, Fort Worth, weekend prior to Labor Day

Scarborough Faire, Waxahachie, late April through early June

Shakespeare in the Park, Dallas and Fort Worth, throughout June

Southwestern Livestock Show & Rodeo, Fort Worth, late January

State Fair of Texas, Dallas, late September and early October

museum inside the vintage railroad station is the official repository of historical records and artifacts of the Katy Railroad Historical Association and will delight any train buff. Open from 10:00 A.M. until 1:00 P.M. and from 2:00 until 4:00 P.M. Monday through Saturday. Admission is free. Right across the street, check out the marvelous inventory at Katy Antique Station (104 East Main Street).

Sherman, 9 miles south of Denison on U.S. Highway 75, is the Grayson County seat and a city of 31,000 people. Settled in 1846, it was named for Sidney Sherman, a Battle of San Jacinto leader and hero credited with the well-known cry, "Remember the Alamo! Remember Goliad!" To see some of the lovely homes and buildings from Sherman's late-nineteenth-century boom, grab a map from the chamber of commerce (307 West Washington Street, Sherman 75090, 903–893–1184), which covers places dating from 1883.

Among buildings of special note in Sherman's downtown is the American Victorian Furniture Museum (201 East Lamar Street, Sherman 75090), housed in a historic church building; Kelly Square (115 South Travis Street, Sherman 75090), a three-story complex of antiques shops, art galleries, and charming cafes in the gorgeous Kelly Building, built in 1915; and the C. S. Roberts House (915 South Crockett Street, Sherman 75090), an Eastlake-style home built in 1886 and maintained today by the Sherman Preservation League.

Many of Sherman's beautiful Victorian homes and buildings—there are thirty-three on the downtown walking map, for starters—are opened to the public during the city's Preservation League Tour of Homes in April and the Pilgrimage of Homes in December. Contact the chamber of commerce for details.

Austin College (900 North Grand, Sherman 75090, 903–892–9101) is the oldest college in Texas operating under an original charter. Several firsts include being the state's first college to grant a graduate degree, the first to start a law school, and the first to have a national fraternity. A bell hanging in the chapel was a gift from Sam Houston, one of the first trustees of the college. Plays and concerts are staged by the theater and music departments, and monthly art exhibits are held.

Directly across the street from Austin College, *Hart's Country Inn* (601 North Grand Street, Sherman 75090, 903–892–2271) occupies a lovely Victorian home that was a hospital upon its erection in 1898. It became a home when the Naylor family bought it in 1905 (and this author's grandfather was raised there), and after loving and historically accurate restoration, a bed-and-breakfast in 1988, now with five individually decorated guest rooms, including a bridal suite. The inn is filled with antiques, many of which guests may buy.

For still another look at history, stop in at the *Red River Historical Museum* (301 South Walnut Street, Sherman 75090, 903–893–7623), which occupies a wonderful 1914 Carnegie Library building, listed on the National Register of Historic Places. Among exhibits are a room of furnishings and artifacts from Glen Eden, the main house of a grand Red River plantation that was dismantled upon the creation of nearby Lake Texoma; a 1900 country store; and an excellent collection of World War II aircraft models. Open Tuesday through Friday 10:00 A.M. until noon and 1:00 until 4:30 P.M., and Saturday and Sunday from 2:00 until 5:00 P.M. Admission is $2.00.

Now you may want to head west on U.S. Highway 82, stopping 33 miles down the road at *Gainesville,* the Cooke County seat and home to 14,000 people. Some of their ancestors were forty-niners headed to California during the gold rush, and some of these were freethinkers in their day: When most Texans wanted secession in the 1860s, Cooke County folks were against it, and some of them created a secret society supporting the Union.

The surrounding area is now renowned for its rich quarter horse ranches, seen on country drives from town. Downtown, however, is a charming, bricked square with its nineteenth-century appeal intact, augmented by a cluster of antiques shops, one of which contains a cute little tearoom.

Stop in at the local chamber of commerce (101 South Culbertson Street, Gainesville 76240, 940–665–2831) and pick up a driving tour map of historic Gainesville. There are thirty-four homes and buildings on the map, including some beautiful homes dating from the 1880s.

Chances are you'll want to spend time exploring the town square, whose centerpiece is the majestic *Cooke County Courthouse,* a four-wing, four-story limestone work with a polygonal, art-glass dome, built in

1910. Look for remaining detail work, such as the mosaic tile in the entryway at Otis Furniture on the west side of the square.

As you make your way around the square, some things to note are the office of KXGM-FM radio, an oldies station on the west side of the square with outdoor speakers to let shoppers hear hits by the Monkees and other groups; Watts Bros. Pharmacy, an old-fashioned drugstore with Elizabeth Arden make-up and a soda fountain, established in 1915, on the northwest corner of the square at Commerce and California Streets; and Val's Antiques, also at Commerce and California, occupying the ground floor of an old brothel and calling itself "the best little antique house in Texas."

Other antiques shops are Miss Pittypat's, on the north side of the square on California Street; Carousel Antique Mall, on the east side of the square on Dixon Street; and Track Side Antique Mall, a few blocks east of the square on California Street at Lindsay Street. A nonantiques shop that's especially appealing is Bella Matiz (on the square's north side, on California Street), a purveyor of Southwestern art, furniture, and jewelry.

Right on the courthouse square, find a pleasant diner called the *Fried Pie Co. & Restaurant* (corner of Commerce and Main Streets). Framed stained glass is hanging in the window and a huge chandelier hangs from an original pressed-tin ceiling. Burgers, club sandwiches, and a salad bar are offered, and delicious slices of homemade fried pies—including peach, cherry, coconut, Dutch apple, and apricot—are $1.35.

Most shoppers today, however, are arriving in droves to spend time and money at the spectacular *Gainesville Factory Shops,* I–35 at exit 501, (940) 668–1888. The retailers with wholesale or better prices—anywhere from 25 to 75 percent off is the norm—number above sixty and include such top-notch names as Ann Taylor, Brooks Brothers, Reebok, Nine West, and Guess?. Plan to go early, as there are more places worth looking into than at the usual outlet mall.

Food of the fast variety is available at that shopping center, but you'll find a far more interesting taste experience down the road in *Muenster,* about 14 miles west of Gainesville via U.S. Highway 82. In this minute German town, you'll easily find the *Center Restaurant & Tavern* right on U.S. 82, (940) 759–2910. It's open for breakfast, lunch, and dinner daily from 6:00 A.M. until 10:00 P.M.; specialties are outstanding pork schnitzel, German potato salad and sauerkraut, homemade sausages, and apple strudel.

On the way to or from Muenster, slow down in the minute town of Lindsey, about 3 miles west of Gainesville on U.S. Highway 82. Have a look inside *St. Peter's Church,* ornately adorned with frescoes, stained-glass windows, and carved altars, imparting a distinctly European look. Much of the work was done by Friedolin Fuchs, a Swiss national who was stranded in Texas during World War I.

Before heading away from Gainesville, make a detour 5 miles north of town on I–35 to the Texas Travel Information Center. Here you can pick up hundreds of pieces of free literature, such as state highway maps, colorful guides, and brochures pertaining to every city and nearly every town in Texas. The travel counselors at these centers are especially helpful. Open daily from 8:00 A.M. until 5:00 P.M.

If German fare doesn't grab you, and the idea of fantastic barbecue piques your interest (and taste buds), you'll want to head for *Tioga,* south from Gainesville on I–35 for 10 miles, then east on Farm Road 922 for 17 miles. Another super-tiny town, this one is on the old M-K-T rail line and is in the heart of that rolling, multimillion-dollar horse ranch country.

The object of this drive is to have a lunch or dinner that will remain long in your memory at *Clark's Outpost,* on Texas Highway 377 at Gene Autry Lane, (940) 437–2414. Looks can be deceiving, and this little brown roadhouse appears to be leaning a bit to one side, but the interior is warm and homey, as is the service. Find smoked brisket, ribs, turkey, and river trout, plus lots of vegetables, great barbecue sauce, and sensational homemade pies. The walls are covered with photos of championship horses from nearby ranches, as well as celebrities—supermodel Christie Brinkley is just one—who love this Texas chow. It's open Monday through Thursday from 11:00 A.M. until 9:00 P.M., Friday and Saturday until 9:30 P.M., and Sunday until 8:30 P.M.

From Tioga drive about 20 miles south on U.S. Highway 377—skirting scenic Lake Ray Roberts—to U.S. Highway 380, and go west about 7 miles to *Denton,* seat of the county bearing the same name and home to 70,000 residents. Besides being home, too, to the University of North Texas, Denton is the site of Texas Women's University, where you'll find *Little Chapel in the Woods,* at Bell and University Streets. Designed and built in 1939 by noted architect O'Neil Ford, it's considered one of the country's finer architectural achievements. Art melds with nature, as the stained-glass window (designed by students) depicts *Woman Ministering to Human Needs.* Open daily from dawn to dusk; telephone (940) 898–3601.

Also on the TWU campus, in the Human Development Building (117 Bell Avenue, Denton 76201, 940–898–3201), the *DAR Museum* houses the inaugural gowns of the first ladies of Texas. The only one of its kind in existence, the collection features either the original garments or faithful copies. Open from 8:00 A.M. until 5:00 P.M. Monday through Friday and by appointment. Admission is free.

Denton's appealing courthouse square earned the town a national designation as a Main Street City. Inside the elaborately designed Denton County Courthouse, which was built between 1895 and 1897, find the county's *Courthouse-on-the-Square* museum (110 West Hickory Street, Denton 76201, 940–565–5667). Exhibits tell the story of the county's history and nineteenth-century life with a period country kitchen, Victorian parlor, farm tools, antiques, textiles, branding irons, guns, dolls, and folk art. Open from 10:30 A.M. until 4:30 P.M. Tuesday through Saturday. Admission is free.

For some cultural contrast, check out *Evers Hardware Store* (109 West Hickory Street, on the south side of the courthouse square, Denton 76201, 940–382–5513). Measuring 25 feet wide, the front of the store is exactly as it was at its opening in 1885. You'll find the merchandise stacked floor to ceiling, with clerks using old rolling ladders to get to top shelves. Open Monday through Saturday 8:00 A.M. until 5:30 P.M.

Shops and sites worth a look on the square include *Stone Soup,* a shop with upscale gifts and interior-decor items on the square's north side at 120 Oak Street; *Recycled Books, CDs, and Records,* a three-story treasure trove in the old 1901 opera house on the northeast corner at 200 North Locust Street; *Austin Street Gallery,* an art space on the east side at 122 North Locust Street; and *Longhorn Gallery,* a sensational art gallery on the southwest corner of Hickory and Elm Streets.

There's a lot of dining right on the square, as well. *The Loop Hole* (119 West Hickory Street, Denton 76201, 940–565–0770) has a menu written in pseudo-legalese, with appetizers called arraignments, and so on. *Denton County Hamburger Company* (113 West Hickory Street, Denton 76201, 940–383–1022) is a quick place to grab a cheeseburger with fries.

Just a block south of the square, *Sweetwater Grill and Tavern* (115 South Elm Street, Denton 76201, 940–484–2888) does a dynamite job with grilled vegetable sandwiches, grilled shrimp over greens, toasted tomato salsa, and bountiful burgers with elaborate toppings.

If you're wanting to spend time looking around the Oak-Hickory Historic District, which offers several buildings seen on a walking tour, as well as a handful of good restaurants and bars, contact the Denton Chamber of Commerce for information at (940) 382–7895. Stay overnight at *The Redbud Inn* (815 North Locust Street, Denton 76201, 888–565–6414 or

940–565–6414), 7 blocks north of the courthouse square. A 1910 Tudor Revival home, this B&B offers five guest rooms, each with claw-foot tubs and antique beds. A full, homemade breakfast is served in the dining room. The owners offer rooms, too, in their Magnolia Inn, next door.

Let's hope it's time to eat again, as this ranch country has plenty of good eats to share. From Denton head 4 miles west on U.S. 380, then take Farm Road 156 south another 4 miles to the hamlet of *Ponder,* home to an excellent steak joint called *Ranchman's Cafe,* right on Farm Road 156 (940–479–2221). A legendary favorite of north Texans, this family place serves a mean steak dinner. The St. Louis beef is cut when you order your steak, cooked exactly to order, and served with salad and baked potato—if you had the foresight to call ahead and reserve your very own spud. Do not, under any circumstances, get too full for dessert: Ranchman's is famous for its homemade pies and cobblers, good enough alone to draw people from Fort Worth and Dallas, both an hour away. The cafe's open daily 8:00 A.M. until 10:00 P.M.

If a cowpoke's experience is what you want after Ranchman's, *Texas Lil's Diamond A Ranch* at Justin, just 7 miles south of Ponder on Farm Road 156, is your destination. A dude's day on this expansive ranch is filled with horseback riding, hayrides, fishing, swimming, campside or ranch house dining, and a variety of entertainment, even golf. Kids will enjoy the petting zoo and the playground. Call ahead for rates and information, (800) LIL–VILL or (940) 430–0192.

A different side trip from Denton is to the town of *McKinney,* a straight shot east of Denton on U.S. 380 about 30 miles, then south on Texas Highway 5 about 2 miles. The Collin County seat has been revived in recent years, with a terrific courthouse square surrounded by delightful shops. The Victorian buildings have been renovated and now offer a full day of shop and cafe browsing. Just a few of the stores to note are Cotton Hearts and Angels Unlimited in the old Ritz Building (103 East Virginia Street); The Little Red Hen (105 East Virginia Street); Austin & Daughters (115 West Virginia Street); Portfolio (104 North Tennessee Street); Canyon Wren's Nature Store (109 South Tennessee Street); and Electric Quilters (211 East Louisiana Street). Several buildings on the square contain antiques malls, such as The Old McKinney Opera House Mall, Estate Antique Mall, and Market on the Square Antique Mall.

Some of the restaurants around the square are The Pantry (214 East Louisiana Street); Backstage Coffee Company (103 East Virginia Street); and Opera House Restaurant (107 North Kentucky Street). A near-downtown lodging is Dowell House Bed and Breakfast (1104 South Tennessee Street, 972–562–2456), an antiques-filled, 1870 home. Local history is detailed at The Old Post Office Museum (105 North Chestnut Street, 972–542–9457), in a 1911 building.

Get a complete guide to the town from the McKinney Chamber of Commerce, 1801 West Louisiana Street, (972) 542–0163 or (888) 649–8499. More than sixty specialty and antiques shops, boutiques, galleries, and cafes are listed.

A quaint but terrific find near McKinney is the town of *Van Alstyne,* north via U.S. 75 about 15 miles, just inside Grayson County, settled around 1846. The primary reason for visiting is to stay at the *Durning House Bed & Breakfast* (205 West Stephens Street, Van Alstyne 75070, 903–482–5188), a sweet, eighty-year-old farmhouse with two guest rooms. Both are filled with antiques and have private baths and cable TV.

Adjacent is *Durning House Restaurant,* a cute dining room offering lunch Wednesday through Friday and dinner on Friday and Saturday. Be sure to get a piece of pie, made by eighty-something-year-old Aunt Opal, who lives nearby.

The Big D

The way to *Dallas* is easy from McKinney: Drive 35 miles south on U.S. Highway 75 and you're there. Stay on I–35 all the way into the city and watch for I–30 East, which you'll be upon when you see downtown and the unmistakable *Reunion Tower*—that big silver ball atop a tall tower. Take I–30 East, avoiding morning or evening traffic hour if possible, and continue a short distance to the exit for *Fair Park.* Follow the directional signs a few blocks until you reach entrances on Parry Street or Cullum Boulevard.

Inside the park, your destination is *The Museum of African-American Life and Culture* (3536 Grand Avenue, Dallas 75210, 214–565–9026), a six-million-dollar storehouse/showcase of ethnic artifacts. The only one of its kind in the entire Southwest, the grand building of ivory-colored stone with a huge rotunda and four vaulted galleries contains a library and research center, as well as remarkable changing exhibits that typically include the work of nineteenth-century Black masters: wood carvings, contemporary paintings, photography, and sculpture. Closed Monday, the museum is open Tuesday through Friday from noon until 5:00 P.M., Friday noon until 9:00 P.M., Saturday 10:00 A.M. until 5:00 P.M. and Sunday 1:00 until 5:00 P.M. Admission is free.

Nearby are other important buildings worth a look. For example, the **Hall of State** (3939 Grand Avenue, Dallas 75210, 214–421–4500) is one of the fantastic art deco buildings erected for the 1936 Texas Centennial exhibition held at Fair Park. Inside find heroes of Texas's fight for independence honored in bronze, including William B. Travis, Gen. Sam Houston, and Stephen F. Austin. Several fascinating murals illustrate the state's history from the pioneer period to the centennial year. The hall is open Tuesday through Saturday from 9:00 A.M. until 5:00 P.M. and Sunday from 1:00 until 5:00 P.M. Admission is free.

From Fair Park it's just a quick drive of a few blocks to **Deep Ellum,** taking First Avenue off of Parry Street out of the park and under I–30. Soon you'll be crossing Commerce Street, then Main Street, and Elm Street, the three big thoroughfares in this unusual and very culturally infused district. Its name comes from the African-American people—many of whom produced landmark blues music—who lived here in the early twentieth century and placed a somewhat Southern twist on "elm." Today it's a sensational neighborhood in which to find odd, unique, and always imaginative dining, clothes, jewelry, home furnishings, artwork, and lots of live music. Vintage brick buildings have been elaborately restored, and interiors have been doused with massive creativity. Whether you're in search of a Native American–designed bed, an early seventies lava lamp, an antique electric fan, a handmade water pitcher, 1920s lace-up boots, postmodern cowboy art, sumptuous barbecued pork ribs, a vegetarian sandwich, a Manhattan on the rocks, a four-layer double-fudge chocolate cake, an oversize cup of caffe latte, or an earful of alternative rock or moody jazz, you will have no trouble finding it in Deep Ellum. Businesses are usually open daily, and most restaurants and nightclubs keep very late hours.

For radically different entertainment in spring, summer, and early fall, make a detour by heading east again on I–30 about 10 miles to I–635,

Please Make Sure Your Tray Tables and Seat Backs Are in the Upright Position

*T*he Dallas/Fort Worth International Airport became the busiest airport in the world in 1998, beating the FAA's prediction that this record would occur in 2000. With a new runway and the increase of airspace capacity over the north Texas area, DFW surpassed Chicago O'Hare in terms of takeoffs and landings. DFW still ranks behind O'Hare and Atlanta in the number of passengers serviced.

which you'll take south 3 miles to the Military Parkway exit. Just ahead on the right you'll see a big, covered arena, home to the **Mesquite Championship Rodeo,** at 118 Rodeo Drive, Mesquite 75149 (972–285–8777). Since 1958 cowboys and cowgirls have considered this a top place to make a name at bull riding, calf roping, and steer wrestling, and spectators have been ever enthusiastic. A barbecue pavilion offers supper—that's what dinner is called in many parts of Texas—at 6:30 P.M. on performance nights. The rodeo is staged for 6,000 fans every Friday and Saturday night from April through September at 8:30 P.M. Admission is charged.

Another attraction that's been a favorite for several generations of Texans is found back in downtown Dallas at the **Farmers' Market,** a rich country tradition deep within the heart of the nation's eighth-largest city. Head back to town on I–30 West and take the downtown exit marked Pearl Street. You'll find the 10-block, open-air market at 1010 South Pearl Street, best if visited

Texas Trivia
Ennis, about 35 miles south of Dallas, hosts the National Polka Festival every May.

early in the day. Some farmers personally bring their produce from around the state, while other vendors are locals who buy from farmers or wholesale nurseries and then sell to the public. Even if you're not in need of fresh fruits, vegetables, herbs, flowers, or plants, the sensory experience is pure invigoration—be sure to load the camera. The market is open daily from 5:00 A.M. until 7:00 P.M. in summer and 6:00 A.M. until 6:00 P.M. in winter. The phone number is (214) 670–5879.

Next stop is also downtown, at the **Belo Mansion,** 2101 Ross Avenue, Dallas 75201. This extraordinarily opulent house was designed by noted architect Herbert Green and completed in 1900. It's the only residence still existing in the city's Central Business District and was home to Col. Alfred H. Belo, founder of the venerable *Dallas Morning News.* Belo died in 1901, and the family retained ownership, leasing it out as a funeral home from 1926 until 1977, when it was purchased by the Dallas Bar Association. Now open as the Dallas Legal Education Center, it's available for free tours by appointment; just call (214) 969–7066.

Barely a block away, the **Dallas Museum of Art** (1717 North Harwood Street, Dallas 75201, 214–922–1200) is a vast facility with collections including pre-Columbian, African, and decorative arts. Upstairs at the museum, an elegant restaurant called Seventeen Seventeen (214–922–1260 or 922–1200) offers lunch and dinner selections including lobster, pasta, roast lamb, Vietnamese chicken salad, and incredible desserts.

Texas Trivia

Speaking of food, there are close to one hundred excellent, nonchain restaurant offerings just north of the museum in the *McKinney Avenue–Cedar Springs* neighborhood. Breakfast, lunch, and dinner are wonderful at Breadwinners (3301 McKinney Avenue, Dallas 75204) and Dream Cafe (in the Quadrangle at 2800 Routh Street, Dallas 75204). Lunch and dinner at Cafe Express (3230 McKinney Avenue, Dallas 75204) means roasted chicken and vegetable sandwiches and salads piled high with grilled fish or meat; Mattito's (3011 Routh Street, Dallas 75204) is the place for fancy versions of Tex-Mex favorites; Pomodoro (2520 Cedar Springs Road, Dallas 75204) is well loved for upscale pizza and pasta; and Thai Taste (1301 North Fitzhugh Avenue at McKinney Avenue, Dallas 75204) is among the top Asian restaurants in town, thanks to owner-chef Annie Wong.

Also in this area, *Hotel St. Germain* (2516 Maple Avenue, Dallas 75204, 214–871–2516) is a spectacular small hotel inside what was a fashionable home when built in 1909. The boutique hotel has won several industry awards for its luxurious lodgings and exceptional restaurant. There are seven suites, with turn-of-the-twentieth-century French antiques, private baths, fireplaces, cable TV, Jacuzzi tubs, and expensive toiletries. There's twenty-four-hour concierge, butler, and room service. Guests choose to have breakfast either in the dining room, the courtyard, or their suites.

A few blocks west of the Dallas Museum of Art find *The Dallas World Aquarium,* at 1801 North Griffin Street, Dallas 75201, a spectacular offering. Bearing the look of a small European museum, it showcases a 65,000-gallon array of saltwater marine life including sharks, stingrays, and reef fish in a reconstructed coral reef ecosystem. Then there are tropical blackfoot penguins in their own terrarium world. A restaurant, called the Eighteen-O-One, is open daily for lunch and Sunday brunch. The aquarium is open Monday through Friday 11:00 A.M. until 6:00 P.M., Saturday 10:00 A.M. until 6:00 P.M., and Sunday noon until 6:00 P.M. Admission is charged. Telephone (214) 720–2224.

Having found the aquarium, you're already in what's known as the *West End Historical District,* a wildly popular place for shopping and dining. Interest in the latter will keep you here for lunch or dinner, and there's an oasis of serenity found at *Lombardi's 311* (311 Market Street at Ross, Dallas 75201, 214–747–0322). Let everyone else crowd into the rollicking beer, spaghetti, steak, or enchilada joints; this delightful Italian cafe provides a welcome respite from the party scene outside. Linger over freshly crafted dishes from Italy's provinces, furnished by unobtrusive, polished servers. The focaccia bread is a favorite, and live jazz is offered most evenings. Open from 11:00 A.M. Monday through Friday and from 5:00 P.M. Saturday and Sunday, the restaurant closes between 10:00 and 11:00 P.M. except on Friday and Saturday, when it is open until midnight.

Leave your car wherever it's parked and walk down Market Street (south) 4 blocks to Main Street, then turn right (west) and proceed another long block. To your left, at the intersection of Main and Houston Streets, is *Old Red,* the imposing red sandstone building that originally was Dallas County's courthouse when erected in 1892. It's quite a spectacle in all its Richardsonian Romanesque glory, complete with scary gargoyles scowling down at you from the corners. This is a great photo opportunity for anybody with a zoom lens.

Right in front of the courthouse, bounded by Houston, Commerce, and Elm Streets, is *Dealey Plaza,* a small and very scenic little park with a reflection pool, trees, and a statue honoring early *Dallas Morning News* publisher and civic leader George Bannerman Dealey. Since November 22, 1963, however, Dealey Plaza has been known as the place where President Kennedy was assassinated. No matter the time of day or night when you visit, you won't be alone: More than thirty years after the tragedy, people of all ages and nationalities still show up to look around, perhaps wondering if some answer could ever be known.

The life, death, and heritage of President Kennedy is detailed in an educational and historical exhibit across the street from the park, the *Sixth Floor: John F. Kennedy and the Memory of a Nation,* a remarkable museum on the sixth floor of the former Texas School Book Depository from which Lee Harvey Oswald allegedly shot the president. Opened in 1988, the exhibit contains historic pictures, artifacts, forty minutes of documentary films, and an award-winning audio tour. Open daily from 9:00 A.M. until 6:00 P.M., the Sixth Floor's address is 411 Elm Street (214–979–6430). Admission is charged.

Something more unusual is *The Conspiracy Museum* (110 South Market Street, Dallas 75201, 214–741–3040), in the first floor of the historic Katy Building. The museum explores assassinations throughout American history and the political motivations that were (possibly) relevant. Creators of this museum contend that Lee Harvey Oswald did not kill JFK, by the way. Open daily from 10:00 A.M. until 6:00 P.M. Admission is $7.00 for adults and $3.00 for children.

A convenient downtown lodging is *Amelia's Place* (1775 Young Street, Dallas 75201, 214–651–1775), a warehouse loft made over into a six-room bed-and-breakfast inn. Guests are just a short walk from City Hall,

Neiman Marcus, and the Farmers' Market. Amelia caters to a diverse clientele but not, in her words, to "snobs or bigots." Her gigantic breakfasts are legendary.

Immediately north of downtown is the uptown area, home to Southern House (2625 Thomas Avenue, Dallas 75204, 214–720–0845), a nice hotel alternative. The three-story contemporary Prairie-style home has been made over into a small inn that's near the Dallas Museum of Art and the oodles of galleries on McKinney Avenue. There are two rooms, one with private bath, in the main house and a one-bedroom apartment for stays of four or more nights. Breakfast is included, and lunch and dinner are available by arrangement.

Dallas's supply of art galleries, theaters, and concert halls is enormous. For a timely schedule of events, pick up free copies of the alternative weeklies, *The Observer* and *The Met*. For a complete guide to all attractions, consult the Dallas Convention & Visitors Bureau, located downtown at 1201 Elm Street, Suite 2000, (214) 746–6677. Visit the Internet site at www.cityview.com/dallas.

Before leaving the Dallas area, consider a worthwhile side trip. Head exactly 30 miles due south of Dallas on I–35 to **Waxahachie,** the Ellis County seat and home to 20,000 citizens. Waxahachie (WOCKS-uh-hatch-ee) is a charming Victorian town built on the rich cattle and cotton businesses here at the turn of the twentieth century. Some 170 of the original, ornate homes with extensive gingerbread detail survive, giving the community its "Gingerbread City" nickname. For a map of historic places on both walking and driving tours, ask at the chamber of commerce, 102 YMCA Drive, (972) 937–2390.

You won't dare miss the **Ellis County Courthouse,** easily the most fabulous of all Texas's many magnificent courthouses. Located at Main and College Streets, the 1896 masterpiece is noted for a spectacular clock tower, balconies, arches, and gargoyles. An intriguing story that's survived the past century says that one of the artisans brought from Italy to craft the stonework became enamored with a Waxahachie beauty and modeled the lovely face above the east entrance after her; she did not return his love, however, and in his anger he created monstrous faces on the rest of the detail.

Waxahachie's celebrated Victorian veneer has appealed to Hollywood in a big way: Among the excellent films shot here are *Places in the Heart, Tender Mercies, The Trip to Bountiful,* and *Bonnie & Clyde.* A brochure outlining the movie sites is also available from the chamber.

Whatever you do in Waxahachie, don't miss a chance to have lunch or dinner at *The Dove's Nest* (105 Jefferson Street, Waxahachie 75165, 972–938–3683). You'll find it immediately south of the courthouse square in what was a hardware store, built in 1913. More sophisticated than most places in a town of this size, this excellent and very attractive dining room offers New American dishes of rabbit, chicken, lamb, pork loin, and fish. The restaurant's lovely cookbook is available. Meals start at about $8.00; it's open for lunch Monday through Saturday.

You'll need the sustenance for all the shopping to be done here on the courthouse square. Among the many choices is the *Taylor & Co. Mercantile Mall* (200 South Rogers Street, Waxahachie 75165), in an 1887 building. A partial list of selections includes antique and vintage furniture in European, American, Texas, and country designs; Depression glass; fine china; crystal; linens; pottery; lamps; books; dolls; toys; and pictures. In the same building you'll find more delectables at The Crazy Horse Cafe & Bakery (972–938–9818).

Overnight stays in Waxahachie are luxurious at bed-and-breakfasts such as *The Bonnynook Inn* (414 West Main Street, Waxahachie 75165, 972–938–7207), where five rooms and suites are elegantly appointed and gourmet breakfasts are served; and at *The Chaska House* (716 West Main Street, Waxahachie 75165, 972–937–3390), with two antiques-filled rooms. Several others, including The Harrison, Millie's Victorian, and Seven Gables, are offered. Inquire at the chamber.

The town's architecture is exhibited in grand style annually on the first Saturday and Sunday in June during the *Gingerbread Trail.* The special tour showcases several homes, the courthouse, two museums, and a fine auditorium. For information and tickets contact the chamber of commerce at (972) 937–2390.

Another annual event bringing throngs to Waxahachie is *Scarborough Faire,* a re-created sixteenth-century English village spread over thirty-five acres of open countryside. It's an impressive production, consisting of more than 400 actors and musicians portraying royalty, peasants, jesters, knights and ladies, and minstrels. Among activities and entertainment are jousting competitions, juggling, sheep-dog demonstrations, magic, and comedy shows. Arts and crafts—some of which aren't entirely Old World—are available, as are all kinds of foods and drink. The faire is held on eight weekends from late April until mid-June; if you go in summer, dress for hot weather. Admission is charged. Call (972) 937–6130 for details.

Don't fill up on the faire's junk fare, however; you need to save room for the wonderful Southern cooking at Waxahachie's **Catfish Plantation,** 814 Water Street, Waxahachie 75165 (972–937–9468). The delightful 1895 house is said to be haunted, but that seems to simply enhance the good dining experience found here. Besides the signature fresh catfish, enjoy sweet potato patties, fried corn, fried chicken, black-eyed peas, bread pudding in rum sauce, and cobbler. It's open Thursday from 5:00 until 8:00 P.M., Friday 11:30 A.M. until 2:00 P.M. and 5:00 until 9:00 P.M., and Sunday from 11:30 A.M. until 8:00 P.M.

Around Cowtown

From Waxahachie your destination is **Arlington,** a fast-growing place of more than a quarter million residents that has the highest average income per household in the state. You'll find it by traveling 42 miles northeast via U.S. Highway 287.

The stunning **Ballpark in Arlington,** home to the Texas Rangers Baseball Club, is situated on I–30 at the Pennant Drive exit. Opened in time for the Rangers's 1994 season, this masterpiece is crafted from the popular Texas pink granite and redbrick to look like a vintage stadium from baseball's glory days much earlier in the twentieth century. The stadium boasts multiple tiers as well as friezes around the facade detailed with Texas longhorns and Texas Rangers, the lawmen, and an interior hall of fame honoring baseball greats. Billed as being revolutionary and unique to the industry, the ballpark has restaurants, sidewalk cafes, bars, various shops,

Bizarre Texas Stuff

ARLINGTON: Frank Smith, curator at the Antique Sewing Machine Museum at 804 West Abram Street, (817) 275–0971, has been described by one observer as "a sewing machine evangelist." And why not? He has amassed more than 300 sewing machines, including some made before the Civil War. One of particular interest is the one used by Frances Bavier, who played Aunt Bea on The Andy Griffith Show.

In March, Smith offers a special exhibit of the Civil War sewing machines; in September, his exhibit features the Elias Howe works, the extremely rare examples made by the man who first came up with the first practical sewing machine. The museum is open Tuesday through Saturday from 9:00 A.M. until 5:00 P.M. and Sunday from 1:00 until 5:00 P.M. Admission is $3.00 for adults and $2.00 for children.

and other kinds of businesses—even a dentist. Around the stadium an expansive park includes Little League fields, picnic areas, a riverwalk, and an amphitheater. The ballpark is home to the *Legends of the Game Baseball Museum and Learning Center* and the *Sports Legacy* art gallery. The history of the game is detailed in an assortment of exhibits, and shoppers can find tons of souvenirs at the adjacent *Grand Slam Shop.* The museum and learning center are open from 9:00 A.M. until 7:30 P.M. Monday through Saturday and from noon until 5:00 P.M. Sunday. The art gallery is open daily from 10:00 A.M. until 6:00 P.M. The Grand Slam Shop hours vary, but it's open daily. All admissions are free. For game times, tickets, and information, call (817) 273–5100.

Fewer than 10 miles east of Arlington in the town of Grand Prairie, visit *Lone Star Park* (Belt Line Road, just north of I–30, 972–263–RACE). Here you'll find world-class thoroughbred and quarter horse racing at the state's top Class 1 track. The Post Time Pavilion is a 36,000-square-foot simulcasting facility with a Las Vegas–style race book, sports bar, and restaurant. Live racing is seen from a multilevel, 280,000-square-foot grandstand with European-style paddock.

And north about 5 miles from Arlington on Texas Highway 360, the *American Airlines C. R. Smith Museum* (Texas 360 at Texas 183, 817–967–1560) is a hugely impressive tribute to the history of flight. Among attractions is a film called *Dream of Flight,* which introduces the exhibits; a pre–World War II DC-3, the 1940 *Flagship Knoxville;* historical photos and equipment; and a fine museum store with books, toys, videos, models, and travel gifts. The museum is open from 10:00 A.M. until 7:00 P.M. Tuesday, from 10:00 A.M. until 6:00 P.M. Wednesday through Saturday, and noon until 5:00 P.M. Sunday. Admission is free.

From the American Airlines museum, your destination is 10 miles north to *Grapevine,* at the intersection of Texas Highways 360 and 114. The town's roots date to negotiating days between Native Americans and settlers; in fact, it was the site of an 1849 treaty signing by Gen. Sam Houston. Don't let its chain restaurants and close proximity to DFW Airport fool you; Grapevine, which boasts a National Register Historic District, is rich with Texas heritage. Pick up a walking tour guide and list of historic sites at the Grapevine Convention & Visitors Bureau in the old Wallis Hotel Building (One Liberty Park Plaza, Grapevine 76051, 817–410–3185) or at the visitors information center in the Grapevine Depot (707 South Main Street, Grapevine 76051).

ONE MAINSTREAM ATTRACTION WORTH
SEEING IN NORTH TEXAS

*It's outrageous, but you have
to see it to believe it. Bass
Pro Shops Outdoor World,
based in Springfield, Missouri, opened a 200,000-
square-foot superstore in
Grapevine in early 1999.
Inside you'll find a trout
stream, waterfalls, aquarium,
full-service restaurant, two-
story archery range, a full-
size log cabin, and every
conceivable item needed for
camping, fishing, and hunting. Located on Texas Highway 26; the store's phone
number is (972) 724-2018.*

The train depot is one end of a popular daily route made from Fort Worth by the vintage Tarantula Train. The Grapevine Heritage Center (817-424-0516) is here, too, with a museum containing castings of dinosaur footprints found at nearby Lake Grapevine. The Heritage Center is home to a blacksmith shop, a railroad foreman's house, and an artisan's shop where old arts and crafts, such as rug hooking, quilting, woodcarving, chair caning, and bootmaking are taught and practiced.

Grapevine's entertainment includes The Grapevine Opry and other musical events at The Palace Theatre (308 South Main Street, Grapevine 76051). Shopping includes The British Emporium (130 North Main Street, Grapevine 76051); Julia's Antiques and Tea Room (210 North Main Street, Grapevine 76051); and Off the Vine (336-A South Main Street, Grapevine 76051), where wines and wine-related gifts are sold.

The wine business is booming in suitably named Grapevine. The three big wineries in town are Delaney Winery & Vineyards (2000 Champagne Boulevard, Grapevine 76051, 817-481-5668); La Buena Vida Vineyards (416 East College Street, Grapevine 76051, 817-481-WINE); and La Bodega Winery and Tasting Room (inside Terminal 2-E, facing Gate 6, Dallas/Fort Worth International Airport, 817-329-3145). Call for tasting and tour times and for fees. Also check in with the Texas Wine and Grape Growers Association at One Liberty Plaza, Grapevine 76051, (817-424-0570) to learn more about Texas's wine industry, now second in the nation behind California.

Slow down a bit, spending a leisurely hour over a sandwich and an ice cream soda at *City Drug Soda Fountain,* 309 South Main Street in downtown Grapevine, or over a plate of pasta at *Ravioli,* 1230 East Worth Street, also in Grapevine's historic district.

It's time for a megadose of serious, albeit very enjoyable, culture, so head on into *Fort Worth,* taking Texas Highway 121 south to Texas Highway 183. Stay on 183, then take I-30 West and exit University Drive, heading north on that street less than a mile to the *Cultural District,* a highly unusual place where four unforgettable, very independent museums are clustered within a 5-block area.

From University Drive, turn left at the Lancaster Avenue light and you'll quickly see the *Kimbell Art Museum,* (3333 Camp Bowie Boulevard, Fort Worth 76107, 817–332–8451). Designed by the famous architect Louis Kahn, the museum was founded by industrialist and entrepreneur Kay Kimbell, who left a wealth of art and money to begin the nation's second-richest privately endowed museum, surpassed only by the Getty in Malibu, California. Within the beautifully vaulted, gray-white building are vast galleries filled with paintings by El Greco, Velázquez, Rembrandt, Cézanne, Picasso, and others, plus varied pieces of pre-Columbian art. World-class exhibits make appearances here on worldwide tours; for information call the museum.

The Kimbell is open Tuesday through Thursday and Saturday from 10:00 A.M. until 5:00 P.M., Friday from noon until 8:00 P.M., and Sunday from noon until 5:00 P.M. Admission is free.

Just a block west, the *Amon Carter Museum* (3501 Camp Bowie Boulevard, Fort Worth 76107, 817–738–1933) is known for its outstanding collection of western art, particularly by Frederic Remington and Charles M. Russell, willed to the city along with a foundation by millionaire Amon G. Carter, the founder of the *Fort Worth Star-Telegram* and dedicated promoter of Fort Worth. Today's Carter Museum collection

June's Texas Anecdotes

*N*ORTH TEXAS: Several summers ago, a friend from New York called to say that a chum from England was making his first cross-country trek through America. Our New York friend was calling pals all over the States to ask if we would show the Englishman around our towns. Happy to oblige, we received the Brit on a hot August evening and immediately took him for a Mexican-food feast. The place we chose was a little family operation in Fort Worth's historic Stockyards district, right on Exchange Avenue, the main thoroughfare. A very good sport, he seemed to genuinely enjoy the spicy salsa, the sizzling fajitas, and the cold Texas beer we ordered. But as he looked out the window next to our table, he looked perplexed. Finally he asked, "Is there a costume party of some sort?" We looked but had no idea what he meant. "Well," he elaborated, "what about all these chaps wearing hats and boots and those big belt buckles?" I told him those were cowboys, probably heading to one of the dance halls or saloons up and down Exchange. "Real cowboys?!" he asked. Yep, the very thing. Our New York friend called us several weeks later to report that after visiting New York, Atlanta, Chicago, Fort Worth, San Francisco, and Los Angeles, our English friend said his favorite stop was our very own Cowtown.

Cowgirls and Cattle Ranchers

*F*ort Worth's renowned Cultural District will make room for two more museums, which will be paired together in the Western Heritage Center. The National Cowgirl Hall of Fame and Museum and the Cattle Raisers' Museum, two existing entities, will team up when the $15 million necessary to build the new center is raised—perhaps by 2002 or 2003.

includes works by such noted American artists as Winslow Homer, Grant Wood, and Georgia O'Keeffe. A sensational bookstore is found here, too. Open Tuesday through Saturday from 10:00 A.M. until 5:00 P.M. and Sunday from noon until 5:00 P.M.; tours are given at 2:00 P.M. daily, except Monday. Admission is free. Note: The Carter will be closed for extensive remodeling and expansion until late 2001.

Right across the street, the **Modern Art Museum of Fort Worth** (1309 Montgomery Street, Fort Worth 76107, 817–738–9215) is the city's oldest museum, begun in 1901 as a gallery at the Carnegie Library. Noteworthy in that it's one of a very small number in the United States with a collection devoted to twentieth-century artists, the museum houses a permanent collection including works by Warhol, Picasso, and Rothko. A new, much larger building will be completed in 2003. Open Tuesday through Friday from 10:00 A.M. until 5:00 P.M., Saturday from 11:00 A.M. until 5:00 P.M., and Sunday from noon until 5:00 P.M. Admission is free.

Next door you'll find Fort Worth's best children's attraction, the **Museum of Science and History** (1501 Montgomery Street, Fort Worth 76109, 817–732–1631), also important for being the largest repository of its kind in the entire Southwest. Numerous exhibits—many of which appeal to children and adults alike—include those on Texas history, fossils and geology, the human body, medical history, and computer science. At the museum's Noble Planetarium, shows include astronomy and lasers; the Omni Theater houses a domed screen 80 feet in diameter, a projector weighing almost a ton and casting the largest film in history, and seventy-two speakers hugging the audience with unbelievable sound. Shows are sensational, dealing with earth science in a thrilling format. Omni shows are offered several times daily; admission is charged; call for times and information. Museum admission is $3.00 for adults and $1.00 for children. Open Monday from 9:00 A.M. until 5:00 P.M., Tuesday through Thursday from 9:00 A.M. until 8:00 P.M., Friday and Saturday from 9:00 A.M. until 9:00 P.M., and Sunday from noon until 8:00 P.M.

The entire Cultural District is electrified from mid-January until early February when the **Southwestern Stock Show and Rodeo** is held at **Will Rogers Coliseum,** facing the Carter and Kimbell Museums at 3301 West Lancaster Avenue, Fort Worth 76107 (817–877–2400). This terrifically Texan event—which includes the world's largest indoor rodeo—celebrated its centennial in 1996. Annual attendance is edging close to one million, with attractions ranging from shows of more than 15,000 animals; livestock auctions; and sales of every sort of western wear, western art, Texas souvenirs, and food to pig races; goat-milking contests; and a carnival. Rodeo tickets sell out early, so order in advance if possible. Grounds admission is $5.00.

A concise look at the industry that originally put Fort Worth on Texas's map is available at the **Cattle Raisers' Museum** (1301 West Seventh Street, Fort Worth 76107, 817–332–7064), just 2 miles east of the Cultural District. The Texas ranching and cattle business is documented from its earliest days through audiovisual and hands-on exhibits, plus historic photographs of such distinguished Texas citizens as Charles Goodnight and Capt. Richard King. Admission is free, and the museum is open Monday through Friday from 8:30 A.M. until 4:30 P.M.

Because so many people make an entire day of touring museums in the Cultural District, it's a good thing there are lots of places to have a great meal within walking distance. Inside the Kimbell Art Museum, there's The Buffet, an upscale place for lunch Tuesday through Sunday and dinner on Friday. Much more casual is Rick's on the Bricks (3716 Camp Bowie Boulevard, Fort Worth 76107), for burgers and such at lunch and dinner daily; Saint Emilion (3617 West Seventh Street, Fort Worth 76107), for elegant, country French dinner daily; Four Star Coffee Bar (3324 West Seventh Street, Fort Worth 76107), for coffee, pizza, and sandwiches daily; and J&J Oyster Bar (612 University Drive, Fort Worth 76107), for good fish at lunch and dinner.

> **Texas Trivia**
>
> *Thousands of cyclists from across the United States converge in Wichita Falls, northwest of Fort Worth, in late August every year for the Hotter 'n Hell Hundred—to ride 100 miles.*

Barely a three-minute drive south of the Cultural District, find the **Fort Worth Zoo** (1989 Colonial Parkway, Fort Worth 76109, 817–871–7050), widely rated among the top five zoos in America. Exceptional, natural habitats for hundreds of animals plus nature shops and cafes are on the grounds. A miniature train is in the adjacent park, taking a tour

Texas Meets Australia

*W*ith the addition of a permanent exhibit in 1998 called Koala Outback, the Fort Worth Zoo became one
of ten zoos in the nation and the only
zoo in Texas to boast such an attraction. The cute marsupials share their
shady habitat with red kangaroos and
yellow-footed rock wallabies.

alongside the Trinity River. The zoo is open from 10:00 A.M. until 5:00
P.M. daily. Admission is $7.00 for adults, $4.50 for children.

Across the street from the zoo, **University Park Village** (on University
Drive just south of I–30) is an upscale complex featuring stores such as
Harold's, Talbot's, Williams-Sonoma, Pottery Barn, Victoria's Secret,
Bath and Body Works, Voyagers Travel Store, Nine West, Ann Taylor, The
Gap, and Starbucks Coffee. Excellent restaurants here are Blue Mesa,
Water Street Seafood, and La Piazza.

Antiques hunters will find Fort Worth has a good selection right in
town. The Antique Connection (7429 East Lancaster Avenue, Fort
Worth 76112, 817–429–0922) has 45 dealers; and Montgomery Street
Antique Mall (2601 Montgomery Street, Fort Worth 76107, 817–735–
9685) has 205 dealers, a nice tearoom for lunch, and an excellent location just a few blocks from the Cultural District's museums.

Now head downtown to **Sundance Square** (the center is at Main and
Fourth Streets), which is undoubtedly the envy of all Texas's larger
cities. This superb and extensive renovation of beautiful Victorian
buildings has revitalized downtown to an extraordinary extent. Day
and night, the 14-block area with redbrick streets is bustling with folks
visiting museums, dining, shopping, and attending plays, concerts, and
movies. Special architecture to note is at the Knights of Pythias building—the first such temple ever built—at 315 Main Street.

At the Caravan of Dreams (312 Houston Street, Fort Worth 76102,
817–877–3000), the city's top venue for national names in jazz, rhythm
and blues, and folk music, there's a rooftop grotto bar for wonderful
downtown views. The Circle Theatre (230 Fourth Street, Fort Worth
76102, 817–877–3040), Casa on the Square (109 East Third Street, Fort
Worth 76102, 817–332–2272), and The Jubilee Theater (506 Main
Street, Fort Worth 76102, 817–338–4411) offer plays and musicals.
Newest is the phenomenally grand Nancy Lee and Perry R. Bass Performance Hall (Fourth and Calhoun Streets, 817–212–4280), the premier
performing space for Fort Worth's opera, symphony, ballet, and national

NASCAR's new Texas Motor Speedway in Fort Worth, which opened in April 1997, has seating for 150,061. That makes it the second-largest sports facility in America.

touring productions. If you want to catch up on current movies, there's the Sundance eleven-theater complex, at Third and Houston Streets, and the Palace, at Third and Calhoun Streets, with nine more screens. Next to the Palace find a cavernous, two-story Barnes & Noble bookstore, which also has a Starbucks Coffee inside.

Sundance Square museums are: Sid Richardson Collection of Western Art (309 Main Street, Fort Worth 76102, 817–332–6554), with Western masterpieces by Charles Russell and Frederic Remington; The Modern at Sundance Square (410 Houston Street, Fort Worth 76102, 817–335–9215), an extension of the Modern Art Museum in the Cultural District, with a superb gift shop; and Fire Station No. 1 (203 Commerce Street, Fort Worth 76102, 817–732–1631), home to a permanent exhibit called "150 Years of Fort Worth Museum." And you can't miss The Chisholm Trail Mural (on the Jett Building at 400 Main Street, Fort Worth 76102), a wonderful, enormous artwork honoring the Fort Worth portion of the Chisholm Trail cattle drives from 1867 to 1875.

A recent addition to Sundance Square is ***Etta's Place*** (200 West Third Street, Fort Worth 76102, 817–654–0267), a bed-and-breakfast inn named for the Sundance Kid's schoolteacher-girlfriend. All ten guest rooms are done in period style, with Texas antiques and reproductions, and come with fresh flowers, candies, and cookies. All have private baths with lotions and bath toys. Breakfast is an elaborate, three-course event, complete with sterling silver, china, and crystal. Hosts will assist with theater and dinner reservations.

The beautiful ***Tarrant County Courthouse,*** 100 Weatherford Street at Main Street, is at the north end of Sundance. The 1893 Renaissance Revival architecture is worth a good look, crafted again from marble and that wonderful Texas pink granite.

Time once was when everyone in Fort Worth went to Dallas to shop, but unless you must have something from Macy's, Cowtown's shopping will keep you happy. (There is a Neiman Marcus on Fort Worth's west side at Ridgmar Mall, of course.) Right in Sundance Square, ***Fort Worth Outlet Square*** is the only known downtown outlet mall in the nation. More than forty retailers' outlets with good discounts include Nine West, Spiegel's, Mikasa, London Fog, Bugle Boy, and Bali. For hours call (817) 390–2666.

The list of Sundance Square's dining options grows all the time. Light fare can be had at Coffee Haus (404 Houston Street, Fort Worth 76102),

Texas Trivia

The small town of Olney, northwest of Fort Worth in Young County, hosts an annual One-Arm Dove Hunt in September. An event of international repute, the hunt attracts arm and hand amputees for two days of fun and fellowship.

and Pizzeria Uno (300 Houston Street, Fort Worth 76102) offers good pizzas and pasta. You will need reservations at Angeluna (215 East Fourth Street, Fort Worth 76102, 817–334–0080), a very hip room for fusion (Asian-Caribbean-continental) cuisine; and Chop House (301 Main Street, Fort Worth 76102, 817–336–4129), where beef tenderloin is outstanding.

Restaurants in or within 3 blocks of Sundance Square with lively bar scenes include 8.0 (111 East Third Street); The Flying Saucer Beer Emporium (111 East Fourth Street); The Pour House Sports Grill (209 West Fifth Street); Razzoo's Cajun Cafe (318 Main Street); and Mi Cocina (509 Main Street).

About 3 miles north of downtown Fort Worth via North Main Street, *The Stockyards National Historic District* supplies a full day or night of history and fun. The district's main intersection is North Main Street and Exchange Avenue, and the visitors center kiosk (817–624–4741) is on East Exchange Avenue between the White Elephant Saloon and Stockyards Station.

In the Stockyards you can visit *Billy Bob's Texas* (Rodeo Plaza, Fort Worth 76106, 817–624–7117), the "world's largest honky-tonk," where top country performers often include Willie Nelson, George Jones, Patty Loveless, Trisha Yearwood, and Jerry Jeff Walker. There are two dance floors, forty bar stations, gift shops, and live bull riding inside, too.

At *Cowtown Coliseum* (121 East Exchange Avenue, Fort Worth 76106, 817–625–1025), home of the world's first indoor rodeo, there's a professional rodeo and Wild West Show every Saturday from April through September. Next door at the Livestock Exchange Building (817–625–5087), built in 1904 as offices for livestock traders, you'll find the *Stockyards Collection Museum,* which chronicles the importance of the Stockyards to Fort Worth's history.

Right across the brick street in Stockyards Station (817–625–9715), souvenirs, gifts, clothing, artwork, food, and drink are found in thirty shops and restaurants in what was once the Stockyards's hog-and-sheep pens. It's also a depot for the Tarantula Train (817–625–RAIL), a vintage, 1896 steam engine making daily excursions to nearby Grapevine.

Wandering down Exchange Avenue you'll find the *White Elephant Saloon* (817–624–9712), a century-old barroom named "One of the Best

100 Bars in America" by *Esquire* magazine. It offers cold beer and margaritas, live music, a lively dance floor, and a breezy beer garden. Across the street from the White Elephant, the historic Stockyards Hotel (109 East Exchange Avenue, Fort Worth 76106, 817–625–6427) is a charming 1907 hotel with fifty-two rooms with period decoration. Just another block west, find Miss Molly's Hotel (109½ West Exchange Avenue, Fort Worth 76106, 817–626–1522), a bed-and-breakfast inn in a restored 1910 building with eight guest rooms.

Plenty of good eating goes on in and around the Stockyards area. For Mexican fare try El Rancho Grande Restaurante (1400 North Main Street, Fort Worth 76106); Joe T. Garcia's Mexican Bakery (2122 North Main Street, Fort Worth 76106); and Joe T. Garcia's Mexican Dishes (2201 North Commerce Street, Fort Worth 76106).

The Fort Worth Convention & Visitors Bureau's office is right in Sundance Square at 415 Throckmorton Street, Fort Worth 76106, (817) 336–8791. Call the events hot line, (817) 332–2000, to hear an update of current happenings. You can also visit the Internet site at www.fortworth.com.

From Fort Worth head west on I–30, then U.S. Highway 180, for about 30 miles to **Weatherford.** The seat of Parker County, Weatherford was established in 1855 and grew in 1857 when the Butterfield Stage was routed through town. Hundreds of lives were lost, however, as pioneers warred with Native Americans in 1877. One of the lasting monuments to the late nineteenth century is the Parker County Courthouse, at the center of town on U.S. Highway 180. Made of locally quarried limestone in 1884, the richly Victorian building cost $55,555.55 to construct.

Three blocks east of the courthouse, you'll find a flurry of activity once a month when **First Monday Trade Days** is in progress. Thousands of folks buying and selling junk, antiques, farm animals, puppies, and food converge for the Friday, Saturday, and Sunday prior to the first Monday of each month. Across the street, the stucco Weatherford Public Market is a 1932 WPA building housing an open-air farmers' market, where produce, plants, honey, seeds, jams, and peanuts are sold by the bushel.

Stroll down to the Weatherford Public Library (1214 Charles Street, Weatherford 76086) and see a *life-size bronze of Peter Pan* out front. The sculpture honors Weatherford's late daughter, Mary Martin, who originated the role of Peter Pan in the Broadway musical. The library's Heritage Gallery houses costumes, photos, sheet music, and other mementos belonging to the actress.

Other important sites include a Queen Anne Victorian home at 202 West Oak Street, which was the boyhood home of former U.S. Speaker of the House Jim Wright; and the Greenwood Cemetery, at Front and Mill Streets. Here you'll find a state historical site, the grave of Oliver Loving, known as the Dean of Texas Trail Drivers, whose story inspired the Pulitzer prize–winning novel, *Lonesome Dove,* written by Texan Larry McMurtry. Loving died after being wounded by Native Americans during a trail drive with his close friend Charles Goodnight; Goodnight, along with Loving's son, returned his body more than 600 miles to be buried, as he had wished, in Weatherford.

There are pleasant antiques shops, as well as homegrown cafes offering Texas and Southern specialties, barbecue, pizza, and Mexican food.

Spend a night or two at the St. Botolph Inn (808 South Lamar Street, Weatherford 76086, 817–594–1455 or 800–868–6520), a gorgeous mansion with six guest rooms with private baths and a one-bedroom carriage house with hot tub. You'll have five hilltop acres to roam and a wonderful swimming pool at your disposal, too.

For information on lodging, dining, historic sites, antiques, and the wonderful Parker County Peach Festival, held every July, contact the Weatherford Chamber of Commerce, 401 Fort Worth Street, Weatherford 76086, (817) 594–3801.

Dinosaurs and Hell's Gates

From Fort Worth the next destination is *Granbury,* a charming 1800s town that was restored in the 1970s to its original Victorian glory. You can reach Granbury by driving south 30 miles from Fort Worth on U.S. Highway 377; note, however, that a slight but most worthy detour can be found 5 miles shy of Granbury. *Acton State Historic Site* is just 2 miles away on Farm Road 4, which intersects U.S. Highway 377. The Acton Cemetery holds a lovely monument to Elizabeth Crockett, widow of Alamo hero Davy Crockett, who moved here after he was killed. The statue rising above her grave shows her with her hand to her brow, watching and hoping he will come home. If you arrive during spring, the cemetery—and all this countryside—will be blanketed in vibrant bluebonnets.

Continue to Granbury then, following signs directing you to the historic downtown, which has been listed on the National Register of Historic Places. The town, after its 1890s heyday, fell into a decline but was grandly resuscitated by a town project in the 1970s that became a model for all Main Street renovation projects in the state. The town of 5,000 is the Hood County seat and a charming escape for a day, but most people stay at least a weekend.

First stop is at *The Nutt House* on the Granbury Town Square (817–573–5612), named, of course, for the Nutt family, who originally owned the building when it was a mercantile in 1893. If ever there were a laid-back country inn, this is it: Rooms have screen doors and ceiling fans, even though the hotel's air-conditioned; a large upstairs landing has tables for playing cards and writing letters; and Hennington's Cafe, an excellent restaurant—drawing diners from all over north Texas—is downstairs. The hotel's popularity necessitated the addition of extra rooms, which are found a block away in the Annex, also on the square, stationed in an old law office.

Lunch and dinner at *Hennington's Cafe at the Nutt House* (817–573–9362) range from chicken and dill dumplings, spicy Thai prawns, and stacked New Mexican enchiladas to hot smoked salmon in avocado with tropical salsa. Closed Tuesday and Wednesday, Hennington's is open Monday and Thursday through Sunday from 11:00 A.M. until 3:00 P.M. and Monday and Thursday through Saturday from 5:00 until 9:00 P.M.

Facing the Nutt House is the *Hood County Courthouse,* built in 1890 and containing its original Seth Thomas clock; past that is *Granbury Opera House,* 116 East Pearl Street, Granbury 76048, built in 1886 and a very popular stage for a variety of musical productions from February through December. For show information and tickets, call (817) 573–9191.

Off the north side of the square, the *Hood County Jail,* 208 North Crockett, Granbury 76048 (817–573–5135), is an 1885 Old West jail crafted of hand-hewn stone. Used as a jail for ninety years, it's now home to the chamber of commerce, but visitors are welcome to look at the old cellblock and hanging tower.

One of the most appealing B&Bs in Granbury is *The Iron Horse Inn* (616 Thorp Springs Road, Granbury 76048, 817–579–5535). The largest historic home in town at 7,000 square feet, the ninety-year-old Craftsman-style house has wood floors throughout; a huge, open staircase; lots of beveled glass in windows and doors; and a large fireplace. Six guest rooms are in the main house and one is in the carriage house. All have private baths or showers and queen-size beds. Breakfasts are served in the dining room and usually consist of quiche, omelets, pancakes or waffles, baked grapefruit, muffins, or coffee cake.

Granbury is known by north Texas weekend explorers for its abundance of reasonably priced antiques stores, tearooms offering wonderful lunches, and bed-and-breakfast lodgings. To get a list, a few good maps, and information, see the Granbury Convention & Visitors Bureau at 100 North Crockett Street, Granbury 76048 (817–573–5548).

The Brazos River cuts its path diagonally across north and central Texas and in Granbury is impounded to make the 8,700-acre Lake Granbury that nearly wraps around the city. There are more than 100 miles of shoreline with parks, swimming beaches, and marinas.

From Granbury follow Texas Highway 144, 17 miles south, and you'll find the bucolic town of **Glen Rose.** Founded in 1849 as a trading post,

Hood County Courthouse

it is now the Somervell County seat and home to 2,000 people. From the 1920s through the 1930s, however, this was a thriving health resort for people who came to sanitariums here to take the rejuvenating waters. One still standing has been transformed into a lovely place to stay today, the *Inn on the River,* at 206 Barnard Street, Glen Rose 76043 (254–897–2101 or 800–575–2101), an extravagantly renovated and decorated nineteen-room bed-and-breakfast lodge. Built in 1919, the inn backs up to the serene Paluxy River and is a romantic place to spend the weekend. Gourmet breakfasts and dinners are offered to guests, and sometimes to nonguests, by reservation only.

Sitting out in the rolling hills of Somervell County, the *Hummingbird Lodge* (Farm Road 203 just off U.S. Highway 67, 254–897–2787) has rustic-but-contemporary buildings of stone and cedar, surrounded by 140 woodsy acres. A hot tub, library with TV/VCR, porch with rockers, living and dining rooms with stone fireplaces, walking trails, fishing ponds stocked with black bass and channel cat, and plenty of bird watching and wildlife spotting keep guests relaxed and amused. Six guest rooms include a king/twin room, which can be made up either way, with a refrigerator. All have private baths and sitting areas, and decor includes Texas period and antique pieces, Oriental rugs, and Mexican tile detail. Breakfast is a buffet affair.

Glen Rose is known best, though, for something much older—actually prehistoric. *Dinosaur Valley State Park,* 4 miles west of town on Farm Road 205 (254–897–4588), is the site of the best-preserved dinosaur tracks, some experts say, in the world. In the solid limestone bed of the Paluxy River, just above its confluence with the Brazos River, the unmistakable prints have been found to be those of the sauropod, a gargantuan creature that ate plants, measured longer than 55 feet, and weighed more than 30 tons. Other tracks have indicated that the duck-billed dinosaur and the theropod also lived in this area. Near the river, a fenced-off area contains two life-size models of the T-rex and the brontosaurus, fiberglass models left over from the Sinclair Oil Corporation's dinosaur exhibit at the 1964–65 New York World's Fair. The park is about 1,500 acres and offers a wild but enchanting shrubby terrain of bluffs and water, ideal for picnicking, camping, and hiking. A dinosaur exhibit at the visitors center is open daily from 8:00 A.M. until 5:00 P.M. Park admission is $5.00 per vehicle.

North Texans also come to Glen Rose throughout the year for the numerous *bluegrass festivals* hosted by Oakdale Park, on Texas Highway 144 about 3 miles south of U.S. Highway 67 (254–897–2321). There are camping facilities, cabins, a swimming pool, and a pavilion here, as well.

Dinosaur Valley State Park

From spring through fall, outdoors lovers flock to this part of the Brazos River for *canoeing* near Tres Rios Park, 2 miles east of town on County Road 312 (254–897–4253). Canoe trips can last a day or a week, depending on your wishes. The park offers information, as well as cabins and camping.

Three miles southwest of town via U.S. Highway 67 (254–897–2960) is the fascinating, renowned *Fossil Rim Wildlife Ranch.* More than 1,000 endangered animals from five continents call this 3,000-acre conservation center home. There's a 9-mile driving tour through the ranch, where visitors see animals roaming at will, among them the white rhino, cheetah, gray zebra, and wildebeest. The scenic overlook near the route's end is an excellent place for photos and reflection, and a restaurant, petting zoo, nature hiking trail, riding stables, and picnic areas are close by. The ranch is open daily from 9:00 A.M. until two hours before sunset. Admission is charged.

The ranch also offers the *Foothills Safari Camp,* a luxury wildlife safari providing guests with posh tents and gourmet meals. Five rooms are also available at the lodge. For inquiries and reservations call (254) 897–2960.

From Glen Rose depart on Texas Highway 144 heading south 23 miles, pick up Texas Highway 6 in the town of Meridian, and follow it south another 12 miles. This places you at the tiny community of *Clifton,* settled in 1854 on the banks of the pretty Bosque (BOS-Kee) River, today the largest town—with about 4,000 residents—in Bosque County. Fishing is a popular pastime here on the Bosque River and nearby at Lake Whitney.

Scandinavian traditions are still observed in Clifton by descendants of the original Norwegian settlers. To see the terrain of this heritage, drive into what's known as Norse Country, along Farm Road 219 west from town and Farm Road 182 north from town. Tours can be arranged through the Clifton Chamber of Commerce, (254) 675–3720. The Norse church, sitting alone in the countryside, is really special.

To explore more of this Norse community, check out the **Bosque County Memorial Museum,** at Avenue Q and West Ninth Street (254–675–3720), a small but informative place with exhibits detailing the founding and growth of the Norse Capital of Texas. You'll see excellent examples of "rosemaling," the Norwegian craft of painting or carving intricate floral detail on all sorts of wooden furnishings. The museum is open Sunday and Thursday from 2:00 until 5:00 P.M. and Friday and Saturday from 10:00 A.M. until 5:00 P.M. Admission is charged.

Your next destination from Clifton takes you along some roughly scenic prairie and ranch land, gently rolling into the west. Drive north along Texas Highway 6, 36 miles to the town of Hico (HY-koe), stopping for a robust breakfast, lunch, or dinner at the **Koffee Kup Family Restaurant,** at the intersection of Texas Highway 6 and U.S. Highway 281 (254–796–4839). Don't try to resist the extraordinary meringue pies—it's impossible.

From Hico drive north on U.S. Highway 281, 47 miles, touring through more rolling, tree-dotted ranch country, until you arrive in **Mineral Wells,** a pretty old town of 14,000 in Palo Pinto County, a wonderful place to pause in your approach to west Texas. Here's another town that saw a boom—this one in the 1880s—thanks to its mysteriously healing waters. Since no one could explain why this mineral-laden water, which didn't have an appealing scent, would make people feel better, it became known as Crazy Water, and everything in town was named similarly, such as the Crazy Hotel, the Crazy Park, and a radio show called "The Crazy Gang."

The boom was highlighted by the building of the elaborate, luxurious Baker Hotel in 1929, but the Depression ended the boom, and today the grand Baker Hotel—which was a copy of the famous Arlington Hotel in Hot Springs, Arkansas—stands deserted. Nevertheless, it's a great photo site rising above the skyline in the middle of town. **The Crazy Water Hotel,** North Oak Street at Northwest Third Street (940–325–4441), is a popular retirement home. Visitors are often allowed access to the seventh-story terrace, from which a good view of the town and the Palo Pinto Mountains just north is available. Mineral Wells's downtown streets have a few good antiques shops with most reasonable prices.

Shopping stops worth noting include *Hanchey Leather Goods* (200 North Oak, Mineral Wells 76067, 940–325–1843), a quality shop selling hand-crafted leather items, from wallets and belts to earrings and watch bands. *W. D. Woodworks* (221 North Oak Street, Mineral Wells 76067, 940–328–0424) allows you to view talented craftspeople producing all sorts of furniture, which you can order and/or buy.

A charming, relaxing place to spend a night or two is *Silk Stocking Row Bed & Breakfast* (415 Northwest Fourth Street, Mineral Wells 76067, 940–325–4101), found inside a fastidiously restored 1904 home. Four guest rooms each have private baths, TV, and either king, queen, or twin beds. A full gourmet breakfast is included with your stay.

If a cheap meal is up your alley and you enjoy an old-fashioned pool hall spirit, by all means drop into Woody's (6105 Highway 80, Mineral Wells 76067, 940–325–9817). A Mineral Wells legend, this little hole-in-the-wall offers a darned good burger from an old griddle, along with an icy-cold beer.

On beautiful west Texas days, when the sun's out and the rivers aren't too low, you should think about taking a little canoe excursion on the beautiful Brazos River. *Rochelle's Canoe Rentals* (Highway 4 at the Brazos River, 940–659–3341 or 940–659–2581) is a friendly outfit that

Bizarre Texas Stuff

*M*INERAL WELLS: *In 1987 Amanda Lollar rescued an injured Mexican free-tailed bat (the state's official flying mammal) on her way to her furniture store. Since then she liquidated her business and turned it into the state's only permanent sanctuary for nonreleasable bats, and she became a state-licensed wildlife rehabilitator. She runs Bat World Living Museum (217 North Oak Street, 940–325–3404), where she provides a home to up to fifteen bat species, including orphaned bat pups, bats used in lab research, wild bats with permanent injuries, and bats confiscated from the illegal pet trade. Inside you can see several wire-mesh cages with bats hanging upside down from special roosts that she designed and her father built. Lollar says she can tell by the bats' eyes or facial expressions if they're feeling sick, and she has inspired her town to go batty, too. More than one hundred bat houses are up on buildings and poles in Mineral Wells; the police department added a roost to its building and painted "Bat Cops" on it, while the bank's bat roost is labeled "Nite Depository." Lollar has also penned two books,* The Bat in My Pocket: A Memorable Friendship, *and* The Crazy Water Town That Went Batty.

will charge you $10 to $20 per person, depending on how long you want to paddle downriver, and they'll pick you up at a designated spot.

Hikers and rock climbers will want to spend at least a day at *Lake Mineral Wells State Park* (Highway 180, 3 miles east of town, 940–328–1171). Crowded with trees and rocks, this scenic spread with a 650-acre lake is popular with nature watchers, too, in search of white-tailed deer, raccoon, and armadillo. The park is the western terminus of the outstanding *Rails-to-Trails* pathway, a 22-mile connection of Mineral Wells and Weatherford, built on an old railbed and opened in 1997 for hikers, cyclists, and horseback riders to enjoy.

Another great place to spend a few days in this area is at *Possum Kingdom Lake State Park,* reached by driving west of Mineral Wells on U.S. Highway 180 for 38 miles until you reach the settlement of Caddo. Then head north 17 miles on Park Road 33, which ends at the park entrance; the park's phone is (940) 549–1803. Near the entrance look for some not-too-shy longhorn cattle; they are part of the official state herd.

The massive lake, a 22,000-acre reservoir formed by damming the beautiful Brazos River, has depths up to 150 feet and the clearest water in the Southwest, making it a popular site for scuba diving, waterskiing, and sailing. An extraordinary cliff formation on the southwestern end of the lake is called Hell's Gates; it's a great photography subject and is magnificent at sunset. Campsites, cabins, marinas, and cafes sit around the 300 miles of shoreline, but the state park's offerings are generally the best. Sitting on the south shore, the 1,500-acre park has superb hiking trails, nice if small beaches, shady and scenic campsites, a playground, canoe rentals, simple cabins, a small store, a long and lighted fishing pier, and countless good places for bank fishing.

A resort on the eastern shores of Possum Kingdom is called *The Cliffs* (940–779–4040 or 888–843–2543). You'll find it along Texas Highway 16, south of Park Road 36. There guests can choose between lodge and condo accommodations and take advantage of the resort's 18-hole, championship golf course; health and beauty spa; tennis and swim center; full-service marina; and private, white-sand beach.

Lunch and dinner is had at the *Rafters Restaurant* (on Scenic Point Cove, 940–779–3177), north of The Cliffs on Texas Highway 16, then west and north on Farm Road 2353 west/north to Park Road 36, which you'll follow west. A relaxed eating and drinking spot housed in a restored Amish barn (relocated from Ohio), the Rafters offers everything from fried catfish and steaks to burgers and homemade pies.

There are modest, old-fashioned lake retreats in the form of cabins and apartments on Possum Kingdom, too. Call the Possum Kingdom Lake Chamber of Commerce at (940) 779–2424 for information.

Hang around the lake a while or go north to *Archer City* and Wichita Falls. From Possum Kingdom, head north on Texas Highway 16 through the town of Graham (that's 14 miles from the lake) and then another 30 miles north until you reach Texas Highway 281. Follow U.S. 281 north another 7 miles to Windthorst, deep in dairy country, then turn west on Texas Highway 25 and travel 11 miles until you reach Archer City.

You've arrived in the hometown of author Larry McMurtry, who penned the Pulitzer prize–winning *Lonesome Dove,* as well as *Terms of Endearment,* and *The Last Picture Show,* which was filmed in this very burgh. Archer City has but 2,000 residents, but thanks to McMurtry, it will prosper.

McMurtry owns and operates *Booked Up* (216 South Center Street, Archer City 76351, 940–574–2511), the nation's largest collection of antiquarian books, found in four stores around the Archer County Courthouse square. The buildings are clearly marked in front; No. 1 holds tomes of African-American studies, law and true crime, sports, and more; No. 2 contains art, architecture, photography, and children's books; No. 3 has books about books, fiction before 1925, and foreign books; and No. 4 ranges from books on dance and drama to journalism and medicine.

Inside the shops is a sheet for visitors with commonly asked questions, such as, "Are these books for sale?" (Answer: Of course); "Where do I

Bizarre Texas Stuff

*A*RCHER CITY: An astoundingly ordinary-looking town of about 1,800, Archer City—roughly 85 miles north of Albany—is quite a bit more than it seems. Thanks to native son Larry McMurtry, author of Lonesome Dove, Terms of Endearment, The Last Picture Show, and other novels, Archer City isn't in danger of disappearing as other rural Texas towns are. Archer City has been used as the filming loca-tion for The Last Picture Show (1971) and its sequel, Texasville (1989), Hollywood's versions of McMurtry's stories. In addition, McMurtry established Booked Up, Inc., in Archer City, a bookstore offering the largest collection of antiquarian books in the United States. Over the years the author has collected the rare, odd, and out-of-print books carried in this store. Find it in several renovated buildings along Main Street.

pay?" (A: In building No. 1); and "When will Mr. McMurtry be here?" (A: At his whim). When he is, he will sign copies of his books. Note that first editions of *Lonesome Dove* sell for $350 to $400.

Next door to one of the shops is **Chalk Hill Grill**, open for breakfast and lunch Monday through Friday and for dinner on Friday and Saturday. Archer City lodgings include the **Spur Hotel** (on the square, 940–574–2501), a 1928 inn originally called the Andrews Hotel, offering eleven rooms with private baths; and **Lonesome Dove Inn** (225 West Main Street, Archer City 76351, 940–574–2700), McMurtry's seven-room bed-and-breakfast lodging in a large, Georgian-style home.

Now turn north on Texas Highway 79, and 25 miles later you'll find yourself in **Wichita Falls,** a city of about 100,000 with an oil-boom heritage, situated on the Wichita River, nearly right on top of the Texas-Oklahoma state line.

Among many historic sites is **Kell House** (900 Bluff Street, Wichita Falls 76301, 940–723–0623), the early twentieth-century home of a city founder who entertained lavishly. The restored home features original period furnishings, a baby grand player piano, seven fireplaces, and hand-stenciled decorations. Open from 2:00 to 4:00 P.M. Tuesday through Friday and Sunday. Admission is $3.00.

At the **Wichita Falls Museum and Art Center** (2 Eureka Circle, Wichita Falls 76301, 940–692–0923), a permanent collection of pre–American Revolution prints are exhibited, and there's a planetarium and a discovery room for kids on-site. Open from 10:00 A.M. until 5:00 P.M. Tuesday through Saturday. Admission is $3.00.

Overnight guests in Wichita Falls can choose from a number of hotels and motels, or they can stay in an elegant, Prairie-style home built in 1919, **Harrison House** (2014 Eleventh Street, Wichita Falls 76301, 940–322–2299). Inside are four guest rooms with shared baths; a full breakfast is included with your stay.

Some of the more popular chow palaces in Wichita Falls are the **Bar-L** (Thirteenth at Travis Street, Wichita Falls 76301, 940–766–0003), a down-home beer-and-barbecue joint that counts McMurtry and sportswriters among its fans; **El Gordo's** (512 Scott Street, Wichita Falls 76301, 940–322–6251), a friendly, fattening Mexican-food spot; and **McBride's Land & Cattle** (501 Scott Street, Wichita Falls 76301, 940–322–2516).

Twenty miles southeast via U.S. 82/U.S. 287 is the town of Henrietta, the seat of Clay County. Folks come here specifically to the charming escape called **Henrietta Township Bed & Breakfast** (102 North Bridge Street,

Henrietta 76365, 940–538–6968). Tucked inside a lovingly restored 1883 building, the B&B offers five antiques-stocked guest rooms, some with antique claw-foot tubs. The hosts frequently offer murder mystery weekends, based on actual events in the area; authentic costumes are included.

OTHER PLACES TO STAY IN NORTH TEXAS

DALLAS

Hotel Crescent Court, 400 Crescent Court, Dallas 75205, (800) 654–6541 or (214) 871–3200. Elegant, Turtle Creek–area lodging with excellent restaurants, shopping, and sensational spa.

Magnolia, 1401 Commerce Street, Dallas 75201, (214) 915–6500 or (888) 915–1110. Renovated 1922 office building–turned–first-class hotel has rooms, suites, dry-cleaning service, and exercise room.

FORT WORTH

Azalea Plantation Bed & Breakfast, 1400 Robinwood Drive, Fort Worth 76111, (800) 687–3529.

B&B at the Ranch, U.S. Highway 287, 1/2 mile north of Saginaw, (817) 232–5522. Located on 20 acres about 120 miles from the Stockyards district, this lodging is a ranch home with four guest rooms with private baths. Guests enjoy a large living room and a gourmet breakfast.

Bloomsbury House, 2251 Lipscomb Street, Fort Worth 76110, (817) 921–2383. A Queen Anne Victorian home, built by a foreman working out of the Fort Worth Stockyards, has been converted to an inn offering three pretty guest rooms with private baths. In back there's a carriage house with a full kitchen, too. Dessert and a full breakfast are included.

Hotel Texas, 2415 Ellis Avenue, Fort Worth 76106, (817) 624–2224.

Texas White House, 1417 Eighth Avenue, Fort Worth 76104, (817) 923–3597. One of Fort Worth's historic landmarks, the 1910 Colonial Revival home is often the site of weddings and receptions. Three guest rooms have period decor and private baths with lotions, bubble bath, thick towels, and–on request–feather beds.

GAINESVILLE

Rose House Bed and Breakfast, 321 South Dixon Street, Gainesville 76240, (940) 665–1010 or (972) 219–4762.

GLEN ROSE

Rough Creek Lodge (restaurant and resort), County Road 2013, Glen Rose 76043, (800) 864–4705.

Wild Rose Inn, 401 Grace Street, Glen Rose 76043, (254) 897–4112.

GRANBURY

Arbor House, 530 East Pearl Street, Granbury 76048, (800) 641–0073.

Captain's House and Cottage B&B, 123 West Doyle Street, Granbury 76048, (817) 579–6664.

Pearl Street Inn Bed & Breakfast, 319 West Pearl Street, Granbury 76048, (817) 579–7465.

OTHER PLACES TO EAT IN NORTH TEXAS

DALLAS

Javier's, 4912 Cole, Dallas 75205, (214) 521–4211. Real Mexican food–meaning from Mexico's interior–includes steak, roasted chicken, fish, and enchiladas with earthy chile treatments. Open for dinner nightly; prices start from about $20 per meal.

Cafe Madrid, 4501 Travis Street, Dallas 75205, (214) 528–1731. Dallas's original tapas bar does a fabulous potato omelet, grilled pork loin, marinated squid, cheeses, and more.

Nuevo Leon, 3211C Oak Lawn Avenue, Dallas 75219, (214) 522–3331. Mexican dishes from the country's interior, including excellent seafood and steaks. Lovely, art-filled interior also appeals.

Tei Tei Robata Bar, 2906 North Henderson Street, Dallas 75206, (214) 828–2400. Sublime, sleek Japanese restaurant beloved for sashimi, super-fresh grilled fish, and the pricey Kobe beef steaks. Amazing sake choices abound.

Sonny Bryan's, 2202 Inwood Road, Dallas 75235, (214) 357–7120. Possibly the best smoked brisket and ribs anywhere in north Texas. Open for lunch only, seven days a week; meals start at about $5.00.

DENTON
The Cupboard Cafe, 200 West Congress Street, Denton 76201, (940) 387–5386. Tucked inside Cupboard Natural Foods, this bright, artful spot does wonders with soups, salads, sandwiches, and desserts for lunch and early dinner daily. Meals average about $6.00.

Mercado Juarez Cafe & Cantina, 419 South Elm Street, Denton 76201, (940) 380–0755.

Place Louisiane Restaurant, 1007 Avenue G, Denton 76201, (940) 483–1411.

The Texican Grill, 111 West Mulberry Street, Denton 76201, (940) 381–6722.

Tom & Jo's Cafe, 702 South Elm Street, Denton 76201, (940) 387–0491.

FORT WORTH
Carshon's Delicatessen, 3133 Cleburne Road, Fort Worth 67110, (817) 923–1907. The only kosher-style restaurant in town; the sandwiches and pies are outstanding. Open for lunch Tuesday through Sunday. Meals start at about $5.00.

Paris Coffee Shop, 700 West Magnolia Avenue, Fort Worth 67104, (817) 335–2041.

Parthenon, 401 North Henderson Street, Fort Worth 76102, (817) 810–0800.

Railhead Smokehouse, 2900 Montgomery Street, Fort Worth 76107, (817) 738–9808. This is the best place in town for smoked ribs, pork, chicken, and cold schooners of beer. Open for lunch and dinner Monday through Saturday; meals start at about $5.00.

GAINESVILLE
Cary's Tearoom in Miss Pittypat's Antique Emporium, 111 West California Street, Gainesville 76240, (940) 668–7344.

GLEN ROSE
Rough Creek Lodge (restaurant and resort), County Road 2013, Glen Rose 76043, (800) 864–4705.

GRANBURY
Cliff's Seafood Restaurant, 4506 Weatherford Highway, Granbury 76048, (254) 573–2543. Catfish is the big favorite at this family place, which serves inexpensive lunch and dinner Wednesday through Sunday.

Pearl Street Pasta House, 101 East Pearl Street, Granbury 76048, (254) 279–7729. Situated in a historic building on the square, this charming spot serves home-style Italian fare daily for lunch and dinner.

MINERAL WELLS
Baris Pizza & Pasta, 2805 Highway 180 West, Mineral Wells 76067, (940) 325–0333.

Longhorn Bar and Grill, 3501 Highway 180 West, Mineral Wells 76067, (940) 325–9882.

POSSUM KINGDOM LAKE
Jackson's Restaurant, Farm Road 2353, (940) 779–4131.

WEATHERFORD
Downtown Cafe, 101 West Church Street, Weatherford 76086, (817) 594–8717.

Mesquite Pit, 1201 Fort Worth Street, Weatherford 76086, (817) 596–7046.

The Texas Panhandle

Romance and longing? For the Texas Panhandle? Why not? The pioneers who settled here came with a dream that—with plenty of muscle and heart—they made come true. Although the earth and the elements had their hard edges, the South, Staked, and High Plains also offered sweet repose. Anyone who read the Pulitzer prize–winning *Lonesome Dove* (or watched the fine television miniseries) will have a sense of déjà vu upon arrival. The *llano estacado* (staked plains) stretch north toward the Cap Rock Escarpment, later yielding to the High Plains. The Canadian River should look familiar—that's the area where a lone Gus used his horse as a fort to fight the Kiowas and where he rescued the tortured Lorena from Blue Duck.

The sixteenth-century Spanish conquistadors were enamored with the endless grasslands and countless buffalo of the Panhandle, as were the Apaches, who were followed by the war-loving Comanches and young American pioneers, determined to find a future. Some would-be Gold Rushers jumped off the Fort Smith–Santa Fe Trail in the Panhandle, and ranchers came sometime after the Comanches were conquered and sent to the Oklahoma Territory. By 1888, thirty-three ranches spread to occupy a land the size of Ireland.

Yucca plants shoot sharply skyward, nettles sprout white blooms, and challas burst with pink blossoms after a rainy spring. It's not unusual to drive an infuriatingly straight highway, then find it inexplicably winding and climbing a bluff before the monotonous view suddenly falls off into a green-and-red valley blanketed in yellow flowers. Purple-red firewheels scale rocky hillsides that are also lined by paths etched by the collared lizard, whose skin ranges from neon green to dusty yellow. Watch out for bushes with three-inch thorns, but rest assured it's okay to eat the tart sumac berries—Native Americans made their version of Kool-Aid from the stuff.

Barbed-wire fences—which originated on ranches in this region—stretch for thousands of miles, attempting to corral this great openness. The sky grows larger every day. A few of the scarce trees have elongated,

The Texas Panhandle

gnarled arms that surely were loved by those who administered outlaw justice. And hilly rises where there were once no trees are now populated by the tenacious mesquite.

Just a few years after the buffalo hunters and ranchers came to Texas a century ago, the Native Americans and buffalo had been exterminated. Indeed, Panhandle cattle-empire builders were successful in their work; for a period, there were three cows to every person. Poking around the same plains today, it's easy to trace history. Little has changed, for one matter, and the region's children are accomplished at preservation and continuation, for another. You'll come away wondering why all westerns aren't filmed here—it's so utterly Texan that other places in the state seem almost fraudulent by comparison.

June's Favorite Attractions in the Texas Panhandle

Allen's Fried Chicken, Sweetwater

Buffalo Gap Historic Village, Buffalo Gap

Cadillac Ranch, Amarillo

Caprock Canyons State Park, Quitaque

Fort Phantom Hill ruins, near Abilene

Llano Estacado Winery, Lubbock

Palo Duro Canyon State Park, Canyon

Panhandle Plains Museum, Canyon

Silver Falls Park, near Crosbyton

The Old Jail Art Center, Albany

Fandangles and Rattlesnakes

Most likely your Panhandle tour will pick up where our north Texas trail left off. But whether you're approaching the northwest section of Texas from Possum Kingdom Lake, just west of Fort Worth, or coming directly from the Dallas–Fort Worth area, you'll want to follow U.S. Highway 180 west from the Metroplex. First stop is Albany, seat of Shackelford County and home to 1,900 Texans, 120 miles west of Fort Worth on U.S. Highway 180.

Albany earned the handle "the home of the Hereford" for being the place where the favorite cattle breed was introduced in Texas's young days. The western heritage associated with the town endures: Hereford and other cattle represent some 90 percent of Shackelford County's agriculture business; historians point out that one of Albany's more famous sons was Edwin Dyess, for whom the Air Force base at Abilene is named; and one of its more infamous guests was prisoner John Selman, who later killed gunman John Wesley Hardin in El Paso.

First stop on the Albany tour is *The Old Jail Art Center,* South Second Street near Walnut Street (915–762–2269), which has achieved status as one of the finer small art museums in the Southwest, having gained a great deal of stature since its 1980 opening. Its staff enjoys bragging that this museum has a larger storage vault than Fort Worth's esteemed Kimbell Art Museum. Several wings have been added to the original structure, which was built in 1877. Some of the masons were paid by the stone, and their initials are visible on many of the large rectangles of stone. The jail once housed the keeper's office, cells, and exercise room, also known as a runaround. Today it contains the remarkable pre-Columbian collection donated by a Mineral Wells resident. Of note are the Chinese terra-cotta tomb figures, dating to 206 B.C., and a Buddhist prayer book from Cambodia dating to the sixteenth century.

In the several new wings added to the jail are such interesting items as art deco doors from the Old Town Drug Store; an exceptional jade and amethyst collection; Picasso drawings; Italian ballroom chairs; and small Henry Moore bronzes. There also are exquisite furnishings, such as a grand piano crafted from tiger-eye oak in 1895. The museum's courtyard is a pretty place for reflection and for the myriad parties held there. Commanding attention in the center is a blockish contemporary windmill carved from native stone by artist Jesus Morales. The museum is open Tuesday through Saturday from 10:00 A.M. until 5:00 P.M. and Sunday from 2:00 until 5:00 P.M. Admission is free.

Just a block away in the City Park on South Main Street at South First Street, the *Georgia Monument* is a touching site. The stark stone memorial commemorates the five companies of volunteers who made the journey from Georgia to fight with the Texans in their revolution. Sadly, the majority were killed with Col. James Fannin in the famous massacre at Goliad; nearly twenty years later the Georgia legislature invoiced Texas for $3,000 for guns but waived payment if the Lone Star State would erect a monument to the victims. Thanks to the citizens of Albany, that was finally accomplished in 1976.

Also downtown at City Park, the *Ledbetter Picket House* occupies the corner of South Main and South First Streets. The restored 1870s frontier ranch has been relocated from near Fort Griffin so people can better inspect the interior, with items from the Ledbetter Salt Works, built in 1860. "Picket" is the term used for the construction style in which walls are built with vertical rather than horizontal boards. To tour this place, make an appointment with the chamber of commerce, (915) 762–2525.

When it's time for a meal, *Fort Griffin General Merchandise Restaurant,* just west of the Albany square on Texas Highway 180 (915–762–3034), is not only a good place to dine but also a self-contained point of interest. Chef and co-owner Ali Esfandiary is a petite, jovial man who is retired from Dyess Air Force Base, but he originally comes from Iran.

THE TEXAS PANHANDLE

JUNE'S FAVORITE ANNUAL EVENTS IN THE TEXAS PANHANDLE

Artwalk, Abilene, second weekend in March

Bob Wills Day, Turkey, last weekend in April

Cowboy Symposium, Lubbock, mid- to late September

Fort Griffin Fandangle, Albany, last two weekends in June

Panhandle South Plains Fair, Lubbock, late September

Punkin Days, Floydada, weekend closest to Halloween

Rattlesnake Roundup, Sweetwater, second weekend in March

Texas Cowboys Reunion, Stamford, first weekend in July

Texas! A Musical Drama, Palo Duro Canyon, June through August

XIT Reunion and Rodeo, Dalhart, first weekend in August

Ali is all smiles and jokes, and as he talks with patrons, it's obvious that he's quite a local favorite. The restaurant is all roadhouse upon first impression, but its interior surprises with homey touches such as curtains and antiques. The menu is fashioned after an old-time newspaper, full of noteworthy items and lore from the nineteenth century. Atmosphere and details aside, the rib-eyes are fork-tender and simply the best in memory, the beautiful prime rib is the size of most placemats, and red snapper and fresh zucchini strips are other delights from the mesquite grill.

Stick around and relax the night away at the *Ole Nail House Inn* on the courthouse square, (915) 762-2928. The comfortable bed-and-breakfast occupies the upstairs of a 1914 home whose former resident was Robert Nail, creator of the town's Fandangle—which we'll soon cover. The three guest rooms are made soft and pretty with flowers, antiques, and fruit baskets. Sunporch breakfast spreads are usually something wonderful such as pecan waffles, bacon, and fresh fruit.

From town head 15 miles north on U.S. Highway 283 to *Fort Griffin State Historical Park* (915–762–3592), occupying 500 acres along the Clear Fork of the Brazos River. The fort was established in 1867 during the federal reoccupation of Texas after the Civil War, and the cavalry stationed here fought Kiowa and Comanche and helped end their domination of north Texas. Some people know the park chiefly as the home of the state longhorn herd, whose story is as impressive as any in the state. Fort Griffin was along one of the routes through which some ten million head of Texas longhorns were driven north to the beef markets a century ago. The longhorn was nearing extinction around 1920, and western author J. Frank Dobie was among a handful of men who helped preserve the stock. Descendants of the Dobie herd live at Fort Griffin, while other animals in the state herd live at state parks including Possum Kingdom, Palo Duro Canyon, and LBJ. By loan agreement, University of Texas mascots bearing the name Bevo are obtained from the Fort Griffin herd.

The park grounds also hold a restored bakery, replicas of other fort buildings, and some ruins, with a model of the fort and an exhibit on fort history inside the visitors center. In addition, there are nature and walking trails, rest rooms, showers, a picnic area, a playground, and campsites, some with water and electricity.

The Chisholm Trail's Western Trail split off and came through Fort Griffin, and, like Fort Worth, this town was one of the West's wildest for gunslingers, gamblers, and outlaws—and that's where the **Fort Griffin Fandangle** comes in. The grand outdoor musical has been staged by locals for more than fifty years and is one of the more endearing annual events in Texas. Lawlessness and the fortitude it took to endure that, as well as isolation and Native American Indian scares, are celebrated in song, dance, and pageantry, with longhorns and horses helping to create the mood. Close to a quarter of the townspeople—about 300—are involved in the spectacle, which takes place the third and fourth weekends in June. The show begins at 8:30 P.M. on pageant nights, with a barbecue dinner taking place earlier. For reservations and information call (915) 762–3642.

If you go back through Albany, then west 8 miles on Texas Highway 6 and south 27 miles on Texas Highway 351, you will arrive in *Abilene,* the Taylor County seat and home to 106,000 residents. A sizable stop on I–20, Abilene is best known as the location of *Dyess Air Force Base,* I–20 at U.S. Highway 277 (915–696–5609 or 915–696–2196), which is a closed base requiring you to obtain a pass at the main gate to enter. Having done that, head for Dyess's *Linear Air Park,* where twenty-five World War II, Korean, and Vietnam War aircraft displayed outdoors include the C-47 Skytrain and B-17 Flying Fortress, plus B-1 bombers for training and combat. The date changes from year to year, but you may be lucky enough to catch an air show featuring the USAF Thunderbirds. Admission is free, and the air park is open during daylight hours.

For another collection head for the *Museums of Abilene,* situated at Grace Cultural Center, 102 Cypress Street, Abilene 79601 (915–673–4587), a cluster of three museums. In the Children's Museum, kids learn, in a participatory way, scientific principles and technology's uses and applications in daily life; at the Fine Arts Museum, exhibits generally include classical to abstract art, using various media; and the Historical Museum profiles Abilene's history, with emphasis on the recent past. Numerous traveling exhibits make stops at this museum center annually. Admission is $3.00 for adults, $2.00 for senior citizens, and $1.00 for children twelve and under; the museums are open Tuesday through Saturday from 10:00 A.M. until 5:00 P.M., for Thursday Family Night from 5:30 to 8:30 P.M., and Sunday from 1:00 until 5:00 P.M.

Be sure the kids get to see the *Abilene Zoo and Discovery Center* (3 miles east of the center of town on Texas Highway 36, in Nelson Park, 915–676–6085). The plains of Texas and Africa are represented by 500 species of animals, including coyotes, javelinas, zebras, ostriches, and bison. The herpetarium houses more than seventy different species of reptiles and amphibians. At the Discovery Center, visitors can learn more about various biomes. Open daily 9:00 A.M. to 5:00 P.M., with extended hours between Memorial Day and Labor Day. Admission is $3.00 for adults and $2.00 for children.

To find western artistry of a slightly different nature, head for *Art Reed Custom Saddles* (361 East South Eleventh Street, Abilene 79602, 915–677–4572). The saddlemaker has been at his craft for more than three decades, building custom saddles from the saddle tree up. Along with western saddles—mostly crafted for ranchers and other cowboys and cowgirls, starting at around $1,500—Mr. Reed makes tack, chaps, and belts. His work is so popular he typically accepts orders for up to six months in advance of delivery. Open Monday through Friday 9:00 to 11:00 A.M. and 2:00 until 5:00 P.M.

It won't take quite as long to claim a pair of custom-made boots at *James Leddy Boots* (1602 North Treadway, Abilene 79601, 915–677–7811), one of the renowned names in Texas cowboy boots. Order now and you should have your eel, snakeskin, calfskin, lizard, or other exotic leather boots within two or three months. Prices start at around $500 and top out at about $3,500. Don't forget to order a belt or wallet to match. Open Monday through Friday 8:30 A.M. until 5:00 P.M.

Sweet Old Baird

The town of Baird, just east of Abilene via I–20, was settled in 1880 and was named the Antiques Capital of West Texas by the state legislature in 1993. In town, you'll find the Old Rock Jail at 100 West Fifth Street, which was moved from the former county seat of Belle Plain; each block was numbered and the jail was rebuilt exactly as it had been. It's used as a Boy Grumpe's, a candy factory at 206 Market Street, which is one of only four candy factories in the United States that produces lollipops for business advertising, and one of only two that puts messages on both the stick and the candy.

Chain motels are plentiful, but you may find a cozier stay at *B. J.'s Bed & Breakfast* (508 Mulberry Street, Abilene 79601, 915–675–5855). Four affordable guest rooms sleep eight guests, with two shared bathrooms. A full breakfast is offered, giving travelers a chance to get to know the hosts and fellow guests.

Two restaurants are on all insiders' must-go lists. Downtown, in easy walking distance of the museums and art galleries, is the *Railhead Grill* (North First and Pine Streets, 915–672–7004), a place serving everything from chicken-fried steak and pot roast to salads. Then there's *Joe Allen's Pit Barbecue* (1233 South Treadaway Boulevard, Abilene 79602, 915–672–6082), a legendary stop for old-fashioned, no-frills Texas 'cue.

Another excellent place to find great cuts of beef is the *Perini Ranch Steakhouse,* situated in *Buffalo Gap Historic Village,* about 6 miles south of the Abilene city limits on Farm Road 89. In this rustic setting, diners enjoy sixteen-ounce roast rib-eyes with cowboy potatoes and ranch beans, or baby-back ribs cooked over mesquite. Open for dinner Wednesday and Thursday and lunch and dinner Friday through Sunday. Call (915) 572–3339 for reservations.

Spend time before dining exploring Buffalo Gap, a restored frontier complex that was once a stopping place along the famous Dodge Cattle Trail, containing relocated historic buildings such as the Taylor County Courthouse and Jail, circa 1879; a railroad depot dating to 1881; Abilene's first blacksmith shop; and Buffalo Gap's own Nazarene Church, built in 1902. A charming trip back in time, Buffalo Gap is open mid-March through mid-November Monday through Saturday from 10:00 A.M. until 6:00 P.M. and Sunday from noon until 6:00 P.M.; and mid-November through mid-March Friday through Sunday 10:00 A.M. to 5:00 P.M. Admission is $4.00 for adults, $3.00 for

We'll Leave the Light on for You

*D*rive 46 miles east of Abilene via I–20 to the town of Cisco in order to visit the Mobley Hotel, 309 Conrad Hilton Avenue (also Texas Highway 6). The old hotel was purchased by Conrad Hilton in 1919, who needed a place to sleep. It became the first in a chain of Hilton hotels when Hilton realized he could make a bundle by letting rooms to oil field workers who would rent by the shift. Today, the restored hotel serves as a chamber of commerce office and community center.

senior citizens, and $1.75 for students. Call the village at (915) 572–3365. The last weekend in April brings the Buffalo Gap Arts Festival, staged in the oak tree shade and featuring art booths and an auction, as well as entertainment ranging from mariachis to barbershop quartets and square dancing.

Another look at history is found north from Abilene 14 miles on Farm Road 600, where the **Fort Phantom Hill Ruins** consist of monolithic, cactus-crowded crumbled masses of stones. These ruins have a particular poignance about them, especially in the day's first or last light—it's easy to imagine that desertion was a problem here because of monotony and loneliness. Dramatic as its name, Fort Phantom Hill was established in 1851 for protection against the Comanches as the westward settlement activity spread. The fort was abandoned in 1854, as the water supply was insufficient; although it mysteriously burned shortly afterward, the fort was later used as a Texas Rangers outpost and as a U.S. Army outpost during the Indian Wars of the 1870s. The ruins lie on private property today, but the owner keeps the site open to the public daily from dawn until dusk. Admission is free.

For fishing or a picnic, head back toward Abilene on Farm Road 600 just 4 miles to 4,200-plus-acre **Lake Fort Phantom,** with 29 miles of shoreline dotted by marinas, boat ramps, primitive campsites, a swimming beach, and an airfield for model planes. Call (915) 676–6217 for information.

Abilene serves as a good pivot point to reach two more marvelous pockets of the Old West. First is **Anson,** 24 miles northwest of Abilene via U.S. Highway 83/277, the seat of Jones County. The town was long known and widely criticized until a few years ago for banning dancing—except at the Christmas Ball—for religious reasons. Times have changed slightly, but most citizens still choose only to go dancin' in Anson for the three days every December when Anson hosts its historic Cowboys' Christmas Ball. Usually held the weekend prior to Christmas, Anson has quite a time letting its citizens cut a rug, and western crooner Michael Martin Murphey has put into song and video the century-old poem honoring the ball, written by rancher Larry Chittenden. If you miss the dancin', check out the other element that drew the locals' ire: The Depression-era mural in Anson's post office offended folks at its 1941 unveiling, as some townspeople felt it was wrong to illustrate the fun people were having on the dance floor. (This *is* the Bible Belt, remember.) See the mural depicting the Christmas Ball in the post office on tiny Main Street (915–823–2241).

Now point your car to our next side trip, to **Stamford,** 17 miles north of Anson on U.S. Highway 277, still in Jones County and with a population

Fort Phantom Hill Ruins

of 3,800. You're in true cowboy country here, as Stamford is home to the Texas Cowboy Reunion held for three days over the weekend closest to July 4. Begun more than sixty years ago, it hosts unquestionably the world's greatest amateur rodeo, drawing more than 500 competitors and thousands of fans. The festival includes chuck wagon meals, a huge western art show, and lots of music. Call the chamber of commerce at (915) 773–2411.

For a better understanding of Stamford's cowboy history, head to the *Texas Cowboy Museum,* 113 South Wetherbee Street, Stamford 79553 (915–773–2411). Well-known cowboy artists have paintings and prints displayed here, and other exhibits include ranch and farm artifacts from a century ago, as well as a blacksmith shop. The museum is open Monday through Friday from 8:00 A.M. until noon and 1:00 until 5:00 P.M. Admission is free.

There may not be a better place to capture on film the heritage of this region than at the *Mackenzie Trail Monument,* at the intersection of U.S.

THE TEXAS PANHANDLE

Texas Trivia

The world's largest (and oldest) rattlesnake roundup is held every March in Sweetwater.

Highway 277 and Texas Highway 6. This immense, sand-colored stone marker was hand carved to depict the days of the famous Mackenzie Trail (1874–1900) and the buffalo, Native Americans, pioneers, and early ranchers who figured into this history. Open at all hours.

Now we're off to rattlesnake country: Head west from Abilene on I–20, following it 42 miles to **Sweetwater,** seat of Nolan County and home to 12,000 salty Texans. The community came about when buffalo hunters in the 1870s camped on Sweet Water Creek simply because they preferred the sweet, clear water there over the area's other, gypsum-flavored streams. The humble beginnings continued with the opening of a dugout trading post in 1877; then the town charter—first established in 1884—failed twice due to blizzard, drought, and resulting evacuation. After the 1902 incorporation held, the area grew during World War II, when the Women's Air Force Service Pilots training program was based at the local **Avenger Field.** The world's first and only all-women military flying school produced a little more than 1,000 pilots out of 25,000 applicants. The thirty-nine who died in service are honored with a bronze statue and a walk of fame on the campus of Texas State Technical College–Sweetwater at Avenger Field, on I–20 West at Sweetwater Municipal Airport, (915) 235–7300. Open during daylight hours.

Plan your arrival in time for lunch, as you wouldn't want to miss a chance to use your boardinghouse reach at **Allen's Fried Chicken,** not unlike Sunday dinner with a big family. For less than $10 you can eat family-style from a long table spread with a plastic tablecloth and set with unmatched plates. For lunch your table will be filled with plates and bowls weighted down with not only fried chicken, but also cream gravy, beef brisket, buttered potatoes, candied sweet potatoes, potato salad, turnip greens, green beans, stewed summer squash, corn, English pea salad, pinto beans, fruit salad, rolls, peach cobbler, and iced tea. The restaurant has been a favorite for forty years and will soon be one of yours. It's at 1301 East Broadway Street, Sweetwater 79556, (915) 235–2060. Open only for lunch Tuesday through Sunday.

If good fortune was in your planning, you'll have arrived in Sweetwater on the second weekend in March—that's when the town is jumping, thanks to some 20,000 or 30,000 folks who show up for the annual **Rattlesnake Roundup.** Some six or seven tons of rattlesnakes are gathered during this, the world's largest such event. Several other Texas towns have followed suit, but Sweetwater's is the oldest, having begun in 1958 when the Jaycees pitched in to help local ranchers and farmers deal with their tremendous rattlesnake problem. The roundup became a festival, and the rest—as is widely said in the western reaches of this state—is history. The weekend is filled with a parade, the Miss Snake Charmer Queen Contest, real hunts for western diamondback rattlers, professional snake-handling demonstrations, snake-milking for medical research, a 10K run, a dance, a tour of rattlesnakes' natural habitats, and a rattlesnake-eating contest. Fried rattlesnake is available, as are numerous other—and less exotic—snacks. And there's a weigh-in and prize ceremony for the most snakes captured and the largest. All the fun takes place at the Nolan County Coliseum at the north end of Elm Street. Call (915) 235–5488 for schedules, details, and ticket information.

Now it's time to head into the Panhandle Plains: take I–20 west 8 more miles till you pick up U.S. Highway 84 and follow it 30 miles north to **Snyder,** found right at the U.S. Highway 180 West exit. This is the seat of Scurry County, with a population of 12,000 and—more importantly— a monument saluting a rare beast, the **White Buffalo Statue,** on the courthouse lawn at College and Twenty-fifth Streets. One of the many, many buffalo hunters who killed off the valuable herds here claimed that among the 22,000 buffalo he killed was a rare albino, shot near Snyder. To honor the herds, Snyder's townspeople put up this life-size replica of the albino buffalo. Some say the beast began as a bull buffalo, but respect for delicate sensitivities rendered it a cow instead.

Also to amuse you is the **Scurry County Museum,** on the campus of Western Texas College on Texas Highway 350 South (915–573–6107). Regional history covers progress from earliest Native American civilization through the oil boom, marked by the county's production of the billionth barrel in 1973. You'll learn more about the buffalo-hunting days, as well as the tumultuous period when the 1876 trading post was plagued by outlaws, a range war raged between ranchers and homesteaders, and cowboys locked up the sheriff in his own jail. Things eventually calmed down early in the twentieth century, just to become upset again when the oil boom nearly quadrupled the population in the early 1950s, and shantytowns popped up at an alarming rate. Decency prevailed, the concerned citizens cleaned up Snyder, and their hometown was declared an All-America City in 1969 by the National Municipal League. The museum is open 8:00 A.M. until 5:00 P.M. Monday through Thursday and 8:00 A.M. until 4:00 P.M. Friday. Admission is free.

On the lighter side of Snyder, there's the **House of Antieks** at 4008 College Street, Snyder 79549, (915–573–4422), an excellent place for clock hunters. Shopkeepers are knowledgeable about the many antique clocks, victrolas, tables, chairs, cabinets, and other home furnishings stocked. Open Monday through Saturday, 9:00 A.M. until 6:00 P.M.

You won't go hungry in Snyder at *The Shack* (right on U.S. Highway 180, 915–573–4921). Open for lunch and dinner, the restaurant offers everything from a rib-eye sandwich, taco salad, and fried chicken to a sixteen-ounce sirloin steak, grilled chicken breast, and fried shrimp. The restaurant also has a small gift shop selling crystal pieces and ceramic figurines.

Cap Rock and Canyons

Now we head into some of the most physically compelling country, if regarded with respect to those who spent lifetimes trying to tame it. Taking country roads at this point is the way to best drink in the often parched land, fascinating to anyone with an eye for prehistoric aesthetics. From Snyder, take Texas Highway 208 north 57 miles to the town of Spur, passing through Clairemont. Now skirting the Cap Rock's eastern edge, head north 20 miles on Farm Road 836 to U.S. Highway 82, then go west just another 6 miles, actually driving onto the famous escarpment. Watch for a roadside park on the left, and you'll have found **Silver Falls Park,** a stop said by many to be the finest of all roadside parks in the vast state. The White River courses through this part of the Cap Rock and its canyon land on its way south to join the Brazos River, and state engineers were wise enough to place picnic tables and carve riverside hiking paths here for journeymakers like yourself. Perhaps you've picked up snacks or sandwiches on the way; this is a perfect place to stretch your legs and take some scenery photos.

It's just another 4 miles west to the town of *Crosbyton,* seat of Crosby County and home to 2,000. It's in the heart of an agricultural land, and the local Associated Cotton Growers is said to be the world's largest cotton-processing plant of stripped cotton, serving more than 500 cotton companies in a 50-mile area. Crosbyton is also home to the *Pioneer Memorial Museum* (101 Main Street, Crosbyton 79322, 806–675–2331). Inside, the pioneer lifestyle is illustrated with home replicas and admirable collections of vintage housewares, arts, and farm equipment. Native American relics and artifacts relevant to the local ecology are exhibited, too. Open Tuesday through Saturday from 9:00 A.M. until noon and 1:00 until 5:00 P.M. Admission is free.

From here head north 23 miles on Farm Road 651 to *Floydada,* seat of Floyd County, home to 3,900 Texans and the undisputed Pumpkin

Texas Trivia

Floydada, a Panhandle town, calls itself Pumpkin Capital, U.S.A, and celebrates in late October with Punkin Days.

Capital of the United States. If it's autumn, you've no doubt seen some awesome pumpkins—they call the hundred-pounders Big Macs—at markets and along roadsides in Texas, and you can bet they came from here. The town's annual **Punkin Days** is a festival held on the courthouse square the weekend closest to Halloween. Stop in for some pumpkin bowling, pie tastings, seed-spitting contests, and carving competitions. Most events are free. Find the fun at Main and Missouri Streets; for details call (806) 983–3434.

Now it's time to cross the Cap Rock again, heading east on U.S. 62/70 from Floydada 24 miles to Matador, where you'll pick up Texas Highway 70 north, following it 28 miles to **Turkey,** a Hall County town and site of the **Bob Wills Museum,** intriguing to anyone with even a passing interest in the music called Texas swing. Found on Sixth Street at Lyles Street (806–423–1253), the collection dedicated to the King of Texas Swing—who was born just outside of town and whose daughter has moved back to Turkey to run the foundation—includes fiddles, boots, hats, recordings, sheet music, and photos belonging to or representing the Texas Playboys. Open Monday through Friday from 9:00 until 11:00 A.M. and 1:00 until 5:00 P.M. and weekends by appointment. Admission is free; however, donations are accepted. Inquire, too, about Bob Wills Day, usually held the last weekend in April, with a parade, fiddlers' contest, dances, and performances by members of the original Texas Playboys.

Texas Trivia

Turkey hosts Bob Wills Day to honor the King of Western Swing each year on the last Saturday in April.

The town is home to, naturally, the **Hotel Turkey,** Third and Alexander Streets, (806) 423–1151 or (800) 657–7110. A couple from north Texas bought the seventy-year-old hotel—now listed on both the Texas Historical Property register and the National Register of Historic Places—in the late 1980s and spent years on a facelift, then sold it to relatives. The comfortable hotel draws plenty of Bob Wills fans, as he played here in the late 1920s, as well as people who simply enjoy old hotels. Guest rooms are filled with original furniture and wallpaper adorned with hand-sewn decorations, while the front parlor downstairs is furnished with century-old sofas, chairs, and tables. The forty-seat dining room is decked out with antique photos of Turkey's residents. Some 1,200 guests stay here each month, and the owners frequently receive gifts such as vintage clothing, gloves, hats, and knickknacks from past guests.

THE TEXAS PANHANDLE

ONE MAINSTREAM ATTRACTION WORTH SEEING IN THE TEXAS PANHANDLE

Plan a visit to the Amarillo Zoo, which features a herd of grazing bison on a twenty-acre range, as well as other "exotic" Texas animals. Open year-round, it's closed on Monday. On Northeast Twenty-fourth Street at U.S. Highway 287, (806) 381–7911.

From Turkey, turn west on Texas Highway 86 and travel 13 miles to Ranch Road 1065, following it north for just over 3 miles till you reach **Caprock Canyons State Park,** just inside Briscoe County and 3 miles beyond the tiny town (population 500) of Quitaque (KIT-a-KWAY). You may want to stock up on some groceries and camping goods in that town or back in Turkey, as this little-known park is an ideal place to kick back a while and savor this rugged country. The views here of mountains, canyons, streams, and indigenous flora and fauna are simply breathtaking, and a visitors center offers an interpretive area plus an archaeological site, with artifacts representing the canyon for some 250 million years. There's a hundred-acre lake for swimming, fishing, and boating, but the real draw—besides the vistas, of course—is the hiking trails, 25 miles of paths coursing through the mountainous, 14,000 acres of parkland. Be on the lookout, especially on mountain trails, for buffalo and antelope, among several species of wild animals. Joining you on the paths may be horseback riders, mountain bikers, or campers who brought their own mounts. Camping is in both primitive and improved campsites. The park is always open, and a small admission fee is charged. Call (806) 455–1492 for information and (800) 792–1112 for reservations.

After the relaxation, you can get to **Amarillo,** seat of Potter County and home to 160,000 people, by driving north from the Caprock park on Texas Highway 86 not quite 9 miles and taking Texas Highway 256 west another 9 miles till you reach Texas Highway 207 north, which will put you on a scenic route across the majestic **Palo Duro Canyon,** which we'll explore in detail later. For now stay on Texas Highway 207, 48 miles till you reach U.S. Highway 287 at the town of Claude, and follow that highway west 28 miles to the Amarillo city limits.

Amarillo's humble beginnings date to its 1887 establishment as Ragtown, a railroad workers' tent camp. Today it's a mammoth center of cattle trade, and there are wonderful places to buy western artwork and clothing. Some lovely historic homes are on view, as are an art museum and a well-known science and technology museum.

To get a taste of Amarillo's tremendous cattle heritage, make your first stop at the city's **Livestock Auction,** held in the stockyards at 100 South Manhattan Street, Amarillo 79105 (806–373–7646) every Tuesday from 10:00 A.M. until 5:00 P.M. As you walk in, the auctioneer's rhythmic patter with odd inflections meets your ears as assorted cows and bulls are moved quickly for viewing through the main room's bottom, from which rise bleachers for spectators and bidders. Outside, the purchased cattle are herded into pens one at a time, usually by a few no-nonsense cowgirls, who are the only indication that anything has changed in the past one hundred years. To understand the significance of this place, note that more than 300,000 cattle are sold here every year, making this the largest individually owned auction in the state. It's the world's largest weekly livestock auction, and annual sales are close to seventy-five million dollars. Even if you miss auction day, you can look around the place; admission is always free.

At the adjacent **Stockyard Cafe,** also at 100 South Manhattan Street, Amarillo 79105, (806–374–6024), you can fill up on cheap but big steaks, home-cooked vegetables, sandwiches, and home-baked pies, sitting down with cowboys and ranchers. It's open for breakfast and lunch Monday through Saturday and for dinner Friday and Saturday only.

Newer to Amarillo but just as important historically is the **American Quarter Horse Heritage Center** at 2601 I–40 East, Amarillo 79104 (806–376–5181). The magnificence of the quarter horse is studied from its days as the working ranch horse of the American West to the equine competitor of the modern world. Its life is examined from the seventeenth century, when the breed was developed in the Western Hemisphere, to the present day. The complex is also the international headquarters of the American Quarter Horse Association, the world's largest horse registry. Open Monday through Saturday from 9:00 A.M. until 5:00 P.M. and Sunday from noon until 5:00 P.M. Call ahead for a guided tour. Admission is $4.00 for adults; $2.50 for children, free for age five and under; and $3.50 for senior citizens fifty-five and older.

For a day of cowboy life, head for the **Bar H Dude Ranch,** an hour's drive east of the city via U.S. Highway 287 in Clarendon (806) 874–2634. Ride horses or haywagons, do a little work with the cowboys and cowgirls, pitch horseshoes, fish, take square dancing lessons, and even stay the night if you like. Call ahead for reservations and prices.

Explore Amarillo's high-tech side at **Don Harrington Discovery Center and Planetarium,** in the fifty-acre Amarillo Garden Center at 1200 Streit Drive, Amarillo 79105 (806–355–9547). Named for a local oil mogul and philanthropist, the complex presents *Panhandle Promise,* a slick, twenty-five-minute show incorporating thousands of slides that illustrate a century of history. "Cowboys are as real as weather," the narrator's voice says, supported by vivid images showing pioneers and their lives through the years that brought drought, devastating winters,

THE TEXAS PANHANDLE

the railroad from Fort Worth, the Depression, Bob Wills, and the legendary Route 66, all in rapid, dramatic bursts. The Discovery Center also presents Smithsonian traveling exhibits and several interactive displays that are enjoyed by children and adults alike.

And in tribute to Amarillo's standing as chief helium producer in the United States, a leggy, four-pronged **Helium Monument** stands in front of the Discovery Center. The structure functions as a futuristic sundial, and its limbs are time capsules filled with newspapers, a Sears catalog, and a piece of apple pie sealed in helium. The Discovery Center is open Tuesday through Saturday from 10:00 A.M. until 5:00 P.M. and Sunday from 1:00 until 5:00 P.M. Admission is charged. Planetarium shows are included with admission.

The quintessential, Texas-size experience is found in lunch or supper at the **Big Texan Steak Ranch,** 7701 I–40 East at Lakeside exit (806–372–6000). Resembling a circus arena, the cavernous interior is fun and fascinating, with a giant wooden Indian, a stuffed grizzly greeting you at the entrance, and big game trophies covering every wall. Chairs and benches are fashioned from horseshoes, of course. The menu is laden with buffalo, rattlesnake, rabbit, calf fries (the most private of calf parts), chicken-fried steak, and rib-eye steak. The fanfare, however, surrounds the presentation of a seventy-two-ounce prime steak dinner that's free if the diner eats the whole thing—with the accompanying salad, shrimp cocktail, baked potato, bread, and butter—in one hour. Some do it, but it's a true challenge. The luckiest diners happen by when the Kawahadi Indian Dancers are scheduled for a performance. The restaurant is open daily for lunch and dinner.

Of course, you'll find plenty of other food around Amarillo that doesn't come in such dramatic portions. Jamaican jerk chicken and pork are the rage at Tazan's Shack at Ocho Rios (3020 West Sixth Street, Amarillo 79106, 806–374–6522), where fried fish and Red Stripe beer keep pace with the lively music and convivial patrons. Or do your carbo-loading on pasta at Macaroni Joe's (in Wellington Square, I–40 at Georgia Street, 806–358–8990). Chicken, shrimp, and every sort of noodle will make your tummy happy. Lunch and dinner are served Tuesday through Saturday, and prices start at about $7.00.

Antiques hounds will love the **Old San Jacinto** area, located on Sixth Street along historic Route 66 (between Georgia and Western Streets). Those in the know think this is becoming the premier antiques center of the Southwest, with dozens of delightful shops selling treasures dating from the turn of the twentieth century. While away the morning or afternoon browsing, then stop at any of the several cafes along the strip. Most shops are open from 10:00 A.M. until 5:30 P.M. Monday through Saturday and from 1:00 until 5:00 P.M. Sunday.

In addition to several hotels and motels, Amarillo offers bed-and-breakfast lodging at **Galbraith House,** 1710 South Polk Street, Amarillo 79105. Built in 1912, the 4,000-square-foot mansion exhibits gorgeous interior work in walnut, oak, and mahogany, as well as Oriental rugs and antiques. Rooms to be enjoyed by guests include the solarium, library, dining and living rooms, in addition to three balconies. There are five guest rooms with private baths, and generous breakfasts may feature casseroles, biscuits and gravy, and pastries. To make reservations call (806) 374–0237.

For all visitor information contact the Amarillo Convention & Visitor Council at (800) 692–1338 or (806) 374–1497. Visit the Internet site at www.amarillo-cvb.org.

Just outside of town, 12 miles to the west on I–40—also the epic Route 66—**Cadillac Ranch** is the unique creation of Stanley Marsh 3 (as he is faithfully called), land and broadcasting baron and easily one of the more powerful of all the personalities of modern Texas. Known always for his noteworthy and eccentric ways, he made his contribution to pop culture in a cotton field with a lineup of ten Cadillacs buried nose-down, exhibiting tail-fin designs from between 1949 and 1963 diagonally into the air. Worth noting is that the cars are buried at precisely the

Bizarre Texas Stuff

*W*ELLINGTON: In some of the wildest lands in Texas lies the seat of Collingsworth County, a town named for the Duke of Wellington. Found about a two-hour drive east of Amarillo and just 13 miles from the Oklahoma state line, it was among the estates on the Rocking Chair Ranch more than a century ago and was called Nobility Ranch by Texas cowboys. And rightly so: Its owners were British noblemen, the Baron of Tweedmouth (Sir Dudley Coutts Majoribanks) and the Earl of Aberdeen (John Campbell Hamilton Golden). This unusual history is detailed at the Collingsworth County Museum, 1404 Fifteenth Street, (806) 447–2352.

Cadillac Ranch

same angle to the ground as the great Cheops pyramids. Graffiti artists have made their own contributions, as the art display—called Amarillo's "bumper crop"—is always open. No admission is charged.

You can take a side trip from Amarillo 38 miles northwest of town on Farm Road 1061 and U.S. Highway 385 to reach **Cal Farley's Boys Ranch,** 2 miles north of U.S. 385 on Spur 233. This 10,000-acre spread was established in 1939 as a ranch home for troubled and needy boys. Now more than 400 boys between the ages of four and nineteen attend classes, live in comfortable dorms, and work in the ranch's dairy, horticulture, custodial, and farming divisions. Nonresidents are welcome to join the boys—who are unfailingly polite and winning—at lunch and for a short tour of the impeccable grounds. A wildlife zoo is open, too. Call ahead for reservations, (806) 372–2341. Admission is free. There's a Labor Day weekend Boys Ranch Rodeo (a small admission fee is charged), drawing some 10,000 spectators to watch the boys take part in their biggest annual function.

The ranch grounds are on the site of **Old Tascosa,** a boom town that busted in 1887 when railroad planners chose to skip it. If the name seems familiar, it's because this was a haunt of outlaws and gunfighters such as Billy the Kid, Pat Garrett, and Len Woodruff. As part of your ranch visit, tour the museum housed in the Old Tascosa Courthouse, where displays illustrate west Texas's role in the days of the Wild West.

From the ranch take Texas Highway 136 north 38 miles to **Alibates National Monument,** a mostly undeveloped site popular with hikers and archaeology buffs. The area atop a high ridge overlooking Lake Meredith contains an ancient quarry of flint, unique for its amazing colors. Farmers and Native Americans distributed Alibates flint over the

Adobe Walls

*H*istory buffs will want to seek out the site of the Battle of Adobe Walls, where two famous Native American battles were fought. In 1864 Col. Kit Carson fought his last fight when his U.S. troops barely escaped defeat by Kiowa and Comanche who had been molesting wagon trains and settlers. Ten years later, in 1874, Quanah Parker and Lone Wolf led a tribe in an attack on a buffalo hunters' camp, but they were eventually scared away when the famous shot by William "Billy" Dixon took a brave from his horse at a distance of roughly ⁷/₈ mile. The Adobe Walls site is roughly 18 miles northeast of Stinnett, which is northeast of Amarillo and near Lake Meredith. Inquire in Stinnett as to local tours.

Southwest and Great Plains from 10,000 B.C. until the nineteenth century. The quarry itself is overgrown with grass and shrubs, so you won't know you've found it until you're in it. The stones are flat, somewhat smooth, and shaded with muted blues and grays, black, maroon, and orange. Nearby, great pits of buffalo bones have been found, along with pottery dating to A.D. 1250. A Native American village was excavated in a 1938–39 project, and pictographs were found in huge dolomite boulders. Ranger-led walks, extremely helpful for visitors, conclude with flint-chipping instruction. Free tours are offered at 10:00 A.M. and 2:00 P.M. during summer and by appointment for the balance of the year. Admission is always free, and the monument is open during daylight hours. Call (806) 857–3151 for information and reservations.

The monument lies on the south shore of Lake Meredith, site of *Lake Meredith National Park.* Fashioned from the Canadian River, the lake is 2 miles wide in places and 14 miles long, offering 100 miles of shoreline. The National Park Service has created eight recreation areas with swimming in a lake and swimming pool, fishing, sailboating, and waterskiing. There are places to play golf and tennis, too. If you've picked up provisions in Amarillo or in nearby Fritch, you can pick a place from several bluffs and canyons around the lake for picnicking and camping. Open at all times, admission is free, but there are fees for boating. Call (806) 857–3151 for information.

Another interesting stop just north of Amarillo is in the town of *Panhandle,* 30 miles northeast of Amarillo on U.S. Highway 60. The Carson County Square House Museum (Fifth and Elsie Streets, 806–537–3524) illustrates the history of the Panhandle, from its early Native American cultures to present-day industries and technology.

The historic Square House was built during the 1880s with wood transported from Dodge City, Kansas. Other parts of the museum include a hall of natural history, two art galleries, railroad exhibits (housed in a caboose), and a barn. Open from 9:00 A.M. until 5:00 P.M. Monday through Saturday and from 1:00 until 5:00 P.M. Sunday. Admission is free, but donations are accepted.

One of Amarillo's better side trips takes you to **Dalhart,** seat of Dallam County, home to almost 69,000 residents. To reach it from the north side of Lake Meredith, follow Ranch Road 1319 north about 11 miles to Texas Highway 152, follow it west 20 miles to Dumas, and then go west on U.S. Highway 87, 39 miles to Dalhart. Or, the route from Amarillo is north on U.S. Highway 287, 49 miles to Dumas and west on U.S. Highway 87, 39 miles to Dalhart. The reason for this journey is to explore the heritage of the world-renowned **XIT Ranch** and today's **XIT Museum.** Here you'll discover the considerable history of the XIT, which was in the 1880s the largest ranch in the world under a single fence, which stretches 6,000 miles. It was created when investors from up north were contracted to erect the three-million-dollar granite capitol building in Austin in exchange for this three million acres of land. The ranch spread across an area that today covers nine counties and was 27 miles in average width and 200 miles long between north and south fences.

The XIT Museum (at 102 East Seventh Street, Dalhart 79022, 806–249–5390) tells the whole story, which involved the employ of 150 cowboys and the running of 150,000 head of cattle. The investors lost interest, however, and sold off the cattle and split the ranch into pieces. The museum lies inside a renovated art deco building and contains photographs, documents, an antique gun collection, and reconstructed

Panhandle's Little Tree

*A*bout 5 miles southwest of the Panhandle town of Panhandle, which is the seat of Carson County, you can visit Thomas Cree's Little Tree, the site of the first tree planted throughout the entire Panhandle. On a plains that was once a sea of grass, pioneer settler Thomas Cree brought a sapling bois d'arc (pronounced "BOE dark") for planting behind his dugout home in 1888. The tree lived until 1969, when an agricultural chemical was accidentally used here; county residents planted a new tree, which sits behind a protective fence at the south edge of U.S. Highway 60. Be sure to note two State Historical Markers and a medallion from the National Men's Garden Clubs of America.

period rooms such as a parlor, bedroom, and kitchen. Native American relics and Peter Hurd paintings are exhibited, as well. The Pioneer Chapel, created from pieces of Dalhart's first six churches, today is frequently the site of weddings. The museum is open Tuesday through Saturday from 9:00 A.M. until 5:00 P.M. Admission is free.

To see more of the XIT legacy, drive to a traffic island adjacent to the underpass at U.S. Highway 87 North and U.S. Highway 385. There you'll find the **Empty Saddle Monument,** honoring all XIT cowboys. The story behind it concerns an XIT cowboy who died just before the annual reunion; his widow requested that his horse be allowed to participate in the parade, and today's parade is always led by a saddled horse without a rider.

Plan your arrival in Dalhart to coincide with the first Thursday, Friday, and Saturday in August, and you'll enjoy the **XIT Rodeo and Reunion,** held in Rita Blanca Park, U.S. Highway 87 South at Farm Road 281 West. This is the world's largest amateur rodeo and features a free barbecue of six tons of beef. The parade, junior rodeo, nightly dance, antique car show, and 5K run add to the revelry. For information and ticket prices, call (806) 249–5646.

The final side trip from Amarillo is a bit ambitious but may be worth it to those who have Irish blood coursing through their veins. **Shamrock,** a town in Wheeler County of 2,200 residents, is located 86 miles east of Amarillo via I–40. This is the site of Texas's own **Blarney Stone,** in Elmore Park, 400 East Second Street. Someone in this town convinced the keepers of the original in County Cork, Ireland, to donate a small piece of their famous rock; it sits on a pedestal and is offered at all hours to anyone who cares to kiss it. Legend holds that those who do are given the gift of eloquence. The Irish celebration of St. Patrick's Day is held annually on the weekend closest to March 17 all over town. There's a carnival, bazaar, old settlers' reunion, beard contest, fiddling contest, chili cook-off, dances, cowboy roping contests, and a Miss Irish Rose pageant. Call the chamber of commerce for ticket information at (806) 256–2501.

Now it's time to make a trek back down the Panhandle, stopping first at **Canyon**—just 16 miles south of Amarillo via I–27—seat of Randall County, home to 11,000 Texans, and site of the exceptional **Panhandle Plains Historical Museum.** Found on the campus of Texas A&M West University, 1 block east of U.S. Highway 87 at 2401 Fourth Avenue (806–651–2244), the museum holds the honor of being the state's largest historical center. Up front, the building's busy 1933 art deco exterior offers friezes depicting an array of Texana designs from spurs to brands. Inside, a time-line approach is used to relate the geological, social, cultural, industrial, and financial development of northwest Texas. Murals in the main hall overwhelm onlookers with an overview, and dinosaurs liven up the geological displays. Pioneer life, Native Americans, and Texas ranching have individual exhibit areas, and the three-floor annex is outfitted with a 1925 cable tool drilling rig. Other oil-patch relics piece together the story of oil and gas discovery and development in west Texas. An art gallery offers permanent and traveling exhibits, and a good gift shop sells souvenirs. Open Memorial Day through Labor Day Monday through Saturday from 9:00 A.M. until 6:00 P.M. and Sunday from 1:00 until 6:00 P.M. From Labor Day to Memorial Day, it's open Monday through Saturday from 9:00 A.M. until 5:00 P.M. and Sunday from 1:00 until 6:00 P.M. Admission is charged.

Then you'll want to continue east of town 12 miles on Texas Highway 217 to *Palo Duro Canyon State Park.* Here the Panhandle's arid climate, chilly mornings, cool evenings, and clean air are pleasingly exaggerated during spring, summer, and fall in the spectacular chasm, cut 120 miles long by a branch of the Red River. Rich in geological, Native American, and pioneer history, the canyon's rock formations rise and fall a little more than 1,000 feet, showing ninety million years of earth formation, baring brilliant walls colored ochre, red, and coral by the spirits of time. The Coronado expedition took shelter here in 1541 while looking for the fabled Quivira, and they decided *palo duro*—meaning hard wood—was appropriate for the tough juniper trees that still flourish here. What's so surprising and invigorating about the Palo Duro Canyon are its green trees and even greener meadows when the rain's been plentiful. Most of the canyon's beauty secrets are revealed in the state park, covering a 16,400-acre portion of the canyon.

An 8-mile paved road takes you rim to floor and affords unforgettable vistas. Hiking, camping, picnicking, and horseback riding are loads of fun. Open daily from 6:00 A.M. until 10:00 P.M. in summer and 8:00 A.M. until 10:00 P.M. the rest of the year; admission is charged. Call (806) 488–2227 for reservations and information.

Inside Palo Duro's park, *The Chuck Wagon* (806–488–2152) sells snacks, drinks, and souvenirs and serves breakfast, lunch, and dinner daily. Visitors also can rent horses year-round for an off-road tour of the canyon. For information call (806) 488–2231.

On summer nights, lightning and thunder explodes, horse hooves pound, Native Americans dance, and eighty voices sing against a 600-foot canyon wall during **TEXAS! A Musical Drama,** a flashy production now thirty years old. Nearly 100,000 people come annually to see the outdoor spectacle, with audience members representing all fifty states and almost a hundred foreign countries. In song and dance, the story presents the struggle, heartbreak, joy, and politics of Panhandle pioneers, and a barbecue dinner is offered prior to the show just outside the canyon floor's amphitheater. The musical begins at 8:30 P.M. nightly except Sunday, from early June until late August. Reservations are necessary and can be made by calling (806) 655–2181. Tickets are generally between $10 and $20 for adults and $5 and $10 for children.

Another splendid way to enjoy Palo Duro Canyon from May until September is at *Cowboy Morning Breakfasts,* booked in Amarillo but enjoyed here at the canyon. The Christian family of the Figure 3 Ranch offers its perch on the canyon's rim for you to enjoy a taste of real ranch life. Cowboys drive a mule-team wagon for a twenty-minute ride in earliest morning light through pasture to the canyon edge. The camp cook prepares sourdough biscuits in iron kettles to go with a spread of other edibles made in skillets over open fires. The food is filling and never runs out. Most partakers can't resist a hike after breakfast, which is best—simply because you can't leave the canyon until you've been in it. The ranch family indulges every tourist's whim, and it's enjoyable to watch a European visitor who's never been near a cowboy or a horse be saddled up for a little walk atop a gentle sorrel. Kids are given a chance to try some roping, and branding exhibitions are followed by cow-chip–tossing competitions. The morning will slip away quickly, but you can always go back for steak dinners on the canyon rim. Required reservations are made by calling (806) 944–5562 or (800) 658–2613; call also for schedules and rates.

Learn to work cattle the way it's been done for about a century and a half by signing on for one of the cattle drives and overnight pack trips offered by the *Elkins Ranch* (806–488–2100), a working cattle operation now in its fifth generation and covering thousands of acres of rugged range and canyon lands. A two-and-a-half-day, two-night roundup and cattle drive push a herd of Corriente longhorns from the floor of Palo Duro Canyon to lush pastures on the canyon's rim. Your package includes riding instruction and basic cowboy skills and meals. These are offered on alternate weeks, Wednesday through Friday, from late May to early October.

A shorter, overnight pack trip takes riders to the rim of Palo Duro Canyon and down inside the canyon. Offered on weeks when there is no cattle drive, the pack trip is Wednesday and Thursday.

If you'd prefer a bit more pampering, you can stay in a motel or book a room at *The Hudspeth House,* Canyon's bed-and-breakfast place at 1905 Fourth Avenue, Canyon 79015, (806) 655–9800. A famous former resident was the late artist Georgia O'Keeffe, who taught at the local university. There are six bedrooms, some with private baths and fireplaces, and decor includes beautiful antiques, tins, plates, dolls, grandfather clocks, and musical instruments. The breakfast table is set with linens, china, and crystal, so you'll enjoy a lavish breakfast or brunch in elegance. A spa, fitness room, sundeck, and gazebo are on the property, as well. Call well in advance for reservations.

The Staked Plains

rom Canyon follow U.S. Highway 60 southwest 30 miles and then take U.S. Highway 385 south 40 miles. At U.S. Highway 70, head west 24 miles to reach *Muleshoe,* seat of Bailey County and home to the peerless *National Mule Memorial*—what else? Found at the intersection of U.S. Highway 84 and Main Street, the memorial to the West's original draft animal is a fiberglass model measuring fifteen hands (5 feet) in height. The mule's statue was built in 1965 thanks to donations from people all over the country—even a mule-driver from the former Soviet Union sent a twenty-cent contribution.

Another 20 miles south on Texas Highway 214, you'll see *Muleshoe National Wildlife Refuge,* the oldest such refuge in Texas, founded in 1935. As it is situated on a central flyway between Mexico and Canada, hundreds of thousands of waterfowl stop by during migration between September and March. The park consists of about 5,800 acres of rolling, mostly treeless sandhills planted with sorghum and wheat (bird food) punctuated by lakes, which are occupied during the season by the country's largest concentration of sandhill cranes. Observation areas are available in the refuge, and picnicking and camping are allowed. Admission is free and the refuge is open Monday through Friday from 8:00 A.M. until 4:30 P.M. for day visitors. Call (806) 946–3341 for information.

Just south of the refuge, pick up Farm Road 37 and follow it almost 20 miles to U.S. Highway 84, which will lead 46 miles to *Lubbock,* nicknamed Hub City, or hub of the Panhandle. Seat of Lubbock County, the city is home to 186,000 people and the expansive Texas Tech University. On its campus you'll find the remarkable *Ranching Heritage Center* at Fourth and Indiana Streets (806–742–2498), a living, authentic center of ranching in the American West. Each year 100,000 people visit here to tour the twelve-acre grounds filled with more than thirty restored structures, dating from 1838 until 1917. Among them you'll find one of seven division headquarters of the XIT Ranch, a century-old schoolhouse, milk and meat houses, a granary, a blacksmith shop, log cabins, a grand Victorian ranch home, a bunkhouse, a barn, and a train depot. There are horseshoeing, bread-making, sheepshearing, spinning, and weaving demonstrations, and changing exhibits include saddles, bronzes, and western art, plus wagons and branding irons. As was the case a century ago, windmills are more plentiful than trees, and the ranching center offers windmills of varying designs. A gallery has been created from a room at the enormous 6666 Ranch, complete with ornate mantle, saddle, brass bed, Oriental rug, grandfather clock, and family portraits. Open Monday through Saturday from 10:00 A.M. until 5:00 P.M. and Sunday from 1:00 until 5:00 P.M. Admission is free.

Also see the ***Museum of Texas Tech University and Moody Planetarium*** (Fourth Street at Indiana Avenue, 806–742–2490), where the history of man is chronicled with an emphasis on the Southwest and its climate. Closed only on Monday, it's open 10:00 A.M. until 5:00 P.M. Tuesday through Saturday, until 8:30 P.M. on Thursday, and 1:00 until 5:00 P.M. on Sunday. Admission to the museum is free and is $1.00 for planetarium shows.

Ranching Heritage Center

Kids and others with curious minds will enjoy *Science Spectrum and Omnimax Theater* (2579 South Loop 289, Lubbock 79423, 806–745–6299). More than seventy hands-on exhibits explain science and technology, and small ones will have fun in the Kidspace area. The thrilling Omnimax Theater programs are a treat for everyone. Open from 10:00 A.M. until 5:30 P.M. Monday through Friday and until 7:00 P.M. Saturday, and from 1:00 until 5:30 P.M. Sunday. Admission is charged. Call for Omnimax Theater fees and film schedules.

Among Lubbock's other interests is that of music, since the city gave the world rock 'n' roll pioneer Buddy Holly. You'll find the *Buddy Holly Statue and Walk of Fame* at Eighth Street and Avenue Q, where an outdoor park honors Holly and other west Texans—including Mac Davis, Waylon Jennings, and Jimmy Dean—who made significant contributions to musical entertainment. It's open twenty-four hours and is free. Buddy Holly's grave is found in the Lubbock Cemetery at East Thirty-fourth Street at Quirt Street. Marked by a small, plain stone, the site is visited by a steady procession of fans, many from the United Kingdom.

Head for *Lubbock Lake Landmark State Historical Site,* North Indiana Street and Loop 289 (806–741–0306), one of the largest and most productive archaeological excavations in North America and thought to be the continent's only place where deposits relate to all cultures known to have lived on the Southern Plains. Covering the periods of the Clovis Man and the Folsom Man, Texas residents of 10,000 to 15,000 years ago, the site's digs have turned up remains of the mammoth, extinct horse, camel, and bison, plus a giant armadillo. New to the park is a pair of sculptures, life-size replicas of a Columbian mammoth and her baby. The mother mammoth weights 6,800 pounds and has a trunk reaching 15 feet into the air, as she "runs" through Yellowhouse Canyon with her 1,200-pound offspring. Follow a 3/4-mile trail through the twenty-acre excavation area and look for interpretive signs along the way. A new interpretive center offers exhibits, a children's center, a gift shop, and an auditorium. Open Tuesday through Saturday from 9:00 A.M. until 5:00 P.M. and Sunday from 1:00 until 5:00 P.M. Admission is $2.00 for adults, $1.00 for students, and free for children five and under.

Children also get a kick out of *Prairie Dog Town,* within Mackenzie State Park at Fourth Street and Avenue A (contact the Lubbock Convention & Tourism Bureau, 800–692–4035 or 806–747–5232). One of the last remaining colonies of its kind in the whole country, it's home to cute little critters who are playful and endlessly amusing and who share their habitat with burrowing owls and a few rabbits. The park also has Joyland, an amusement park; a golf course; picnic areas; and the Yellowhouse Canyon Lakes, where you can enjoy waterfalls, footbridges, fishing, and hiking trails. Open until midnight; admission is free. (Hours at Joyland vary; call 806–763–2719 for information.)

Texas's oldest and most award-winning winery is here in Lubbock. Find **Llano Estacado Winery** just over 3 miles east of U.S. Highway 87 on Farm Road 1585 (806–745–2258). Winery founders discovered ideal conditions in the loose, sandy soil, hot days, and cool nights of the Panhandle Plains. Some fifteen or more varieties are grown at a time, and eleven or twelve different wines—plus one sparkling wine—are bottled each year. Plan to spend an hour here touring the winery and tasting four wines. Open Monday through Saturday from 10:00 A.M. until 5:00 P.M. and Sunday from noon until 5:00 P.M.; tours are free and are offered every half hour, with the last tour at 4:00 P.M. daily.

Visit also **Cap Rock Winery** (U.S. Highway 87 south from South Loop 289 about 6 miles to Woodrow Road, 806–863–2704). The tasting room and gift shop are open from 10:00 A.M. until 5:00 P.M. Monday through Saturday and from noon until 5:00 P.M. Sunday; tours are offered and admission is free.

Good food keeps Texas Tech students and others happy at places such as **County Line** (Farm Road 2641, 1/2 mile west of I–27 North, 806–763–6001). The setting includes a pond and waterfowl, but great eats include smoked prime rib, grilled beef tenderloin, pork ribs, and smoked chicken. Open for lunch and dinner daily, meals start at about $8.00.

June's Texas Anecdotes

*P*ANHANDLE: *Buddy Holly died before I knew any tunes other than* Jesus Loves Me *and* The Eyes of Texas Are Upon You *(the first songs my mother taught me, in that order). But since I saw the 1979 film* The Buddy Holly Story, *it has remained one of my very favorite films. I find it extraordinary that the son of a very ordinary Lubbock family achieved so much in a career and laid groundwork for landmark artists such as the Beatles, before being killed at the tender age of twenty-three. When I visited the 8½-foot bronze statue of Holly in Lubbock, I felt a great thrill. I was even more moved upon visiting his grave site, as others have before me: There, on top of the headstone engraved with a guitar and musical notes, are flowers and guitar picks, left by his fans.*

Make like the locals and hang out at Spanky's Sandwich Shop (811 University Drive, Lubbock 79401, 806-744-5677), where the Texas Tech faithful line up for great burgers, fried cheese, and ice-cold beer.

For more information on Lubbock and the area, contact the Lubbock Convention & Tourism Bureau at (800) 692-4035 or (806) 747-5232.

Southeast of Lubbock 42 miles on U.S. 84, the town of *Post*—seat of Garza County and one of Texas's more famous speed traps—is located, thanks to cereal magnate C. W. Post, who bought nearly a quarter of a million acres here and founded Post City in 1907 with the intent of developing his own utopia. He built a sanitarium, hotel, business district, cotton gin and textile plant, and farm homes, but his project never saw true success because he couldn't make it rain, and the lack of water during the 1911 drought was devastating. He died in 1914, but his statue on the courthouse lawn keeps something of his memory alive.

Post is home to the *Garza Theater* (226 East Main Street, Post 79356, 806-495-4005), which was one of the first movie houses in west Texas when it opened in 1920 with silent films. It was adapted to sound in 1929 but closed in 1957. In 1986 it was renovated and reopened for use by a local theater production group. Musicals and plays are presented some weekends, and a barbecue dinner is usually offered, as well. Call for schedules and ticket information.

About 6 miles southeast of town on U.S. Highway 84, find the *Llano Estacado Marker,* one that helps travelers more easily understand the geography of this remarkable area. It details the flat-topped mountains of the Cap Rock Escarpment and the Staked Plains, or llano estacado.

From Post you can trace the lowest reaches of the Cap Rock as it unwinds to the Panhandle's reach into deep west Texas. Follow Farm Road 669 as it meanders along mesas and buttes, about 70 miles south to *Big Spring.* This is the Howard County seat and home to 23,000, and where a nice resting spot is *Comanche Trail Park.* Find this beauty at Whipkey Drive off U.S. Highway 87, immediately south of Farm Road 700 (915-264-2345). A large spring indeed is the focus of this 480-acre park, which offers a swimming pool, lighted tennis courts, an 18-hole golf course, small fishing lake, playground, hiking and biking trails, nature trails, a flower garden, and improved campsites. In summer you'll especially enjoy the huge amphitheater—cut from native limestone during the Depression—which hosts summer concerts. Admission is free, and the park is open from dawn until 10:00 P.M. daily.

OTHER PLACES TO STAY IN THE TEXAS PANHANDLE

ABILENE

Embassy Suites Hotel, 4250 Ridgemont Drive, Abilene 79606, (915) 698–1234. Adjacent to the Mall of Abilene, this three-story hotel has one-bedroom suites, an indoor pool, steam room, whirlpool, and restaurant open for lunch and dinner. Complimentary beverages are offered in the afternoon and evening.

AMARILLO

The Big Texan Motel, I–40 at Lakeside Drive, Amarillo 79104, (806) 372–5000. Next to the Big Texan Steak Ranch, this two-story complex has a funny Old West facade, fifty-four guest rooms, and swimming pool.

Parkview House, 1311 South Jefferson Street, Amarillo 79104, (806) 373–9464. Two guest rooms have private baths, and three have shared baths. Guests are offered a hot tub and sauna, plus a full breakfast.

LUBBOCK

Country Place Bed & Breakfast, Route 1, Box 459, Wolfforth 79382, (806) 863–2030.

Residence Inn by Marriott, 2551 South Loop 289, Lubbock 79423, (806) 745–1963. Two-story complex features eighty rooms with fireplaces and some two-bedroom suites, heated pool, and complimentary drinks in the evening.

OTHER PLACES TO EAT IN THE TEXAS PANHANDLE

ABILENE

Cypress Street Station, 158 Cypress Street, Abilene 79601, (915) 676–3463. Charming restaurant inside a vintage storefront offers pretty pasta dishes as well as grilled chicken, fish, and beef plates.

AMARILLO

Blackstone Restaurant, 202 West Tenth Avenue, Amarillo 79101, (806) 372–7700

Jackson Square Fountain and Grill, Fourteenth and Van Buren Streets, Amarillo 79101, (806) 337–4156.

Sakura, 4000 Soncy Street, Amarillo 79101, (806) 358–8148.

LUBBOCK

Cagle Steaks, 118 Farm Road 179 North, Lubbock 79416, (806) 795–3879.

J&J Bar-B-Q, 1306 Texas Street, Lubbock 79401, (806) 744–1325. Brisket sandwiches, smoked sausage, and tender ribs, as well as old-fashioned counter service and a friendly atmosphere, have kept this place popular for decades. Open for lunch, Monday through Friday.

Gordito's, 7006 University Drive at South Loop 289, Lubbock 79413, (806) 745–5582; and Nineteenth Street at West Loop 289, Lubbock 79413, (806) 791–0888.

Grapevine Cafe and Wine Bar, 2407-B Nineteenth Street, Lubbock 79413, (806) 744–8246.

Hub City Brewery, 1807 Buddy Holly Drive, Lubbock 79401, (806) 747–1535.

SWEETWATER

Jack's Family Steak House, 2005 Lamar Street, Sweetwater 79556, (915) 235–1777.

Ranch House Cafe, 703 Southwest Georgia Street, Sweetwater 79556, (915) 235–6341.

Williams Bar-B-Que, 1211 Elm Street, Sweetwater 79556, (915) 235–9607.

Wildest West Texas

Early life in west Texas wasn't easy, and seeing the land even today is proof. The land is lonely, honest, tough—like the pioneers who conquered it, the cowboys who worked it, the people who call it home. Everywhere you look, the long histories of Native Americans, cavalry units posted at forts to protect pioneers and settlers, and oil-field discoveries bringing startling fortunes are unfolded.

The country wasn't always harsh. Sixteenth-century explorer Cabeza de Vaca wrote in his diary that he walked around completely unclothed in the soothing surroundings, and the earliest ranchers wrote that grasses here grew as high as cows' bellies. But herds of several thousand head of cattle were allowed to graze uncontrolled, and the ground was left bare. Apaches didn't mind the desolation, and outlaws were grateful for it. The open skies and spaces of west Texas invited pioneers to forge a new existence. Those hardy settlers who didn't find this part of the Rio Grande utterly impassable assigned names to spots like Camp Misery and Murder's Cove. They were preceded, of course, by the Comanches, whose war trails can still be seen. In 1882 the Southern Pacific Railroad connected the Trans-Pecos towns of Alpine and Marfa to its line, and Terlingua, a bit south, became the quicksilver (mercury) mining center of Texas. Faint remains of those and other long-past ventures can be found in the area.

West Texas's great wealth of natural history is defined, revealed, and studied in the sensational form of Big Bend, a name for a region, a national park, and—for many—a state of mind. Within the elbow of the Rio Grande, where it pushes deeper into Mexico, 800,000 acres were set aside by the national park service in 1944 for preservation of a complex array of huge canyons, numerous clusters and stretches of mountains, and exotic plant and animal life. Many who live here say it claims a place in the soul, and even geology textbooks found in area shops contain descriptions with mystical undertones; one Native American legend holds that after the Great Creator made Earth with its stars, fish, sea, and birds, he threw all his leftover stony, dusty materials into one heap—the Big Bend. Because it's such a long way from anywhere, the Big Bend is

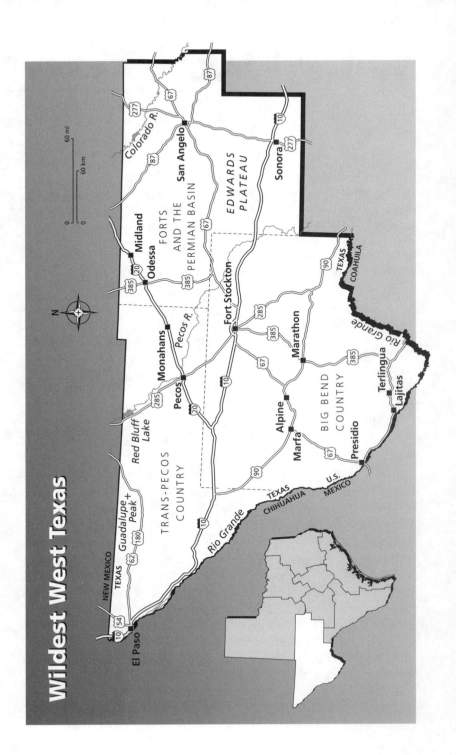

Wildest West Texas

one of the ten least visited parks in the nation, and that's what makes it all the more desirable.

So it's time to embrace the Chihuahuan Desert— roll down the windows and smell the cool scent of sagebrush. Walk around, but watch your step and keep quiet so deer will appear. Wear sturdy boots for protection and train an eye to the roadsides, as rattlers may dart out and recoil just as rapidly; that other brownish streak of movement into the brush was the regional mascot, the roadrunner. Low-slung mountain ranges, bearing names from Christmas to Chisos to Chinati, first appear like little more than bluish shadows nudging the horizon. Broom-weed lies low in oversized patches of vivid yellow in fall, and robust bluebonnet blooms spring forth with zeal in February. Rafters floating along the Rio Grande marvel at the changing purples, tangerines, and corals in massive canyon walls, and formations of tuff, a hardened ash from volcanic activity millions of years ago, rise like deformed sand castles, followed by layered pink and gray rock cliffs, interrupted with soft carpets of grassy hills. Travelers from as far away as Japan and Germany, as well as those from far-flung corners of Texas, express awe at towering hills of rock, mountain lion warning signs, tough gray-green scrubland, and lush riverside grasses and palms.

Names of places and life forms often ring of the Spanish-Mexican culture or are pioneer impressions of the land itself—to wit, Rosillos Mountains, Mesa de Aguila, Dagger Flat, Dugout Wells, Mule Ear Peaks. And there is such diverse vegetation; most eye-catching are the sotol, century plant, Spanish dagger, and ocotillo, the latter featuring tall spines sprouting bright green, tiny leaves just after the late summer rainy season and brilliant scarlet blooms in spring. The lechuguilla blooms pinkish orange in spring, too, progressing from top to bottom. In some contrast the Davis Mountains north of the Big Bend wrap comforting arms about you, and the Limpia River is still the crystal, gentle vision it was when settlers arrived 130 years ago. Frontier life is present in a hotel and a distinguished cavalry post. Just don't try to rush through this generous corner of the state, because it takes time to feel and see. West Texas is by turns dusty and sensual, sweltering and refreshing— but always gratifying in a deeply spiritual way.

JUNE'S FAVORITE ATTRACTIONS IN WILDEST WEST TEXAS

Cowboy and His Horse Statue, Ballinger

Davis Mountain State Park, Fort Davis

Fort Concho National Historic Landmark, San Angelo

Front Street Books, Alpine

Gage Hotel, Marathon

Hot Springs, Big Bend National Park

Lajitas Stables, Lajitas

McKittrick Canyon, Guadalupe Mountains National Park

Presidio County Courthouse, Marfa

Sarah's Cafe, Fort Stockton

Forts and the Permian Basin

ou'll likely pick up this reach into the Texas "badlands" where you left off at the end of the Panhandle, striking southeast from Big Spring on U.S. 87—better stock the cooler with cold drinks and snacks, as this is the first of several somewhat long but always satisfying hauls. Drive 86 miles on this one highway, leaving Howard County, crossing Sterling and a corner of Coke Counties, to ease into Tom Green County and its seat, *San Angelo*. Home to more than 90,000 Texans, the town grew from the exceptional *Fort Concho,* founded in 1867 where the north and middle branches of the lovely Concho River meet. Local lore holds that one of the town's first personalities was the Fighting Parson, who held church in the town's gaming halls; the only time anyone ever objected, the parson gave the protester a knock in the head with the butt of his six-shooter. An early cattle- and sheep-ranching center, San Angelo today is the country's largest primary wool and mohair market and a significant livestock auction site.

Old Fort Concho is one of the state's best preserved frontier military forts, a forty-acre National Historic Landmark with twenty-three original and restored buildings quite close to downtown. It served for twenty-two years for the army, stationed here to keep peace on the frontier. Among the cavalry and infantry forces there were the heroic Buffalo Soldiers, black troops named as such out of admiration by their Native American enemies. The fort today contains three museums, featuring frontier life exhibits, officers' quarters, enlisted men's barracks, and a chapel. Throughout the year, special events and demonstrations and reenactments are held at the fort. Christmas at Old Fort Concho is a particularly colorful event, with artists, dancers, and musicians adding to the celebration. Open Tuesday through Saturday from 10:00 A.M. until 5:00 P.M. and Sunday from 1:00 until 5:00 P.M. A small admission fee is charged. Fort Concho is located at 213 East Avenue D, (915) 657–4441 or (915) 657–4444.

The newest addition to the local landscape is the *San Angelo Museum of Art* (One Love Street, San Angelo 76903, 915–653–3333), a $6 million masterpiece in its own right. The swooping roofline resembles a saddle, fittingly, and interior works range from classic paintings to contemporary ceramics.

Still in the frontier vein but more expressive in some ways is *Miss Hattie's Museum,* 18 East Concho Street, San Angelo 76903 (915–653–0112). One of several bordellos that thrived along this street, it was opened in 1896 and was a successful "gentlemen's social center" until the Texas Rangers closed it in 1946. Still in its original location, Miss Hattie's has

WILDEST WEST TEXAS

June's Favorite Annual Events in Wildest West Texas

Border Folk Festival,
El Paso, Labor Day weekend

*Christmas at Old Fort
Concho,* San Angelo, first
weekend in December

*Confederate Air Force
Air Show,* Midland, October

*Fiesta del Concho, San
Angelo,* third weekend in June

*International Good
Neighbor Day Fiesta,*
Big Bend National Park,
late October

Marfa Lights Festival,
Marfa, Labor Day weekend

Shakespeare Festival,
Odessa, late April

*Texas Cowboy Poetry
Gathering,* Alpine,
first weekend in March

Viva El Paso!, El Paso,
June through August

been restored to its former glory, complete with furnishings, plus clothing worn by the girls and the cowboys, soldiers, and businessmen who were patrons. Open Tuesday through Saturday from 10:00 A.M. until 5:00 P.M. Admission is charged.

While you're downtown, check out the **Cactus Hotel** (36 East Twohig Street), Conrad Hilton's fourth hotel—reportedly his most ornate—built in 1929 for $900,000. Rising fourteen stories high with lavish ornamentation, the hotel is home today to a coffee shop, old-fashioned barber shop, and the **San Angelo Children's Art Museum** (915–659–4391). Exhibits here encourage children to participate, think, and be creative. There's a picture-book library and a gift shop on-site. The museum is open from 1:00 to 5:00 P.M. Tuesday through Friday and Sunday, and from 10:00 A.M. to 5:00 P.M. on Saturday.

The pretty Concho River is the setting downtown for the **River Walk,** a landscaped and lighted stretch of more than 4 miles of river winding beneath huge pecan trees through parks, gardens, gorgeous homes, fountains, and waterfalls. If you're looking for nine holes of golf, miniature golf, children's play areas, hot air balloon races, walkathons, or marathons, this is the place to find them.

You'll want to take along a camera to photograph the beautiful **Pearl of the Concho,** a magical sculpture of a mermaid created by the late Jane Charless Beck, found in the Concho River near Celebration Bridge. A bit larger than life-size, the bronze mermaid holds in her outstretched hand a Concho pearl, the freshwater gem found only in these waters.

Note that from Celebration Bridge you can walk to historic Fort Concho along **El Paseo de Santa Angela,** a walkway with pecan-tree shade, fountains, historic ranch buildings, and a windmill. The short route follows a footpath used by soldiers at the fort all those years ago.

For San Angelo information contact the convention and visitors bureau at (800) 375–1206.

Consider a night or two spent in comfort at **Chaparral Ranch Bed & Breakfast,** 32 miles directly east of San Angelo in Paint Rock, which you can reach via Ranch Road 380. The hosts, who live on the property, can accommodate up to fifteen guests on sleeper sofas and beds in three rooms, each with a private bath. There's continental breakfast, or you can fix your own full breakfast in a separate kitchen—everything's supplied. Call (915) 732–4225 for reservations.

Nearby are the *Painted Rocks,* a collection of Native American pictographs thought to be more than 1,000 years old displayed in their natural setting. Call ahead to reserve tours (915–732–4376 or 915–732–4418) and to see if river excursions, taking in both pictographs and native wildlife, are scheduled.

Also in the tiny town of Paint Rock, you'll find *Ingrid's Custom Hand-Woven, Inc.* (U.S. Highway 83, 915–732–4370), a shop where crafters hand-weave rugs and saddle blankets on old-fashioned looms. You can see how the artists finish the items with latch hooks or by hand-knotting the fringes. Open from 8:00 A.M. until 4:30 P.M. Monday through Friday, and on Saturday during the Christmas season.

An interesting side trip to make while you're in the neighborhood—relatively speaking, as the neighborhoods out here are pretty big—is one for a photo op at the town of *Ballinger,* 36 miles northeast of San Angelo via U.S. Highway 67 in Runnels County. The county seat and town of 4,000 is worth finding for the *Cowboy and His Horse Statue* on the courthouse lawn, at the intersection of U.S. Highway 83 and U.S. Highway 67. The handsome memorial was sculpted by the acclaimed Pompeo Coppini, who was commissioned by the family of Charles H. Noyes, a local cowboy killed in a range accident.

About 45 miles south of San Angelo is the town of *Eldorado,* jumping-off point for stays at the X Bar Ranch (P.O. Box 696, Eldorado 76936, 915–853–2688). Three generations of the Meador family run this fifth-generation ranch, where you can enjoy bird-watching and explore mountain-bike trails also used by cattle, sheep, deer, and turkey. You can see how wool is grown and shorn and how it is then cleaned, spun, and woven into beautiful blankets and socks at the Eldorado Woolen Mill. Lodging includes cabins that sleep one to four people and lodges that sleep up to twelve. Meals, entertainment, swimming, nature study, and horseback riding can be packaged.

Still another diversion in this neck of west Texas is found in *Sonora,* a 63-mile drive due south of San Angelo on U.S. Highway 277. Go 8 miles west of Sonora on I–10 and take exit 392 to the Caverns of Sonora (915–387–3105 or 915–387–6507). The founder of the National Speleological Society said of this site, "This is the most indescribably beautiful cavern in the world. Its beauty cannot be exaggerated, even by Texans," which is saying something. Cave experts say some of the delicate crystal growths are "impossible." Ceilings, walls, and floors are covered by phenomenal formations, millions of years in the making, that are seen on guided tours. Do note that the tours can be strenuous for some visitors and that everyone should wear rubber-soled shoes. The park contains picnic grounds, camping areas, shower facilities, and a gift shop. A covered wagon dinner theater is offered Friday and Saturday evenings from mid-June through mid-August. Open daily, hours vary according to season. For admission fees and tour times, call ahead.

From San Angelo, the next destination is **Midland,** on I-20, 112 miles northwest via U.S. Highway 87 and Texas Highway 158. The seat of Midland County, with a population of about 90,000, Midland lies on the old Chihuahua Trail, the Emigrant Road to California, and the Comanche War Trail. Its name came from its position between Fort Worth and El Paso. Founded in 1885 by midwestern farm families, agriculture was its means of support until the 1923 discovery of oil in the region's lucrative Permian Basin. The skies over this incredibly flat land are pointed to by skyscrapers built on the oil booms and by those boom-producing oil derricks.

First stop is **Permian Basin Petroleum Museum, Library, and Hall of Fame** (1500 I-20 West, Midland 79701, 915-683-4403), a complex devoted to fossil-fuel origins, discovery, and resulting industries. This is where you can understand the significance of the wealthy Permian Basin, told in paintings and exhibits. There's a marine diorama of the prehistoric Permian Sea, containing 200,000 replicas of sea creatures; a re-created 1920s boomtown; an assortment of antique rigs; and a display on oil and gas well fires. Open Monday through Saturday from 9:00 A.M. until 5:00 P.M. and Sunday from 2:00 until 5:00 P.M. Admission is charged.

Midland is also home to the beloved **American Airpower Heritage Museum and Confederate Air Force Headquarters,** at the new Midland International Airport, 9600 Wright Drive, Midland 79701 (915-563-1000). Widely considered the nation's best and most complete collection of flyable World War II combat aircraft, this moving museum was founded by dedicated pilots who wanted to make sure future generations would understand the importance of such astounding American air power. The museum is committed to acquiring, restoring, and preserving at least one example of each type of World War II plane. The array today includes—among many—the P-40 Warhawk, P-38 Lightning, P-47 Thunderbolt, P-51 Mustang, P-36 King Cobra, F4F Wildcat, F6F Hellcat, F4U Corsair, plus the British Supermarine Spitfires, a German Messerschmitt, and several Japanese planes. Also find a B-17 Flying Fortress, B-29 Superfortress, and a D-47 Skytrain. The second weekend in October, you can see these craft in flight demonstrations at the CAF "Airsho," and don't miss the museum's thirty-minute film on the Ghost Squadron, shown daily at the museum. Open Monday through Saturday from 9:00 A.M. until 5:00 P.M. and Sunday from noon until 5:00 P.M. Admission is $4.00 for adults, $3.00 for seniors, and $2.00 for children.

Another Midland museum to take in is *The Museum of the Southwest* (1705 West Missouri Avenue, Midland 79701, 915–683–2882). Art and archaeology exhibits make up the permanent collection, a children's museum and a planetarium are on-site, and visiting exhibits are of the caliber of Ansel Adams's photography in a 1934 mansion bearing a National Historic Site marker. Open from 10:00 A.M. to 5:00 P.M. Tuesday through Saturday and 2:00 until 5:00 P.M. Sunday. Admission is free.

Before any more travel, take a break for eats at the *Blue Star Inn* (2501 West Wall Street, Midland 79701, 915–682–4231). The town's oldest restaurant has long been a reliable standby for excellent Cantonese dishes and charbroiled steaks—a combination not altogether unusual in west Texas. Open daily for lunch and dinner.

American Airpower Heritage Museum and Confederate Air Force Headquarters

For more information contact the Midland Chamber/Convention & Visitors Bureau (800–624–6435; www.visitmidlandtx.com).

Hitting the road again, we go 20 miles west on I–20 to Midland's sister city, **Odessa,** seat of Ector County, with a population also of 90,000. Established in 1881, Odessa was named by railroad workers from the Ukraine for their home city, which this prairie land resembled.

Lest you think oil country is without culture, Odessa offers its very own **Globe Theatre of the Southwest,** 2308 Shakespeare Road, Odessa 79761 (915–332–1586), on the Odessa College Campus. A nearly perfect replica of William Shakespeare's Globe Theatre in London, this one also was built specifically to host only plays by the Bard. His works are performed throughout the year, with much celebration made of the Spring Shakespeare Festival, held close to his birthday, April 23. Another replica, the Anne Hathaway Cottage, is home to a Shakespeare library and archives. Free tours are given between 9:00 A.M. and 5:00 P.M. Monday through Friday.

Odessa has another distinction in its **Presidential Museum,** 622 North Lee Street, Odessa 79761 (915–332–7123), the only facility in existence dedicated solely to the office of the U.S. presidency. The campaign and election processes are both studied, and collections of campaign memorabilia, presidential medals, and an array of first-lady inaugural gowns in miniature replicas are all quite interesting. Traveling exhibits are almost always on show, as well. Open Tuesday through Saturday from 10:00 A.M. until 5:00 P.M. Admission is charged.

For another glimpse of history, visit Odessa's **Parker House Museum** (1118 Maple Street, Odessa 79761, 915–335–9918), kept within the 1935 home that was headquarters for a giant ranching operation owned and run by Jim and Bessie Parker. The restored home showcases the life of this ranching family, whose empire covered some 175 sections of land in Andrews and Ector Counties. The house is open on Thursday, Friday, and Saturday only. Call for hours and special exhibit information.

Fans of kitsch won't want to leave town without having pictures taken with what is (reportedly) the **World's Largest Jack Rabbit,** a 10-foot-tall statue at 802 North Sam Houston Street, Odessa 79761. You'll see plenty of his ilk in the wild, but none are quite this big.

For more information call the Odessa Convention and Visitors Bureau at (800) 780–4678, or visit the Web site at www.odessacvb.com.

Before departing this area, take a side trip west via I–20 just 30 miles to **Monahans Sandhill State Park,** immediately north of the interstate

(915–943–2092). As you're driving west, you'll cross over a tiny corner of Crane County and drive into Ward County. That's when the flat barren land gives way to hundreds, maybe thousands, of sand dunes, just like those at the coast. You almost think that the beach must be nearby. Wind-sculpted sand dunes resembling those in the Sahara spread over a 4,000-acre park area but also extend into New Mexico. Most of the dunes are still active, growing and assuming various shapes, and are odd also for their proliferating Harvard oak forest, covering 40,000 acres in all. The trees aren't immediately seen, as they grow no more than 3 feet in height, yet their roots reach some 90 feet into the ground. The park's interpretive center offers illustrations of the dunes' history, as well as that of the ranchers, Native Americans, and oil prospectors who once called this area home. There's a 2-mile drive around the dunes leading to picnic and hiking areas and campgrounds, plus a 1/4-mile nature trail allowing you on the dramatic mountains of sand. Inside the interpretive center you can rent huge, flat plastic disks (think of an enormous Frisbee) for $1.00 for sliding down the dunes. The shop also sells books on area geology, plants, and animals, as well as souvenir T-shirts. The park is open daily from 8:00 A.M. until 10:00 P.M., and the center is open from 8:00 A.M. until 5:00 P.M. Admission is charged.

In the town of **Monahans,** founded in 1881 as a stop on the Texas and Pacific Railroad and situated today just a couple of miles west of the state park via Business Interstate 20, you'll find a handful of places to grab a bite. Texas Highway 18, a north-south thoroughfare, is the town's main street and home to The Corner Gift Shop and Soda Fountain, Howard's Drive-In, and Hero's Pizza. While you're here, don't miss the **Million Barrel Museum** (U.S. Highway 80/Business Interstate 20, 915–943–8401), located in the town's 1928 oil storage facility and an adjacent, relocated railroad hotel. Antique oilfield equipment and other period artifacts are displayed.

Transportation in the Days before Shock Absorbers

*T*he town of Monahans, famous for its miles of white-sand dunes, is home to the Butterfield Overland Stagecoach & Wagon Festival, usually held during the first weekend of August. The celebration of long, bygone stagecoach days features everything from a parade, live music, and street dancing to bull riding and barbecue.

Now it's time to venture south a while, traveling down U.S. Highway 385 for 53 miles to the town of McCamey, where you'll pick up Farm Road 305 for 19 miles, then make a 4-mile jaunt west on U.S. Highway 190 to I–10. Now head back southeast 33 miles via I–10, Texas Highway 349, and Texas Highway 290 to our destination, **Fort Lancaster State Historic Site.** The site is worth finding if you like ruins, as this briefly occupied fort has a poignancy lingering amidst its rubble. Founded in 1855 to protect the many settlers traveling the San Antonio–El Paso road, it was abandoned during the Civil War and only momentarily used again after the war's end. It had an important role, however, on the frontier, a story told in the modern interpretive center on-site. Open Wednesday through Sunday from 8:00 A.M. until 5:00 P.M. Admission is free. Call (915) 836–4391 for information.

If you're a real fort fan, continue east another 30 miles on I–10 to the lonely town of **Ozona,** the Crockett County seat, with a population of 5,000. Unique for being the only town in the county—a county that's larger than the state of Delaware, by the way—and the largest unincorporated town in the nation, Ozona also offers the **Crockett County Museum** (404 Eleventh Street, Ozona 76943, 915–392–2738). Housed there are artifacts and relics pertaining to Native Americans, the Spanish, and pioneers that were found at Fort Lancaster. Open Monday through Friday from 2:00 until 5:00 P.M. and by appointment. Admission is free, but donations are welcome.

Big Bend Country

West of Fort Lancaster 67 miles via I–10 is **Fort Stockton,** seat of Pecos County. This town of 8,500 residents began with the establishment of Camp Stockton in 1858 by troops forming from the First and Eighth Infantries of the U.S. Army. The town grew into its modern form after the Yates oil field discovery in 1925 in the eastern part of the county. The massive drilling rigs are still part of the skyline, but historical sites are the reason for stopping.

The first thing to catch your attention in town, however, is the unforgettable **Paisano Pete,** pure Texas kitsch on Main Street immediately south of U.S. Highway 290 at Farm Road 1053. *Paisano* means "companion" in Spanish, and this statue of a roadrunner is 11 feet tall and 22 feet long, making Pete the largest companion of his kind in the world. You'll see these creatures everywhere in west Texas, but you will never see another like Pete, so take this photo now—otherwise, no one back home will believe you.

To explore the admirable local history, have a look around the **Annie Riggs Memorial Museum** (301 South Main Street, Fort Stockton 79735, 915–336–2167). Housed in an 1899 hotel and a popular stop on the Overland-Butterfield Stage line, the museum was named for a colorful local figure—a twice-divorced, hard-working woman who ran the hotel for more than twenty-five years. The building, called territorial in design, features adobe brick and wood with a wraparound veranda and heavy gingerbread trim. The local historical society assembled the collection here, but the salt cedar that Annie planted in the courtyard was already in place. The parlor boasts one of the first pianos brought west of the Pecos River, as well as a giant cranberry-glass chandelier made in Ohio before the Civil War. The hotel's fifteen rooms are filled with relics, such as an 1880s baby christening gown, a man's collar box, furniture, lanterns, and a profusion of kitchen and outdoor cooking gadgets, as well as artifacts relating to the area's archaeology, geology, ranching, and religion. Open in summer Monday through Saturday from 10:00 A.M. until 8:00 P.M. and Sunday from 1:30 until 8:00 P.M.; and the rest of the year Monday through Saturday from 10:00 A.M. until noon and 1:00 until 5:00 P.M., and Sunday from 1:30 until 5:00 P.M. A small admission fee is charged.

Paisano Pete

Immediately adjacent to the Annie Riggs is the **Courthouse Square,** surrounded by wonderfully restored old buildings important to the history of Pecos County. These include the 1883 courthouse, an 1875 Catholic church, the 1883 schoolhouse, and the Zero Stone, a marker placed by a survey party in 1859 that was used as a point of origin for all land surveys in this part of west Texas for many years. There's also the photogenic Grey Mule Saloon, now a private residence.

One of Texas's premium vineyards is found at **Ste. Genevieve Wines,** about 25 miles west of Fort Stockton via I–10 (915–395–2417 or 915–395–2484). Tastings and tours are held at 10:00 A.M. on Saturday or by special appointment. Tour buses depart Fort Stockton Chamber of Commerce, 222 West Dickinson Street (915–336–8525, ext. 208) on Saturday morning by reservation. Call for rates and information.

Before leaving Fort Stockton, don't forget to have a sturdy Mexican plate lunch or dinner at **Sarah's Cafe** (106 South Nelson Street, Fort Stockton 79735, 915–336–7124). Located about 10 blocks south of Dickenson Street (a main thoroughfare), the cafe opened in 1929 and is run today by the wonderfully friendly Cleo, Mike, and Michael Castelo, the descendants of Sarah Ramirez Nunoz. It's now the oldest restaurant in town operating in the same location, with friendly service and super tacos, enchiladas, chalupas, and nachos. Open for lunch and dinner Monday through Saturday.

For more information call the Fort Stockton Visitors Center at (915) 336–8052. Ask about a sixteen-point driving-tour map and audio cassette.

If you're searching for a truly remote hideout, you probably can't find anything more so than the **Parker Ranch Bed & Breakfast** (County Road 310 at Iraan, 915–639–2850), 2 miles east of the town of Iraan, which is 59 miles east of Fort Stockton via U.S. Highway 190. Tucked into the Pecos River Valley, the expansive ranch home is a twenty-room, Spanish Colonial design built in 1929 and surrounded by palm trees. It would seem sort of a Hollywood creation, this tile-roofed, stucco wonder rather in the middle of nowhere in west Texas.

Built by O. W. Parker, the ranch is neighbors with Yates Field, which hosted one of the large and most famous oil booms in Texas. Today the ranch is owned and run as a B&B by Parker's granddaughter, Dickie Dell Ferro, who offers three bedrooms with private baths and two with a shared bath. Overnight stays are inexpensive and include a breakfast of biscuits or muffins with eggs and sausage or bacon. If your preference is yogurt and cereal, she'll do that instead.

Now to delve deeper into the land of the Big Bend, follow U.S. Highway 385 south 58 miles, cutting through the Glass Mountains and arriving in the Brewster County town of *Marathon,* with a population of 800. This is definitely a place to set a spell, as we sometimes say in west Texas. And there's no place better to do that than at the *Gage Hotel,* right in the middle of town on U.S. Highway 90 (800–884–4243). This 1927 creation by west Texas architect Henry Trost exudes the Old West in mood and looks, with a recent updating that delivered beautiful landscaping, a gorgeous swimming pool, and all sorts of decor for rooms and public areas, such as branding irons, chaps, saddles, horseshoes, and spurs. A new, $1 million adobe wing added rooms, all of which are more luxurious—some have fireplaces and parlors—than those in the original building. The dining room is worth writing home about, be assured: Southwestern dishes with sophisticated treatment include the pork chops with chipotle sauce and garlic mashed potatoes, grilled quail, shrimp enchiladas, and rainbow trout. Watch the sun fall from the sky on a front-porch rocker or ask the management to arrange a raft, jeep, or hunting trip for you.

Captain Shepard's Inn (Avenue D and Second Street, 800–884–4243) is a large, two-story adobe house built in 1889 by Albion Shepard, who came to Marathon in 1881 as a surveyor for the Southern Pacific Railroad. He became the town's first postmaster and a sheep rancher. It's managed today by the Gage Hotel owner. This inn offers five guest rooms and a two-bedroom carriage house, all with private baths and private porches. Period antiques fill the house, and there are two common areas with televisions and telephones, to be shared by guests. A continental breakfast is included with stay.

Travelers who haven't visited Marathon in a while might be astounded by the town's growth. Since J. P. Bryan of Houston bought the Gage Hotel in 1978 and supervised its marvelous expansion in recent years, he has also bought up most all the other buildings in town for renovation as art studios and galleries, boutiques and gift stores, and cafes. Whereas Marathon had been simply a launching point for journeys deep into the Big Bend region, it's now a place where travelers can hang out for a couple of days before continuing.

Bryan's vision for the still-sleepy town—you'll see goats and chickens and windmills in residents' yards, and there are virtually no stop signs or street signs to be found—has resulted in the opening of Johnny B's Soda Fountain; Gage Gear, which sells hats, book bags, shirts, and such with Gage Hotel logos; Front Street Books, selling new and used books; Weeks & Litschauer Gallery and Studio; and the V6 Collection, Bryan's store, which sells watercolor prints, Mexican glassware, and home decor in the ranch/cowboy vein.

These are all within a few steps from the front door of the Gage. Other new businesses opened in the past year or two are Sotol Gallery Fine Art Photography gallery, Angelo & Diane's Italian Cafe, and Chisos Gallery. Most businesses are open Thursday through Sunday.

Crossing the railroad tracks that run in front of the Gage, parallel to U.S. Highway 90, you'll see Dry Bean Cowboy Cafe, a rustic, two-story house with a big porch, featuring steaks and potatoes, homemade desserts and breads, as well as outside dining by candlelight. The Dry Bean offers a chuck wagon supper and show on Friday and Saturday nights.

The Dry Bean is just a block west of Evans Gallery, whose sign offers a cheery crescent moon lighted in gold, and whose interior exhibits the work of established and emerging fine-art photographers.

About a mile west of the Gage, the *Marathon Motel* (U.S. Highway 90; 915-386-4241) consists of several old, white-stucco cottages painted with terra-cotta trim. It's cheap and it's the best—if only—alternative when the Gage is full or too expensive. The rooms are very basic, but the view from the porches of these little casitas gazes southward toward the Woods Hollow and Santiago mountain ranges, which rise in a series of heights like waves rolling in from an archaeological ocean.

If you'd rather camp nearby and save your money for later Big Bend adventures, consider *Stillwell's Store,* the only camping option near the park's northern entrance. It's 40 miles south of Marathon via U.S. Highway 385, then 6 miles southeast via Farm Road 2627 (915–376–2244). The drive itself helps you become even more acclimated to the spreading region; just about 15 miles south of Marathon on U.S. Highway 385, the scrubby, hunchbacked mountains come upon you, huge and enveloping. Here, you'll find 25,000 acres for primitive camping, as well as RV hookups. Camping is anywhere from $3.50 to $15.00, and the store has plenty of provisions. An on-site bonus is *Hallie Stillwell's Hall of Fame,* a great little collection of Big Bend antiques and artifacts from the turn of the twentieth century, kept in a building next to the store. Admission is free—you just ask the storekeepers for a key. Stillwell's Store is generally open daily from 7:00 A.M. until 8:30 P.M., but you might call ahead just to be sure.

Also en route to the national park, in a scenic area called Heath Canyon, is *Spring Creek Ranch Remuda* (U.S. Highway 385 south of Marathon, 915–376–2260), a treasure for folks who want to experience a working west Texas ranch. You can take one of two horseback rides, each lasting between two and three hours, and you're welcome to join a cowboy cookout, which includes Texas steak, homemade bread, potato salad, beans, and desserts. The ranch owners ask that you bring a hat or cap, boots, "a tough posterior, and a good attitude." Horseback rides are $35 per person, and the cookout is $25 per person. Reservations are required.

Now it's time to make the big move to the incomparable *Big Bend National Park.* The northern entrance is where U.S. Highway 385 reaches its southern terminus, 40 miles south of Marathon. On your drive down, note the Woods Hollow Mountains encroaching on the highway from the east. This image of purplish blue mountains slumping low against the horizon will become very familiar to you as you explore this magnificent region.

Once inside the park boundaries, you'll immediately come upon *Persimmon Gap Visitor's Center,* with bathrooms, water fountains, books, and park literature. Another 26 miles south, you'll come to *Panther Junction,* site of *Big Bend National Park Headquarters* (915–477–2251) and the point at which the park's three main paved roads meet. You'll stop here for a variety of reasons: The required $10-per-vehicle fee is paid here; an abundance of free and inexpensive vital pamphlets and brochures regarding roads, sightseeing, flora and fauna, hiking, camping, lodging, and ranger-led activities is offered; necessary backcountry permits are issued; and a huge relief map of the park helps you better understand the undertaking ahead of you. This is also the place to inquire about weather, river, and road conditions. Less than a mile west, you'll find a gas station–convenience store.

Having gathered the copious amounts of information that define the park, you are ready to dig in. From Panther Junction, your most immediate option for exploring is to head east on the paved road. It ends at *Rio Grande Village,* near Boquillas Canyon; here you'll find flat, grassy stretches of RV camping with full hookups and a shower house, and a store selling snacks, camping permits, and bottled water.

About 3 miles upriver, 2 miles off the main road, is an abandoned resort called *Hot Springs,* a place that was all the rage in the 1920s. The drive down here cuts through dry, white limestone and shale shelves, and the road finally turns to white, powdery sands. The rest can be seen on foot. Out of nowhere appears a long-abandoned, whitewashed stone structure bearing a sign, POST OFFICE. Past that, a vacant rock lodge shaded by a grove of palm trees looks down the sandy path to the river and the therapeutic hot springs on the river's edge. Several healthy cows will probably stare vacantly at you from across the river in Mexico, but pay them no mind and go on exploring the few remains of the bathhouse in the water. When the river is low, those 108-degree waters still soothe tired bones. Ease down onto a small sitting area and feel the gush of hot water—moving at a rate of 250,000 gallons daily—revive your body and spirit.

Boquillas Canyon points up the Sierra del Carmen, rising 8,500 feet into the Mexican sky, blanketed by pine and fir forests. A great two-hour hike into the canyon delivers sensational views and a wonderful sand dune to play on. Across the river, the Mexican village of **Boquillas** welcomes you for a diversion in another culture altogether. Park on the Texas side, tip the kind Mexican attendant with a dollar or a spare Coke or sandwich, then follow a little path to the river, where you'll hop in a rowboat to be ferried across. The fare is $2.00 per person. Once in Mexico, you mount a donkey (that's $3.00) for a ride into the adobe village above you. Most tourists enjoy a simple meal of bean-and-cheese quesadillas at Don Jose Falcon's and a look around. People are friendly, and this is a nice break from everyday life.

Other options to consider exploring in the park's eastern area are those off-road adventures, such as hiking or biking. It's a good idea to make sure your vehicle is ready for the dirt roads first, and rangers can supply you with that information. Some excursions include the trek into **Dagger Flat,** reached from the Old Ore Road that splits off from the main road into the park from the north. It's a little-sought delight on a graded dirt road and an excellent primer to the extraordinary desert vegetation so abundant here. The 7-mile road leads to a strange grove of massive dagger yucca, shooting nearly a dozen feet into the air; these are stunning, especially when topped with blossoms in spring. Hike around here if you're armed with a guidebook.

Texas Trivia
West Texas was the first viticultural area in what's now the United States: In 1662, a century before Junipero Serra planted the first vines in California, Franciscan padres from Mexico established vineyards in the El Paso area to produce sacramental wines.

Another detour to make off the main road is into **Dugout Wells,** reached by leaving the road that took you to Rio Grande Village. Here is a microcosm of the diverse Big Bend, as hardwoods commingle with all sorts of desert plants, in the company of a windmill and desert critters that are most commonly spied at sunup or sundown. Watch for the marker for the Chihuahuan Desert Nature Trail, a simple ½-mile path bearing descriptive signs regarding the odd plants you see.

Heading west to the park's center by paved road, you will reach **Chisos Basin,** situated in a 1,500-foot depression—hence, the basin. It rests right in the middle of the mile-high Chisos Mountains and is the busiest part of Big Bend National Park, since this is where the park's only lodging and dining facilities are. It's also the coolest part of the park, and in summer everyone comes here for relief from the heat. As you drive up the twisting road to the Basin, you'll see a marked change in scenery. Here, there are trees—rich, rare shade is provided by evergreen and deciduous trees. The Basin's *Chisos Mountain Lodge* (915–477–2291) is often booked months in advance, and the comfortable rooms with spectacular views are the reason. The restaurant here offers above-average food for breakfast, lunch, and dinner daily. The adjacent store sells candy, some camping supplies, drinks, bandanas, and postage stamps.

The Basin also has lots of campsites up numerous hillsides, but those, too, are often booked far in advance; for spring break, the park's busiest period, reservations are made a year in advance. Unfortunately, there is no longer horseback riding inside the park. Excellent riding opportunities await, however, in Study Butte and Lajitas.

Hikers will enjoy the route from the Basin to the South Rim and to the popular Lost Mine Trail, which can be a two- to four-hour hike but the easiest in these mountains. This is an area where extensive wildlife is sighted, including the black bear. Rangers advise hikers to take along one gallon of water per person. Photographers will take a special interest in *The Window,* a narrow slit of a gorge through which all Basin drainage flows to a 75-foot fall below. When there is heavy rain in the mountains and rocks rush and bounce through The Window, it's easy to see how the Basin was formed. *Mule Ear Peaks,* southwest of the South Rim, draws both hikers and photo buffs to its twin angular rock fragments and remains of volcanic rock flow. This is a 4-mile hike that takes three or four hours to complete.

Southeast of the Basin is *Mariscal Canyon,* where the Rio Grande's southernmost dip cuts through 1,600-foot limestone walls of the Mariscal Mountains. You can explore this canyon, which is littered with abandoned quicksilver mining structures, if you're a very serious, experienced hiker. This, along with other canyons pushing against the park from Mexico, is discovered most often on rafting trips. Among the nearby rafting outfitters offering trips lasting from a half day to several days—with hiking, lunch, and camping options—are Texas River Expeditions in Terlingua (915–371–2633); Rio Grande Adventures in Terlingua (800–343–1640); Far Flung Adventures in Terlingua (915–371–2489); and Big Bend River Tours (800–545–4240). Guides are not only adept at the rowing and navigation of white water, but also are trained to give you all the information you want regarding history, geology, plant and animal life, photography, and folklore. Exquisite riverside meals and entertainment can be arranged through these rafting companies, too. Tours on land are also offered by Texas Jeep Expeditions in Terlingua (915–371–2633) and Far Flung Adventures.

In the park's southwestern section, the village of *Castolon* is reached on a 22-mile paved road branching off from the main park road. Old cavalry barracks sit deserted where a U.S. Army garrison and trading post was active from 1914 until 1916. A little store sells a few basics, such as T-shirts, snacks, books, souvenir coffee cups, and paper products. Grab some sandwich meat, cheese, and a loaf of bread for a picnic at Cottonwood Campground, adjacent to Castolon. There's superb scenery, too, down the 14-mile Maverick Road, but you need to ask a ranger if it's passable.

Morning is ideal for exploring *Santa Elena Canyon,* when the sunlight exposes walls of rose and rust. On the Texas side, the wall you can ascend of steep cement steps is called Mesa de Áquila, and the sheer cliff on the Mexican side is called Sierra Ponce. Santa Elena Canyon is the one most often seen on the shorter raft trips.

This is but a scant overview of a tremendously complex park. If you're itching to explore the lesser-known places bearing names like Devil's Den, Telephone Trail, and Grapevine Hills, ask at the headquarters for appropriate maps and information. The rangers can also provide you with names and phone numbers of personable, knowledgable guides for hire.

Barely 2 miles west of the western park boundary on Ranch Road 170 at Texas Highway 118, *Study Butte* is a 24-mile drive from the park headquarters and has lodging and food. Pronounced STEW-dee B'yewt, this is where travelers relax at the Big Bend Motor Inn and Mission Lodge (both 915–371–2218 or 800–848–BEND), offering clean rooms, gift shop, swimming pool, TV, gas, convenience store, and an above-average diner—but keep in mind, it's one of the few reliable games in town. You can have any sort of breakfast from 6:00 until 11:00 A.M.; after that, it's burgers, tacos, enchiladas, chicken-fried steak, nachos, and club sandwiches. It's rather on the expensive side ($6.00 for a plate of three tacos and $7.00 for a burger with fries), but you have to keep in mind how far from the world this all is. *Roadrunner Deli,* next to the store, sells gourmet coffees, bagels, and elaborate or simple picnic lunches. At the Study Butte Store, you can buy gas, drinks, snacks, and lottery tickets; there's a liquor store adjacent, and the Maverick Rock Shop is facing this on the south side of the road. Other nearby lodging choices are the Chisos Mining Company Motel and Curio Shop (915–371–2254), not quite a mile away; Terlingua Ranch Motel (915–371–2416), 30 miles north and east of Study Butte; and the Longhorn Ranch Motel (915–371–2541), 12 miles north of Study Butte. These are good to know about, since the park's lodging tends to be full. Both Terlingua Ranch Lodge and the Longhorn Ranch Motel have their own restaurants, and Longhorn Ranch Motel also has a swimming pool, as does Big Bend Motor Inn—a definite plus at least six months of the year.

Just west of Study Butte is a fork in the highway, where Texas Highway 170 continues due west and Texas Highway 118 reaches northward to Alpine. At the fork is the Terlingua Post Office and the Quicksilver Bank, with the area's only ATM. Bankers' hours here are serious: 8:00 until 11:00 A.M. and 2:00 until 4:30 P.M. Monday through Friday and until 6:00 P.M. on Thursday. Near the fork also is Big Bend Stables (915–371–2212), where you can book horseback rides to see pictographs and quicksilver mines for an hour to three hours or all day.

As you make this drive west on Texas Highway 170, you might try to tune into 1240 AM, an oldies radio station that often plays "A Theme from A Summer Place," "Ballad of the Green Berets," and the Turtles' "Happy Together." The farther west you drive, you'll only be able to pick up a lively Mexican station from Presidio/Ojinaga, and that's just sometimes.

Just 4 miles west on Ranch Road 170 from Study Butte, *Terlingua* (pro-nounced Tur-LING-gwuh) is called a ghost town—although it isn't anymore. This is a celebrated chili cook-off site where things are really wild in November, and a place to find photo ops in ruined houses, a jail, and a rocky cemetery bearing aged wooden crosses. You'll see the turn off Highway 170 at the sign announcing TERLINGUA GHOST TOWN; as the road climbs into a hilly area, you'll notice a new, small business complex offering a barbecue place called When Pigs Fly, as well as Quicksilver Gift Shop and Totem Gift Shop.

At the heart of Terlingua, beyond the cemetery, is an aging building housing Terlingua Trading Co., Far Flung Adventures, Dos Amigos Art Gallery, and the sensational *Starlight Theatre* (915–371–2326), the latter a spruced-up old movie house now operating as a great bar and restaurant, open Thursday through Sunday evenings.

Past the porch bearing a sign admonishing, NO DOGS ON PORCH!!! and the ubiquitous guy sitting on the porch bench happily drinking his Budweiser, smoking a cigarette, and contentedly staring off toward the horizon is a nice trove of shopping inside Terlingua Trading Co. Here you can buy every manner of T-shirt; lots of western, Mexican, and folk music on CD and cassette tape; Mexican glassware; trinkets crafted from rock and stone; and stuffed animals.

An entire room in the back is devoted to books on regional interest and culture, geology, nature, and travel. Another wall is covered with cookbooks from around Texas, Mexico, and the Southwestern U.S.

For soft adventure tours to see canyons, mountains, and the San Carlos village, just across the river in northern Mexico, book a daylong trip with *San Carlos Excursions* in Terlingua (915–424–3221). You'll travel with a small group in a comfortable Suburban; the $75 fee includes lunch.

Between Terlingua and Study Butte there's the dependable *La Kiva* (915–371–2250), a very cool and funky rock cave sort of establishment, entered underground and built into the side of Terlingua Creek. The bar is inside and an amazing patio is outdoors—you have to see it to understand it. Barbecue and steaks are the fare; open for dinner only.

Another 13 miles west on Ranch Road 170, you'll come to *Lajitas on the Rio Grande,* a re-created western town that's really a resort created by a Houston developer. But Lajitas didn't originate as a commercial brainstorm. Back when Pancho Villa and friends were making life so tough on the area's settlers, the U.S. Army put a post out here in 1895. It was so remote, however, that little happened in the way of growth until the resort was established in 1977. Now it's a lodging center for the area, with choices including a motel, bunkhouse, hotel, and condos, with period reproduction furniture. Lajitas has a nine-hole golf course, riding stables, tennis courts, an airstrip, restaurants, bars, drugstore and soda fountain, liquor store, art gallery, and gift shops. Plans call for

Bizarre Texas Stuff

*L*AJITAS: Whether or not cows can fly, it's certain that goats can drink beer. Proof is found at the Lajitas Trading Post, (915) 424–3234, where the mayor—a goat named Clay Henry Jr.—guzzles beer on a daily basis. His predecessor, Mayor Clay Henry, was a huge hit with tourists who would stop in for a beer and see the mayor's pen littered with beer cans and bottles.

When the curious would ask, someone at the trading post would kindly put a beer up to the goat's mouth, whereupon the goat would get a grip on the bottle with his mouth, tip his head back, and down the whole thing. It's said that old age, rather than liver problems, finally took Clay Henry a few years ago, but soon C. H. Jr. was filling his shoes. Or hooves, as it were.

additional golf and upscale dining. For lodging call (915) 424–3471. For tours of Big Bend Ranch State Park and into northern Mexico, call Big Bend Adventures, (915) 371–2771. For rafting call Big Bend River Tours, (800) 545–4240.

Even if it weren't the only outfit around, *Lajitas Stables* (888–508–7667 or 915–424–3238) is one of the best horseback riding businesses anywhere. Owned for over a decade by Linda Walker, who moved to the Big Bend area from Colorado nearly twenty years ago and was formerly a professional barrel racer, the outfit has grown from eight or ten horses to more than fifty. Linda also owns Big Bend Stables in Study Butte. You can book anything from a one-hour ride to a five-day journey, with longer trips involving both camping and a bed-and-breakfast stay at a luxurious place in Mexico.

Linda's offerings also include two cattle drives every year in Big Bend Ranch State Park, which she says is probably the best deal in Texas. Riders who want to get in touch with real cowboy life spend a few days rounding up some 150 to 200 head of longhorn and "do everything," she says, from holding to branding calves. "Everyone finds his or her comfort zone," Linda says. "The point is to find it and push it on the drive."

Of special interest is the *Barton Warnock Environmental Education Center* (915–424–3327), immediately east of Lajitas, a wonderful museum with old photographs, fossils, and an arboretum. It's open from 8:00 A.M. until 5:00 P.M. Admission is free.

Lajitas is also the home base for ventures into the state's largest park, the new *Big Bend Ranch State Park,* a 270,000-acre spread adjacent to Lajitas. Here you'll find abundant fascination in the form of wildlife, mountains, a herd of Texas longhorns, geological formations, and exotic plants and animals. There are three primitive camping areas and three hiking trails; admission is $5.00 per vehicle. The park is open daily from 8:00 A.M. until 5:00 P.M. Call (915) 229–3416 or (915) 424–3327 for information. There are monthly bus tours with a chuck wagon lunch, too; call (915) 424–3327 well in advance to reserve.

A terrific way to see the glories of Big Bend Ranch State Park is on horseback, thanks to riding trips by P&J Tours, (512) 398–7627 or (281) 486–8070. A pair of professional photographers, Peggy Parks and Jim Carr, lead six to eight weekend-long trips in spring and fall through the park. Groups are usually of about twenty people, which typically include adventurous souls from around Texas. Participants sleep in bunkhouses, eat at picnic tables in a mess hall or out on the trails, and do some hiking in addition to riding. Horsemanship isn't necessary, but it's helpful. These trips are about $475 per person and include food and lodging.

As Ranch Road 170 continues to unwind west from Lajitas, the road is called *El Camino del Rio,* Spanish for "the river road." It's been widely called one of the most scenic drives in the nation, while technically it's known as the 55 miles of Ranch Road 170 between Study Butte and Presidio. El Camino del Rio traces the Rio Grande in a series of dips, climbs, and twists, marked most dramatically by *The Hill,* a mile-high climb with an average grade of 15 percent. That's steep, and there are extraordinary photography spots. Adobe homes dot the hilltops, peering out over the river, and intriguing little metal teepees are part of a highway department roadside park, complete with picnic tables. Drive slowly to savor the scenery and to avoid the horses and cows usually wandering in the road.

Just shy of *Presidio,* 50 miles west of Lajitas, *Fort Leaton State Historic Site* is on Ranch Road 170 (915–229–3613). The private fort and trading post was originally a Spanish mission founded in 1759 but was taken over in 1848 by frontiersman Ben Leaton, who monopolized profitable trade with the Native Americans in the area. The adobe fortress now holds a museum covering Leaton's controversial personal and business ethics, along with the area's Mexican, Native American, and pioneer heritage. Exhibits offer bilingual signage and include natural history, along with chronology of commerce, settlement, and cattle and silver industries. A slide show covers the desert ecology. Open daily from 8:00 A.M. until 5:00 P.M. Admission is charged.

Presidio sits in some of the most rugged land Texas can offer, an isolated Rio Grande settlement that's often mentioned in the news as having the hottest temperature in the country. Besides that, it's the self-proclaimed Onion Capital of the World and a good jumping-off place for travelers wishing to journey southwest into Mexico to tour the magnificent Copper Canyon; for information on such trips, call Sanborn Escorted Tours, (888) 883–6910, or Tour Masters, (800) 729–1406.

If you arrive in Presidio hungry, head right to *El Patio Restaurant* (513 O'Reilly Street, Presidio 79845, 915–229–4409), an inexpensive, family-run spot serving fajitas, enchiladas, tacos, and other Mexican specialties, as well as salads, soups, and ice cream. It's open for breakfast, lunch, and dinner daily. For more Presidio information and help with planning trips into Mexico, contact the *Presidio Chamber of Commerce,* (915) 229–3199.

Presidio's sister city across the Rio Grande is the Mexican village of *Ojinaga,* good for a beer and a spot to eat at La Fogata or Los Comales. Also look for pottery and other clay crafts at Casa de Artesanias and bakery delights from Panaderia Ideal.

If you're in pursuit of something more remote than you ever dreamed possible, continue west from Presidio via Texas Highway 170 about 36 miles to the speck of a town called Ruidosa. From there you'll veer onto rough Hot Springs Road for another 7 miles until you reach *Chinati Hot Springs* (Pinto Canyon Road, 915–229–4165), one of the most restorative places on Earth. Towering cottonwood trees line a running stream, and hot mineral baths will help work out your troubles. There are campgrounds as well as cabins, lodge rooms, and bunkhouse beds. It's open daily to overnight guests and open Thursday through Monday for day guests.

Texas Trivia

In May 1996, Martha Stewart and her staff traveled to Marfa to shoot a five-page barbecue layout for her magazine. Grady Spears, executive chef at Reata in Alpine and Fort Worth, provided recipes and labor.

From Presidio, follow U.S. Highway 67 north 61 miles, looking first to the west along the drive at the slumping Chinati Mountains, followed by the Cuesta del Burro Mountains. Keep an eye out for the sign indicating Lincoln's profile in a mountain formation to the west; sure enough, there's a clear profile of a reclining Abe's face. Soon after that, look to the east side of the highway for Shafter Ghost Town. A turn from the highway will take you into a small, nearly abandoned historic mining town with scenic stone building ruins. Be sure you have film on hand.

Another turn to watch for from U.S. 67—about 25 miles north of Presidio—is that to *Cibolo Creek Ranch,* the most luxurious, remote resort in Texas (see end of chapter for details). Watch carefully and you'll spot some pronghorn antelope hopping and bounding along in the tall grasses to the east. You'll wind up in the ultra-western town of *Marfa,* seat of Presidio County and home to 2,400. The town is becoming well known for a mysterious phenomenon called the *Marfa Ghost Lights.*

If you're around for Labor Day, you'll get to help celebrate the *Marfa Lights Festival,* which includes a fun run, street dance, food and arts booths, parade, evening concert, Mexican folkloric dancers, and mariachi musicians. For details call the chamber of commerce, (915) 729–4942.

By daylight, Marfa shows off its beautiful *Presidio County Courthouse,* at the north end of Highland Street, a stone-and-brick creation in the Second Empire design, built in 1886. The view of the surrounding land is stunning from the dome up top, which is open Monday through Friday from 8:30 A.M. until 4:30 P.M. Admission is free.

A few yards away, the *El Paisano Hotel,* North Highland Street at West Texas Street (915–579–3145), is a beautiful example of Trost architecture dating from 1927; it has hosted Franklin D. Roosevelt, Harry S. Truman, and John F. Kennedy, among other dignitaries. Bearing state and national historical markers, the hotel is beloved by movie buffs for having been the home of Elizabeth Taylor, Rock Hudson, James Dean, and Dennis Hopper, plus all the other actors who appeared in the epic film *Giant,* filmed close by. Past the fountained courtyard, inside the Spanish-detailed hotel lobby, there are glass-fronted cases of *Giant* memorabilia, including signed photos of the cast, clippings from *Life* magazine, and numerous news clippings regarding the shoot.

Marfa's blend of raw landscape and pure solace have made it a magnet for creative forces. The late American sculptor Donald Judd moved to Marfa in 1972 and created *Chinati Foundation* in 1986 as an art museum dedicated to permanent installations of very large works of art in fifteen buildings and scattered around the grounds of the former army post called Fort D. A. Russell. The museum is about a mile south of town and is open from 1:00 to 5:00 P.M., Thursday through Saturday. For information call (915) 729–4362.

Bizarre Texas Stuff

*M*ARFA: *Nobody seems to know why, but there have been some strange lights appearing off the horizon near Marfa since the late 1800s. Various stories and theories circulate about what the Marfa Ghost Lights are, but not even the scientists who have studied them have come up with a sure explanation. Most people who have observed them say the lights sometimes glow softly and then brighten to the intensity of a searchlight. You can see for yourself by driving (after dark, of course) west from Marfa on U.S. Highway 90/67 about 8 miles, then pull over on the south shoulder of the road where a sign indicates the official viewing area. Look southwest toward the Chinati Mountains and just wait. You'll probably wait just a little while, then—poof! There's the first one, a little ball of light in the distance, bobbing just the tiniest bit. Then—poof! It splits into two slightly wavering, shimmering spheres. More will likely appear, but maybe not. Ask the folks around town about all the theories, and decide for yourself. The Marfa Chamber of Commerce has information at (915) 729–4942.*

Other artistic sites in town include *Evan Hughes Studio* (123 North Highland Avenue, Marfa 79843, 915–729–3121), part-time home of a Brooklyn-based furniture designer and sculptor; and *Hegy Propellors* (507 West Lincoln Street, Marfa 79843, 915–729–4249), the home-studio of Jim Corder, who runs a family business of handcarving wooden propellors for antique and homemade aircraft.

If you get high on golf, head 2 miles east from downtown on Oak Street, and you'll find the *Marfa Municipal Golf Course* (915–729–4942), the highest golf course in Texas, sitting almost a mile in elevation above sea level. There are nine holes open to the public, and green fees are $8.00. Open daily from 8:00 A.M. until 5:00 P.M.

For a more in-depth look at the region, head west on U.S. Highway 90/67 for 26 miles to *Alpine,* seat of Brewster County and home to 6,000 west Texans and Sul Ross State University, right on U.S. Highway 90. On the campus you'll find the *Museum of the Big Bend* (915–837–8143), which contains a small but impressive collection of artifacts from the Spanish explorers, Native Americans, ranchers, and cavalry soldiers who figured into the history of the region and national park. A reconstructed frontier general store, stagecoach, and blacksmith shop are exhibited, as well as traveling art exhibits. The collection of western belt buckles is amazing. Open Tuesday through Saturday from 9:00 A.M. until 5:00 P.M. and Sunday from 1:00 until 5:00 P.M. Admission is free, but donations are accepted.

Two miles west of town on U.S. Highway 90, *Apache Trading Post* (915–837–5149) is located in a log cabin and is a treasure chest of sorts, stocked with genuine Native American–crafted jewelry in silver and turquoise; pottery; rugs; agate necklaces; belt buckles and bolo ties; postcards, posters, and calendars; cactus jams and jellies; Mexican pottery and moccasins; arrowheads and geodes; and books on geology, natural history, Big Bend history, and folklore. Open Monday through Saturday from 9:00 A.M. until 6:00 P.M. and Sunday from 1:00 until 6:00 P.M.

Rock hounds will enjoy a trip to *Woodward Agate Ranch,* south of Alpine 16 miles on Texas Highway 118 (915–364–2271). More than seventy varieties of cutting stones on this 4,000-acre ranch include gemstones such as red plume, pom pom agates, amethysts, and opals. Ranch managers will tell you where to find the best stones, which cost 50 cents per pound. Open dawn till dusk; remember to bring a hat, sunscreen, and water.

Stick around a while and maybe rest up at *Holland Hotel* (209 West Holland Avenue, Alpine 79830, 800–535–8040 or 915–837–3844), a historic, three-floor hotel with twelve restored rooms and two suites. The Holland, once a favorite railroad hotel, is smack in the middle of historic downtown. Even high in the hotel's tiny "penthouse"—a cute little hideout for those who don't mind a steep staircase—you can still hear the train whistling by every couple of hours. A tiny sign on the bedstand, accompanied by two little packages of ear plugs, reads, WE THINK OUR TRAIN IS VERY QUAINT. BUT IF EARS IT PAINS, PLUG 'EM AND IT CAIN'T.

In this charming downtown neighborhood are a host of shops and galleries. Among these, find **Front Street Books** (121 East Holland Avenue, Alpine 79830, 915–837–3360), an excellent bookstore selling plenty of Big Bend and west Texas titles, maps, natural history guides, rare and out-of-print books, as well as notecards, books on tape, *New York Times*, and used books. It's open until 7:00 P.M. Monday through Saturday.

If you're needing a beautifying pick-me-up, check into **Americana** next door to the Holland Hotel (207 West Holland Avenue, Alpine 79830, 915–837–1773), a boutique and salon offering hair care, skin treatments, and nail services.

Also downtown, **Rinconada** (401 North Fifth Street, Alpine 79830, 915–837–9179) sells fine Southwestern paintings, pottery, and sculpture, sterling silver jewelry, antiques, and toys. And if you're looking for Native American art, check out **Kiowa Gallery** (105 East Holland Avenue, Alpine 79830, 915–837–3067).

To celebrate Alpine's growing arts community, there's an annual **Gallery Night** held in November, during which more than twenty galleries keep special evening hours and invite you to stroll and peruse special exhibits. For details on this event, and to get a wonderful walking-tour map of Alpine, visit the **Chamber of Commerce** at 106 North Third Street, Alpine 79830, or call (915) 837–2326.

For a quiet meal, try the Bistro at the Holland Hotel (209 West Holland Avenue, Alpine 79830, 915–837–3844), which spreads through the vintage hotel lobby and replaces Kate's. Oysters on the half-shell— yes, in the barren west Texas desert—gourmet burgers, quiche, and lovely desserts are among the favorite selections. Lunch and dinner are served daily.

If you're ready for more adventure, head out for Jeff Davis County and its county seat, **Fort Davis,** north 26 miles via Texas Highway 118. A cavalry post was established in 1855, the town later became a haven for sufferers of respiratory problems, and commercially grown Delicious apples eventually became a primary industry. The highest town in

Texas at just over 5,000 feet, Fort Davis is cool enough to warrant wearing at least a sweater eleven months out of the year.

A good home base in town is *The Hotel Limpia,* on the square in the middle of the tiny town (915–426–3237 or 800–662–5517). The hotel was built in 1912 by the Union Trading Company, was recently remodeled, and is a member of the Historic Accommodations of Texas. There's an upstairs balcony and an enclosed veranda full of rocking chairs, potted flowers, and oak tables—plus a lovely view of the sunset. The front desk's stained-glass detail and an old ranch house door add to the period mood. High-ceilinged rooms and suites are filled with antique oak furnishings, and the big main lounge has a native-stone fireplace. The Limpia's lodgings have been expanded to include—in addition to the main hotel and the annex out back—the Mulhern House, a renovated adobe home built in 1905, now offering three suites; Limpia Cottage, with its back pressed to the mountains; and the Dr. Jones House, a 1903 home that was recently restored.

The Limpia's dining room features home cooking, with steaks, chicken, sandwiches, and soups, plus good pies and breakfast and lunch buffets. Also part of the Limpia are Sutler's Club, a friendly little place to wet your whistle; the Hotel Limpia Gifts, a pretty store specializing in glassware and home furnishings; and Javelinas to Hollyhocks, an artistic boutique selling books and maps, candles, pewter photo frames, and sweatshirts.

The best orientation to the area's wonders is found by driving the *74-Mile Scenic Loop Road,* beginning and ending in Fort Davis. An array of mountain vistas, Madera Canyon, and roadside parks bounded by ancient boulders are the rewards for following Texas Highway 17 south of town just 2 miles to Texas Highway 166 west to Texas Highway 118, then southeast back to Texas Highway 17 and Fort Davis.

Then it's time to see the reason Fort Davis came into being: As Indian raids increased with the numbers of settlers arriving or traveling through this part of the state, usually en route from San Antonio to El Paso, a cavalry post was built in 1855. *Fort Davis National Historic Site* is the restored site, named for U.S. Secretary of War Jefferson Davis, who ordered the army's posting here. Active from 1854 until 1891, with lapses during the Civil War, when fire destroyed the fort, it was home to twelve cavalry and infantry companies—numbering up to 800 men—stationed here in fifty buildings. The renovated stone-and-adobe remains sit in a scenic box canyon, sheltered on the west by towering cliffs, and are as complete and impressive as any in the Southwest. This indoor-outdoor museum was also the post for Black troops from the Ninth,

WILDEST WEST TEXAS

Tenth, Twentieth, and Twenty-fourth U.S. Cavalries. As was the case at Fort Concho, the enemy Comanche and Apache soldiers named these men the Buffalo Soldiers, which has been interpreted as a term of respect.

During the summer a living-history program demonstrates pioneer and fort life with costumed participants; the fort's Labor Day celebration draws as many as 2,000 spectators, and a special Black History event is a February highlight. Otherwise, the place is easily seen on self-guided tours with a slide-show introduction. A bugle sounds twice daily, starting the audio of a formal ceremony on the parade yard. Images of hundreds of mounted and marching soldiers in full dress are easy to see in the mind's eye. The commander's house was occupied the longest by Col. Benjamin H. Grierson, and his original furnishings show luxury's spotty hand in a usually mundane frontier post life. Antiques, silver, and linens decorate the parlor and dining areas; giant beds and ornate wardrobes are characteristic in the oversize bedrooms. A museum in the main building contains a display illustrating Trans-Pecos frontier days, the overland gold rush, stagecoach and Indian raiding routes, plus artifacts such as an officer's scabbard, pistol, and musket. A gift shop sells books and more books, including Old West cookbooks, art books, and children's coloring books. Open daily in summer from 8:00 A.M. until 6:00 P.M. and the rest of the year 8:00 A.M. until 5:00 P.M. Admission is $2.00 for adults and free for those younger than seventeen and older than sixty-two. Situated immediately north of town on Texas Highway 118, (915) 426–3224.

You can be enveloped in the area's solitude and natural beauty by a stay in *Davis Mountains State Park,* 4 miles north of town on Texas Highway 118 (915–426–3337). Sandwiched ideally between the grassy desert plains and the fragrant, woodsy mountains, this 2,700-acre park offers numerous hikes, from easy to challenging, as well as a rewarding Skyline Drive. Camp if you like, or call ahead for a room at the very cozy *Indian Lodge,* a pueblo-style motel with plenty of amenities, plus the hand-carved cedar furniture fashioned by Civilian Conservation Corps workers, who also built the lodge in the 1930s. The park is open daily for day use from 8:00 A.M. until 10:00 P.M. and at all hours for campers. Admission is charged.

Or hang your hat at the *Prude Ranch,* also just north of town on Texas Highway 118 (915–426–3202 or 800–458–6232). A working ranch run by the same friendly west Texas family and open to guests since 1921, it offers bunkhouse and motel-style lodging, horseback riding, tennis, Jacuzzi, and plenty of ranch-hand chow. To honor the ranch's centennial (it was founded in 1897), the Texas State Historical Commission bestowed a historical marker in 1997 that details the ranch's history.

Another site worth a look is the **Neill Doll Museum,** on Court Avenue at Seventh Street (915–426–3969), doubling as a bed-and-breakfast home. Inside the restored, 1898 home built as a summer retreat for a Galveston family, there are more than 300 cataloged antique dolls dating from the mid-1800s, including Victorian clown dolls, German bisque dolls (1890–1910), and an 1835 lady doll in white dress with red velvet sash, Marie Antoinette hair, and pearl choker. The young Princess Elizabeth and Prince Phillip dolls are striking likenesses. Open in summer Tuesday through Saturday from 10:00 A.M. until 5:00 P.M. and Sunday from 1:30 until 5:00 P.M. The rest of the year it's open by appointment. Admission is charged.

Stargazing travelers won't waste time driving up to the **McDonald Observatory,** a University of Texas operation reached by driving from Fort Davis 17 miles northwest on Texas Highway 118, then 2 miles southeast on Spur 78. Sitting atop 6,800-foot Mount Locke, the observatory features a 107-inch telescope, plus tours for visitors to see its 160 tons of moving parts. Programs at the visitors center include solar viewings, and star parties are staged Tuesday, Friday, and Saturday evenings for looking at celestial objects through small telescopes. Even if you're not in time for a viewing, pay a visit anyway to see the fascinating, thirty-minute video on the universe, produced by NASA. A great gift shop with unusual goods is on-site. The visitors center is open daily from 9:00 A.M. until 5:00 P.M. Solar viewing programs are offered at 11:00 A.M. and 3:30 P.M. Admission is free; call (915) 426–3640 for details.

If you're hungry, looking for a comfortable place to sleep, or in search of good postcards or a western belt, head to **The Old Texas Inn,** right on the town square (915–426–3118). Inside there's an honest-to-goodness soda fountain, making great breakfasts, lunches, and dinners—the old-fashioned burgers, malts, and ice-cream floats are hard to beat. The gift shop sells souvenirs, and the lodgings are upstairs. Six rooms are available, each with a private bath. Stop in or call daily from 7:30 A.M. until 5:00 P.M., or until 9:00 P.M. in summer.

Trans-Pecos Country

*D*riving north from Fort Davis along Texas Highway 17, the gorgeous winding road courses through slumping rock formations as it follows Limpia Creek; if you take along some snacks you can stop at one of several roadside picnic sites and enjoy the scenery in relative quiet, as there isn't a lot of traffic along the route. Watch on the east side of the road for a 1956 Texas Historical Marker, noting Wild Rose Pass.

From Fort Davis the next stop is **Balmorhea State Park,** north on Texas Highway 17, 39 miles away. Truly unusual in this modern day is a pool like the one here: Said to be the world's largest spring-fed swimming pool, Balmorhea's measures nearly two acres, is thirty feet deep, and contains three and a half million gallons of water. Talk about cool—the water is between 72 and 76 degrees year-round, so your only swimming opportunities fall between the end of May and Labor Day. In addition to a vintage bathhouse and concession stand, you'll find tent and RV campsites and a small hotel on site. The grounds are green and roomy, so even if you miss the pool season, this is a delightful place to kick back and plot your next move down the road. Call (915) 375–2370 for reservations. Open daily from dawn till dusk. Admission is charged for park entry and pool use.

Keep your eyes peeled in this area for some of the purely Texan things that make this part of the world something you won't forget. On the section of Texas Highway 17 that is the main street in Balmorhea, for example, there's a yellow road sign with just a turkey on it—as in, turkey crossing. And on Texas Highway 17 between Balmorhea and Pecos, look at the tops of telephone poles. More than likely, you'll see a hawk perched on high, looking for lunch in the fields.

If you've come at the right time, this is the point at which to make a detour 33 miles north on Texas Highway 17 to Pecos, home on July 4th to the world-famous **West of the Pecos Rodeo.** The massive affair has been held annually since June 1883, when cowhands from the Hashknife, W, Lazy Z, and NA ranches argued in Red Newell's saloon over which had the best ropers and riders among its brethren. Ever since, the summer holiday has been set aside for competitors in saddle-bronc riding, steer

Sorry, No Muppets Here

*T*he Winkler County seat of Kermit became a boomtown in 1926, when oil was discovered nearby in the Permian Basin. If you're passing through, stop to see the town's oldest structure, the Medallion Home, built in 1907 about 5 miles south of town. It was dismantled and moved into Kermit in 1910 and was occupied until deeded to the city in 1967. Find it in Pioneer Park. (915) 586–2507.

roping, bulldogging, and plenty of other tough events. Things have progressed considerably since that first rodeo, when 1,000 spectators showed up to watch the cowhands compete for a $40 prize—the numbers have increased by the thousands. Pecos, known far and wide also for its cantaloupes, hosts its Cantaloupe Festival the first weekend in August, as well as a World Championship Bar-B-Q Contest the first weekend in October. For tickets and information call the tourism office at (915) 445–2406, or stop by at 111 South Cedar Street.

Should you decide to stick around and explore Pecos for a spell, pay a visit to the *West of the Pecos Museum* (First Street at U.S. 285/Cedar Street, 915–445–5076), occupying the old Orient Hotel. You can see bullet holes from the last gunfight in town, which took place some 120 years ago, and explore fifty rooms on three floors filled with area relics, as well as period exhibits pertaining to such folks as the local sheriff, doctor, rodeo queens, Rotarians, and so on. A popular exhibit is the replica of the Jersey Lilly Saloon, where Judge Roy Bean reigned as the Law West of the Pecos down in the town of Langtry. Another exhibit honors Clay Allison, the gentleman gunfighter who "never killed anybody who didn't need killing." The museum is open 9:00 A.M. to 5:00 P.M. Tuesday through Saturday and from 1:00 until 4:00 P.M. on Sunday.

All this is bound to work up a hunger, so it's a good thing the *La Nortena Tamales* (212 East Third Street, Pecos 79772, 915–445–3273) is right around the corner. It's nothing fancy, but the homemade tamales are rewarding. Nearby, there's *Leroy's BBQ* (900 West Third Street, Pecos 79772, 915-445-5110), an old family spot serving barbecue and Mexican food.

Whatever the season, your path from Balmorhea is northwest to *Guadalupe Mountains National Park.* You can reach it by driving west for 71 miles, through parts of Reeves, Jeff Davis, and Culberson Counties to the town of Van Horn. Here, you'll turn north on Texas Highway 54 and go 55 miles to the park. Note that once inside the park, you've entered Mountain Daylight Time. This former ranch land is blessed with 80 miles of hiking trails, assorted mountains (some up to 8,700 feet high), breathtaking overlooks, ancient canyons colored in ridges of brilliant oranges and reds, abandoned ranches, springs, and spectacular foliage in autumn—all of it a photographer's delight. Because of its remote position, this isn't ever a crowded park; those mountaintop pine-and-fir forests are usually just yours to relish. The only company you might have is that of mountain lions, elk, wild turkeys, and black bears. More tame in the way of wildlife are cacti blooming with purple, pink, and ruby flowers. Stop at the visitors center first and inquire about ranger-guided hikes, programs in the amphitheater, and the best places to view or photograph McKittrick Canyon, El Capitan, and Guadalupe Peak. Camping is available at Pine Springs and Upper Dog Canyon campgrounds in the park. The headquarters visitors center is open daily from 7:00 A.M. until 6:00 P.M. in summer, and 8:00 A.M. until 4:30 P.M. the balance of the year. Admission is free; call (915) 828–3251.

If you head west on U.S. Highway 62/180, 70 miles to Farm Road 2775, then make a turn north and follow it 8 miles to *Hueco Tanks State Park,* you'll find odd, blobbish rock formations with caves and cliffs containing some 2,000 ancient Native American pictographs, some from the Apaches, as well as ruins of an old Butterfield stage station. The park's name comes from the vast, natural rainwater basins, or *huecos* (WHAY-coes) in Spanish, making this spread a giant oasis for dwellers and travelers for as long, some studies reveal, as 10,000 years. Camping, picnicking, rock climbing, nature study, and rock art tours are offered. Open daily in daylight hours and at all times for campers. Admission is charged. Call (915) 857–1135 for information.

Don't You Walk on By . . .

In Wink there's the Roy Orbison Museum, named for the native son and rock 'n' roll legend who became famous for "Pretty Woman," "Only the Lonely," and many other popular songs. See memorabilia from his youth and his career, including albums and singles and his trademark sunglasses. For tours call (915) 527–3622.

Your final area for west Texas exploration is *El Paso,* 30 miles west of the Hueco Tanks turnoff, via U.S. Highway 62/180. Jammed into a pass of the mile-high Franklin Mountains, the ancient city clings to and curves around the mountains' base. Inspirations all around are as Native American and pioneer as they are Mexican and Spanish. Combined with Juarez, El Paso's twin across the Rio Grande, the population pushes one and a half million—and some days there's the smog to prove it. In spite of all those people, El Paso feels wide open and very much a part of the Wild West. The purple-and-orange-layered sunsets soften the craggy mountains, giving them a blue cast and the city a somber backdrop. Annual visitors number around fifteen million, due in part to the sunshine, which brightens at least 300 days each year. The story goes that World War II servicemen stationed at massive Fort Bliss discovered the margarita, but they were preceded in discoveries by the sixteenth-century Spanish conquistadors who found this pass of the north from Mexico, and so named the place for its use.

Older even than California's, *El Paso's historic missions* occupy a lower valley along El Camino Real, or the Royal Highway used by the missionaries and conquistadors and the longest historic road in the United

States. The first to explore is the *Ysleta Mission,* situated at Zaragosa and Alameda, next to the Tigua Indian Reservation, which we'll cover soon. Founded by Franciscan padres in 1680, this one has been rebuilt several times and is thought to be the nation's oldest mission and possibly the oldest continuously used parish in the nation. Don't be confused, but the church's official name is Our Lady of Mount Carmel, yet there's a St. Anthony statue on the outside, as he is the patron saint of the Tigua Indians, who fled New Mexico during the Pueblo Revolt in the seventeenth century. All missions are open daily from 8:00 A.M. until 5:00 P.M. Admission is free.

Socorro Mission, 3 miles southeast of Ysleta Mission on Farm Road 258, was also founded in 1680. This one is of the classic, stark adobe design, and its ornate, hand-hewn roof beams are the oldest in Texas. Travel 5 miles southeast next to *San Elizario Presidio Church,* also on Farm Road 258, to see the 1770s architecture in a lovely courtyard. This is still an active Catholic church. Note that drives to the missions are prettiest in autumn, when cotton fields are overrun with white bolls, pecan groves stretch without end, and row upon row of chiles and onions burst in reds and greens. Farmers are usually found on roadsides tending their stands, selling roasted chiles or big, fat *ristras,* those hanging bunches of chiles that are very fashionable in southwestern decor.

For a deeper look into history surviving to the modern day, visit the *Tigua Indian Reservation* (119 South Old Pueblo Road, El Paso 79907, 915–859–3916). Also called Ysleta del Sur Pueblo, this is the home of descendants of those Tiguas who fled during the Pueblo Revolt in New Mexico more than 300 years ago. There's a living-history pueblo, with demonstrations of pottery, jewelry, and weaving crafts, plus bread baking in dome-shaped ovens. Tribal dances are performed during special events, while the twenty-first century threatens to impose itself, as the Tiguas prepare to bring high-stakes gambling to the reservation to increase tourism income. In the Cultural Center, a cafe serves fajitas, puffy Indian tacos, and the hottest bowls of green and red chile (much like stew on fire) on Earth. You can find fairly good deals on pottery and silver jewelry here, too. Open daily from 8:00 A.M. until 5:00 P.M. Admission is free, but donations are accepted.

Of two scenic drives, the *Scenic Road* is shorter and easier to access. Drive behind the Sun Bowl and wind between formidable walls of rock

Tigua Indian Reservation

for 2 miles west to east, from Rim Road to Richmond Avenue. From Murchison Park at the road's apex 4,200 feet high, your vista includes two cities, three states, and two countries. You can see a stone peg that marks the end of the Rocky Mountains, a giant Christ statue on Sierra del Cristo Rey, and several war memorials. Sadly, you may also see a fair amount of graffiti and trash.

The other route is the more lengthy *Transmountain Drive,* a highway cutting through Smugglers Gap in the North Franklin Mountains. The summit is almost a mile above sea level, and the Wilderness Park is up there with great Chihuahuan Desert hiking trails. A nature trail passes replicas of a Pueblo ruin, kiva, and pithouse. The view of mountains reveals geologic history—gray shades indicate where ancient inland sea waters lapped, and reds are the leavings of volcanic lava flows.

The *Franklin Mountains State Park* is in this area, too. The 24,000-acre wilderness offers mountain bikers, hikers, and horseback riders more than 100 miles of trails. After $1.5 million in improvements, the park is now open to overnight campers, too. Guided tours led by park rangers are given the first and third weekends of each month. Call (915) 566–6441 for reservations.

Take off for an Old West retreat by visiting *Indian Cliffs Ranch at Cattleman's Steakhouse,* 30 miles east of town on I–10 and 5 miles north on Farm Road 793 (915–544–3200). The multi-level complex is part sprawling ranch, part adobe, part movie set, and all romance. Long-horn cattle and buffalo graze here, but primarily it's a place of entertainment and social interest. There's a restaurant with huge steaks and Mexican dishes, a gift shop with plenty of jewelry, and a terrace from which to watch achingly beautiful sunsets over a spread of cacti and corrals. A ride aboard a wagon pulled by huge Belgian horses takes you to Fort Misery, an 1860s fort replica for overnight guests and campfire dinners. Call ahead for activities schedules and reservations.

In town, El Paso's cultural offerings are as diverse as they are plentiful. Downtown find *The Bridge Center for Contemporary Arts* (127 Pioneer Plaza, El Paso 79901, 915–532–6707), a nonprofit gallery featuring work in contemporary and experimental art by emerging and nationally recognized artists. Open from 11:00 A.M. until 5:30 P.M. Tuesday through Saturday. Across the street have a look inside the *Camino Real Paso Del Norte Hotel* (101 South El Paso Street, El Paso 79901, 915–534–3000), built in 1912 and listed on the National Register of Historic Places. The eighty-year-old Tiffany glass dome is a commanding sight in the hotel's elegant Dome Bar. Guests here over the years have included Pancho Villa, President Taft, and "Blackjack" Pershing.

Three fine museums are *El Paso Museum of Art,* now in its new home (1 Arts Festival Plaza, El Paso 79901, 915–532–1707), featuring

June's Texas Anecdotes

*W*EST TEXAS: One of the dearest people I've had the pleasure to work with at the Star-Telegram *was a lovely lady named Claire, who apprenticed under my grandmother at the newspaper many years ago. Claire, all 4 feet and 10 inches of her, was probably in her late seventies when we joined a group of travel writers for a west Texas tour. The day we visited the cavernous market in Juarez, Claire and I did a bit of shopping before she announced that she would meet me back at the bus at the appointed hour for the return to* our El Paso hotel. There was nothing strange about this; Claire had recently done her share of traveling in Egypt and France and the Amazon region, where she would wander off on her own without mishap. But when our group was ready to leave, everyone seemed upset that Claire wasn't there. I simply looked at José, our 6-foot-6, barrel-chested Tigua Indian guide, and asked him if there was a bar nearby that served a good brand of Scotch. "Of course!" he said, and there she was, ready to go.

the Kress Collection of European Art, with masterpieces from the thirteenth to the eighteenth centuries; *El Paso Museum of History* (I–10 at the Avenue of the Americas, El Paso 79901, 915–858–1928), where colorful exhibits detail the history of Native Americans, conquistadors, vaqueros, cowboys, and Cavalrymen who played a role in taming the Southwest; and the *Magoffin Homestead* (1120 Magoffin Street, El Paso 79901, 915–533–5147), a state historical park featuring the adobe hacienda built by settler Joseph Magoffin in 1875, with some original period furnishings.

Two more museums, the *Fort Bliss Replica Museum* (915–568–4518) and *The U.S. Army Air Defense Museum* (915–568–5412) are found at Fort Bliss on Pleasanton Road, near the airport. The largest air defense center in the world, the base was founded in 1849 and named after Lt. Col. William Wallace Smith Bliss. Both museums are wonderful in detail. Call for hours. Admission is free, but donations are accepted.

A fine addition to the city's cultural assets is the *El Paso Holocaust Museum and Study Center* (401 Wallenberg Drive, El Paso 79901, 915–833–5656). A re-creation of a death camp, a transport train, aerial photos, and death camp pajamas are among the exhibits of this important museum, which serves as an educational facility by providing public speakers who were liberators or are survivors of World War II concentration camps. The museum is open from 1:00 to 4:00 P.M. Tuesday, Wednesday, Thursday, and Sunday.

At the *Border Patrol Museum* (4315 Transmountain Road, El Paso 79924, 915–759–6060), visitors learn about the U.S. Border Patrol's history since the days of the Old West. Exhibits include aircraft and vehicles used by the patrol, surveillance equipment, confiscated items, and more.

You can find a little bit more history at *Concordia Cemetery* (just northwest of the intersection of I–10 and U.S. Highway 54), a graveyard begun in 1856. Find the section that was El Paso's "Boot Hill," where illustrious gunfighter John Wesley Hardin is buried.

Duffers can revel in the dry, mountain air at two renowned courses. PGA champ Lee Trevino made famous the historic *Emerald Springs Golf Course* about 20 miles east of town (take I–10 East to Horizon City, 915–852–9110), built 25 years ago on an actual desert spring. Another top-ranked course in Texas is *Painted Dunes Desert Golf Course* (12000 McCombs Road, El Paso 79934, 915–821–2122), surrounded by desert plants and purple-blue mountains.

People drive from all over west Texas and southern New Mexico to while away days just eating and shopping in El Paso. Among the favorite places to eat is the **H&H Car Wash and Coffee Shop** (701 East Yandel Street, El Paso 77902, 915–533–1144), an old-fashioned institution where you can have your car hand-washed while the kitchen staff inside makes you an unforgettable meal. Best bets are the *carne picada,* or sautéed beef tips with tomato, onion, and jalapeño, or the amazing huevos rancheros and other spicy breakfast treats.

Easily as popular is **Forti's Mexican Elder** (321 Chelsea Street, El Paso 79905, 915–772–0066), a friendly, pretty, family-run spot with a tiled interior, a dining room with a fountain, and wonderful food. Best bets include the cool salad of chicken and avocado and the excellent enchiladas and burritos.

Jaxon's (1135 Airway, El Paso 79925, 915–778–9696) is a cheerful microbrewery and restaurant, where the menu specializes in steaks, fajitas, pasta, seafood, and vegetable dishes. Open for lunch and dinner daily, meals start at about $10.

It's possible to do nothing for days but shop for wonderful Texas and Mexican gifts and goods in El Paso. The first two of several stores of special note is **Justin Boot Factory Outlet** (7100 Gateway East at I–10, 915–779–5465), a superstore selling a complete line of boots as well as belts, hats, and all kinds of western accessories; and **Lucchese Boots** (6601 Montana Avenue, El Paso 79925, 915–778–8060), the factory store for the famous bootmaker, established in 1883. You'll find boots at up to 50 percent off retail prices, as well as cool, old photographs; boot casts; and memorabilia of famous people who have boasted a pair of Luccheses. **Tony Lama Factory stores** (call for directions to three locations, 915–772–4327) sell leather western boots made right in El Paso. **El Paso Chile** (909 Texas Avenue, El Paso 79901, 915–544–3434) is a booming family business selling salsas, barbecue sauces, margarita mix, gift baskets, and cookbooks. **Old El Paso Traders** (1201 Airway Boulevard, El Paso 79925, 915–779–5815) is where you'll find saddle blankets, rugs, Minnetonka moccasins, cow skulls, peace pipes, weavings, kachina dolls, pottery, mandellas, and Southwestern art.

More home decor is to be had at **Casa Rustica** (6600 Montana Avenue, El Paso 79925, 915–532–7866), a showplace of hand-crafted, rustic furnishings patterned after popular Mexican styles in warm woods. **Galeria San Ysidro** (801 Texas Avenue, El Paso 79901, 915–544–4444) is a three-story treasure chest of antiques, lamps, hand-crafted wrought-iron decorative pieces, and collectibles from Mexico, Spain, India, and North Africa.

For a look at the Texas-Mexico connection, visit the **Chamizal National Memorial** (800 South San Marcial, El Paso 79901, 915–534–6668). Built on land that became part of the United States when the Chamizal border dispute with Mexico was settled in 1963, the grounds cover fifty-five acres and feature a museum and an amphitheatre. Open daily from 8:00 A.M. until 5:30 P.M. Admission is free.

And because no visit to El Paso is complete without exploring its international other half, a visit to **Juarez** is in order. Without the international border, it would be impossible to tell where one city ends and the other begins, they are such mirror images of each other. Spanish and English are spoken interchangeably, American dollars and Mexican pesos are spent indifferently. Locals from both sides make business-lunch and shopping trips back and forth, often several times daily. You can walk across, take a taxi, or board the El Paso-Juarez Trolley, which leaves the Civic Center Plaza on Santa Fe Street hourly. Tickets are $10, or free for children three and under.

For age-old Spanish entertainment, visit the **Plaza Monumental Bullring** (located at Paseo Triunfo de la Republica #4630, 1 block from the Rio Grande Mall), where live, traditional bullfights are held in the spring and summer. Three matadors fight two bulls each in this longstanding Spanish and Mexican sport, and matches last about two hours. Do spend the extra money for tickets on the shady side of the arena on hot days. Buy tickets at the International Hotel at 113 West Missouri in downtown El Paso, (915) 544–3300. Transportation from El Paso can be arranged through Rancho Grande Tours, (915) 771–6661.

Also in Juarez, the **Museo de Arte** (Avenida Lincoln at Avenida Ignacio Mejia) is operated by the National Institute of Fine Arts. Exhibits change every two months; it's open from 11:00 A.M. until 7:00 P.M. Tuesday through Sunday, and admission is 75 cents. Other museums include **Museo de Historico de Ciudad Juarez** (Avenida Juarez at Avenida 16 de Septiembre), with exhibits on the history of Juarez and the state of Chihuahua, the Mexican Revolution, and the exploits of Pancho Villa; and the **Museo de Antropoligia** (in Chamizal Park), usually offering anthropological and archaeological exhibits.

The area's oldest surviving church is **Our Lady of Guadalupe Mission** (2 blocks west of Avenida Juarez on Avenida 16 de Septiembre), the first mission in the area. The existing church dates from 1668 and was the result of combined labor by Mexicans, Mansos Indians, and the Spanish. Next door is the Juarez Cathedral, with a neoclassical facade.

Juarez is quite the shopping and dining mecca, ideal for morning, afternoon, or all-day excursions. The city market, on Avenida 16 de Septiembre, is a huge spread, with baskets, pottery, jewelry, clothing, blankets, and snacks. It's important to go to Juarez with a big appetite, as the food is good and plentiful.

Casa Mendoza, immediately behind the City Market, is a family operation established in 1942. The large curio shop stocks jewelry, pottery, onyx, blown glass, and clay ceramic pots. It's open daily except Sunday. Another good store to find is ***Decor*** (Avenida Ignacio Mejia and Avenida Lincoln), a three-story place stocked with furniture, glass, ceramics, jewelry, and more. It's open daily.

Old Juarez is well represented on Avenida Juarez—just a few steps from one of the international bridges, in fact—at a terrific place called the ***Kentucky Club*** (629 Avenida Juarez, Juarez). Legend holds that the margarita was invented here; that may or may not be, but you'll be delighted by taking your seat at the original, heavily polished bar and watching Lorenzo the bartender craft a perfect one for you, as he's done every day for the past fifty-four years. Afterward, linger next door over a dinner of steak and enchiladas at Martino's, a 1950s throwback where white-jacketed waiters, heavily starched table linens, and campy light fixtures wrap you inside a delightful time warp.

OTHER PLACES TO STAY IN WILDEST WEST TEXAS

ALPINE

Antelope Lodge, 2310 West U. S. Highway 90, Alpine 79830, (800) 880–8106 or (915) 837–2451. Stucco cottages with kitchenettes are offered at budget rates. Units have one, two, or three bedrooms.

BALMORHEA

San Solomon Courts, inside the state park, (915) 375–2370. All eighteen adobe units are within a few steps of the celebrated pool. Some have kitchenettes.

EL PASO

Camino Real Hotel, 101 South El Paso Street, El Paso 79901, (915) 534–3000. This beautiful hotel, begun in 1912, has a luxury floor, where rooms have honor bars, refrigerators, and VCRs. In all there are 360 rooms. A coffee shop, an upscale restaurant and bar, and a small swimming pool are on the premises.

Cowboys & Indians Board and Bunk, twenty-five minutes from downtown El Paso in Santa Teresa, (505) 589–2653. Spreading over three desert acres, this retreat offers sensational mountain views and four rooms with private baths and patios, queen beds, coffeemakers, and private entrances in adobe quarters. Breakfast is included with stay, and horseback riding, hot-air ballooning, and golf can be arranged.

FORT DAVIS

The Veranda, 1 block west of courthouse, (915) 426–2233. Opened in 1883 as the Lempert Hotel, this adobe building with 2-foot-thick walls has wood floors, high ceilings, period furniture, porches, courtyards, and gardens. There are seven rooms, all with private baths, ranging from the large bedroom with two double beds and a fireplace inlaid with quartz to the two-room king suites with mountain views. There's also a private carriage house in an orchard of apricot and peach trees. Breakfast is included with stay.

Webster House, 3 blocks south of courthouse, (800) 752–4145 or (915) 426–3143. A century-old home built in the Territorial Victorian style, this frontier adobe structure offers its guests three spacious bedrooms, two sitting areas, two full baths, a modern kitchen and laundry room, and shady porch. There's also a private cottage on the property, with one bedroom, full bath, and a kitchen.

MARATHON
Heath Canyon Guest Ranch, Farm Road 2627, 28 miles east of U.S. 385, near Marathon, (915) 376–2235. Bunkhouse rooms, access to Black Gap Wildlife Management Area, and fishing on the Rio Grande are offered. The Open Sky Cafe is on-site, offering dinners of Mexican specialties Wednesday through Sunday.

MARFA
Cibolo Creek Ranch, 30 miles south off Texas Highway 17, (915) 358–4696.

A 25,000-acre working ranch with horseback riding, it offers tours of lands where bison, elk, and longhorn roam. The ranch consists of three lavishly restored, nineteenth-century forts named El Cibolo, La Cienega, and La Morita. El Cibolo, the largest, has eleven guest rooms, which start at $200 and top out at $500 or so (meals are included), and has a heated pool, Jacuzzi, stocked reservoir, and an exceptional museum. Decor in all areas is a tasteful, stylish blend of western and Mexican designs.

ODESSA
Mellie Van Horn's Historic Inn and Restaurant, 903 North Sam Houston Street, Odessa 79761, (915) 337–3000. This restored, historic inn was a boarding house from 1938 to 1975. Today's version offers sixteen guest rooms and sixteen baths.

OTHER PLACES TO EAT IN WILDEST WEST TEXAS

ALPINE
Frontier Bar-B-Q, in the Alpine Inn, 2000 U.S 90 East, Alpine 79830, (915) 837–9914. Chicken, beef, and baked beans are popular at this inexpensive joint overlooking the motel pool.

Outback Bar and Grill, 300 South Phelps Street at Avenue G, Alpine 79830, (915) 837–5074. Not connected to the national steak house chain, this unpretentious restaurant does a bang-up job with half-pound burgers topped with bacon, cheese, green chiles, and avocados; as well as fajitas; steaks; and Italian dishes. Service here is exceptionally good. Open daily for lunch and dinner, the Outback features live music after 9:30 P.M. Thursday through Saturday.

Twin Peaks Restaurant, 2700 West Highway 90, Alpine 79830, (915) 837–1500. Breakfasts at this diner include the standards as well as Mexican egg dishes. Lunch and dinner offerings range from tortilla soup, stuffed potatoes, and nachos to baby back ribs, brisket, chicken-fried steak, and fried catfish. Closed Monday.

BALLINGER
Lowake Steak House, about 25 miles south via U.S. Highway 67 and Farm Road 381, (915) 442–3201. This legendary steak joint has unbeatable T-bones, rib eyes, filets, and strips, plus the best onion rings and baked potatoes. Open for lunch and dinner Tuesday through Sunday, meals average $10.

EL PASO

Bill Parks Bar-B-Q, 3130 Gateway East, El Paso 79905, (915) 542–0960. If you're tiring of Mexican spices and yearn for something different, this place has pure Texas barbecue as well as bonafide, Deep South goodies such as black-eyed peas, collard greens, sweet potato pie, and corn bread. Open Monday through Saturday for lunch and early dinner.

Dona Lupe Cafe, 2919 Pershing Avenue, El Paso 79903, (915) 566–9833 or (915) 564–9467. A former 1960s drugstore soda fountain in the historic Five Points district has been a mainstay for homemade chiles rellenos and other Mexican specialties for nearly fifty years. Open for lunch and dinner daily.

FORT DAVIS

Blue Mountain Diner, Highway 118 at Highway 17, (915) 426–2479. Gourmet breakfast creations include quiche with fresh fruit, a croissant sandwich with cheese and bacon or sausage, and homemade waffles with applewood-smoked bacon. Lunch items range from sandwiches or roast beef and Muenster cheese, chili, and spinach salad with sun-dried tomatoes to homemade pizzas and wrap sandwiches.

Open daily for lunch and dinner, the cafe also serves dinner on Friday and Saturday night.

MARATHON

The Oasis Cafe, on U.S. Highway 90 just west of the Gage Hotel, (915) 386–4521. This cafe offers Mexican plates as well as burgers and chicken-fried steak.

MIDLAND

Sedona Grill, 2101 West Wadley Street, Midland 79705, (915) 570–9600. Shrimp tacos, green chile empanadas (savory turnovers), and tortilla soup have patrons panting at this southwestern cuisine hot spot. Lunch and dinner are served and prices are moderate.

Old Monterrey Cafe, 523 East Illinois Street, Midland 79701, (915) 570–6169. Fans of this newer effort love the cheese enchiladas in red chile sauce, the chile relleno stuffed with beef, and the fajitas. Open for lunch and dinner; prices are moderate.

The Wild Scallion, 4400 North Midland Drive, Midland 79707, (915) 520–5455. Mightily upscale continental dining offerings include duck breast in a soy-ginger treatment, beef tenderloin, and a nice wine list. Expect an expensive ticket; open for lunch and dinner.

ODESSA

Manuel's Mexican Food, East Second Street/Business Interstate 20, Odessa 79761, (915) 333–2751. This might be the one, true, must-go place in town. You can't miss the sprawling orange brick place with the vintage signs from the 1950s. Popular since before anyone can remember, this is the place for giant Mexican plates as well as steaks. Open for lunch and dinner Tuesday through Sunday, and only lunch on Monday.

The Permian Basin Hamburger Co., 520 North Grant Street, Odessa 79761, (915) 333–4971. This is a quaint diner in the heart of old downtown, which serves breakfast and lunch Monday through Friday.

Rockin' Q Smokehouse, 3812 Penbrook Street, Odessa 79762, (915) 552–7105. Delectable pork ribs and beef brisket are smoked over a hickory fire for tasty delights. Open for lunch and dinner daily; moderate.

PECOS

Cattleman's Restaurant, 425 West Third Street, Pecos 79772, (915) 445–3433. A longtime west Texas favorite, this no-frills, old-fashioned cafe serves Mexican plates, steaks, and catfish. It's open for lunch and dinner Monday through Saturday.

Index

INDEX

INDEX

INDEX

INDEX

INDEX

INDEX

About the Author

A sixth-generation Texan and Fort Worth native, June Naylor has written for the *Fort Worth Star-Telegram,* a Knight Ridder newspaper, since 1984, starting in sports and writing for the state and metro desks before moving to the travel section in 1985 to write stories about Texas, the Southwest, the U.S., and the world. She added dining and food to the mix in 1987, and currently writes about dining, food, and travel for the *Star-Telegram's* features sections. A contributor to numerous magazines and travel and dining Web sites, June co-hosts a weekly food and travel radio show in the Dallas/Fort Worth area and is writing a Texas cookbook with noted Texas chef Grady Spears.

The author of Globe Pequot's *Quick Escapes® Dallas/Fort Worth, Romantic Days and Nights® in Dallas/Fort Worth* and *Recommended Bed & Breakfasts™ Southwest,* June has received several writing and photography awards from the Society of American Travel Writers. She is currently chairperson of the organization's Central States Chapter and is a founding member of the Association of Women in Journalism.